POLITICAL MARKET PLACE USA

George Thomas Kurian
and
Jeffrey D. Schultz

ORYX PRESS

POLITICAL
MARKET
PLACE

POLITICAL
MARKET
PLACE
USA

by
George Thomas Kurian
and
Jeffrey D. Schultz

ORYX PRESS

The rare Arabian oryx is believed to have inspired the myth of the unicorn. This desert antelope became virtually extinct in the early 1960s. At that time several groups of international conservationists arranged to have 9 animals sent to the Phoenix Zoo to be the nucleus of a captive breeding herd. Today the oryx population is over 1,000, and over 500 have been returned to the Middle East.

© 1999 by George Thomas Kurian and Jeffrey D. Schultz
Published by The Oryx Press
4041 North Central at Indian School Road
Phoenix, Arizona 85012-3397

Published simultaneously in Canada
Printed and bound in the United States of America

♾ The paper used in this publication meets the minimum requirements of the American National Standard for Information Sciences—Permanence of Paper for Printed Library Materials, ANSI Z39.48-1984.

Library of Congress Cataloging-in-Publication Data
Kurian, George Thomas
    Political market place USA / by George Thomas Kurian and
Jeffrey D. Schultz.
        p. cm
        Includes indexes.
        ISBN 1-57356-226-2 (alk. paper)
        1. United States—Politics and government. 2. Politics,
Practical—United States. 3. Mass media—Political aspects—United
States. I. Schultz, Jeffrey D. II. Title.
JK271 .K87 1998
323'.042'02573—dc21   98-33513
                                                                                              CIP
                                                                                              Rev.

Table of Contents

Preface

Political Market Place USA is an annual directory, sourcebook and desk reference for all Americans interested in politics, elections, legislative bodies, political parties, and campaigns for political office. It is designed as an educative and empowering tool, providing information on resources available to citizens to help them make informed political decisions and gauge political trends. It is also an inventory of resources available to political professionals, legislators, public officials and journalists who monitor and analyze political events.

American politics encompasses a rich and varied tableau of powerful social and economic forces, identities and movements. It has been said that with the advent of C-Span, the Internet, sound bites and political commercials, politics is not what it used to be and will never be the same again. In these extraordinary times, the world of politics has been buffeted by unlikely events, and political ideology has been transformed by the disarray and irrelevance of traditional political parties. The very language of politics and the sources of collective identity have been recast. The older definition of politics in formal binary terms of left and right no longer applies as new solidarities have emerged based on gender, race, ethnicity and religion. The political landscape has changed and is continuing to change as special interests erode ideological allegiances. There is a new accountability for political actors and new rules for the political game. *Political Market Place USA* is a road map of the New Politics, profiling the institutions and ideas that drive politics in the United States.

The New Politics involves all the citizens of the republic in a way the Old Politics never did. Politics has become too important to be left to the politicians. *Political Market Place USA* is

therefore addressed not merely to candidates, legislators, and officeholders of political parties but also to journalists, researchers, teachers and students in high schools, colleges and universities as well as grassroots political activists.

The cutoff date for the material in this book was June 1, 1998. Every effort has been made to make this work current as of this date. (Later information, where available, has been included where such inclusion was required for fullness of treatment.)

The sections of the book have been arranged according to a standard, but not rigid, classification system. This system has been devised not only for ease of consultation but also to facilitate comparisons among political organizations and activities.

In addition to the 19 directory-style sections, there is a section that contains political statistics and one that has the most recent State of the Union Address and the Republican Response. The volume also has three overview articles that address larger sections of the book. These three overviews cover political associations, elections, and the media.

To aid the reader in navigating the political market place, three indexes have been compiled: Name/Organization, Geographic, and Key Subject.

The editors have made every effort to check the accuracy of the entries and to make the data as reliable as possible, but despite all precautions, errors may occur. Please feel free to advise the editors of any necessary revisions so that they may be corrected in a subsequent edition. The editors would also like to thank Jeff Coburn, Bill Baron, Nancy Schultz, and Cheryl Gilbert for their help.

The Democratic Party

Democratic National Committee
430 South Capitol Street SE
Washington, DC 20003
(202) 863-8000
(202) 863-8174 (Fax)
http://www.democrats.org

The Democratic National Committee (DNC) is located below the national convention in the party hierarchy, but because the convention meets only for a short time every four years, the committee is responsible for carrying out the convention's mandates and tending to much of the national party's day-to-day business. Although the Democratic state and local party organizations are located below the national party committee, giving the Democratic Party organization the appearance of having a hierarchical structure, power is not and has never been concentrated in the DNC. Party reform and renewal greatly strengthened the DNC, but power within the party remains decentralized similar to the distribution of power within the larger political system.

Before 1968, seats on the DNC were distributed in accordance with the principle of federalism: each state was afforded equal representation. Following the party reform movement, the DNC enlarged its membership from 165 men and women in 1968 to 431 in 1995. Two hundred seats are divided among the states and American territories using a formula that considers the size of each state's population and its level of electoral support for Democratic candidates. An additional 157 seats are reserved for each state and territorial party's chair, the next-highest-ranking party

officer of the opposite sex, and others who are selected by virtue of their political office or membership in an affiliated Democratic organization, such as the Democratic Governors' Association or the National Conference of Democratic Mayors. The Young Democrats, College Democrats, and National Federation of Democratic Women each elect three members. The final 65 seats are reserved for individuals who serve in an at-large capacity to help ensure broad representation of the party's constituencies. States are allowed to choose from several methods the procedures they use to select their representatives to the DNC. The most commonly used methods are selection in a primary convention, by a state party central committee, and at a state party convention.

DNC chairs are not required to be committee members, and they rarely are. They are officially selected by committee, but in reality, chairs are chosen by the party's presidential nominee and then ratified by the committee's members. If the nominee wins the general election, then the DNC chair continues to serve at the president's pleasure. In the event the nominee loses the election, DNC members typically select a new chair to replace their nominee's choice. DNC members also select the committee's other officers, including its vice chair, secretary, treasurer, and executive committee members. Many but not all of these officials are drawn from the DNC's ranks.

In addition to its members, who generally meet twice a year, the DNC has a professional staff of campaign strategists, public relations experts, attorneys, fundraisers, and other political operatives who carry out most of the committee's activities. Some DNC research and strategic activities are carried out by a network of private consultants hired on retainer and by interest groups that donate polls, sponsor conferences, and provide other political services. The size of the DNC's staff expands and contracts with the four-year presidential election cycle, as does the level of services it purchases or receives from outside groups.

ELECTION ACTIVITIES

Most of the DNC's election efforts are concentrated on presidential elections. Federal law and tradition limit the committee's activities in elections. The DNC neither selects nor backs candidates for the Democratic nomination, but it plays a major role in establishing the guidelines under which Democratic presidential nominations are contested. It is also responsible for organizing and making most of the financial arrangements for the party's national convention.

Once the convention adjourns, the DNC works to help elect its nominee in the general election. Major party presidential nominees have their own campaign organizations, and those who accept public subsidies (all have done so since the funds from the presidential election campaign fund were first made available in 1976) are prohibited from accepting money from a national committee or any other source. As a result, national committees are relegated to supporting roles in their presidential nominee's campaign, providing issue research and technical, strategic, and legal advice. In addition, the DNC spearheads a "coordinated campaign" designed to mobilize Democratic voters on behalf of the entire party ticket. The coordinated campaign consists

mainly of strategically targeted voter registration and get-out-the-vote drives. It also includes television, radio, and other advertisements that the DNC uses to reinforce the Democratic presidential nominee's message and to communicate an overall image of the party to voters.

The DNC is less active in subpresidential elections, leaving the bulk of the election activities in these races to the candidates' campaign organizations, the congressional and senatorial campaign committees, and state and local party organizations. The national committee helps to recruit Democratic candidates for the House, Senate, and statewide offices and runs training seminars for candidates and campaign managers. It also finances public opinion polls, contracts for focus group research, and distributes valuable information on major campaign issues.

OTHER ACTIVITIES

When a Democrat occupies the Oval Office, the DNC plays an important supporting role for his administration. The committee provides polling information and strategic advice, and finances the president's and other White House officials' travel to politically oriented events. In recent years, it has also run public relations campaigns to support the president's major legislative initiatives. In 1993, for example, the DNC aired television advertisements in support of President Clinton's health care package.

MEMBERS OF THE
DNC EXECUTIVE COMMITTEE

National Chair: Steve Grossman
General Chair: Roy Romer
Vice Chair: Gloria Molina
Vice Chair: Linda Chavez Thompson
Vice Chair: Bill Lynch
Vice Chair: Lottie H. Shackelford
Vice Chair, President of Association of State Democratic Chairs: Gary J. LaPaille
Treasurer: Carol Pensky

Secretary: Kathleen M. Vick
Deputy Chair: Mazie Hirono

Congressional Representatives: Senator Thomas A. Daschle and Representative Steny H. Hoyer
Democratic Governors' Association: Pedro Rossello

STATE DEMOCRATIC PARTIES

Alabama

Joe Turnham, Chair
PO Box 928
Auburn, AL 36831-0928
(334) 821-4500
(334) 887-1875 (Fax)

Amy Burks, Vice Chair
1206 York Place SW
Decatur, AL 35603
(205) 353-0283
(205) 353-8691 (Fax)

Alabama Democratic Party
290 21st Street North, Suite 405
Birmingham, AL 35203
(205) 326-3366
(205) 324-3320 (Fax)
Executive Director: Giles Perkins

Alaska

Deborah Bonito, Chair
6447 Colgate
Anchorage, AK 99504
(907) 338-7251
(907) 333-9389 (Fax)

Don Lowell, Vice Chair
PO Box 71114
Fairbanks, AK 99707
(907) 488-2879

Alaska Democratic Party
1441 West Northern Lights, Suite C
Anchorage, AK 99503
(907) 258-3050
(907) 258-1626 (Fax)
Executive Director: Joelle Hall

American Samoa

Moaaliitele Tu'ufuli, Chair
PO Box 4581
Pago Pago, AS 96799
(011) 684-633-4656

Sinira T. Fuimaono, Vice Chair
PO Box 855
Pago Pago, AS 96799
(011) 684-633-1091

Democratic Party of American Samoa
PO Box 5169
Pago Pago, AS 96799
(011) 684-633-4656
(011) 684-633-1998 (Fax)
Executive Director: Clair Reid

Arizona

Mark Fleisher, Chair
13635 North 49th Street
Scottsdale, AZ 85254
(602) 813-2400
(602) 996-0475 (Fax)

Betty Liggins, Vice Chair
2111 East Sunland Vista
Tucson, AZ 85713
(520) 624-9980

Arizona Democratic Party
2005 North Central, Suite 180
Phoenix, AZ 85004
(602) 257-9136
(602) 257-8268 (Fax)
Executive Director: Melodee Jackson

Arkansas

Bynum Gibson, Chair
PO Box 680
Dermott, AR 71638
(870) 538-5900
(870) 538-3582 (Fax)

Julia Peck Mobley, Vice Chair
PO Box 1998
Texarkana, AR 75504
(870) 773-4561
(870) 772-6914 (Fax)

Arkansas Democratic Party
1300 West Capitol
Little Rock, AR 72201
(501) 374-2361
(501) 376-8409 (Fax)
Executive Director: Dawne Vandiver

California

Art Torres, Chair
911 20th Street
Sacramento, CA 95814
(310) 724-5800
(310) 724-5828 (Fax)

Alicia Wang, Vice Chair
2350 Anza Street
San Francisco, CA 94118
(415) 750-1126
(415) 751-7881 (Fax)

California Democratic Party
911 20th Street
Sacramento, CA 95814
(916) 442-5707
(916) 442-5715 (Fax)
Executive Director: Kathy Bowler

Colorado

Phil Perington, Chair
770 Grant Street, Suite 228
Denver, CO 80203

(303) 860-1998
(303) 832-3062 (Fax)

Linda Cacchione, Vice Chair
5509 West Jackson Creek Road
Sedalia, CO 80135
(303) 660-2025
(303) 688-4343 (Fax)

Colorado Democratic Party
770 Grant Street, Suite 200
Denver, CO 80203
(303) 830-8989
(303) 830-2743 (Fax)
Executive Director: Darryl Eskin

Connecticut

Edward L. Marcus, Chair
111 Whitney Avenue
New Haven, CT 06510
(203) 787-5885
(203) 789-8705 (Fax)

Patricia Paniccia, Vice Chair
25 Easton Road
Monroe, CT 06468
(203) 946-2000
(203) 498-2002 (Fax)

Connecticut Democratic Party
380 Franklin Avenue
Hartford, CT 06114
(860) 296-1775
(860) 296-1522 (Fax)
Executive Director: Robert Ives

Delaware

Richard H. Bayard, Chair
PO Box 25130
Wilmington, DE 19899
(302) 655-5000
(302) 658-6395 (Fax)

Leah Betts, Vice Chair
113 Magnolia Street

Milton, DE 19968
(302) 684-4774

Delaware Democratic Party
240 North James Street, Suite 100-A
Newport, DE 19804
(302) 996-9458
(302) 996-9405 (Fax)
Executive Director: Jim Purcell

Democrats Abroad

Sally McNulty, Chair
50 Springfield Road
London, NW8 OQN, UK
(44) 171-624-8741
(44) 171-372-6254 (Fax)

Joseph Smallhoover, Vice Chair
5 rue Bargue
75015 Paris, France
(33) 1-5561-1049

Democrats Abroad
7400 Rebecca Drive
Alexandria, VA 22307
(703) 768-3174
(703) 768-0920 (Fax)
Executive Director: Thomas Fina

District of Columbia

Amanda Hatcher Lyon, Chair
5900 3rd Street NE
Washington, DC 20011
(202) 529-7582
(202) 554-8820 (Fax)

Richard Rausch, Vice Chair
220 2nd Street SE, Suite 201
Washington, DC 20003
(202) 547-4401

D.C. Democratic Party
499 South Capitol Street SW
Washington, DC 20003
(202) 554-8790

(202) 554-8820 (Fax)
Executive Director: Sherre Washington

Florida

Terrie Brady, Chair
PO Box 1758
Tallahassee, FL 32302
(904) 396-4063
(904) 396-9389 (Fax)

Jon Ausman, Vice Chair
2202 Woodlawn Drive
Tallahassee, FL 32303-3915
(904) 385-4488
(904) 385-6689 (Fax)

Florida Democratic Party
PO Box 1758
Tallahassee, FL 32302
(904) 222-3411
(904) 222-0916 (Fax)
Executive Director: Scott Falmlen

Georgia

Vacant Chair

Pauline Woods, Vice Chair
505 East 51st Street
Savannah, GA 31405
(912) 238-3034

Georgia Democratic Party
1100 Spring Street, Suite 710
Atlanta, GA 30309
(404) 885-1998
(404) 873-4396 (Fax)
Executive Director: Steve Anthony

Guam

Pilar Lujan, Chair
PO Box 1889
Agana, Guam 96910

(011) 671-789-0213
(011) 671-789-0569 (Fax)

Frank Meno, Vice Chair
PO Box 2950
Agana, Guam 96910
(011) 671-472-8931
(011) 671-477-6425 (Fax)

Guam Democratic Party
PO Box 2950
Agana, Guam 96910
(011) 671-472-8931
(011) 671-477-6425 (Fax)
Executive Director: Joaquin "Kin" Perez

Hawaii

Marilyn Bornhorst, Chair
1525 Oneele Place
Honolulu, HI 96822
(808) 596-2980
(808) 596-2985 (Fax)

Martin Rice, Vice Chair
5117 Lokene Street
Kapaa, HI 96746
(808) 822-7171

Hawaii Democratic Party
777 Kapiolani Boulevard
Honolulu, HI 96813-5211
(808) 596-2980
(808) 596-2985 (Fax)

Idaho

A.K. Lienhart Minnick, Chair
1094 Hearthstone Drive
Boise, ID 83702-1828
(208) 345-3036
(208) 343-5737 (Fax)

Ron Beitelspacher, Vice Chair
PO Box 415
Grangeville, ID 83530
(208) 983-2535

Idaho Democratic Party
PO Box 445
Boise, ID 83701
(208) 336-1815
(208) 336-1817 (Fax)
Executive Director: Karen White

Illinois

Gary LaPaille, Chair
180 West Washington, Suite 1100
Chicago, IL   60602
(312) 960-2215
(312) 960-2220 (Fax)

Iola McGowan, Vice Chair
5839 West Midway Park
Chicago, IL 60644
(773) 261-8426
(773) 261-2002 (Fax)

Democratic Party of Illinois
489 Merchandise Mart
Chicago, IL 60654
(312) 464-1900
(312) 464-1907 (Fax)

Indiana

Joe Andrew, Chair
1 North Capitol, Suite 200
Indianapolis, IN 46204
(800) 223-3387
(317) 231-7129 (Fax)

Pam Carter, Vice Chair
1 North Capitol, Suite 200
Indianapolis, IN 46204
(317) 634-9777
(317) 636-9061 (Fax)

Indiana Democratic Party
1 North Capitol, Suite 200
Indianapolis, IN 46204
(800) 223-3387
(317) 231-7129 (Fax)
Executive Director: Mike Harmless

Iowa

Mike Peterson, Chair
5661 Fleur Drive
Des Moines, IA 50321
(515) 244-7292
(515) 244-5051 (Fax)

Anne Pedersen, Vice Chair
506 33rd Street
Ft Madison, IA 52627
(319) 372-3705
(319) 372-7033 (Fax)

Iowa Democratic Party
5661 Fleur Drive
Des Moines, IA 50321
(515) 244-7292
(515) 244-5051 (Fax)
Executive Director: Mike Peterson

Kansas

Dennis Langley, Chair
12703 High Drive
Leawood, KS 66209
(913) 234-0425
(913) 234-8420 (Fax)

Velda Duette, Vice Chair
1535 SW Cheyenne Hills Road
Topeka, KS 66604-4022
(913) 296-7387

Kansas Democratic Party
PO Box 1914
Topeka, KS 66601
(913) 234-0425
(913) 234-8420 (Fax)
Executive Director: Brett Cott

Kentucky

Ronald B. McCloud, Chair
PO Box 694
Frankfort, KY 40602
(502) 695-4828

Sandra Higgins Stinson, Vice Chair
170 Buckner Ridge Lane
Madisonville, KY 42431
(502) 821-1869

Kentucky Democratic Party
PO Box 694
Frankfort, KY 40602
(502) 695-4828
(502) 695-7629 (Fax)
Executive Director: Nicki Patton

Louisiana

Ben L. Jeffers, Chair
263 3rd Street, Suite 102
Baton Rouge, LA 70801
(504) 336-4155
(504) 336-0046 (Fax)

Mary Lou Winters, Vice Chair
PO Box 1860
Columbia, LA 71418
(318) 649-2722
(318) 649-6812 (Fax)

Louisiana Democratic Party
263 3rd Street, Suite 102
Baton Rouge, LA 70801
(504) 336-4155
(504) 336-0046 (Fax)
Executive Director: Trey Ourso

Maine

Christopher Hall, Chair
PO Box 218
Bristol, ME 04539
(207) 622-6233

Elizabeth Wooster, Vice Chair
PO Box 231
Waldoboro, ME 04572
(207) 832-7764
(207) 832-7435 (Fax)

Maine Democratic Party
PO Box 5258
Augusta, ME 04332-5258
(207) 622-6233
(207) 622-2657 (Fax)
Executive Director: Craig Schuler

Maryland

Peter J. Krauser, Chair
9200 Basil Court, Suite 300
Largo, MD 20774
(301) 925-4900
(301) 925-9752 (Fax)

Mary Jo Neville, Vice Chair
140 Main Street, Suite 300
Annapolis, MD 21401
(410) 263-6600
(410) 263-7391 (Fax)

Maryland Democratic Party
188 Main Street, Suite 1
Annapolis, MD 21401
(410) 280-8818
(410) 280-8882 (Fax)
Executive Director: Anne T. MacKinnon

Massachusetts

Joan Menard, Chair
129 Portland Street, 6th Floor
Boston, MA 02114
(617) 722-2080
(617) 722-2339 (Fax)

Raymond Jordan, Vice Chair
11 Ingersoll Grove
Springfield, MA 01109
(413) 788-0206
(413) 732-0840 (Fax)

Massachusetts Democratic Party
129 Portland Street, 6th Floor
Boston, MA 02114
(617) 742-6770

(617) 742-6598 (Fax)
Executive Director: Gus Bickford

Michigan

Mark Brewer, Chair
606 Townsend
Lansing, MI 48933
(517) 371-5410

Flora Walker, Vice Chair
1034 North Washington
Lansing, MI 48906
(517) 487-5081
(517) 487-3970 (Fax)

Michigan Democratic Party
606 Townsend
Lansing, MI 48933
(517) 371-5410
(517) 371-2056 (Fax)
Executive Director: Sylvia Perkins

Minnesota

Dick Senese, Chair
352 Wacouta Street
St Paul, MN 55101
(612) 293-1200

Gail Huntley, Vice Chair
1924 Wallace Avenue
Duluth, MN 55803
(218) 724-6568

Minnesota Democratic Party
352 Wacouta Street
St Paul, MN 55101
(612) 293-1200
(612) 293-0706 (Fax)
Executive Director: Kathy Czar

Mississippi

Johnnie E. Walls, Chair
163 North Broadway

Greenville, MS 38701
(601) 335-6001
(601) 378-8958 (Fax)

Michele Wilson, Vice Chair
3146 Brushy Creek Road
Lucedale, MS 39452
(601) 947-3862

Mississippi Democratic Party
PO Box 1583
Jackson, MS 39215
(601) 969-2913
(601) 354-1599 (Fax)
Executive Director: Vacant

Missouri

Joe Carmichael, Chair
908 South Augusta Drive
Springfield, MO 65809-1504
(417) 864-5956
(417) 864-8001 (Fax)

Janis Londe, Vice Chair
33 North Maple Avenue
Webster Groves, MO 63119
(314) 961-8205

Missouri Democratic Party
PO Box 719
Jefferson City, MO 65102
(573) 636-5241
(573) 634-8176 (Fax)
Executive Director: Sean Gagen

Montana

Bob Ream, Chair
PO Box 802
Helena, MT 59624
(406) 442-9520

Monica Lindeen, Vice Chair
1626 Heath Street
Huntley, MT 59624
(406) 348-2000

Montana Democratic Party
PO Box 802
Helena, MT 59624
(406) 442-9520
(406) 442-9534 (Fax)
Executive Director: Brad Martin

Nebraska

Deb Hardin Quirk, Chair
PO Box 1142
Hastings, NE 68902
(402) 463-6651
(402) 463-6652 (Fax)

Frank LeMere, Vice Chair
600 Pioneer Place
South Sioux City, NE 68776
(402) 878-2242
(402) 878-2504 (Fax)

Nebraska Democratic Party
985 South 27th Street
Lincoln, NE 68510
(402) 434-2180
(402) 434-2188 (Fax)
Executive Director: Ken Haar

Nevada

Paul Henry, Chair
3790 South Paradise Road, Suite 130
Las Vegas, NV 89109
(702) 737-8683

Carol Cos, Vice Chair
3376 Lagomarsino Court
Sparks, NV 89431
(702) 356-1428

Nevada Democratic Party
3790 South Paradise Road, Suite 130
Las Vegas, NV 89109
(702) 737-8683
(702) 765-7109 (Fax)
Executive Director: Brooks Stratmore

New Hampshire

Jeff Woodburn, Chair
150 North Main Street
Concord, NH 03301
(603) 463-7575
(603) 225-6797 (Fax)

Mary Rauh, Vice Chair
PO Box 279
Sunapee, NH 03782
(603) 763-4106
(603) 763-5674 (Fax)

New Hampshire Democratic Party
150 North Main Street
Concord, NH 03301
(603) 225-6899
(603) 225-6797 (Fax)
Executive Director: Jim Boyle

New Jersey

Thomas Giblin, Chair
150 West State Street
Trenton, NJ 08608
(609) 392-3367
(609) 396-4778 (Fax)

Nilsa Cruz Perez, Vice Chair
514 Cooper Street
Camden, NJ 08102
(609) 541-1251
(609) 541-3415 (Fax)

New Jersey Democratic Party
150 West State Street
Trenton, NJ 08608
(609) 392-3367
(609) 396-4778 (Fax)
Executive Director: Rick Thigpen

New Mexico

Ray Sena, Chair
1600 Lena Street
Santa Fe, NM 87502

(505) 982-4311
(505) 983-5918 (Fax)

Sheryl Williams, Vice Chair
4616 Crest SE
Albuquerque, NM 87108
(505) 256-4240
(505) 256-4416 (Fax)

Democratic Party of New Mexico
5317 Menaul NE
Albuquerque, NM 87110
(800) 624-2457
(505) 830-3645 (Fax)
Executive Director: Vacant

New York

Judith Hope, Chair
60 Madison Avenue, Suite 1201
New York, NY 10010
(212) 725-8825
(212) 725-8867 (Fax)

John Sullivan, Executive Committee Chair
94 East Bridge Street
Oswego, NY 13126-2203
(315) 342-4871
(315) 343-1097 (Fax)

New York Democratic Party
60 Madison Avenue, Suite 1201
New York, NY 10010
(212) 725-8825
(212) 725-8867 (Fax)
Executive Director: David L. Cohen

North Carolina

Barbara Allen, Chair
PO Box 12196
Raleigh, NC 27605
(919) 821-2777
(919) 821-4778 (Fax)

David P. Parker, Vice Chair
PO Box 112

Statesville, NC 28687
(704) 871-0300
(704) 871-1589 (Fax)

North Carolina Democratic Party
PO Box 12196
Raleigh, NC 27605
(919) 821-2777
(919) 821-4778 (Fax)
Executive Director: Vacant

North Dakota

Shirley Dykshoorn, Chair
301 3rd Avenue NW
Mandan, ND 58554
(701) 663-3693

Richard Anderson, Vice Chair
6454 County Road 60
Litchville, ND 58461
(701) 883-5516

North Dakota Democratic Party
1902 East Divide Avenue
Bismarck, ND 58501
(701) 255-0460
(701) 255-7823 (Fax)
Executive Director: Jerry Kelsh

Ohio

David J. Leland, Chair
37 West Broad Street, Suite 430
Columbus, OH 43215
(614) 221-6563
(614) 221-0721 (Fax)

Ruby Gilliam, Vice Chair
2024 Leisure Road NW
Minerva, OH 44657
(216) 868 7634

Ohio Democratic Party
37 West Broad Street, Suite 430
Columbus, OH 43215
(614) 221-6563

(614) 221-0721 (Fax)
Executive Director: Amy Young

Oklahoma

Robert S. Kerr III, Chair
PO Box 25426
Oklahoma City, OK 73125
(405) 239-2700
(405) 236-8009 (Fax)

Debbe Leftwich
2125 SW 85th
Oklahoma City, OK 73159
(405) 239-7141
(405) 236-8009 (Fax)

Oklahoma Democratic Party
PO Box 25426
Oklahoma City, OK 73125
(405) 239-2700
(405) 236-8009 (Fax)
Executive Director: Pat Hall

Oregon

Marc Abrams, Chair
1753 NW Aspen Avenue
Portland, OR 97210
(503) 227-2672
(503) 227-2281 (Fax)

Arlene Collins, Vice Chair
1900 SW Vermont
Portland, OR 97219
(503) 246-5438
(503) 246-5642 (Fax)

Oregon Democratic Party
711 SW Alder, Suite 306
Portland, OR 97205
(503) 224-8200
(503) 224-5335 (Fax)
Executive Director: Robert Sacks

Pennsylvania

Christene Tartaglione, Acting Chair
Main Capitol Building, Room 458
Harrisburg, PA 17120
(717) 787-1141
(717) 772-2756 (Fax)

Vacant Vice Chair

Pennsylvania Democratic Party
510 North 3rd Street
Harrisburg, PA 17101
(717) 238-9381
(717) 233-3472 (Fax)
Executive Director: Kerry Kirkland

Puerto Rico

William Miranda Marin, Chair
PO Box 6263
Caguas, PR 00726
(787) 746-6100
(787) 746-6562 (Fax)

Mercedes Otero deRamos, Vice Chair
2002 Concha Expina Street El Senorial
San Juan, PR 00926
(787) 723-0277
(787) 723-0366 (Fax)

Puerto Rico Democratic Party
Esquire Building, 6th Floor
Ponce DeLeon Avenue and Vela Street
Hato Rey, PR 00918
(787) 751-8371
(787) 764-3341 (Fax)
Executive Director: Eliseo Roques

Rhode Island

Richard James, Chair
10 Davol Square, Suite 300
Providence, RI 02903
(401) 722-0811
(401) 726-5095 (Fax)

Edna O'Neill Mattson, Vice Chair
74 Maplewood Drive
North Kingstown, RI 02852
(401) 333-7077
(401) 825-2265 (Fax)

Rhode Island Democratic Party
10 Davol Square, Suite 300
Providence, RI 02903
(401) 459-3800
(401) 459-3803 (Fax)
Executive Director: Jeffrey Keller

South Carolina

Dick Harpootlian, Chair
PO Box 1987
Columbia, SC 29202
(803) 252-4848
(803) 252-4810 (Fax)

Carol F. Khare, Vice Chair
1521 Glenwood Road
Columbia, SC 29204
(803) 799-7550
(803) 771-7442 (Fax)

South Carolina Democratic Party
PO Box 5964
Columbia, SC 29250
(803) 799-7798
(803) 765-1692 (Fax)
Acting Executive Director: Brent Weaver

South Dakota

Kathleen Piper, Chair
PO Box 43
Yankton, SD 57078
(605) 665-7700
(605) 665-0127 (Fax)

Jack Billion, Vice Chair
1600 South 4th Avenue
Sioux Falls, SC 57105
(605) 331-4729
(605) 373-8893 (Fax)

South Dakota Democratic Party
PO Box 737
Sioux Falls, SD 57101
(605) 335-7337
(605) 335-7401 (Fax)
Acting Executive Director: Steve Dick

Tennessee

J. Houston Gordon, Chair
1808 West End Avenue, Suite 515
Nashville, TN 37203
(615) 327-9779

Bobbie Caldwell, Vice Chair
530 Riverside Drive
Clinton, TN 37716
(423) 457-0037
(423) 457-0343 (Fax)

Tennessee Democratic Party
1808 West End Avenue, Suite 515
Nashville, TN 37203
(615) 327-9779
(615) 327-9759 (Fax)
Acting Executive Director: Bob Corney

Texas

Bill White, Chair
415 Louisiana, Suite 3000
Houston, TX 77002
(713) 739-6517
(713) 400-6296 (Fax)

Clara Caldwell, Vice Chair
2118 Endicott Lane
Sugarland, TX 77478
(713) 491-9800
(713) 291-9191 (Fax)

Texas Democratic Party
919 Congress Avenue, Suite 600
Austin, TX 78701
(512) 478-9800
(512) 480-2500 (Fax)
Executive Director: Jorge A. Ramirez

Utah

Meghan Zanolli Holbrook, Chair
775 North Hilltop Road
Salt Lake City, UT 84103
(801) 539-0622
(801) 328-1238 (Fax)

Rod Julander, Vice Chair
1467 Penrose Drive
Salt Lake City, UT 84103
(801) 626-6697
(801) 626-7130 (Fax)

Utah Democratic Party
455 South 300 East, Suite 102
Salt Lake City, UT 84111
(801) 328-1212
(801) 328-1238 (Fax)
Executive Director: Todd Taylor

Vermont

David Curtis, Chair
PO Box 1142
Burlington, VT 05402
(802) 660-4900

Cindy Metcalf, Vice Chair
43 Central Street
Randolph, VT 05060
(802) 728-5163

Vermont Democratic Party
PO Box 1142
Burlington, VT 05402
(802) 660-4900
(802) 660-2828 (Fax)
Executive Director: Tom Hughes

Virginia

Sue Wrenn, Chair
4 Wolfe Street
Alexandria, VA 22314
(703) 299-9771
(703) 299-8832 (Fax)

W. Raymond Colley, Vice Chair
1105 Dalebrook Drive
Alexandria, VA 22308
(703) 360-4640

Virginia Democratic Party
1108 East Main Street, 2nd Floor
Richmond, VA 23219
(804) 644-1966
(804) 343-3642 (Fax)
Executive Director: Judy Napier

Virgin Islands

Marylyn Stapleton, Chair
PO Box 3739 Charlotte Amalie
St Thomas, VI 0080
(809) 777-4577
(809) 775-7832 (Fax)

Gerard Luz James II, Vice Chair
PO Box 4617, C. Sted
St Croix, VI 00822
(809) 778-8663
(809) 778-8661 (Fax)

Virgin Islands Democratic Party
PO Box 5994, Sunny Isle
St Croix, VI 00823
(809) 778-5830
(809) 778-1454 (Fax)
Executive Director: Mario deChabert

Washington

Paul Berendt, Chair
PO Box 4027
Seattle, WA 98104
(206) 583-0664
(206) 583-0301 (Fax)

Ya Yue J. Van, Vice Chair
NE 1630 Lower Drive
Pullman, WA 99163
(509) 332-2112
(509) 334-6958 (Fax)

Washington Democratic Party
PO Box 4027
Seattle, WA 98104
(206) 583-0664
(206) 583-0301 (Fax)
Executive Director: Robin Brand

West Virginia

Thomas P. Maroney, Chair
608 Virginia Street East
Charleston, WV 25301
(304) 346-9629
(304) 346-3325 (Fax)

Emilie Holroyd, Vice Chair
1428 Main Street
Princeton, WV 24740
(304) 425-5694
(304) 487-0854 (Fax)

West Virginia Democratic Party
405 Capitol Street, Suite 501
Charleston, WV 25301
(304) 342-8121
(304) 342-8122 (Fax)
Executive Director: Debbie McCormick

Wisconsin

Terri Spring, Chair
6304 Johnson Street
McFarland, WI 53558
(608) 838-2020

Bill Murat, Vice Chair
PO Box 111
Stevens Point, WI 54481
(608) 267-9649

Wisconsin Democratic Party
222 State Street, Suite 400
Madison, WI 53703
(608) 255-5172
(608) 255-8919 (Fax)
Executive Director: Larry Martin

Wyoming

Matilda Hansen, Chair
1306 Kearney
Laramie, WY 82070
(307) 745-7296
(307) 742-2554 (Fax)

Harold Bovee
22 Ridge Road
Torrington, WY 82240
(307) 532-4826

Wyoming Democratic Party
PO Box 5044
Cheyenne, WY 82003
(307) 637-8940
(307) 637-8947 (Fax)
Executive Director: Phoebe Bollin

AFFILIATED ORGANIZATIONS

Association of State Democratic Chairs
430 South Capitol Street SE
Washington, DC 20003
(202) 479-5121
(202) 479-5123 (Fax)

Association of State Executive Directors
2005 North Central, Suite 180
Phoenix, AZ 85004
(602) 257-8268

Democratic Congressional Campaign Committee
430 South Capitol Street SE
Washington, DC 20003
(202) 863-1500
(202) 485-3512 (Fax)

Democratic Governors' Association
430 South Capitol Street SE
Washington, DC 20003
(202) 479-5153
(202) 479-5156 (Fax)

Democratic Leadership Council
518 C Street NE
Washington, DC 20002
(202) 567-0007
(202) 544-5002 (Fax)

Women's National Democratic Club
1526 New Hampshire Avenue NW
Washington, DC 20036
(202) 232-7363
(202) 986-2791 (Fax)

The Republican Party

Republican National Committee
Dwight D. Eisenhower Republican Center
310 1st Street SE
Washington, DC 20003
(202) 863-8500
(202) 863-8820 (Fax)
http://www.rnc.org

The Rules of the Republican Party state that the national committee is responsible for the "general management of the Republican party subject to direction from the national convention." In reality, day-to-day management of the RNC falls to the chair, who acts as chief executive officer. Over the years, the RNC assumed the characteristics of a large corporation with myriad tasks, including the following:

1. Fund Raising. The Finance Division is responsible for raising and spending funds contributed to the Republican National Committee and development of the direct-mail campaign.

2. Voter List Development. This includes the creation of a computer-generated list of 100 million names to assist the RNC in its get-out-the-vote drives during presidential election years.

3. Voter Contact Programs. This involves direct solicitation of voters by mail coordinated by the RNC and state and local parties.

4. Technical Services. This includes candidate seminars, hiring professional poll takers to measure voter response to targeted Republican candidates and issues, providing legal help in complying with state and federal election laws (especially campaign finance statutes), preparation of print and electronic media advertising, as well as redistricting and other computer-based electioneering programs.

5. Generic Advertising. Television advertising to promote the Republican Party.

6. Communications. This includes "opposition research" on Democratic opponents and issuing "line-of-the-day" messages to Republican candidates so that the party can present a coordinated message on national and local media outlets—especially on television and radio talk programs.

7. Speaker's Bureau. More than 500 speakers are made available by the RNC to raise money for and speak on behalf of state and local Republican office seekers.

8. State and Local Party Development. The RNC provides financial grants and regional

directors to assist state and local parties in developing stronger organizations.

9. Managing the National Convention. The RNC is responsible for selecting the site of and managing the party's quadrennial presidential nominating convention.

SIZE OF THE REPUBLICAN NATIONAL COMMITTEE

In addition to the chair and the permanent staff, the RNC is overseen by a board of directors. Until the 1960s, national committee membership consisted of two persons from each state (one male, one female). In 1968 the committee was expanded to include state chairs (a concession to the Republican Party's newfound southern strength). Under rules adopted in 1988, the national committee totals 165—including 1 national committeeman and committeewoman from each state, the District of Columbia, Guam, Puerto Rico, American Samoa, and the Virgin Islands (110) and the 50 state chairs plus representatives from the District of Columbia and the U.S. territories (55).

Four selection methods are used: (1) partisan primary election, (2) state party convention, (3) state party central committee, or (4) the state party's delegation to the national convention. National committeemen and women serve for four years; state party chairs serve for the length of their tenure. A study of committee members conducted in the 1960s found that most were college educated, more than 45 years old, Protestant, and white-collar professionals (with a high percentage being lawyers or business owners).

The composition of the RNC reflects its "confederate" nature, as deference is usually given to the mores of individual state parties. Unlike the Democratic National Committee, the RNC has refrained from intruding into the presidential nominating procedures of the individual states. To date, the greatest effort to control the presidential nominating contest was made by the Delegates and Organization

Committee (the "DO Committee"), which was established by the RNC in 1968.

Among the DO Committee's recommendations were (1) open meetings should be held throughout the delegate selection process in order to assure that all qualified Republicans could participate in the nominating process; (2) no fees should be assessed against prospective convention delegates; (3) no proxy voting should be permitted; (4) "automatic delegates"—that is, those who became delegates by virtue of holding a particular party or elective office—should not be seated; (5) each convention committee should be expanded to include one delegate from each state who is under 25 years of age and one delegate from a designated minority group; (6) each state should be encouraged to seek equal representation between men and women in its national convention delegation; (7) states should be required to seek delegate representation by persons less than 25 years of age in proportion to their voting strength in the general population; and (8) the RNC should assist states in their efforts to inform citizens on the delegate selection process.

The 1972 Republican National Convention adopted all of the DO Committee's recommendations with the exception of that calling for proportional representation of young people. But the RNC has refrained from further intrusion into state delegate selection procedures. With so many states scheduling their presidential primaries in the first few months of 1996, however, Haley Barbour, then chair of the RNC, proposed another RNC-sponsored commission to examine delegate selection procedures with an eye toward greater national party control.

MEMBERS OF THE RNC EXECUTIVE COMMITTEE

Chair: Jim Nicholson
Co-Chair: Pat Harrison
Secretary: Linda Shaw
Treasurer: Alec Poitevint

General Counsel: Mike Grebe
Chair of the Chairs: Rusty Paul
Finance Chair: Mel Sembler
Budget Chair: Ron Carlson
NFRW: Marilyn Thayer

Vice Chair, Midwestern: Mary Alice Lair
Vice Chair, Midwestern: Jack Meeks
Vice Chair, Northeastern: Chris DePino
Vice Chair, Northeastern: Jody Dow
Vice Chair, Southern: Mike Duncan
Vice Chair, Southern: Flo Traywick
Vice Chair, Western: Blake Hall
Vice Chair, Western: Jan Larimer

Midwestern: Connie Nicholas
Midwestern: Ron Schmidt
Northeastern: Herb Barness
Northeastern: Sara Gear
Southern: Rusty Paul
Southern: Quineta Wylie
Western: Arlene Ellis
Western: Mike Hellon

Appointed: Mary Dambman
Appointed: Sue Akey
Appointed: Duane W. Acklie

STATE REPUBLICAN PARTIES

Alabama Republican Executive Committee
PO Box 320800
Birmingham, AL 35232
(205) 324-1990
(205) 324-0682 (Fax)

Executive Director: Bill Harris
National Committeewoman: Bettye Fine Collins
National Committeeman: W. Edgar Weldin Sr.
State Chair: Roger McConnell

Republican Party of Alaska
1001 West Fireweed Lane
Anchorage, AK 99503
(907) 276-4467
(907) 276-0425 (Fax)

Executive Director: Vacant
National Committeewoman: Edna DeVries
National Committeeman: Wayne A. Ross
State Chair: Pete Hallgren

Republican Party of American Samoa
PO Box 3564
Pago Pago, AS 96799
(684) 622-7848
(684) 633-4149 (Fax)

Executive Director: John Ah Sue
National Committeewoman: Amata Radewagen
National Committeeman: Vacant
State Chair: Tautai A. F. Faalevao

Arizona Republican Party
3501 North 24th Street
Phoenix, AZ 85016
(602) 957-7770
(602) 224-0932 (Fax)

Executive Director: Jane Lynch
National Committeewoman: Lori Marsh
National Committeeman: Michael T. Hellon
State Chair: Michael T. Hellon

Republican Party of Arkansas
1201 West 6th Street
Little Rock, AR 72201
(501) 372-7301
(501) 372-1656 (Fax)

Executive Director: Richard Bearden
National Committeewoman: Mildred Oman
National Committeeman: Sheffield Nelson
State Chair: Lloyd Stone

California Republican Party
1903 West Magnolia
Burbank, CA 91506

(818) 841-5210
(818) 841-6668 (Fax)

Executive Director: Richard Lambros
National Committeewoman: Barbara Alby
National Committeeman: Timothy J. Morgan
State Chair: Michael J. Schroeder

Republican State Central Committee of Colorado
1275 Tremont Place
Denver, CO 80204
(303) 893-1776
(303) 629-0459 (Fax)

Executive Director: Chris Baker
National Committeewoman: Mary Dambman
National Committeeman: Jim Nicholson
State Chair: Steve Curtis

Connecticut Republican State Central Committee
97 Elm Street
Hartford, CT 06106
(860) 547-0589
(860) 278-8563 (Fax)

Executive Director: George Gallo
National Committeewoman: Jo McKenzie
National Committeeman: John Miller
State Chair: Chris DePino

Delaware Republican State Committee
2 Mill Road, Suite 108
Wilmington, DE 19806
(302) 651-0260
(302) 651-0270 (Fax)

Executive Director: Vacant
National Committeewoman: Priscilla B.
    Rakerstraw
National Committeemen: Laird Stabler Jr.
State Chair: Basil Battaglia

District of Columbia Republican Committee
600 Pennsylvania Avenue SE, Suite 300
Washington, DC 20003
(202) 608-1407
(202) 608-1428 (Fax)

Executive Director: Vacant
National Committeewoman: Ann F. Heuer
National Committeeman: Harry M. Singleton
State Chair: Julie Finley

Republican Party of Florida
719 North Calhoun Street
Tallahassee, FL 32302
(904) 222-7920
(904) 681-3768 (Fax)

Executive Director: Randy Enright
National Committeewoman: Carole Jean Jordan
National Committeeman: Mel Sembler
State Chair: Tom Slade

Georgia Republican Party
5600 Roswell Road East, Suite 200
Atlanta, GA 30342
(404) 257-5559
(404) 257-0779 (Fax)

Executive Director: Joe King
National Committeewoman: Carolyn Meadows
National Committeeman: Alec Poitevint
State Chair: Rusty Paul

Republican Party of Guam
PO Box 2846
Agana, GU 96932
(671) 472-3558
(671) 734-2001 (Fax)

Executive Director: Vacant
National Committeewoman: Doris F. Brooks
National Committeeman: Edward Calvo
State Chair: Fred Castro

Republican Party of Hawaii
50 South Beretania, Suite C211D
Honolulu, HI 96813
(808) 526-1755
(808) 545-4039 (Fax)

Executive Director: Jesse Yescalis
National Committeewoman: Miriam Hellreich
National Committeeman: Howard Chong Jr.
State Chair: Donna L. Alcantara

Idaho Republican State Central Committee
PO Box 2267
Boise, ID 83701
(208) 343-6405
(208) 343-6414 (Fax)

Executive Director: Andrew Arulanandum
National Committeewoman: Cindy Moyle
National Committeeman: Blake Hall
State Chair: Ronald McMurray

Illinois Republican State Central Committee
188 West Randolph Street, Suite 627
Chicago, IL 60601
(312) 201-9000
(312) 201-1271 (Fax)

Executive Director: Christine Dudley
National Committeewoman: Mary Jo Arndt
National Committeeman: Robert Kjellander Jr.
State Chair: Harold B. Smith Jr.

Indiana Republican State Central Committee
200 South Meridian, Suite 400
Indianapolis, IN 46225
(317) 635-7561
(317) 632-8510 (Fax)

Executive Director: Vacant
National Committeewoman: Diane K. Adams
National Committeeman: Robert J. Hiler Jr.
State Chair: Michael McDaniel

Republican Central Committee of Iowa
521 East Locust Street
Des Moines, IA 50309
(515) 282-8105
(515) 282 9019 (Fax)

Executive Director: Keith Fortmann
National Committeewoman: Phyllis L. Kelly
National Committeeman: Stephen W. Roberts
State Chair: Steve Grubbs

Kansas Republican State Committee
2348 South Topeka Boulevard
Topeka, KS 66611
(913) 234-3456
(913) 234-3436 (Fax)

Executive Director: Kris Van Meteren
National Committeewoman: Mary Alice Lair
National Committeeman: Dwight Sutherland
State Chair: David G. Miller

Republican Party of Kentucky
PO Box 1068
Frankfort, KY 40602
(502) 875-5130
(502) 223-5625 (Fax)

Executive Director: Randy Kammerdiener
National Committeewoman: Betty L. Holmes
National Committeeman: Robert M. Duncan
State Chair: Tom Jensen

The Republican Party of Louisiana
7916 Wrenwood Boulevard, Suite E
Baton Rouge, LA 70809
(504) 928-2998
(504) 928-2969 (Fax)

Executive Director: Jeff Crouere
National Committeewoman: Patricia B. Brister
National Committeeman: Roger Villere Jr.
State Chair: Mike Francis

Maine Republican Party
100 Water Street

Hallowell, ME 04347
(207) 622-6247
(207) 623-5322 (Fax)

Executive Director: Rick Tyler
National Committeewoman: Doris M. Russell
National Committeeman: Kenneth M. Cole III
State Chair: Kevin Keogh

Republican State Central Committee of Maryland
1623 Forest Drive, Suite 400
Annapolis, MD 21403
(410) 269-0113
(410) 269-5937 (Fax)

Executive Director: Jim Burton
National Committeewoman: Ellen R. Sauerbrey
National Committeeman: Richard P. Taylor
State Chair: Joyce Terhes

Massachusetts Republican State Committee
21 Milk Street, 4th Floor
Boston, MA 02109
(617) 357-1998
(617) 357-1975 (Fax)

Executive Director: Marc DeCourcey
National Committeewoman: Jody Dow
National Committeeman: Ron Kaufman
State Chair: Jean A. Inman

Michigan Republican State Committee
2121 East Grand River
Lansing, MI 48912
(517) 487-5413
(517) 487-0090 (Fax)

Executive Director: Greg Brock
National Committeewoman: Sharon A. Wise
National Committeeman: Charles Yob
State Chair: Elisabeth DeVos

The Republican Party of Minnesota
480 Cedar Street, Suite 400
St Paul, MN 55010
(612) 222-0022
(612) 224-4122 (Fax)

Executive Director: Tony Sutton
National Committeewoman: Evie Axdahl
National Committeeman: Jack Meeks
State Chair: William A. Cooper

Mississippi Republican Party
PO Box 60
Jackson, MS 39205
(601) 948-5191
(601) 354-0972 (Fax)

Executive Director: Randy Eberts
National Committeewoman: Stephanie Punches
National Committeeman: Haley R. Barbour
State Chair: Mike Retzer

Missouri Republican State Committee
PO Box 73
Jefferson City, MO 65102
(573) 636-3146
(573) 636-3273 (Fax)

Executive Director: John Hancock
National Committeewoman: Roberta C. Moore
National Committeeman: Hillard F. Selck
State Chair: John C. Cozad

Montana Republican State Central Committee
1419-B Helena Avenue
Helena, MT 59601
(406) 442-6469
(406) 442-3293 (Fax)

Executive Director: Tricia Pearson
National Committeewoman: Ione Brownson
National Committeeman: Tim Babcock
State Chair: Susan C. Aleksich-Akey

Nebraska Republican State Central Committee
421 South 9th Street, Suite 233
Lincoln, NE 68508
(402) 475-2122
(402) 475-3541 (Fax)

Executive Director: Beth Thompson Smith
National Committeewoman: Patricia Dorwart
National Committeeman: Duane W. Acklie
State Chair: Charles W. Sigerson Jr.

Republican State Central Committee of Nevada
6114 West Charleston Boulevard
Las Vegas, NV 89102
(702) 258-9182
(702) 258-9352 (Fax)

Executive Director: Dan Burdish
National Committeewoman: Barbara
    Vucanovich
National Committeeman: Tom Wiesner
State Chair: John Mason

New Hampshire Republican State Committee
134 North Main Street
Concord, NH 03301
(603) 225-9341
(603) 225-7498 (Fax)

Executive Director: Vacant
National Committeewoman: Ruth L. Griffin
National Committeeman: Thomas D. Rath
State Chair: Stephen Duprey

New Jersey Republican State Committee
28 West State Street, Suite 305
Trenton, NJ 08608
(609) 989-7300
(609) 989-8685 (Fax)

Executive Director: Rocco Iossa
National Committeewoman: Judith H. Stanley

National Committeeman: David Norcross
State Chair: Garabed Haytaian

Republican Party of New Mexico
PO Box 36900
2900 Juan Tabo Street NE, Suite 116
Albuquerque, NM 87112
(505) 298-3662
(505) 292-0755 (Fax)

Executive Director: Kevin Moomaw
National Committeewoman: Rosalind F. Tripp
National Committeeman: Manuel Lujan Jr.
State Chair: John Dendahl

New York Republican State Committee
315 State Street
Albany, NY 12210
(518) 462-2601
(518) 449-7443 (Fax)

Executive Director: Brendan Quinn
National Committeewoman: Georgette
    Mosbacher
National Committeeman: Joseph Mondello
State Chair: William Powers

North Carolina Republican Executive Committee
PO Box 12905
1410 Hillsborough
Raleigh, NC 27605
(919) 828-6423
(919) 899-3815 (Fax)

Executive Director: Lee Currie
National Committeewoman: Linda O. Shaw
National Committeeman: Ferrell Blount
State Chair: Samuel T. Currin

North Dakota Republican State Committee
PO Box 1917
101 East Broadway Avenue
Bismarck, ND 58501

Executive Director: Gary Porter
National Committeewoman: Connie Nicholas
National Committeeman: Steve Easton
State Chair: Gary Porter

Republican State Central & Executive Committee of Ohio
211 South 5th Street
Columbus, OH 43215
(614) 228-2481
(614) 228-1093 (Fax)

Executive Director: Thomas Whatman
National Committeewoman: Martha C. Moore
National Committeeman: Michael F. Colley
State Chair: Robert T. Bennett

Republican State Committee of Oklahoma
4031 North Lincoln Boulevard
Oklahoma City, OK 73105
(405) 528-3501
(405) 521-9531 (Fax)

Executive Director: Quineta Wylie
National Committeewoman: Bunny Chambers
National Committeeman: Lynn Windel
State Chair: Quineta Wylie

Oregon Republican Party
PO Box 1450
Beaverton, OR 97075-1450
(503) 520-1996
(503) 644-0210 (Fax)

Executive Director: Marge Hughes
National Committeewoman: June S. Hartley
National Committeeman: Dennis A. Smith
State Chair: Deanna Smith

Republican State Committee of Pennsylvania
112 State Street
Harrisburg, PA 17101
(717) 234-4901
(717) 231-3828 (Fax)

Executive Director: Vacant
National Committeewoman: Christine Toretti
National Committeeman: Herbert Barness
State Chair: Alan P. Novak

The National Republican Party of Puerto Rico
502 Hostos Avenue
Hato Rey, PR 00918
(787) 754-0144
(787) 767-6866 (Fax)

Executive Director: Cesar Cabrera
National Committeewoman: Zoraida F. Fonalledas
National Committeeman: Edison Misla-Aldarondo
State Chair: Luis A. Ferre

Rhode Island Republican State Central Committee
551 South Main Street
Providence, RI 02903
(401) 453-4100
(401) 453-0066 (Fax)

Executive Director: Vacant
National Committeewoman: Eileen G. Slocum
National Committeeman: Michael A. Traficante
State Chair: Joan B. Quick

South Carolina Republican Party
1508 Lady Street
Columbia, SC 29201
(803) 988-8440
(803) 988-8444 (Fax)

Executive Director: Trey Walker
National Committeewoman: Cindy Costa
National Committeeman: Buddy Witherspoon
State Chair: Henry McMaster

South Dakota Republican Party
PO Box 1099
Pierre, SD 57501

(605) 224-7347
(605) 224-7349 (Fax)

Executive Director: Patrick Davis
National Committeewoman: Mary Jean Jensen
National Committeeman: Ronald G. Schmidt
State Chair: Joel Rosenthal

Tennessee Republican State Executive Committee
PO Box 150368
Nashville, TN 37215
(615) 292-9497
(615) 292-9619 (Fax)

Executive Director: Brad Todd
National Committeewoman: Lill Coker
National Committeeman: John L. Ryder
State Chair: Jim Burnett

Republican Party of Texas
211 East 7th Street, Suite 620
Austin, TX 78701
(512) 477-9821
(512) 480-0709 (Fax)

Executive Director: Wayne Hamilton
National Committeewoman: Susan Feldtman
National Committeeman: Tim Lambert
State Chair: Susan Weddington

Utah Republican Party
117 East South Temple
Salt Lake City, UT 84111
(801) 533-9777
(801) 533-0327 (Fax)

Executive Director: Spencer Stokes
National Committeewoman: Arlene Ellis
National Committeeman: John Price
State Chair: Rob Bishop

Vermont Republican State Committee
43 Court Street

Montpelier, VT 05602
(802) 233-3411
(802) 229-1864 (Fax)

Executive Director: Ruth Stokes
National Committeewoman: Sara M. Gear
National Committeeman: Allen Martin
State Chair: Daniel R. Hillard

The Republican Party of the Virgin Islands
PO Box 11195
St Thomas, VI 00801
(340) 777-7600
(340) 777-6876 (Fax)

Executive Director: Alston "Bruce" Brewster
National Committeewoman: Lilliana Belardo de O'Neal
National Committeeman: Holland L. Redfield II
State Chair: James M. Oliver

Republican Party of Virginia
115 East Grace Street
Richmond, VA 23219
(804) 789-0111
(804) 343-1060 (Fax)

Executive Director: Chris Lacivita
National Committeewoman: Flo Traywick
National Committeeman: Morton Blackwell
State Chair: J. Randy Forbes

Republican State Committee of Washington
16400 Southcenter Parkway, Suite 200
Seattle, WA 98188
(206) 575-2900
(206) 575-1730 (Fax)

Executive Director: Frank Bickford
National Committeewoman: Gretchen Horton
National Committeeman: Ron Carlson
State Chair: Dale Foreman

Republican Executive Committee of West Virginia
1620 Kanawha Boulevard E, Suite 4B
Charleston, WV 25311
(304) 344-3446
(304) 344-3448 (Fax)

Executive Director: Betty White
National Committeewoman: Donna Boley
National Committeeman: Bill Pauley
State Chair: David Richard Tyson

Republican Party of Wisconsin
PO Box 31
Madison, WI 53701
(608) 257-4765
(608) 257-4141 (Fax)

Executive Director: Dana Walch
National Committeewoman: Mary F. Buestrin
National Committeeman: Michael W. Grebe
State Chair: David Opitz

Wyoming Republican State Committee
400 East 1st Street, Suite 314
Casper, WY 82601
(307) 234-9166
(307) 473-8640 (Fax)

Executive Director: Mary McIntyre
National Committeewoman: Jan Larimer
National Committeeman: Tom Sansonetti
State Chair: Wallace Ulrich

AFFILIATED ORGANIZATIONS

College Republican National Committee
450 East Maple Avenue, Suite 308
Vienna, VA 22180
(703) 319-0280
(703) 319-0203 (Fax)

National Federation of Republican Women
124 North Alfred Street
Alexandria, VA 22314
(703) 548-9688
(703) 548-9836 (Fax)

National Republican Congressional Committee
320 1st Street SE
Washington, DC 20003
(202) 479-7000
(202) 863-0693 (Fax)

National Republican Senatorial Committee
425 2nd Street NE
Washington, DC 20002
(202) 675-6000
(202) 675-6068 (Fax)

Republican Governors Association
310 1st Street SE
Washington, DC 20003
(202) 863-8587
(202) 863-8659 (Fax)

Ripon Society
227 Massachusetts Avenue NE, Suite 201
Washington, DC 20002
(202) 546-1292
(202) 547-6560 (Fax)

Third Parties
National and State Bodies

While the American political system is fundamentally a two-party system, there have been throughout history third parties. Generally, third parties fall into three general categories. The first is a doctrinal party that focuses on a minority of individuals on the political fringes of the left wing such as the socialist and communist parties or the right wing such as the American Party.

The second group are issue parties that arise over a particular issue. Prior to the Civil War, for instance, several single issue parties emerged specifically to address the question of slavery. Today, parties like the Greens are fundamentally single issue parties.

The third type of third party is the personality party. This party forms around the ideas of a single individual and usually does not exist after that individual ceases to be its candidate. Teddy Roosevelt's Bull Moose Party of 1912 and Ross Perot's Reform Party are examples of this type. The Reform Party, however, is trying to become a more broad-based party.

There are several reasons why third parties have not fared well in the American political system. The first reason is that the United States has a single member, plurality electoral system. Unlike many European countries that have proportional representation, American elections only reward those who come in first in elections.

While the electoral system may account for the biggest reason for the failure of third parties, there are others, including: state laws make it difficult for third parties to get on ballots; public funding of the two dominant parties often gives additional aid to them; the news media is often skeptical of third parties and their candidates, giving them little coverage; and the two dominant parties often adjust their positions to defuse the need for a third party.

Despite the many factors that exist against third parties in America, there is no shortage of them. The following list contains third parties of all types. Some are loosely organized, while others have a network of state and local affiliations.

American Independent Party
1084 West Marshall Boulevard
San Bernardino, CA 92045
(909) 882-9829
E-mail: sdaip@earthlink.net
Chairman: Merton Short
Website: http://www.wordpr.com/aip

f. 1967 for the Wallace Campaign of 1968, Affiliated with the US Taxpayers Party at the national level; Publications: *The California Statesman*.

American Party
PO Box 597
Provo, UT 84603
Website: http://www.wavefront.com/~contra-m/cm/features/cm04-american.html.

f. 1972 as a small conservative splinter group supporting Sen. Jesse Helms (R-SC) and Gov. Mel Thomson (R-NH) of the American Independent Party.

American Reform Party
2828 Morning Glow Drive, Suite 202
Memphis, TN 38018
(901) 382-7393
(901) 382-7393 (Fax)
E-mail: rwitherspoon@worldnet.att.net
Chair: Linda Witherspoon
Website: http://www.americanreform.org.

f.1997 as a splinter group from Reform Party. The group objected to H. Ross Perot's control of the party and the lack of national organization.

Anti-Lawyer Party
6308 24th Avenue
Kenosha, WI 53140

Archonist Club
682 Callahan Place
Mendota Heights, MN 55118
Regent: Cheryl Andrea Bruhn

f. 1967; A civic, quasi-religious organization of Christian persuasion that advocates socio-political decisions be based upon the merits of logic and morality, with due regard for Scriptures, science, history, and managerial principles.

Black Panther Party
7911 MacArthur Boulevard
Oakland, CA 94605

Boston Tea Party
1051 North Grand Avenue
Mesa, AZ 85201

Communist Party-USA
235 West 23rd Street
New York, NY 10011
(212) 989 4994
(212) 229 1713 (Fax)
E-mail: cpusa@rednet.org
Chair: Gus Hall
Website: http://www.hartford-hwp.com/cp-usa/

f. 1919; Seeks to achieve a socialist society; Publications: *Jewish Affairs* (bimonthly); *People's Weekly World* (weekly); *Political Affairs* (monthly).

Arizona District CPUSA. PO Box 26912, Tucson, AZ 85726. Tel: (520) 623-5280.

Communist Party of Southern California. 1251 S Street, Andrews Place, Los Angeles, CA 90019. Tel: (213) 733-3415.

Communist Party of Northern California. 1206 Fruitvale Avenue, Oakland CA 94601. Tel: (510) 532- 0105.

Communist Party of Colorado. PO Box 4602, Boulder, CO 80306. Fax: (303) 772-7253 E-mail: elikeche@worldnet.att.net.

Communist Party of Connecticut. PO Box 1437, New Haven, CT 06506. Tel: (203) 624-4254 E-mail: ct-cpusa@ pobox.com. Website: http://www.hartford-hwp.com/ct-cpusa/.

Communist Party of Illinois. 3116 South Halsted Street, Chicago, IL 60608. (312) 842-5770 E-mail: cpi@rednet.org. Website: http://miso.wwa.com/~ksm/index.html.

Communist Party of Indiana. PO Box 575, Gary, IN 46401. E-mail: kaczocha@ netnitco.net.

Communist Party of Maryland. 408 Park Avenue, Suite 200, Baltimore, MD 21202. Tel: (301) 685-1914.

Communist Party of Massachusetts. 550 Massachusetts Avenue, 2nd Floor, Cambridge, MA 02139. Tel: (617) 287-9672 E-mail: jacruz@argo.net.

Communist Party of Michigan. 16145 Woodward, Highland Park, MI 48203. Tel: (313) 883-3244.

Communist Party of Minnesota. E-mail: svbx43a@prodigy.com. Website: http://global-reach.com/cp-minn/.

Communist Party, Missouri-Kansas District. PO Box 8093, St Louis, MO 63156.

Communist Party of New Mexico. c/o Friends of the PWW, PO Box 613, Albuquerque, NM 87103. E-mail: emilshaw @rt66.com.

Communist Party of New York. 235 West 23rd Street, 6th Floor, New York, NY 10011. Tel: (212) 924-0550. E-mail: dmallisk@mhv.net. Website: http://www1.mhv.net/~dmallisk.

Communist Party of North Carolina. PO Box 671, Carrboro, NC 27510-0671. E-mail: hoseahudsonclub@mindspring.com.

Communist Party of Ohio. 4307 Lorain Avenue, Cleveland, OH 44113. Tel: (216) 281-7141 E-mail: 10356.2672@compuserve.com.

Communist Party of Eastern Pennsylvania. 4515 Baltimore Avenue, Philadelphia, PA 19143. Tel: (215) 222-8895. or 801 South 47th Street, Philadelphia, PA 19143. Tel: (215) 387-7200.

Communist Party of Western Pennsylvania. 5024 Penn Avenue, Pittsburgh, PA 15224. Tel: (412) 661-6115 E-mail: dwinebr696@aol.com.

Communist Party of Rhode Island. Center for Workers Education, PO Box 25015, Providence, RI 02905.

Communist Party of Texas. PO Box 226147, Dallas, TX 75222. E-mail: comment2.juno.com.

Communist Party of Washington. 1406 18th Avenue, Seattle, WA 98122. Tel: (206) 329-9171 E-mail: marca@earthlink.net.

Communist Party of Wisconsin. E-mail: dialectical@msn.com.

Confederate National Congress
HCR 33, PO Box 450
Elkins, AR 72717
President: Frank Starr

f. 1867; Works for Southern independence through re-establishment of Confederate States of America; Publications: *CSA Information Agency News* (quarterly).

Conservative Party of Massachusetts
Belmont, MA 02178
(617) 489-4842

Conservative Party of New York
486 78th Street
Brooklyn, NY 11209
State Chair: Michael R. Long

f. 1962; Dedicated to individual liberty, limited constitutional government and national defense.

Constitution Action Party
PO Box 5705
Arlington, VA 22208
Chair: Frank Creel
Website: http://www2.arinet/home/cap

Seeks replacement of the income tax with a progressive corporate income tax.

Democratic Socialists Party
180 Varick Street
New York, NY 10014
(212) 727-8610
(212) 727-8616 (Fax)
Chair: Alan Charney
Website: http://www.dsausa.org/ index.html.

f. 1900; Principal US affiliate of the Socialist International which is dedicated to the progressive movement for social change by establishing an openly socialist presence in American society and politics.

Alaska Chapter. PO Box 70252, Fairbanks, AK 99707. Fax: (907) 479-9466. E-mail: niilosoc@mosuitonet.com. Chair: Niilo Koponen.

Arkansas Chapter. 2218 Scott, Little Rock, AR 72206. Tel: (501) 372-2152. Chair: Jason Murphy.

Northern California Region. PO Box 162394, Sacramento, CA 95816. Tel: (916) 448-3484. Chair: Javier Sepulveda.

Southern California Region. PO Box 291864, Los Angeles, CA 90029. Tel: (213) 951-1960. Chair: Tim Parks.

Colorado Chapter. PO Box 748, Boulder, CO 80306-0748. Tel: (303) 666-5064 E-mail: mciver@cs.colorado.edu. Chair: William McIver.

Carbondale IL Chapter. PO Box 2201, Carbondale, IL 62902. Tel: (618) 549-1409 E-mail: eghughes@midwest.net. Chair: E.G. Hughes.

Chicago IL Chapter. 1608 North Milwaukee Avenue, Suite 403, Chicago, IL 60647.

Tel: (312) 384-0327 E-mail: robertmroman@ delphi.com. Chair: Robert Roman.

Indianapolis IN Chapter. 5613 East Washington, Suite12, Indianapolis, IN 46219. Tel: (317) 352-8261. Chair: Nancy Nann.

Iowa Chapter. 112 South Dodge, Iowa City, IA 52240. Tel: (319) 338-4551 E-mail: jlcox@blue.weeg.uiowa.edu. Chair: Jeff Cox.

Baltimore MD Chapter. 3704 Yolando Road, Baltimore, MD 21218. Tel: (410) 235-3504. Chair: Richard Bruning.

Boston MA Chapter. 11 Garden Street, Cambridge, MA 02138. Tel: (617) 354-5078. Chair: Gayle Neave.

Ann Arbor MI Chapter. PO Box 7211, Ann Arbor, MI 48107. Tel: (313) 677-8470. Chair: Eric Ebel.

Detroit MI Chapter. 20247 Kelly Road, Detroit, MI 48225. Tel: (810) 759-1200 E-mail: raronso@cms.cc.wayne.edu. Chair: Roger Robinson.

Twin Cities Chapter. 695 Ottawa Avenue, St Paul, MN 55107. Tel: (612) 224-8262. Chair: Dan Frankot.

St Louis MO Chapter. 3323 Magnolia, St Louis, MO 63118. Tel: (314) 773-0605 E-mail: radrathke@aol.com. Chair: Dave Rathke.

New Hampshire Chapter. One Mill Street, Suite 325, Dover, NH 03820. E-mail: jgidding@mv.mv.com. Chair: Don Taylor

Central NJ Chapter. 81 Moore Street, Princeton, NJ 08540. Tel: (609) 783-1853 E-mail: pmann@access.digex.net. Chair: Bernie Backer.

Northern NJ Chapter. PO Box 32238, Midtown Station, Newark, NJ 07102. Tel: (201) 345-7171. Chair: Stanley Sheats.

Albuquerque NM Chapter. 6008 Ponderosa NE, Albuquerque, NM 87110. Tel: (505) 881-4687. Chair: Gerry Bradley.

Ithaca NY Chapter. 1426 Hanshaw Road, Ithaca, NY 14850. Tel: (607) 257-2520 E-mail: talt@igc.apc.org. Chair: Sylvia G. Wahl.

Nassau County NY Chapter. 662 Howard Avenue, West Hempstead, NY 11552. Tel: (516) 538-8246. Chair: Mark Finkel.

New York NY Chapter. 180 Varick Street, New York, NY 10014. Tel: (212) 727-2207 E-mail: dsa@igc.apc.org. Chair: Marsha Borenstein.

Columbus OH Chapter. 824 Kerr Street, Columbus, OH 43215. Tel: (614) 297-0710 E-mail: freeper@aol.com. Chair: George Boas.

Philadelphia PA Chapter. PO Box 58544, Philadelphia, PA 19102. Tel: (215) 702-9739 E-mail: quinnkm@aol.com. Chair: Kathy Quinn.

Pittsburgh PA Chapter. PO Box 5122, Pittsburgh, PA 15206. Chair: Bill Wekselman.

Austin TX Chapter. 2409 West 8th Street, Austin, TX 78703. Tel: (512) 320-0257. Chair: Dick Fralin.

Houston TX Chapter. 10915 Wickersham, Houston, TX 77042. Tel: (713) 268-1617. Chair: Elroy Sullivan.

Charlottesville VA Chapter. 104 Diamond Road, Troy, VA 22974. Tel: (804) 295-8884 E-mail: cnk2r@poe.acc.virginia.edu. Chair: Claire Kaplan.

Richmond VA Chapter. PO Box 5011, Richmond, VA 23220. Tel: (804) 355-6618. Chair: Irene Ries.

Seattle WA Chapter. 6221 Greenwood Avenue North, Seattle, WA 98103. Tel: (206) 784-9695 E-mail: csalins@scn.org. Chair: Craig Salins.

Expansionist Party
446 West 46th Street
New York, NY 10036
(212) 265-1081
(212) 265-1081 (Fax)
Chair: L. Craig Schoomaker

f. 1977; Interested in expanding the US geographically.

Grassroots Party of Minnesota
PO Box 6197
Minneapolis, MN 55406
(612) 722-4GRP
E-mail: grp@visi.com
Chair: T. Christopher Wright
Website: http://www.visi.com/~grp

f. 1986; opposes mandatory drug sentencing, seeks universal health care and supports the legalization of marijuana.

The Greens/Green Party USA
PO Box 100
Blodgett Mills, NY 13738
(607) 756-4211
E-mail: gpusa@igc.apc.org
Website: http://www.greens.org/gpusa/

f. 1984; nonviolent, environmental party.

Green Party of Alaska. 2611 Northrup Place, Anchorage, AK 99508. Tel: (907)

278-7436 E-mail: greenak@alaska.net. Contact: Jim Sykes.

Arizona Green Party. PO Box 60173, Phoenix, AZ 85082. Tel: (602) 814-9297. Contacts: Jon or Lisa Broderick. Website: http://home.sprynet.com/sprynet/azgp.

Green Party of California. 1108 10th Street, Suite 482, Sacramento, CA 95814. Tel: (916) 448-3437.

Green Party of Colorado. Tel: (303) 575-1631 E-mail: muzzin@igc.apc.org. Contact: Mark Ruzzin.

Green Party of Connecticut. PO Box 874, Storrs, CT 06268. Website: http://www.ntplx.net/~droberts/ctgreens.html.

Green Party of Florida. PO Box 10294, Pensacola, FL 32524. Tel: (904) 474-1495 E-mail: jdardis@earthlink.net. Contact: John Ardis.

Green Party of Georgia. PO Box 5455, Atlanta, GA 30307. Tel: (770) 368-7137 E-mail: ggp@greens.org.

Green Party of Hawaii. PO Box 3220, Kailua Kona, HI 96745. Tel: (808) 324-7336. State Co-Chair: Ira Rohter; Website: http://www.greenhawaii.org.

Green Party of Illinois. 716 Maxwell Street, Chicago, IL 60607. Tel: (312) 226-3248. Website: http://www.pg.net/users/g/greens/index.htm.

Green Party of Kentucky. 3205 Fallshore Court, Louisville, KY 40220. Tel: (502) 495-0856 E-mail: al_vater@usa.pipeline.com. Chair: Richard W. Bohlman.

Green Party of Louisiana (Delta Greens). 7725 Cohn Street, New Orleans, LA 70118. Tel: (504) 861-8832 E-mail: clark@beta.loyno.edu. Treasurer: John

Clark. Website: http://www.geocities/rainforest/1387/.

Green Party of Maine. 283 Water Street, Augusta, ME 04330. Tel: (207) 623-1919.

Green Party of Maryland. PO Box 461, College Park, MD 20740. Tel: (301) 277-3720 E-mail: dmoore@ crosslink.net. Chair: David K. Moore. Website: http://www.cpcug.org/user/kopp/bob/mdgreens/.

Green Party of Massachusetts. PO Box 43, Lawrence, MA 01842. Tel: (978) 688-2068 E-mail: massgreens@ipc.apc.org.

Green Party of Minnesota. PO Box 582931, Minneapolis, MN 55458. Tel: (612) 871-4585. Website: http://www.jimn.org/gpm/.

Green Party of Michigan. 548 South Main Street, Ann Arbor, MI 48104. Tel: (313) 663-3555. Website: http://ic.net/~harvey/greens/.

Green Party of Missouri. PO Box 1958, Columbia, MO 65205.

Nevada Green Party. PO Box 9127, Reno, NV 89507. Tel: (702) 784-4611 E-mail: jones@scs.unr.edu. Chair: Helen Jones.

Green Party of New Jersey. PO Box 9802, Trenton, NJ 08650. Tel: (609) 278-4467 Fax: (609) 393-5343 E-mail: organizer@juno.com. Chair: Madelyn Hoffman. Website: http://www.gphj.org.

Green Party of New Mexico. 1001 Yale Boulevard SE, Albuquerque, NM 87106. Tel: (505) 473-3621 E-mail: nmgp@nmgp.org.

Green Party of New York. 63-36 98th Place, Suite 5J, Rego Park, NY 11374. Tel: (888) NY4-GREENS E-mail: levner

@panix.com. Clearinghouse Coordinator: David Levner.

Green Party of North Carolina. Tel: (919) 933-5562 E-mail: marcoplos@ aol.com. Chair: Mark Marcoplos. Website: http://www.jwp.bc.ca/rbueker/nc-greens/.

Green Party of Ohio. Tel: (216) 631-0557 E-mail: dellison@igc.apc.org. Contact: David Ellison. Website: http://www.envirolink.org/greens/ohio/.

Green Party of Pennsylvania. PO Box 7413, Lancaster, PA 17604. Tel: (717) 394-9100 E-mail: ajgoeke@igc.apc.org. Chair: Tom Linzey.

Green Party of Rhode Island. PO Box 1151, Providence, RI 02901. Tel: (401) 658-3884. Secretary: Chuck Bradley.

Green Party of Virginia. 8 River Ridge Road, Verona, VA 24482. Tel: (504) 248-7721 E-mail: eric@rockbridge.net. Contact: Sherry Stanley. Website: http://ns.rockbridge.net/greens/.

Green Party of Washington. Tel: (206) 324-5675 E-mail: benburg@ u.washington.edu. Chair: Scott Denburg. Website: http://vader.boutell.com/seagreens.

Green Party of Wisconsin. 1001 East Keefe Avenue, Milwaukee, WI 53212. E-mail: peterson@win.bright.net. Contact: Jeff Peterson. Website: http://www.excel.net/~pdrewry/wigreen.htm.

International Green Party
1295 Marshall Boulevard, Suite 512
Aurora, IL 60505.
(708) 898-5122
(708) 898-5122 (Fax)
Chair: Randall Toler
f. 1973; Promotes ecological issues; Publica-

tions: *Green Party Newsletter* (quarterly); *International Green Manifesto* (quinquennial).

Jewish Labor Bund
21 East 21st Street
New York, NY 10010
(212) 475-0059
Secretary: Benjamin Nadel

Pioneer in modern socialism and associate member of Socialist International; Publications: *Report and Resolutions of the 7th World Conference of the Jewish Labor Bund.*

Labor Party
PO Box 53177
Washington, DC 20009
E-mail: lpa@labornet.org
Website: http://www.igc.apc.org/lpa/

Seeks full employment, the protection of the environment and the protection of workers' rights including the right to strike.

Arizona Chapter. PO Box 42003-602, Phoenix, AZ 85080. E-mail: aenglish@ crl11.crl.com. Contact: Andrew English.

East Bay Chapter. PO Box 8266, Berkeley, CA 94707-8266.

Frank Little Chapter. PO Box 5077, Fresno, CA 93755. Tel: (209) 226-2078 E-mail: clr2@labornet.org.

Golden Gate Chapter. PO Box 423047, San Francisco, CA 94142-3047. E-mail: bwiles@labornet.org.

Los Angeles Metro Chapter. PO Box 26446, Los Angeles, CA 90026. Contact: Kathleen O'Nan.

San Diego Chapter. PO Box 16235, San Diego, CA 92176. Contact: Ali Hebshi.

Tri-County Chapter. PO Box 488, Santa Barbara, CA 93102. E-mail: mshone@ labornet.org. Contact: Mya Shone.

Colorado Chapter. 20531 East Coolidge Place, Aurora, CO 80011. Sec-Treas: Dale Carpenter.

Connecticut Chapter. PO Box 340, Kensington, CT 06037.

Washington DC Chapter. PO Box 2273, Washington, DC 20013-2273.

Greater Deerfield Chapter. 6800 Royal Palm Boulevard, Margate, FL 33063. Contact: Gene Lowey.

Central Illinois Chapter. 1536 North Taylor Avenue, Decatur, IL 62526. Contact: Paul Kendall.

Chicago Chapter. 3245 West 64th Street, Chicago, IL 60629-2747. Contact: Frank Rosen.

Eastern Iowa Chapter. 222 3rd Street SE, Suite 408, Cedar Rapids, IA 52401. Contact: Sylvia Kelley.

Southern Maine Labor Party. PO Box 1812, North Berwick, ME 04104.

Baltimore Chapter. 4702 Lavington Place, Baltimore, MD 21236. Contact: Mike Libber.

Massachusetts Chapter. 30 Winter Street, 9th Floor, Boston, MA 02108-4720. Contact: Frank Borges.

Detroit Chapter. 26555 Evergreen Road, Suite 200, Southfield, MI 48076-4225. E-mail: fvitale@igc.apc.org.

Washtenaw County Chapter. PO Box 7788, Ann Arbor, MI 48107. Contact: Michael Kinnucan.

Twin Cities Chapter. PO Box 583461, Minneapolis, MN 55458. E-mail: elymn@ net1.net-info.com. Secretary: Brien Link.

Kansas City Area Chapter. PO Box 30127, Plaza Station, Kansas City, MO 64112. Treasurer: Tony Saper.

Central New Jersey Chapter. 20 Pine Knoll Drive, Lawrenceville, NJ 08648. Contact: Eric Lerner.

New Jersey Chapter. 511 Westminster Avenue, Elizabeth, NJ 07208. Chair: Kathy King.

New Mexico Chapter. PO Box 12546, Albuquerque, NM 87195. Treasurer: Jon Thomas-Weger.

Buffalo Chapter. 441 Massachusetts Avenue, Buffalo, NY 14213-2303. E-mail: garywelborn@compuserve.com. Contact: Gary Welborn.

Capital District Chapter. 55 Grant Avenue, PO Box 13570, Albany, NY 12212. Contacts: David Patrick or Glenn Goliber.

Central New York Chapter. 106 Washington Street, Ithaca, NY 14850. Contact: Howard Botwinick.

Higher Education Chapter. 28 West 96th Street, Suite 7, New York, NY 10025. Contact: Elaine Harger.

New York Metro Chapter. 220 East 23rd Street, Suite 707, New York, NY 10010. Treasuer: Robert Spencer.

Ocean Front Chapter. 251 Amherst Street, Brooklyn, NY 11235. Co-Chair: Philip Metling.

Richmond County/Staten Island Chapter. 41 Belmont Place, St George, NY 10301. Chair: Ed Wlody.

Rochester Labor Council Chapter. 30 North Union Street, Rochester, NY 14607. Sec-Treas: Jon Garlock.

Rochester Chapter. 96 Magee Avenue, Rochester, NY 14613. Contact: Tom Fitzpatrick.

North Carolina Piedmont Triad Chapter. PO Box 20002, Greensboro, NC 27420. Contact: Frank Brayant.

North Carolina Triangle Chapter. 2736 Dogwood Road, Durham, NC 17705. Contact: Jack Holtzman.

Cleveland Chapter. PO Box 5652, Cleveland, OH 44101. Contact: Maryanne Young.

Toledo Chapter. PO Box 971, Toledo, OH 43697-0971.

Columbia/Willamette Valley Chapter. PO Box 4732, Portland, OR 97208. E-mail: lsundet@cybernw.com

Lehigh Valley/Brennan Chapter. PO Box 1547, Bethlehem, PA 18018-1547. E-mail: meglo01@moravian.edu. Contact: Gary Olson.

Metro Pittsburgh Chapter. 100 North Bellefield Avenue, Pittsburgh, PA 15213.

Philadelphia Chapter. PO Box 34142, Philadelphia, PA 19101. Chair: Jim Moran.

Western Pennsylvania Chapter. PO Box 11354, Pittsburgh, PA 15238. Chair: Ed Grystar.

Rhode Island Chapter. 1201 Elmwood Avenue, Providence, RI 02907. Chair: Stephen Dennis.

Bexar County Chapter. 931 West Harding Boulevard, San Antonio, TX 78221-1818. Contact: Paul Pipkin.

North Texas Chapter. 1126 Pioneer Drive, Dallas, TX 75224-1255. Contact: Gary Kennedy.

Utah Chapter. 1141 North Redwood Road, Suite 86, Salt Lake City, UT 84116. Chair: Bill Hoyle.

Vermont Chapter. Bear Swamp Road RR 5, PO Box 2147, Montpelier, VT 05602. E-mail: chrisr@sun.goddard.edu. Contact: Hal Leyshon.

Seattle Chapter. PO Box 61087, Seattle, WA 98121. Chair: Lou Truskoff.

South Central Wisconsin Chapter. 925 Haywood Street, Suite 1, Madison, WI 53715. Chair: Mike McCallister.

La Raza Unida Party
483 5th Street
San Francisco, CA 91340
(818) 365-6534
Chair: Xenaro G. Ayala

f. 1972; Seeks greater governmental representation for Latinos through the electoral process; Publications: *El Sembrador* (monthly); *La Nacion* (monthly); *La Semilla* (quarterly).

League of Revolutionaries for a New America
PO Box 3524
Chicago, IL 60654
(312) 486-3551
(312) 486-1728
Organizing Secretary: JoAnn Capalbo

f. 1995 as the successor to the Communist Labor Party; Seeks revolutionary change of the current political and economic system; Publications: *People's Tribune* (bi-monthly newspaper); *Tribuno del Pueblo* (Spanish edition).

Liberal Party of New York State
381 Park Avenue South
New York, NY 10016

Libertarian Party
2600 Virginia Avenue NW, Suite 100
Washington, DC 20037
(202) 333-0008
(800) 682-1776
(202) 333-0072
Chair: Steve Dasbach
Website: http://www.lp.org

f. 1971; Believes that each individual has the absolute right to exercise complete domain over his or her own life, liberty and property.

Libertarian Party of Alabama. 1019 Old Monrovia Road, Suite 219, Huntsville, AL 35806. Tel: (888) 838-1775 E-mail: stephendow@aol.com. Chair: Stephen Dow. Website: http://www.al.lp.org.

Libertarian Party of Alaska. 3901 Barbara Drive, Anchorage, AK 99517. Tel: (907) 566-1235 E-mail: anc4hemp @alaska.net. Chair: Len Karpinski. Website: http://www.alaska-libertarian.org.

Libertarian Party of Arizona. PO Box 501, Phoenix, AZ 85001. Tel: (602) 248-8425 E-mail: mongoose@indirect.com. Chair: Mike Dugger. Website: http://www.primenet.com/~idic/azlp.html.

Libertarian Party of Arkansas. PO Box 1579, Little Rock, AR 72203. Tel: (501) 340-3933 or (888) 894-1836 E-mail: cliffb@ausistotle.net. Chair: Cliff Biedenharm. Website: http://www.arlp.simplenet.com/.

Libertarian Party of California. 655 Lewelling Boulevard, Suite 362, San Leandro CA 94570. Tel: 310 477 6491 or 800 637 1776 E-Mail: chair@ca.lp.org.

Chair: Mark Hinkle. Website: http://www.ca.lp.org.

Libertarian Party of Colorado. 720 East 18th Avenue, Suite 309, Denver, CO 80203. Tel: (303) 837-9393 E-mail: sdj@rmll.com. Chair: Sandra Jones. Website: http://www.pageplus.com/~lpcolorado.

Libertarian Party of Connecticut. PO Box 551, East Granby, CT 06026. Tel: (860) 423-0230 or 9449 or (800) 364-0023 (CT only) E-mail: ceve@lpet.org. Chair: Carl Vassar. Website: http://www.lpct.org.

Libertarian Party of Delaware. PO Box 1472, Dover, DE 19903. Tel: (302) 455-1162. E-mail: sensor@dol.net. Chair: Mike Sensor. Website: http://www.magpage.com/lpd/.

Libertarian Party of Washington, DC. PO Box 12075, Washington, DC 20005. Tel: (202) 483-6401 E-mail: 104702.3320@compuserv.com. Chair: Daniel Smith.

Libertarian Party of Florida. PO Box 3012, Winter Park, FL 32790-3012. Tel: (800) 478-0555 or (407) 297-9188. E-mail: bdcollar@ix.netcom.com. Chair: Brian Collar. Website: http://www.lpf.org/.

Libertarian Party of Georgia. 1874 Piedmont Road, Suite 590-E, Atlanta, GA 30324. Tel: (800) 257-2493 or (404) 888-9468 Fax: (404) 874-8339 E-mail: lpga@juno.com. Chair: Montague L. "Cosmo" Boyd. Website: http://www.ga.lp.org.

Libertarian Party of Hawaii. 1125 South King Street, Suite 202, Honolulu, HI 96814. Tel: (808) 597-8008 E-mail: rogert@pixi.com. Chair: Roger Taylor. Website: http://www.geocities.com/CapitolHill/2118/.

Libertarian Party of Idaho. PO Box 15582, Boise, ID 83715. Tel: (208) 344-6230 E-mail: sparrow@cyberhighway.net.

Chair: Chris Struble. Website: http://www.prime,net.com/~slack/lpidaho.

Libertarian Party of Illinois. 175 West Jackson Boulevard, Suite 1166, Chicago, IL 60604. Tel: (800) 735-1776 or (312) 360-1040. Fax: (312) 360-9413. E-mail: lpi@il.lp.org. Chair: Mike Ginsberg. Website: http://www.il.lp.org/.

Libertarian Party of Indiana. 606 Wilshire Avenue, West Lafayette, IN 47906. Tel: (800) 814-1776 E-mail: 75267.3243@compuserve.com. Chair: Robert Shuford. Website: http://www.lpin.org/.

Libertarian Party of Iowa. PO Box 2282, Ames, IA 50010-2282. Tel: (515) 268-1962. Chair: Dick Kruse. Website: http://www.commonlink.com/~olsen/LPI/lpi.html.

Libertarian Party of Kansas. PO Box 3735, Wichita, KS 67201. Tel: (913) 862-4846 or (800) 335-1776 (KS only) E-mail: slider714@aol.com. Chair: Seth Warren. Website: http://www.eskimo.com/~lpk.

Libertarian Party of Kentucky. 137 Creekport Drive, Columbia, KY 42728-2120. Tel: (502) 384-6139 E-mail: ctwimmer@duo-county.com. Chair: Carl T. (Tom) Wimmer. Website: http://www.ky.lp.org/.

Libertarian Party of Louisiana. PO Box 66301, Baton Rouge, LA 70896. E-mail: pmill32182@aol.com. Chair: Jenny Millette. Website: http://www.la.lp.org.

Libertarian Party of Maine. PO Box 6677, Portland, ME 04101. Tel: (207) 780-1776 E-m: liberty@midcoast.com. Chair: Richard Eaton. Website: http://www.midcoast.com/manselibertarian.

Libertarian Party of Maryland. 4323 Rosedale Avenue, Bethesda, MD 20814. Tel: (301) 951-0539 or (410) 628-1141 or (800) MLP-1776 E-mail: chair@md.lp.org.

Chair: Jesse Markowitz. Website: http://www.md.lp.org.

Libertarian Party of Massachusetts. PO Box 2610, Boston, MA 02208. Tel: (617) 625-1100 E-mail: chowell@la-ma.org. Chair: Carla Howell. Website: http://www.la-ma.org.

Libertarian Party of Michigan. 11700 Merriman Road, Livonia, MI 48150. Tel: (800) 343-1364 E-mail: tobrien321@aol.com. Chair: Tim O'Brien. Website: http://www.coast.net/~lpm/.

Libertarian Party of Minnesota. PO Box 580774, Minneapolis, MN 55458. Tel: (612) 788-2660 or (800) 788-2660 Fax: (612) 874-6803 E-mail: ChasDTest@aol.com. Chair: Charles D. Test. Website: http://www.lpmn.org.

Libertarian Party of Mississippi. 3520 Terry Road, Suite 160, Jackson, MS 39212. Tel: (601) 362-2923. Chair: Mark G. Bushman.

Libertarian Party of Missouri. PO Box 3231, St Louis, MO 63130. Tel: (314) 997-8585 E-mail: jimgivens@aol.com. Chair: Jim Givens. Website: http://www.geocities.com/CapitolHill/1865.

Libertarian Party of Montana. PO Box 4803, Missoula, MT 59806. Tel: (406) 721-9020. Chair: Mike Fellows. Website: http://www.geocities.com/CapitolHill/6177.

Libertarian Party of Nebraska. RR 32, PO Box 285-C, Omaha, NE 68142. Tel: (402) 331-5040. Chair: Andy Miller. Website: http://www.phonet.com/~bsimon/liberty.htm/.

Libertarian Party of Nevada. PO Box 3752, North Las Vegas, NV 89036. Tel: (702) 251-7123 Fax: (702) 626-2501 E-mail: james@lpn.sparks.nv.us. Chair: James Dan. Website: http://www.lpnevada.org.

Libertarian Party of New Hampshire.
PO Box 5293, Manchester, NH 03108. Tel:
(800) 559-LPNH or (603) 627-3666 E-mail:
dandon@scout.netis.com. Chair: Danielle
Donovan. Website: http://www.lpnh.org.

Libertarian Party of New Jersey. PO
Box 56, Tennent, NJ 07763. Tel: (800)
201-NJLP E-mail: jpresser@netaxs.com.
Chair: Janice Presser. Website: http://
www.njlp.org.

Libertarian Party of New Mexico. 1380
Rio Rancho Boulevard, Suite 182, Rio
Rancho, NM 87124. Tel: (505) 891-4541 E-
mail: tintoys@rt66.com. Chair: Ron
Bjornstad. Website: http://www.lpnm.org/.

Libertarian Party of New York. PO Box
1664, New York, NY 10013. Tel: (914)
679-8340. Chair: Jim Harris. Website: http:/
/civic.li/lpny/.

Libertarian Party of North Carolina. PO
Box 817, Garner, NC 27529. Tel: (800)
292-3766 E-mail: cspruyt@eos.ncsu.edu.
Chair: Chris Spruyt. Website: http://
www.lpnc.org/lpnc.

Libertarian Party of North Dakota. PO
Box 9002, Fargo, ND 58106. Tel: (701)
241-9687. Chair: Martin Riske. Website:
http://fm-net.com/subnosa/lpnd.html.

Libertarian Party of Ohio. 415 Pinebluff
Drive, Loveland, OH 45140. Tel: (800)
669-6542 E-mail: JMatheney@aol.com.
Chair: Jack Matheney. Website: http://
www.lpo.org.

Libertarian Party of Oklahoma. PO Box
14042, Tulsa, OK 74159. Tel: (918) 835-
7988. Chair: Michael Clem. Website:
http://www.geocities.com/CapitolHill/4397.

Libertarian Party of Oregon. PO Box
40471, Portland, OR 97204. Tel: (800)
829-1992 Fax: (503) 640-8717 E-mail:
kbanett@spiritone.com. Chair: Kristopher

Barrett. Website: http://www.teleport.com/
~lpol.

Libertarian Party of Pennsylvania. 1227
Pine Street, Philadelphia, PA 19107. Tel:
(215) 732-6155 or (215) 732-6244 E-mail:
tjmoir@aol.com. Chair: Tim Moir. Website:
http://www.lppa.org/.

Libertarian Party of Rhode Island. 5
Thurston Avenue, Newport, RI 02840-
1728. Tel: (401) 848-9733 E-mail: rilee@
wsii.com. Chair: Robert Rilee. Website:
http://www.lpri.org/.

South Carolina Libertarian Party. PO
Box 50643, Columbia, SC 29250. Tel: (803)
254-3204 E-mail: rtravis@awod.com.
Chair: Rodney Travis. Website: http://
www.awod.com/sclp/.

Libertarian Party of South Dakota. PO
Box 9341, Rapid City, SD 57709. Tel:
(605) 352-4559. Chair: Jim Christen.
Webiste: www.geocities.com/CapitolHill/
5525.

Libertarian Party of Tennessee. PO
Box 8154, Hermitage, TN 37076. Tel:
(615) 773-7090. Chair: Scott Benson.
Website: www.mindspring.com/~cole/
lptn.html.

Libertarian Party of Texas. PO Box
56426, Houston, TX 77256. Tel: (800) 422-
1776 or (512) 467-1776 E-mail:
jay.d.manifold@mail.sprint.com. Chair: Jay
Manifold. Website: http://www.tx.lp.org.

Libertarian Party of Utah. PO Box
526025, Salt Lake City, UT 84152. Tel:
(800) 280-7900 E-mail: lputah@
inconnect.com. Chair: Jim Dexter.
Website: http://www.inconnect.com/lputah.

Libertarian Party of Vermont. PO Box
5475, Burlington, VT 05402. Tel: (802)
863-8123 E-mail: secur@sover.net. Chair:

Christopher Costanzo. Website: http://www.catamount.com/utlp.

Libertarian Party of Virginia. PO Box 28263, Richmond, VA 23228-0263. Tel: (800) 619-1776 E-mail: vetodj@cais.com. Chair: Dana Johansen. Website: http://www.lpva.com/.

Libertarian Party of Washington. PO Box 20732, Seattle, WA 98102. Tel: (800) 353-1776 Fax: (206) 747-6881 E-mail: chair @lpws.org. Chair: Mary Maas. Website: http://www.lpws.org.

Libertarian Party of West Virginia. PO Box 75423, Charleston, WV 25375. Tel: (800) 950-3421 E-mail: lpwv@almost-heaven.com. Chair: John K. Brown. Website: http://www.almost-heaven.com/lpwv/.

Libertarian Party of Wisconsin. PO Box 20815, Greenfield, WI 53220. Tel: (800) 236-9236 E-mail: jimueller@execpc.com. Chair: Jim Mueller. Website: http://www.lpwi.org.

Libertarian Party of Wyoming. 2362 Glendale Avenue, Casper, WY 82601. Tel: (307) 265-4459 Fax: (307) 265-4459 E-mail: stever@trib.com. Chair: Steve Richardson. Website: http://www.geocities.com/CapitolHill/1799.

Light Party
20 Sunnyside Avenue, Suite A-156
Mill Valley, CA 94941
(415) 381-2357
(415) 381-2645 (Fax)

Seeks health, peace, and freedom for all.

Mississippi Freedom Democratic Party
PO Box 10837
Jackson, MS 39209

Multipartisan Coalition
1226 Cherokee Avenue West
St Paul, MN 55118
Prolocutor: Floyd R. Nelson

Discontented Democrats, Republicans and Archonists who advocate positions based on Christian principles and middle-class values.

National Black Independent Political Party
370 St Nicholas, Suite 2
New York, NY 10027

National Hamiltonian Party
24669 West 10 Mile Road, Suite 3
Southfield, MI 48034
(313) 352-7196
Executive Director: Michael Kelly

f. 1965; Seeks to bring nobility, ability and dignity to government through its membership of aristocracy and educated citizens; Publications: *The Hamiltonian* (periodic).

National Party
PO Box 86221
Los Angeles, CA 90086
(909) 624-8474
E-mail: pendragn@cyberg8t.com
Website: http://www.cyberg8t.com/natlprty/

White fundamental rights group seeking reform on immigration, arms and nationalistic economic policies.

National Patriot Party (or Patriot Party)
16 South Broadway
Wind Gap, PA 18091
(800) 288-3201
E-mail: salitj@aol.com
Chair: Jackie Salit

Website: http://www.usglobenet.com/patriot/
patriot.html

f. 1994. Seeks responsible government that
emphasizes individual liberty and tolerance of
others; Publications: *Patriot News* (bi-monthly
newsletter).

**National Socialist White People's Party
(American Nazi Party)**
Website: http://www.nswpp.org

No presidential candidate since 1964. White
political radicals of unmixed, non-Semitic
European descent.

National States' Rights Party
PO Box 4063
Marietta, GA 30061
Chair: J.B. Stoner

f. 1958; A patriotic white racist political order;
Publications: *Personal Newsletter* (monthly);
Thunderbolt (monthly).

National Woman's Party
144 Constitution Avenue NE
Washington, DC 20002
(202) 546-1210
(202) 543-2365 (Fax)
Coordinator: Lou Ann J. Broad

f. 1913; Devoted to equality for all women.

Natural Law Party
51 West Washington Avenue
Fairfield, IA 52556
(800) 332-0000 or (515) 472-2040
(515) 472-2011 (Fax)
E-mail: info@natural-law.org
Website: http://www.natural-law.org

Stands for prevention-oriented government,
conflict-free politics, and solutions to social
problems that bring the nation in harmony with
the natural law.

New Alliance Party
200 West 72nd Street, Suite 30
New York, NY 10023

New Democratic Movement
PO Box 295, 39 Bowery
New York, NY 10002

New Order
PO Box 27486
Milwaukee, WI 53227

f. 1983; A national socialist organization that
seeks to embody the philosophy of Adolf Hitler.

New Party
88 3rd Avenue, Suite 313
Brooklyn, NY 11217
(800) 200-1294
E-mail: newparty@iqc.apc.org
Chair: Tom Israel
Website: http://www.newparty.org

f. 1978; Progressive political party seeking
universal tax-supported health-care, abolition of
death penalty and compulsory service in armed
services worldwide.

Pacific Party
PO Box 9272, University Station
Portland, OR 97207
(505) 293-5888

Non-affiliated green party.

Pansexual Peace Party
E-mail: eris@neosoft.com
Chair: Judy Brugger
Website: http://www.neosoft.com/~eris/PPP/.

Patriot Party of Virginia
PO Box 610
Herndon, VA 22070
(800) 713-4154
E-mail: bweiner@vais.net.

Peace and Freedom Party
PO Box 2325
Aptos, CA 95001
(408) 688-4268
E-mail: emcfarla@sonic.net
Website: http://www.sonic.net/~emcfarla/
pfpage.html

f. 1967; Seeks the release of Watergate tapes, jailing of George Bush for JFK assassination, reduced Pentagon budget, 30-hour work week, 50% capital tax on 1000 richest families, end of poverty, racism, and sexism, end of individual income tax and the IRS, and the lowering of the voting age to 13; Publications: *Leaflets* (monthly); *Nixon and Bush: How the CIA Ambushed JFK* (video).

Populist Party
PO Box 76737
Washington, DC 20013
or
PO Box 15499
Pittsburgh, PA 15237
(412) 443-7300
Chair: Donald B. Wassall

f. 1891, revived 1987; Advocates a nationalist philosophy; Publications: *The Populist Observer* (monthly).

Pot Party
PO Box DC
Pacific Grove, CA 63950
Cheif: Nathan Brown
Website: http://www.mbay.net/~usapor/pot.htm

f. 1995; Seeks to legalize and mandate marijuana growth.

Progressive Labor Party
150 West 28th Street, Suite 301
New York, NY 10001-6103
(212) 255-3959
(212) 255-2574 (Fax)
E-mail: plp@plp.org
Chair: Milton Rosen
Website: http://www.plp.org

f. 1962; Works to establish communism; Publications: *Al Tahadi* (Arabic bimonthly); *Challenge/Desafio* (bilingual weekly); *The Communist Magazine* (bilingual quarterly); *Le Defi* (French monthly).

> **Progressive Labor Party of Northern California.** PO Box 10788, Grand Lakes Station, Oakland, CA 94610.
>
> **Progressive Labor Party of Southern California.** 2601 B. Martin Luther King Jr Boulevard, Los Angeles, CA 90018. Tel: (213) 293-4538.
>
> **Progressive Labor Party of Connecticut.** PO Box 4245, Hartford, CT 06147.
>
> **Progressive Labor Party of Hawaii.** PO Box 62, Hailua, HI 96734.
>
> **Progressive Labor Party of Illinois.** PO Box A3156, Chicago, IL 60690. Tel: (312) 663-4138 Fax: (312) 663-9742.
>
> **Progressive Labor Party of Maryland.** PO Box 13426, Baltimore, MD 21203.

Progressive Labor Party of Massachusetts. PO Box 836, Boston, MA 02120.

Progressive Labor Party of Michigan. PO Box 03251, Highland Park, MI 48203.

Progressive Labor Party of Minnesota. PO Box 580215, Minneapolis, MN 55458.

Progressive Labor Party of Missouri. PO Box 2915, St Louis, MO 63130.

Progressive Labor Party of New Jersey. PO Box 6165, Newark, NJ 07106.

Progressive Labor Party of New York. PO Box 808, Brooklyn, NY 11202. Tel: (212) 255-3959 Fax: (212) 255-3959.

Progressive Labor Party of Ohio. PO Box 02074, Columbus, OH 43202.

Progressive Labor Party of Pennsylvania. PO Box 53705, Philadelphia, PA 19105.

Progressive Labor Party of Washington. PO Box 22935, Seattle, WA 98122.

Progressive Labor Party of Washington, DC. PO Box 366, Hyattsville, MD 20871.

Progressive Labor Party of Wisconsin. PO Box 3001, Madison, WI 53704.

Prohibition Party
PO Box 2635
Denver, CO 80201
(303) 572-0646 or (303) 237-4947
E-mail: earldodge@aol.com
National Chair: Earl F. Dodge

f. 1869; Primarily opposes the manufacture and sale of alcoholic drinks; also opposes abortion, drug abuse and euthanasia; Publications: *National Statesman* (monthly).

Reform Party
PO Box 96
Dallas, TX 75221
(800) 967-7289
(214) 450-8823 (Fax)
Executive Director: Russell Verney
Website: http://www.reformparty.org/

f. 1992 as United We Stand; 1992 and 1996 Reform Party supporting H. Ross Perot's campaigns. Seeks more effective government.

Reform Party of Alabama. PO Box 11623, Birmingham, AL 35202. Tel: (205) 655-7894. Chair: Bob Belcher.

Reform Party of Alaska. 2709 West 34th Street, Anchorage, AK 99517. Tel: (907) 248-4185 or (907) 248-8534 E-mail: akrefparty@aol.com. Chair: Steven Carlisle.

Reform Party of Arizona. PO Box 3103, Scottsdale, AZ 85257. Tel: (520) 778-4544 E-mail: chair@arizona.reformparty.org. Chair: Eugene Kerkman.

Reform Party of Arkansas. 4213 Roundtop Drive North, Little Rock, AR 72117. Tel: (501) 945-0277 E-mail: missginger@msn.com. Chair: Billie D. Deeter.

Reform Party of California. 4718 Merudan Avenue, MSC 228, San Jose, CA 95118. Tel: (408) 997-9267.

Reform Party of Colorado. 709 Grape Street, Denver, CO 80220. Tel: (303) 399-8532 Fax: (303) 355-9394 E-mail: chair@colorado.reformparty.org. Chair: Rosemarie Sax. Website: http://www.colorado-reformparty.org.

Reform Party of Connecticut. 14 Pleasant Street, Cromwell, CT 06416. Tel: (860) 635-8972 Fax: (860) 635-7624 E-mail: chair@connecticut.reformparty.org. Chair: Bob

Davidson. Website: http://www.conix.com/~urban/ptyindex.html.

Reform Party of Delaware. 42 Doncaster Road, New Castle, DE 19720. Tel: (302) 328-1233 Fax: (302) 328-6794 E-mail: frank5963@aol.com. Chair: Frank Sims.

Reform Party of District of Columbia. PO Box 58112, Washington, DC 20037-8112. Tel: (202) 728-3835 E-mail: chair@dc.reformparty.org. Chair: Donna Waks.

Reform Party of Florida. 3 North Madison Street, Suite 23, Quincy, FL 32351. Tel: (904) 875-2565 or (904) 627-2040 E-mail: chair@florida.reformparty.org. Chair: Carl Owenby Jr. Website: http://www.florida.reformparty.org.

Reform Party of Georgia. 11 Overlook Drive, Newnan, GA 30265-1266. Tel: (770) 251-7764 E-mail: chair@georgia.reformparty.org. Chair: Anne Merkl.

Reform Party of Hawaii. 46-081 Konohiki Street, Apt 3554, Kaneohe, HI. Tel: (808) 247-8685 E-mail: wumc@gte.net. Chair: Bill or Patti Russell.

Reform Party of Idaho. PO Box 2222, Boise, ID 83701. Tel: (208) 388-1200 Fax: (208) 388-1201 Chair: Gary Allen.

Reform Party of Illinois. PO Box 5296, Aurora, IL 60507. Tel: (630) 554-0661 Fax: (630) 554-0911 E-mail: illinoisrp@aol.com. Chair: David Cherry. Website: illinois.reformparty.org/ill.htm.

Reform Party of Indiana. 8513 Lamira Lane, Indianapolis, IN 46234-1845. Tel: (317) 293-8623 Fax: (317) 388-1344 E-mail: chairman@indiana.reformparty.org. Chair: Rick Harte.

Reform Party of Iowa. 209 North 2nd Street, Marshalltown, IA 50158. Tel: (515) 753-0036 E-mail: chair@iowa.reformparty.org. Chair: Ronn Young.

Reform Party of Kansas. Topeka, KS. Tel: (913) 267-4417 Fax: (913) 267-3906 E-mail: chair@kansas.reformparty.org. Chair: Darrel King. Website: http://www.tri.net/reformks/.

Reform Party of Kentucky. 8913 Lippincott Road, Louisville, KY 40222. Tel: (502) 425-3608 Fax: (502) 425-3608 E-mail: chair@kentucky.reformparty.org. Chair: Jeannette Lenczyk.

Reform Party of Louisiana. Tel: (504) 454-0584 Fax: (504) 455-4273 E-mail: chair@louisiana.reformparty.org. Chair: Dede Mule.

Reform Party of Maine. PO Box 1938, Ogunquit, ME 03907. Tel: (207) 882-6582. Chair: Wendell Kinney. Website: http://pages.map.com/bkpowell/merpage.html.

Reform Party of Maryland. Annapolis, MD 21401. Tel: (888) 637-3367 E-mail: chair@maryland.reformparty.org. Chair: Rachel Mann.

Massachusetts Reform Party. PO Box 1408, Boston, MA 02205. Tel: (413) 783-2918 Fax: (413) 782-9909. Chair: Phil Bator.

Reform Party of Michigan. 5260 Northland Drive NE, Dept F-187, Grand Rapids, MI 49525. Tel: (616) 361-3663 Fax: (616) 361-1811 E-mail: chair@michigan.reformparty.org. Chair: Brian Nylaan. Website: michigan.reformparty.org/ml.htm.

Reform Party of Minnesota. 2211 Oliver Avenue North, Minneapolis, MN 55411. Tel: (612) 522-6957. Chair: Eric Pone.

Reform Party of Mississippi. Tylertown, MS. Tel: (800) 851-0545 Fax: (601) 876-

2342 E-mail: uniref@aol.com. Chair: Ted Weill.

Reform Party of Missouri. 12211 Oak Ridge Road, Independence, MO 64052. Tel: (816) 461-7400 Fax: (816) 461-7400 E-mail: chair@missouri.reformparty.org. Chair: Larry Terry.

Reform Party of Montana. PO Box 3511, Bozeman, MT 59772. Tel: (800) 232-8522 Fax: (406) 585-9384. Chair: Bob Abbott.

Reform Party of Nebraska. 1022 South 41st, Omaha, NE 68105-1808. Tel: (402) 342-5731 E-mail: secretary@nebraska.reformparty.org. Secretary/Treasurer: Kay Neil.

Reform Party of Nevada. 4255 South Channell Drive, Suite 55, Las Vegas, NV 89119. Tel: (702) 650-9011 E-mail: chair@nevada.reformparty.org. Chair: Janet Alicesun.

Reform Party of New Hampshire. PO Box 922. Londonderry, NH 03053. Tel: (603) 434-8624 Fax: (603) 425-2292 E-mail: chair@newhampshire.reformparty.org. Chair: Daron Libby.

Reform Party of New Jersey. Voice: (609) 616-9067 Fax: (609) 354-8274 E-mail: chair@newjersey.reformparty.org. Chair: Pat Benjamin.

Reform Party of New Mexico. 107 East 6500 Montgomery Boulevard NE, Albuquerque, NM 87190. Tel: (505) 881-3714 Fax: (505) 881-1896. Chair: Alberta Hoffswell.

Independence Party of New York. 755 Waverly Avenue, Suite 309, Holtsville, NY 11742. Tel: (516) 447-1938 Fax: (516) 447-1957 E-mail: nysindpty@aol.com. Chair: Jack R. Essenberg. Website: http://www.arnfire.com.

Reform Party of North Carolina. PO Box 6796, South Brunswick, NC 28470. Tel: (910) 287-5411 E-mail: chair@northcarolina,reformparty.org. Chair: Dror Bar-Sadeh.

Reform Party of North Dakota. Tel: (800) 897-8263 Fax: (701) 281-9653. Chair: Daryl or Jan Hanson.

Reform Party of Ohio. PO Box 340288, Columbus, OH 43234. Tel: (614) 760-9401 E-mail: chiar@ohio.reformparty.org. Chair: Sandy Reckseit. Website: http://members.tripod.com/~reformohio.

Reform Party of Oklahoma. PO Box 50440, Tulsa, OK 74120-0440. E-mail: chair@oklahoma,reformparty.org. Chair: Jack Newkirk. Website: http://www.spellbinder.com/reformok.

Reform Party of Oregon. PO Box 26, Phoenix, OR 97535. Tel: (541) 535-7237 Fax: (541) 535-5336 E-mail: chair@oregon.reformparty.org. Chair: Micki Summerhays.

Reform Party of Pennsylvania. 72 Fernwood Avenue, Bartonsville, PA 18321. Tel: (717) 629-8766 Fax: (717) 629-8035 E-mail: chair@pennsylvania.reformparty.org. Chair: Thomas J. McLaughlin. Website: http://home,ptd.net/~tomrake.

Reform Party of Rhode Island. PO Box 1549, North Kingstown, RI 02852. Tel: (401) 295-8495 E-mail: chair@rhodeisland.reformparty.org. Chair: June Spink. Website: http://members.aol.com/halger2/ri-reform-party.html.

Reform Party of South Carolina. Forty Oaks Farm, Campobello, SC 29322. Tel: (864) 542-8972 E-mail: chair@southcarolina.reformparty.org. Chair: Betty Montegomery.

Reform Party of South Dakota. 114 Hillcrest Drive, Rapid City, SD 57701. Tel: (604) 355-9758. Chair: David Seals.

Reform Party of Tennessee. 1408 Bowman Lane, Brentwood, TN 37027. Tel: (615) 370-4344 Fax: (615) 370-9724 E-mail: chiar@tennessee.reformparty.org. Chair: Kathryn H. Siebel. Website: http://www.geocities.com/Capitol Hill/5396/.

Reform Party of Texas. PO Box 453052, Garland, TX 75045. Tel: (972) 248-1934 Fax: (972) 248-1547 E-mail: ptruachair@texas.reformparty.org. Chair: Paul Truax.

Reform Party of Utah. PO Box 71416, Salt Lake City, UT 84171. Tel: (801) 943-9665 Fax: (801) 943-6776 E-mail: chair@utah.reformparty.org. Chair: Claire Geddes.

Reform Party of Vermont. PO Box 7, Bellows Falls, VT 05101. Tel: (802) 463-3738 or (802) 463-3428. Chair: Russ Capron.

Reform Party of Virginia. PO Box 8067, Yorktown, VA 23693. Tel: (804) 567-7085 E-mail: chair@virginia.reformparty.org. Chair: Sue Harris DeBauche. Website: http://www.naxs.com/people/megoats/homepage.htm.

Reform Party of Washington. 1122 East Pike Street, Suite 539, Seattle, WA 98122. Tel: (206) 625-3303 E-mail: chair@washington.reformparty.org. Chair: Stan Emert.

Reform Party of West Virginia. 2045 Parkwood Road, Charleston, WV 25314. Tel: (304) 343-6096 Fac: (304) 346-9209. Chair: Ed DelGrande.

Reform Party of Wisconsin. 2134 15th Avenue, Cameron, WI 54822. Tel: (715) 458-2180 E-mail: chair@wisconsin.reformparty.org. Chair: Nora Gerber. Website: http://www.excel.net/~rpw.

Revolutionary Communist Party
RCP Publications
Public Relations Office
PO Box 3486
Chicago, IL 60654
(312) 227-4066
(312) 227-4497 (Fax)
Chairman: Bob Avakian
National Spokesman: Carl Dix (212-713-5084)

f. 1975; Promotes Marxism-Leninism-Maoism by working to prepare for armed proletarian revolution; Publications: *RW* (weekly); *Revolution* (occasional).

Social Democrats, USA
815 15th Street NW
Washington, DC 20005
(202) 638-1515
(202) 347-5585 (Fax)
President: Donald Slaiman
Executive Director: Rita Freedman

f. 1972; succeeded Socialist Party est. in 1901.

Socialist Equality Party
PO Box 48377
Oak Park, MI 48237
E-mail: icfi@wsws.org
Website: http://www.wsws.org

Originally named the Workers League--first fielded a Presidential nominee in 1984. They changed their name to Socialist Equality Party in 1994. The Michigan-based SEP regularly fields congressional and local candidates in several states (mainly in the Midwest).

Socialist Labor Party
111 West Evelyn Avenue, Suite 209
Sunnyvale, CA 94086-0517
(408) 245-2047
(408) 245-2049 (Fax)

E-mail: labornet@igc.apc.org
National Secretary: Robert Bills
Website: http://gopher://gopher.slp.org:7019/.

f. 1876; Advocates creation of classless, socialist, industrial democracy; Publications: *National Convention Reports* (biennial); *The People* (semimonthly).

Socialist Party, USA
516 West 25th Street, Suite 404
New York, NY 10001
(212) 691-0776
(212) 691-0776 (Fax)
E-mail: hammer@socialist.org
National Co-Chairs: David McReynolds, Kari
   Fisher

f. 1901; Seeks the establishment of a socialist democracy; Publications: *The Socialist* (bimonthly).

Socialist Workers Party
1573 North Milwaukee
PO Box 478
Chicago, IL 60622
(773) 772-0551
E-mail: 105162.605@compuserv.com
National Secretary: Jack Barnes
Website: http://pages.prodigy.com/AHSG60C/index.html

f. 1938; Seeks to abolish capitalism and establish a workers' and farmers' government.

Socialist Workers Party of Northern California. 3284 23rd Street, San Francisco, CA 94110. Tel: (415) 282-6255.

Socialist Workers Party of Southern California. 2546 West Pico Boulevard, Los Angeles, CA 90006. Tel: (213) 380-9640.

Socialist Workers Party of Georgia. 803 Peachtree Street NE, Atlanta. GA 30308. Tel: (404) 724-9759.

Socialist Workers Party of Illinois. 545 West Roosevelt Road, Chicago, IL 60607. Tel: (312) 829-7018.

Socialist Workers Party of Massachusetts. 780 Tremont, Boston, MA 02118. Tel: (617) 247-6772.

Socialist Workers Party of Michigan. 7414 Woodward Avenue, Detroit, MI 48202. Tel: (313) 875-0100.

Socialist Workers Party of Minnesota. 2490 University Avenue West, St Paul, MN 55114. Tel: (612) 645-1674.

Socialist Workers Party of New Jersey. 141 Halsey Street, Newark, NJ 07102. Tel: (201) 643-3341.

Socialist Workers Party of New York. 14 Charles Lane, Manhattan, NY 10001. Tel: (212) 242-5530.

Socialist Workers Party of North Carolina. 2000 South Eugene Street, Greensboro, NC 27406. Tel: (336) 242-5530.

Socialist Workers Party of Ohio. 1832 Euclid Avenue, Cleveland, OH 44115. Tel: (216) 861-6150.

Socialist Workers Party of Pennsylvania. 1103 East Carson Street, Pittsburgh, PA 15203. Tel: (412) 381-9785.

Socialist Workers Party of Texas. 3260 South Loop West, Houston, TX 77025. Tel: (713) 349-0222. or 6969 Gulf Freeway, Houston, TX 77087. Tel: (713) 644-9066.

Socialist Workers Party of Utah. 147 East 900 South, Salt Lake City, UT 84111. Tel: (801) 355-1124.

United States Pacifist Party
5729 South Dorchester Avenue
Chicago, IL 60637
(773) 324-0654
(773) 324-6426 (Fax)
E-mail: blyttle@igc.apc.org
Acting Secretary: Bradford Lyttle
Website: http://www.geocities.com/Capitol Hill/
lobby/4826/

f. 1983; Advocates a zero military budget, immediate nuclear weapons disarmament, and an end to hunger and poverty through support of the United Nations; Publications: *US Pacifist Party Report* (monthly).

US Taxpayers Party
450 Maple Avenue East
Vienna, VA 22180
(800) 2-VETO-IRS
E-mail: lmuller@iquest.com
Chair: Howard Philips
Website: http://www.USTaxpayers.org/

f. 1974 as Conservative Caucus; Seeks to restore American jurisprudence to its Biblical premises and limit federal government to constitutional boundaries.

United Workers Party
GPO Box 1565
New York, NY 10001.

Workers Party
PO Box 25716
Chicago, IL 60625
(312) 409-1127
E-mail: wp-usa@universe.digex.net
Website: http://www.universe.digex.net/~wp-usa/

The WP-USA is a hard-core Marxist-Leninist political party founded in 1992 (sharing much of the CPUSA's ideology). While the WP-USA

has yet to field any candidates, the party publishes a bi-weekly newspaper, *The Worker* and a quarterly journal, *The Worker Magazine*.

Workers World Party
55 West 17th Street
New York, NY 10011
(212) 627-2994
(212) 675-7869 (Fax)
E-mail: wwp@workers.org
Chair: Monica Moorehead
Website: http://www.workers.org/

f. 1961; Fights for a socialist society.

Los Angeles CA Chapter. 422 South Western Avenue, Suite 202, Los Angeles, CA 90020. Tel: (213) 487-2368.

San Francisco CA Chapter. 3181 Mission, Suite 29, San Francisco, CA 94110. Tel: (415) 826-4828.

Washington, DC Chapter. PO Box 57300, Washington, DC 20009. Tel: (202) 588-1205.

Atlanta GA Chapter. PO Box 424, Atlanta, GA 30301. Tel: (404) 662-6417.

Chicago IL Chapter. PO Box 6510, Chicago, IL 60680. Tel: (312) 435-0942.

Baltimore MD Chapter. 426 East 31st Street, Baltimore, MD 21218. Tel: (410) 235-7040.

Boston MA Chapter. 31 Germania Street, Boston, MA 02130. Tel: (617) 983-3835 Fax: (617) 983-3836.

Detroit MI Chapter. 1947 Grand River, Suite 201, Detroit, MI 48226. Tel: (313) 962-4979 Fax: (313) 961-8977.

Buffalo NY Chapter. 349 Niagara Street, Buffalo, NY 14201. Tel: (716) 855-3055 Fax: (716) 852-3402.

New York NY Chapter. 55 West 17th Street, New York, NY 10011. Tel: (212) 627-2994 Fax: (212) 675-7869.

Rochester NY Chapter. 36 St Paul Street, Room 304, Rochester, NY 14604. Tel: (716) 232-9050.

Cleveland OH Chapter. 13018 Buckeye Road, Cleveland, OH 44120. Tel: (216) 921-8130 Fax: (216) 921-8130.

Philadelphia PA Chapter. PO Box 8486, Philadelphia, PA 19101. Tel: (610) 352-3625.

State College PA Chapter. PO Box 10963, Calder Square, State College, PA 16805. Tel: (814) 237-8695 Fax: (814) 237-0683.

Providence RI Chapter. c/o 1043 Broad Street, Providence, RI 02905. Tel: (401) 467-2288.

Houston TX Chapter. PO Box 52115, Houston, TX 77052. Tel: (713) 861-5965.

Richmond VA Chapter. PO Box 27814, Richmond, VA 23261. Tel: (804) 788-6819 Fax: (804) 358-5427.

Seattle WA Chapter. 1218 East Cherry, Suite 201, Seattle, WA 98122. Tel: (206) 325-0085.

Milwaukee WI Chapter. PO Box 16483, Milwaukee, WI 53216.

World Socialist Party of the United States
PO Box 405
Boston, MA 02272
(617) 628-9096

(617) 628-5239 (Fax)
Editor: Ronald Elbert

f. 1916; Advocates the establishment of a society based upon common ownership and wealth distribution; Publications: *The Futility of Reformism* (book); *Internationales Freieswort: Journal of Bund Demokratischer Sozialisten* (German quarterly); *The Socialism of Bernard Shaw* (book); *Socialist Standard: Journal of the Socialist Party of Great Britain* (monthly); *State Capitalism* (book); *World Socialist Review: Journal of World Socialism in the U.S.* (quarterly); *World Without Wages* (book).

Overview: Political Associations and the Political Market Place

Perhaps as a result of America's stubbornly two-party system of politics, extra-political organizations like political associations have become important components in the process of democracy. Alexis de Tocqueville, the noted French political observer of America, wrote in *Democracy in America* (1835) that the formation of associations--not just political ones--was a unique characteristic of Americans. Today, more than 150 years after Tocqueville noted the American tendency to form associations, he would be little surprised by the plethora of organizations and the multitude of forms that they take.

Political associations play important roles in our political system. The organizations represent their members in a number of political activities including testifying at hearings, helping to draft legislation, litigating against the government, and protesting actions. In addition to representation, political associations increase political participation by motivating members to become active. They disseminate information about candidates and issues of concern. They help build the political agenda of the government and then monitor its enactment and enforcement.

Tocqueville understood that while political associations did not have power to directly make laws, "they have the power of attacking those which are in force and of drawing up beforehand those which ought to be enacted." More important, Tocqueville saw the power of associations as "a necessary guarantee against tyranny of the majority."

In addition to political associations, Americans have other groups that serve similar purposes. These include political action committees (PACs), political science research institutes, and think tanks. Political action committees are the result of attempts by the federal government to limit and to account for money that was being spent on political campaigns. While the section of the Federal Elections Campaign Act of 1971 that addressed the formation of PACs was at first little noticed or employed, there are currently more than 4,000 registered PACs that have memberships drawn from unions, corporations, and political associations. Even specific politicians have established PACs in order to advance their particular agendas.

Critics of the PAC system have complained that PACs have flooded elections with money. While there is a growing number of PACs and a corresponding increase in the amount of money given by PACs, the 1971 act that established them has also led to a decrease in the ability of individuals to donate to political campaigns. The typical campaign for US Senate received only 22 percent of campaign funds from PACs. The vast majority (60 percent) was still raised through individual contributions.

Both political science research institutes (PSRIs) and think tanks offer to the democratic process information, opinions, and agendas. These organizations often engage in primary research that helps formulate policy objectives for national, state, and local officials. The conservative think tank, The Heritage Foundation, played a key role in helping to formulate the public policy objectives of the administration of President Ronald Reagan. It was often noted that if one wanted to know what the administration thought, one should check Heritage's findings and publications. While no such direct link existed, it shows that these organizations can have a serious impact on American politics.

Additionally, these organizations work to help

form public opinion that a particular position should be adopted. However, unlike political associations and PACs, these groups are generally not open to membership. Rather, PSRIs and think tanks are generally made up of active political scholars. The research reports that are generated from these organizations are often shaped by the political perspective of the organization itself and its associates. Despite the bias of any one of these organizations, the sheer number of them produces a complex and often contradictory market place of ideas. These groups play a critical role in offering policy alternatives, research findings, and public opinion insight.

Therefore, political associations and the various other forms they take in our modern democracy are important parts of our political system. Publius, writing in *The Federalist Papers*, reminds us of the critical benefit that taking "in a greater variety of parties and interests; you make it less probable that a majority of the whole will have a common motive to invade the rights of other citizens." The political market place of ideas is key to our political freedom.

Political Associations

Political associations are organizations of individuals who have voluntarily come together because of common social, economic, or cultural experiences, ideas, and concerns. These groups often have nonpolitical primary purposes for forming and engage in politics to advance their particular agenda.

9 to 5, National Association of Working Women. 614 Superior Avenue NW, Suite 852, Cleveland, OH 44113. Tel: (216) 566-9308 Fax: (216) 566-0192. Executive Director: Ellen Bravo; f. 1973; Seeks to gain better pay and greater opportunities for women in the workplace; Publications: *The 9 to 5 Guide to Combating Sexual Harassment*; *9 to 5 Newsletter* (5/year); *9 to 5 Women's Guide to Office Survival*.

Accion International (ACCION). 120 Beacon Street, Somerville, MA 02143. Tel: (617) 492-4930 Fax: (617) 876-9509. Website: http://www.accion.org. President and CEO: Michael Chu; f. 1961; Works to improve the socioeconomic well-being of low income Americans; Publications: *ACCION International Bulletin*; *ACCION International Publications*.

Accuracy in Media (AIM). 4455 Connecticut Avenue NW, Suite 330, Washington, DC 20008. Tel: (202) 364-4401 or (800) 787-0044 Fax: (202) 364-4098 E-mail: ar@take.aim.org. Website: http://take.aim.org. Executive Director: Donald K. Irvine; f. 1969; Nonpartisan news media watchdog organization; Publications: *AIM Report* (semimonthly); *Index of AIM Reports* (annual).

Act Up. 135 West 29th Street, 10th Floor, New York, NY 10001. Tel: (212) 564-2437 Fax: (212) 594-5441. Website: http://www.actupny.org. Manager: Walt Wilder; f. 1987; Committed to increasing public awareness and government involvement in the fight against AIDS; Publications: *Act Up Americans* (catalog); *Act Up Reports* (quarterly); *AIDS, Act Up and Activism* (handbook).

Africa Network (AN). PO Box 1894, Evanston, IL 60204. Tel: (708) 328-9305 Fax: (708) 328-9333. Secretary: Y.B. Holly; f. 1981; Works to promote human rights and oppose apartheid in South Africa; Publications: *Africa Network Directory of Resources* (periodic).

Alliance for Consumer Rights (ACR). 132 Nassau Street, 2nd Floor, New York, NY 10038. Tel: (212) 349-9204 Fax: (212) 267-7931; f. 1985; Seeks to promote the rights of the consumer and expand the US tort system; Publications: *ACR Bulletin* (quarterly).

Alternatives for Simple Living. 3617 Old Lakeport Road, PO Box 2857, Sioux City, IA 51106. Tel: (712) 274-8875 Fax: (712) 274-8875 E-mail: iversens@aol.com. National Coordinator: Gerald Iverson; f. 1973; Seeks to exchange materialistic lifestyles for lifestyles of voluntary simplicity; Publications: *Alternative Celebrations Catalog*.

American Agri-Women Resource Center (AAWRC). 17265 East Highway 4, Stockton, CA 95215. Tel: (209) 465-4840. Chair: Laura

Tower; f. 1974; Concerned with the advancement of women and of agricultural production within the free enterprise system; Publications: *The Voice* (quarterly).

American Association for Public Opinion Research (AAPOR). PO Box 1248, Ann Arbor, MI 48106. Tel: (313) 764-1555 Fax: (313) 764-3341 E-mail: aapor@umich.edu. Administrator: Marlene Bednarz; f. 1947; Comprised of individuals interested in the public opinion and social research; Publications: *AAPOR Newsletter* (quarterly); *Agencies and Organizations Represented in AAPOR Membership* (annual); *Public Opinion Quarterly*.

American Association of Political Consultants (AAPC). 900 2nd Street NE, Suite 204, Washington, DC 20002. Tel: (202) 371-9585 Fax: (202) 371-6751 E-mail: aapcmail@aol.com. President: Ralph D. Murphine; f. 1969; Provides a vehicle for the exchange of information, resources, and ideas among persons involved in political activity; Publications: *Membership Roster* (annual); *Politea* (quarterly).

American Association of Pro Life Obstetricians and Gynecologists (AAPLOG). 850 Elm Grove Road, Elm Grove, WI 53122. Tel: (414) 789-7984 Fax: (414) 782-8788. Contact: Dan Martin; f. 1973; Obstetricians and gynecologists who oppose abortion and seek to assist unwed mothers who choose to have their babies.

American Business Conference (ABC). 1730 K Street NW, Suite 1200, Washington, DC 20006. Tel: (202) 822-9300 Fax: (202) 464-4070. President: Barry K. Rogstad; f. 1981; Concerned with tax policy, regulation, and international trade issues to preserve the free enterprise system; Publications: *Capital Gains: Economic Growth and Jobs*; *Commitment to Growth: American Business Conference and Challenge of Economic Policy*; *Winning in the World Market*.

American Center for International Leadership (ACIL). 2200 South Josephine Street, Denver, CO 80208. Tel: (303) 733-6143 Fax: (303) 733-6122. President: Stephen Hayes; f.

1985; Seeks to promote respect and understanding between potential US and foreign leaders; Publications: *International Leadership* (quarterly).

American Civil Liberties Union (ACLU). 132 West 43rd Street, New York, NY 10036. Tel: (212) 944-9800 Fax: (212) 869-9065. Website: http://www.aclu.org/. Executive Director: Ira Glasser; f. 1920; Seeks to protect the rights set forth in the Bill of Rights of the US Constitution; Publications: *Civil Liberties* (quarterly); *First Principles* (monthly).

American Conservative Union (ACU). 1007 Cameron Street, Alexandria, VA 22314-2426. Tel: (703) 836-8602 Fax: (703) 836-8606 E-mail: acu@conservative.org. Website: http://www.conservative.org. Executive Director: Jeff Hollingsworth; f. 1964; Seeks to mobilize conservatives to further the cause of conservatism; Publications: *Annual Rating of Congress*; *Battleline* (monthly).

American Constitutional Law Foundation (ACLF). PO Box 9383, Denver, CO 80209-0383. Tel: (303) 744-6449 Fax: (303) 744-6581. Executive Director: William Orr; f. 1989; Works to protect the First Amendment right to petition the government; Publications: *We the People* (quarterly).

American Council for Capital Formation (ACCF). 1750 K Street NW, Suite 400, Washington, DC 20006. Tel: (202) 293-5811 Fax: (202) 785-8165 E-mail: info@accf.org. Website: http://www.accf.org. President: Mark Bloomfield; f. 1973; Seeks to communicate the capital formation issue to the public, national opinion leaders, and members of Congress; Publications: *Capital Formation* (monthly).

American Council for Health Care Reform (ACHCR). 4200 Wilson Boulevard, Suite 750, Arlington, VA 22203. Tel: (703) 908-9220 Toll-Free: (800) 240-6423 Fax: (703) 908-9467. President: William Shaker; f. 1982; Seeks to eliminate costly federal and state health care regulations and laws.

American Council of Young Political Leaders (ACYPL). 1612 K Street NW, Suite 300, Washington, DC 20006. Tel: (202) 857-0999 Fax: (202) 857-0027 E-mail: acypl@erols.com. Executive Director: Gerry Cobb; f. 1966; Promotes understanding between younger political leaders of all countries; Publications: *Network* (quarterly).

American Defense Institute (ADI). 1055 North Fairfax Street, 2nd Floor, Alexandria, VA 22314. Tel: (703) 519-7000 Fax: (703) 519-6392. E-mail: ebml@americandefinst.org. Executive Director: Dorothy McDaniel; f. 1983; Nonpartisan public policy foundation supporting a strong national defense; Publications: *ADI Briefing* (periodic).

American Family Association (AFA). PO Drawer 2440, Tupelo, MS 38803. Tel: (601) 844-5036 Fax: (601) 844-9176. Executive Director: Donal E. Wildmon; f. 1977; Promotes the "biblical" ethic of decency in American society with a primary emphasis on television and other media; Publications: *AFA Journal* (monthly).

American Farmland Trust (AFT). 1920 N Street NW, Suite 400, Washington, DC 20036. Tel: (202) 659-5170 Fax: (202) 659-8339. President: Ralph E. Grossi; f. 1980; Dedicated to stopping the loss of productive farmland and promoting a healthy environment through responsible farming; Publications: *American Farmland* (quarterly).

American Freedom Coalition (AFC). 7777 Leesburg Pike, Suite 314N, Falls Church, VA 22043. Tel: (703) 790-8700 Fax: (703) 790-8711. President: Robert G. Grant; f. 1986; Promotes commonly held traditional American values.

American Gathering of Jewish Holocaust Survivors (AGJHS). 122 West 30th Street, Suite 205, New York, NY 10001. Tel: (212) 239-4230 Fax: (212) 279-2926. Executive Director: Arie Bucheister; f. 1980; Seeks to perpetuate the remembrance of the Holocaust and to combat anti-Semitism; Publications: *Together* (quarterly).

American Immigration Control Foundation (AICF). PO Box 525, Main Street, Monterey, VA 24465. Tel: (703) 468-2022 Fax: (703) 468-2024. President: John Vinson; f. 1983; Americans concerned with the need for immigration control and the problems caused by immigration; Publications: *Border Watch* (monthly).

American Israeli Civil Liberties Coalition (AICLC). 275 7th Avenue, Suite 1776, New York, NY 10001. Tel: (212) 696-9603 Fax: (212) 257-7749. Executive Director: Lesly I. Lempert; f. 1981; Seeks to promote basic civil liberties among Israelis; Publications: *American-Israeli Civil Liberties Coalition Newsletter* (3/year).

American Jewish Alternatives to Zionism (AJAZ). 347 5th Avenue, Suite 900, New York, NY 10016. Tel: (212) 213-9125 Fax: (212) 213-9142. President: Elmer Berger; f. 1960; Anti-Zionist Americans who are concerned with the impact of Zionism on the US and in the Middle East.

American League of Lobbyists (ALL). PO Box 30005, Alexandria, VA 22310. Tel: (703) 960-3011. Executive Director: Patti Jo Barber; f. 1978; Registered lobbyists and others interested in the lobbying profession; Publications: *ALL News* (monthly).

American Life Lobby (ALL). PO Box 1350, Stafford, VA 22554. Tel: (703) 659-4171 Fax: (703) 659-2586. Website: http://www.all.org. President: Judie Brown; f. 1979; Seeks to gain passage of a Human Life Amendment to the US Constitution that would grant personhood to the unborn and make abortion and euthanasia illegal; Publications: *Communique* (periodic).

American National Metric Council. 1735 North Lynn Street, Suite 950, Arlington, VA 22209-2022. Tel: (703) 524-2007 Fax: (703) 524-2303. President: G.T. Underwood; f. 1973; Seeks to coordinate the transition to the metric system in the US; Publications: *Metric Reporter* (monthly).

American Pro Life Council (APLC). 1612 South Prospect Avenue, Park Ridge, IL 60068.

Tel: (708) 692-2183. President: John de Paul Hansen; f. 1980; Promotes pro-life insurance, credit unions, and other programs whose profits are used for pro-life causes; Publications: *By Laws*.

American Security Council (ASC). 5545 Security Circle, Boston, VA 22713. Tel: (703) 547-1750 or (202) 296-9500 Fax: (703) 547-9737. Executive Director: Greg Hilton; f. 1955; Studies national security and promotes a strong national defense; Publications: *National Security Report* (monthly).

American Society for the Defense of Tradition, Family and Property (TFP). PO Box 1868, York, PA 17405. Tel: (717) 225-7147 Fax: (717) 225-7382. President: Raymond E. Drake; f. 1973; Seeks to defend the ideals of tradition, family, and property and oppose the socialist and Marxist views of life; Publications: *Tradition, Family, Property Magazine* (bimonthly).

American-Arab Relations Committee (AARC). PO Box 416, New York, NY 10017. Tel: (212) 972-0460 Fax: (212) 682-1405. President: Dr. M.T. Mehdi; f. 1964; Concerned with improving American-Arab relations and establishing a peaceful and democratic Palestine; Publications: *Islam in America* (weekly).

Americans Against Union Control of Government (AAUCG). 527 Maple Avenue East, Vienna, VA 22180. Tel: (703) 242-3575 Fax: (703) 242-3579. President: David Y. Denholm; f. 1973; Seeks to fight against union influence in government; Publications: *Political Insider* (monthly); *Forewarned* (monthly).

Americans for a Sound AIDS/HIV Policy (ASAP). PO Box 17433, Washington, DC 20041. Tel: (703) 471-7350 Fax: (703) 471-8409. President: W. Shepherd Smith Jr.; f. 1987; Advisory board assisting in the formulation of public policy on HIV/AIDS; Encourages public awareness and early diagnosis; Promotes health care access to persons infected with HIV/AIDS. Publications: *AIDS/HIV News* (bimonthly), *Guide to Federal Funding of HIV Disease* (periodic).

Americans for Customary Weight and Measure (ACWM). Old Stone Farm, Wiscasset, ME 04578. Tel: (207) 882-5554 or (207) 882-6066. Chair: Seaver W. Leslie; f. 1978; Believes that the metric system should not be promoted by the government; Publications: *Footprint* (semiannual); *Why America Should Not Go Metric* (book).

Americans for Democratic Action (ADA). 1625 K Street NW, Suite 210, Washington, DC 20006. Tel: (202) 785-5980 Toll-Free: (900) 787-2734 Fax: (202) 785-5969 E-mail: adaction@ix.netcom.com. Website: http://hogod.b9.battelle1.american.edu/ada.htm. Director: Amy Isaacs; f. 1947; Seeks to formulate liberal domestic and foreign policies and put them into effect through the political process; Publications: *ADA Today* (quarterly); *ADA Voting Record* (annual); *ADAction News and Notes* (weekly); *Legislative and Membership Alerts* (periodic).

Americans for Religious Liberty (ARL). PO Box 6656, Silver Spring, MD 20916. Tel: (301) 598-2447 Fax: (301) 438-8424. Executive Director: Edd Doerr; f. 1980; Dedicated to protecting the constitutional principle of separation of church and state, as well as religious, intellectual, and personal freedoms; Publications: *Voice of Reason* (quarterly).

Americans for Tax Reform (ATR). 1320 18th Street NW, Washington, DC 20036. Tel: (202) 785-0266 Fax: (202) 785-0261. President: Grover Norquist; f. 1985; Seeks a pledge from all incumbents and candidates that they will oppose all income tax increases; Publications: *Memos* (bimonthly).

Americans for the National Voter Initiative Amendment (ANVIA). 3115 N Street NW, Washington, DC 20007. Tel: (202) 333-4846. Director: Edward A. Dent; f. 1979; Seeks an amendment to the US Constitution that will permit direct voter action to initiate legislation at both the state and federal levels.

Americans United for God and Country (AUGC). PO Box 183, Merion Station, PA 19066. Tel: (215) 224-9235. Executive Director: Leslie Harris; f. 1977; Seeks to promote patriotism and love of God and country with the use of federal tax credits to help finance private schools.

Amnesty International of the USA (AIUSA). 322 8th Avenue, New York, NY 10001. Tel: (212) 807-8400 Toll-Free: (800)-AMNESTY Fax: (212) 627-1451. Website: http://www.organic.com.amnesty. Executive Director: William F. Schultz; f. 1961; Opposes torture and works for the release of prisoners held for non-violent crimes; Publications: *Amnesty Action* (3/year); *Amnesty International Report* (annual).

Anti-Defamation League (ADL). 823 United Nations Plaza, New York, NY 10017. Tel: (212) 490-2525 Fax: (212) 867-0779. Website: http://www.adl.org. Director: Abraham H. Foxman; f. 1913; Seeks to stop the defamation of Jewish people and to secure justice and fair treatment for all citizens; Publications: *ADL on the Frontline* (bimonthly); *Dimensions* (semiannual); *Facts* (quarterly); *Latin American Report* (quarterly); *Law* (quarterly); *Law Enforcement Bulletin* (semiannual); *Middle East Insight* (quarterly); *PLO Watch* (periodic).

Arab American Institute (AAI). 918 16th Street NW, Suite 601, Washington, DC 20006. Tel: (202) 429-9210 Fax: (202) 429-9214. President: James Zogby; f. 1985; Encourages Arab-Americans to be active in the political process; Publications: *Issues* (bimonthly); *Update* (monthly); *Who We Are, What We Want: An Arab-American Issues Agenda*.

Association of World Citizens (AWC). 55 New Montgomery Street, Suite 224, San Francisco, CA 94105. Tel: (415) 541-9610 Fax: (415) 227-4878 E-mail: worldcit@best.com. Website: http://www.worldcitizens.org. President: Douglas Mattern; f. 1975; Proposes to establish a world community, end the arms race, protect the environment, and work to meet basic human needs; Publications: *World Citizen* (2-3/year).

Automotive Consumer Action Program (AUTOCAP). National Automobile Dealers Association, 8400 Westpark Drive, McLean, VA 22102. Tel: (703) 821-7144. Manager: Lesly J. Hardesty; f. 1973; Provides car dealers and customers with consumer dispute resolution assistance; Publications: *Automotive Customer Relations Directory* (annual).

BankCard Holders of America (BHA). 524 Branch Drive, Salem, VA 24153. Tel: (540) 389-5445 Fax: (540) 389-3020. Executive Director: Ruth Susswein; f. 1980; Educates the American public about the wise and careful use of credit; Publications: *BankCard Consumer News* (bimonthly); *Information Briefs* (periodic); *Low Rate/No-Fee Credit Card List* (quarterly); *Money Management Guide* (annual).

Black Awareness in Television (BAIT). 13217 Livernois, Detroit, MI 48238-3162. Tel: (313) 931-3427. Website: http:///www.project-bait.com. Director: David Rambeau; f. 1970; Produces black media programs and seeks exposure for black-produced products and black performing artists; Publications: *Thedamu Arts Magazine* (annual).

Black Citizens for a Fair Media (BCFM). 156-20 Riverside Drive, Suite 13L, New York, NY 10032. Tel: (212) 568-3168. President Emma L. Bowen; f. 1971; Works to improve programming, employment and training opportunities of blacks; monitors the media's compliance with FCC equal opportunity regulations.

Black Rock Coalition (BRC). PO Box 1054, Cooper Station, New York, NY 10276. Tel: (212) 713-5097 E-mail: brcny@aol.com. Website: http://users.aol.com/brciny/home.html. Executive Officer: Beverly Jenkins; f. 1985; Works to foster change in the conventional operation and classification of black music and musicians within the entertainment industry; Publications: *BRC Newsletter* (monthly).

Black Silent Majority Committee of the USA (BSMC). PO Box 5519, San Antonio, TX 78201. Tel: (210) 340-2424 Fax: (210) 340-3816. Director: Clay Clairborne; f. 1970; Seeks to show the world that there is a black majority in the US which is patriotic and believes in saluting the flag, paying taxes, and attending church; Publications: *The Crusader* (quarterly).

Black Women's Roundtable on Voter Participation (BWRVP). 1629 K Street NW, Suite 801, Washington, DC 20006. Tel: (202) 659-4929 Fax: (202) 659-5025. Executive Director: James Ferguson; f. 1983; Seeks to forward the causes of social justice and economic equality through increased participation in the political process.

Bread for the World (BFW). c/o Dorota Munoz, 1100 Wayne Avenue, Suite 1000, Silver Spring, MD 20910. Tel: (301) 608-2400 Toll Free: (800) 822-7323 Fax: (301) 608-2401 E-mail: bread@igc.org. Website: http://www.bread.org. President: David Beckmann; f. 1973; Christian organization dedicated to the struggle against hunger and poverty; Publications: *Background Paper* (5/year); *Bread* (8/year); *Hunger Report* (annual).

Bretton Woods Committee (BWC). 1990 M Street NW, Suite 450, Washington, DC 20036. Tel: (202) 331-1616 Fax: (202) 785-9423. Executive Director: James C. Orr; f. 1984; Seeks to inform and educate the public regarding the activities of the World Bank, International Monetary Fund, and other multinational development banks.

Business Executives for National Security (BENS). 1615 L Street NW, Suite 330, Washington, DC 20036. Tel: (202) 296-2125 Fax: (202) 296-2490 E-mail: bens@bens.org. Website: http://www.bens.org. Chairman: Stanley Weiss; f. 1982; Promotes the idea that national security is linked with economic strength and sound business practices; Publications: *Policy Action Report*; *Treadline* (quarterly).

Campaign for UN Reform (CUNR). 713 D Street SE, Washington, DC 20003. Tel: (202) 546-3956 Fax: (202) 543-4878 E-mail: cunr@aol.com. Executive Director: Eric Cox; f. 1976; Seeks to make reform of the United Na-

tions a major political issue in the US; Publications: *Global Statesmanship of America's Senators*; *Global Statesmanship of the US Congress*.

Campaign to Boycott SDI. c/o John B. Kogut, 1110 West Green Street, University of Illinois, Urbana, IL 61801. Co-Founder: John B. Kogut; f. 1985; Scientists and engineers who have agreed not to accept money for contracts or research related the Strategic Defense Initiative; Publications: *Status Report on the Boycott of Star Wars Research by Academic Scientists and Researchers*.

Cardinal Mindszenty Foundation (CMF). PO Box 11321, St Louis, MO 63105. Tel: (314) 727-6279 or (314) 727-5849 Fax: (314) 727-5897 E-mail: info@mindsenty.org. Website: http://www.mindsenty.org. President: Eleanor Schlafly; f. 1958; Conducts educational and research activities regarding Communism; Publications: *Mindszenty Report* (monthly).

Catholics for a Free Choice (CFFC). 1436 U Street NW, Suite 301, Washington, DC 20009. Tel: (202) 986-6093 Fax: (202) 332-7995. Website: http://www.lgc.apc.org/catholicvote/pageone.html. President: Frances Kissling; f. 1972; Catholics that support the right to legal reproductive healthcare, particularly abortion; Publications: *Conscience: a Newsjournal of Prochoice Catholic Opinion* (quarterly).

Center for a New Democracy (CND). 410 7th Street SE, Washington, DC 20003. Tel: (202) 543-0773 Fax: (202) 543-2591. Executive Director: Donna F. Edwards; f. 1991; Supports citizens' groups that are working to reform campaign finance laws and enhance democratic participation; Publications: *CND Update* (monthly).

Center for Constitutional Rights (CCR). 666 Broadway, 7th Floor, New York, NY 10012. Tel: (212) 614-6464 Fax: (212) 614-6499. Executive Director: Ron D. Daniels; f. 1966; Dedicated to advancing the rights guaranteed by the United States Constitution and the Universal Declaration of Human Rights of the United Nations; Publications: *CCR News* (semiannual); *Docket Report* (annual).

Center for Corporate Public Involvement (CCPI). 1001 Pennsylvania Avenue NW, Washington, DC 20004. Tel: (202) 624-2425 Fax: (202) 624-2319. Director: Samuel M. Ulm; f. 1971; Guides health insurance companies on using their corporate, financial, and human resources to deal with community and social problems; Publications: *Response* (quarterly); *Social Report* (annual).

Center for Defense Information (CDI). 1500 Massachusetts Avenue NW, Suite 24, Washington, DC 20005. Tel: (202) 862-0700 Fax: (202) 862-0708 E-mail: cdi@igc.apc.org. Director: John J. Shanahan; f. 1972; Seeks to make independent, informed analysis of US defense policies available to journalists, public officials, scholars, and the general public; Publications: *Defense Monitor* (10/year); *CDI Military Almanac*; *War Without Winners* (video).

Center for Economic Conversion (CEC). 222 View Street, Mountain View, CA 94041. Tel: (415) 968-8798 Fax: (415) 968-1126. Executive Director: Michael Closson; f. 1975; Dedicated to building a stable, peace-oriented economy; Publications: *Base Conversion Handbook; Economic Conversion Update*; *Positive Alternatives* (quarterly).

Center for Financial Freedom and Accuracy in Financial Reporting (CFFAFR). PO Box 37812, Cincinnati, OH 45222. Tel: (513) 621-7177 or (513) 621-9400 Toll-Free: (800) 543-0486 Fax: (513) 345-4727 E-mail: crimpol@eos.net. Executive Officer: Lawrence T. Patterson; f. 1975; Seeks to protect Social Security and ensure financial freedom; Publications: *Criminal Politics* (newsletter).

Center for Law and Religious Freedom (CLRF). 4208 Evergreen Lane, Suite 222, Annandale, VA 22003. Tel: (703) 642-1070 Fax: (703) 642-1075. Website: http://www.iccnet.org. Director: Steven T. McFarland; f. 1975; Seeks to educate the public on issues related to religious

freedom and to train lawyers to handle religious freedom legal cases; Publications: *Center for Law and Religious Freedom Focus*: *On Justice, Reconciliation, and Religious Freedom* (periodic); *Defender* (bimonthly); *Juris: For Jurisprudence and Legal History* (periodic).

Center for Libertarian Studies (CLS). 875 Mahler Road, Suite 150, Burlingame, CA 94010. Tel: (415) 348-3000. President: Burt Blumert; f. 1976; Promotes the analysis of social and political problems from a Libertarian point of view; Publications: *Discovering Self-Government: a Bible Based Study Guide*; *The Liberator* (quarterly); *OPH Manual*; *Self-Government: An Idea Whose Time Has Come* (video).

Center for Media and Public Affairs (CMPA). 2100 L Street NW, Suite 300, Washington, DC 20037. Tel: (202) 223-2942 Fax: (202) 872-4014. Co-Director: Dr. S. Robert Lichter; f. 1986; Studies the effects of how the media treats social and political issues; Publications: *Media Monitor* (bimonthly).

Center for Religion, Ethics and Social Policy (CRESP). Cornell University, Anabel Tayer Hall, Ithaca, NY 14853. Tel: (607) 255-5027 or (607) 255-6022 Fax: (607) 255-9985 E-mail: msw16@Cornell.edu. Director: Mary S. Webber; f. 1971; Promotes individual, social, and ecological advancement toward a more humane and equitable future; Publications: *CRESP Annual Report*; *CUSLAR Newsletter* (bimonthly); *EcoVillage at Ithaca* (quarterly); *Peace, Environmental and Social Justice Group Directory* (annual).

Center for Reproductive Law and Policy (CRLP). 120 Wall Street, New York, NY 10005. Tel: (212) 514-5534 Fax: (212) 514-5538. President: Janet Benshoof; f. 1992; Seeking to secure women's reproductive freedom; Publications: *Reproductive Freedom News* (biweekly).

Center for Responsive Politics (CRP). 1320 19th Street NW, 7th Floor, Washington, DC 20036. Tel: (202) 857-0044 Fax: (202) 857-7809 E-mail: info@crp.org. Website: http://ww.crp.org.

Executive Director: Ellen S. Miller; f. 1983; Works in the area of campaign finance and ethics to promote a more effective Congress; Publications: *The Price of Admission: An Illustrated Atlas to Campaign Spending in the 1988 Congressional Elections*; *Enhancing the Mediaís Role in Congressional Campaigns*; *Open Secrets: The Dollar Power of PACs in Congress*; *Soft Money: A Loophole for the 80's*.

Center for Science in the Public Interest (CSPI). 1875 Connecticut Avenue NW, Suite 300, Washington, DC 20009-5728. Tel: (202) 332-9110 Fax: (202) 265-4954 E-mail: espi@cspinet.org. Executive Director: Michael Jacobson; f. 1971; Concerned with the effects of science and technology on society; Publications: *Nutrition Action Healthletter* (10/yr).

Center for Study of Responsive Law (CSRL). PO Box 19367, Washington, DC 20036. Tel: (202) 387-8030 Fax: (202) 234-5176. Director: John Richard; f. 1969; Seeks to raise public awareness of environmental and consumer issues.

Center for the Defense of Free Enterprise (CDFE). Liberty Park, 12500 NE 10th Place, Bellevue, WA 98005. Tel: (206) 455-5038 Fax: (206) 451-3959. Vice President: Ron Arnold; f. 1976; Defends and promotes the principles of the American free enterprise system; Publications: *Advise and Consent* (periodic); *The Private Sector* (quarterly); *Wise Use of Conservation Memo* (quarterly).

Center for the Study of Democratic Institutions (CSDI). 10951 West Pico Boulevard, 3rd Floor, Los Angeles, CA 90064. Tel: (213) 474-0011 Toll-Free: (800) 336-1007 Fax: (213) 474-8061. Executive Officer: Nathan Gardels; f. 1959; Investigates critical issues that are confronting the world today; Publications: *New Perspectives Quarterly* (journal).

Center for the Study of Democratic Societies (CSDS). PO Box 475. Manhattan Beach, CA 90266. Tel: (213) 374-2737 Fax: (213) 374-8984. Director: Robley Evans George; f. 1969; Re-search and educational institution dedicated to the necessary examination and explanation of the properties and possibilities of democratic societies; Publications: *Center for the Study of Demo-cratic Societies: The Center Review* (periodic).

Center for the Study of Human Rights (CSHR). Columbia University, 1108 International Affairs Building, New York, NY 10027. Tel: (212) 854-2479 Fax: (212) 316-4578. Executive Director: Dr. J. Paul Martin; f. 1977; Promotes teaching and research in the field of human rights; Publications: *Center for the Study of Human Rights Newsletter* (quarterly); *Conference Proceedings* (annual).

Center for Third World Organizing (CTWO). 1218 East 21st Street, Oakland, CA 94606-3132. Tel: (510) 533-7583 Fax: (510) 533-0923. Con-tact: Francis Calpotura; f. 1980; Monitors dis-crimination and supports low-income minority organizations; Publications: *CTWO Times* (3/year); *Directory of Church Funding Sources* (peri-odic); *Issue Pac* (quarterly).

Center for Voting and Democracy. 6905 5th Street NW, Suite 200, Washington, DC 20012. Tel: (202) 882-7378 or (202) 828-3062 Fax: (202) 726-8127 E-mail: cudusa@aol.com. Website: http://www.igcapc.org/cvd/. President: Matthew Cossolotto; f. 1992; Interested in promoting proportional representation voting systems; Publications: *Voting and Democracy Report* (annual); *Voting and Democracy Review* (quar-terly).

Center for Women Policy Studies (CWPS). 2000 P Street NW, Suite 508, Washington, DC 20036. Tel: (202) 872-1770 Fax: (202) 296-8962 E-mail: cwpsx@aol.com. President: Rayna Green; f. 1972; Educates the public and policymakers regarding issues of women's equal-ity; Publications: *Center for Women Policy Studies Publications Catalog*.

Center of Concern (CC). 3700 13th Street NE, Washington, DC 20017. Tel: (202) 635-2757 Fax: (202) 832-9494. Executive Director: James E. Hug; f. 1971; Promotes issues such as economic justice, poverty, and social development through grassroots and international efforts; Publications: *Catholic Social Teaching: Our Best Kept Secret*; *Center Focus* (bimonthly).

Center on Budget and Policy Priorities (CBPP). 777 North Capitol Street NE, Suite 705, Washington, DC 20002. Tel: (202) 408-1080 Fax: (202) 408-1056 E-mail: center@center.cbpp.org. Executive Director: Robert Greenstein; f. 1981; Seeks to promote understanding of the impact of federal and state spending programs for poor and moderate income families and individuals; Publications: *Women, Infants, and Children Newsletter* (monthly).

Center to Prevent Handgun Violence (CPHV). 1225 I Street NW, Suite 1100, Washington, DC 20005. Tel: (202) 289-7319 Fax: (202) 408-1851. Chair: Sarah Brady; f. 1983; Provides legal representation to victims of handgun violence and lobbies for federal gun control laws; Publications: *CPHV: Rx for Gun Violence* (quarterly); *Legal Action Report* (newsletter).

Central Committee for Conscientious Objectors. 1515 Cherry Street, Philadelphia, PA 19102. Tel: (215) 563-8787 Fax: (215) 567-2096 E-mail: ccco@libertynet.org. Website: http://www/libertynet.org/ccco.; f. 1948; Provides draft and military counseling and counter-recruitment counseling; Publications: *Advice for Conscientious Objectors in the Armed Forces*; *Anti-JROTC Organizing Kit* (quarterly); *Choosing Peace* (handbook); *The Objector* (quarterly).

Children's Legal Foundation (CLF). 2845 East Camelback Road, Suite 740, Phoenix, AZ 85016. Tel: (602) 381-1322 Fax: (602) 381-1613. President: Bradley J. Boland; f. 1957; Seeks to enact legislation controlling obscenity and pornography and materials which it deems harmful to juveniles; Publications: *The CLF Reporter* (quarterly).

Christian Americans for Life (CAFL). PO Box 977, Tulsa, OK 74102. Tel: (918) 438-4234 Fax: (918) 438-4235. CEO: Billy James Hargis; f. 1972; Seeks to end abortion and educate to

support adoption as an alternative; Publications: *Hotline* (monthly).

Christian Anti-Communism Crusade (CACC). PO Box 890, 227 East 6th Street, Long Beach, CA 90810. Tel: (310) 437-0941 Fax: (310) 432-2074. President: Fred C. Schwartz; f. 1953; Purpose is to support national and international anti-communist education and activities; Publications: *New Letter* (monthly); *The Three Faces of Revolution*; *What is Communism?*; *Why Communism Kills*; *Why I Am Against Communism*; *You Can Trust the Communists (to be Communist)*.

Christian Coalition (CC). 1801 Sarah Drive, Suite L, Chesapeake, VA 23320. Tel: (804) 424-2603 Fax: (804) 424-9068. Website: http://www.cc.org. Executive Director: Randy Tate; f. 1989; Seeks to stop the "moral decay" of government and promote the election of moral legislators and legislation; Publications: *Christian America* (bimonthly).

Citizens Against Government Waste (CAGW). 1301 Connecticut Avenue NW, Suite 400, Washington, DC 20036. Tel: (202) 467-5300 or (202) 543-3363 Toll Free: (800) BE-ANGRY Fax: (202) 467-4253 Website: http://www.ccrkba.org. President: Thomas A. Schatz; f. 1984; Seeks to eliminate waste, mismanagement, and inefficiency in government spending; Publications: *Burning Money: The Waste of Your Tax Dollars*; *Congressional Pig Book Summary* (annual); *Government Wastewatch* (quarterly); *Prime Cuts* (annual); *Wastewatch Journal* (annual).

Citizens Committee for the Right to Keep and Bear Arms (CCRKBA). Liberty Park, 12500 NE 10th Place, Bellevue, WA 98005. Tel: (206) 454-4911 Fax: (206) 451-3959. Website: http://www.ccrbba.org. Executive Director: Ken Jacobson; f. 1971; Concerned with protecting the Second Amendment right to bear arms; Publications: *Point Blank* (monthly); *Politically Correct Guns*; *Gun Rights Fact Book*.

Citizens for a Debt Free America (CDFA).
2550 South Sunny Slope Road, New Berlin, WI
53151. Tel: (414) 782-1305. Coordinator: Kay M.
Fishburn; f. 1983; Seeks to eliminate the national
debt with private donations to the US Treasury;
Publications: *Silver Linings* (quarterly).

Citizens for a Sound Economy (CSE). 1250 H
Street NW, Suite 700, Washington, DC 20005-
3908. Tel: (202) 783-3870 Fax: (202) 783-4687.
President: Paul Beckner; f. 1984; Seeks to
advance an understanding of the market system to
produce a strong economy; Publications: *Citizen's
Guide to Deficit Reduction* (monograph);
Capital Comment (periodic); *Economic Perspective* (periodic); *Issues and Answers* (bimonthly);
Legal Perspective (periodic); *Myths About
Foreign Investment* (monograph); *On Alert for
Americais Taxpayers* (monthly).

Citizens' Energy Council (CEC). PO Box U,
Hewitt, NJ 07421. Tel: (201) 728-2232 Fax: (201)
728-7664. National Coordinator: Larry Bogart; f.
1966; Monitors and reports on activities of the
Nuclear Regulatory Commission and other events
related to nuclear energy; Publications: *The
Messenger* (monthly).

Clearinghouse on Women's Issues (CWI).
PO Box 70603, Friendship Heights, MD 20813.
Tel: (202) 362-3789 Fax: (202) 632-3789. President: Ruth G. Nadel; f. 1972; Clearinghouse for
national, regional, state, and local women's and
civil rights organizations; Publications: *CWI
Newsletter* (9/year).

Clergy and Laity Concerned (CALC). 340
Mead Road, Decatur, GA 30030. Tel: (404) 377-
1983 Fax: (404) 377-5367. Co-Chair: Marian
Willingham; f. 1965; Seeks to bring moral, ethical,
and religious values to bear on issues of human
rights, racial equality, and gender justice, militarism, and economic justice at home and abroad;
Publications: *CALC Report* (quarterly).

Close Up Foundation. 44 Canal Center Plaza,
Alexandria, VA 22314. Tel: (703) 706-3300 Toll-
Free: (800) 336-5479 Fax: (703) 706-0000.
Website: http://www.closeup.com. President:

Stephen A. Janger; f. 1970; Promotes civic
awareness and encourages participation in the
democratic process through non-partisan education programs; Publications: *Current Issues*
(annual); *Reinventing Citizenship: New Roles
for Every American* (annual); *The Source Book.*

**Coalition for Consumer Health and Safety
(CCHS).** 1424 16th Street NW, Suite 604,
Washington, DC 20036. Tel: (202) 387-6121 Fax:
(202) 265-7989 E-mail: dneidle@essential.org.
Website: http://www.essential.org/cchs. Chair:
Stephen Brobeck; f. 1988; Consumer, health and
insurer groups committed to advancing consumer
health and safety; Publications: *Consumer Health
and Safety Agenda* (periodic); *Consumer
Health and Safety: Progress and Properties for
Congress and Federal Agencies* (annual);
Consumer Health and Safety Update (quarterly).

Coalition for Religious Freedom (CRF). 5817
Dawes Avenue, Alexandria, VA 22311-1114.
Executive Director: Dan Holdgreiwe; f. 1984;
Seeks to preserve the First Amendment freedom
of religion; Publications: *Religious Freedom Alert*
(8-10/year).

**Coalition for the Strategic Defense Initiative
(CSDI).** 2800 Shirlington Road, Suite 405A,
Arlington, VA 22206. Tel: (703) 671-4111 Fax:
(703) 931-6432. Executive Director: J. Milnor
Roberts; f. 1985; Seeks to create public support
for the Strategic Defense Initiative; Publications:
Civilian-Based Defense (quarterly); *National
Security Through Civilian-Based Defense.*

Coalition to Stop Gun Violence (CSGV). 1000
16th Street NW, Suite 603, Washington, DC
20036. Tel: (202) 530-0340 Fax: (202) 530-0331.
Executive Director: Michael K. Beard; f. 1975;
Seeks to ban the sale and possession of handguns
in America.

**Comision Femenil Mexicana Nacional
(CFMN).** 379 South Loma Drive, Los Angeles,
CA 90017. Tel: (213) 484-1515 Fax: (213) 484-
0880. President: Nina Aguayo Sorcin; f. 1970;
Advocates Latina and Hispanic women's rights.

Committee for a Voluntary Census (CVC). PO Box 338, Warminster, PA 18974. Tel: (215) 675-3080. Director: Donald Ernsberger; f. 1970; Believes that census questions that go beyond asking the whole number of persons in each state are unconstitutional and a violation of privacy and supports laws which make responding to such questions strictly voluntary; Publications: *Newsletter* (5 per year during each census year).

Committee for Economic Development (CED). 2000 L Street NW, Suite 700, Washington, DC 20036. Tel: (202) 296-5860 Fax: (202) 223-0776. President: Sol Hurwitz; f. 1942; Conducts research and formulates policy recommendations on national and international economic issues; Publications: *Statements on National Policy*.

Committee of Concerned Scientists (CCS). 53-34 208th Street, Bayside, NY 11364. Tel: (718) 229-2813 Fax: (718) 229-7540 E-mail: ccs@cims.nyu.edu. Executive Director: Dorothy Hirsch; f. 1972; Seeks to preserve the scientific and human rights of the world's scientists.

Committee to Protect Journalists (CPJ). 330 7th Avenue, 12th Floor, New York, NY 10001. Tel: (212) 465-1004 Fax: (212) 465-9568 E-mail: info@cpj.org. Website: http://www.cpj.org. Executive Director: William A. Orme Jr.; f. 1981; Supports journalists who have been subjected to human rights abuses and promotes the freedom of the press; Publications: *Attacks on the Press* (annual); *Dangerous Assignments* (quarterly).

Committee to Restore the Constitution (CRC). 2218 West Prospect Road, PO Box 986, Fort Collins, CO 80522. Tel: (303) 484-2575. Director: Archibald E. Roberts; f. 1965; Seeks to restore the Constitution by eliminating the deficit, the United Nations and the Federal Reserve System; Publications: *CRC Bulletin* (monthly).

Community Associations Institute (CAI). 1630 Duke Street, Alexandria, VA 22314. Tel: (703) 548-8600 Fax: (703) 684-1581 Website: http://www.caionline.com. Executive VP: Bar-

bara Byrd-Lawler; f. 1973; Encourages the successful operation and management of all types of residential community housing and seeks to foster effective community associations; Publications: *Board Briefs* (bimonthly); *Common Ground* (bimonthly); *Community Association Law Reporter* (monthly); *Ledger Quarterly*.

Concerned Educators Against Forced Unionism (CEAFU). 8001 Braddock Road, Suite 500, Springfield, VA 22160. Tel: (703) 321-8519. f. 1975; Works to give educators the right to accept or reject unionism; Publications: *CPER Easy Reference Pocket Guide Series; CPER Journal* (bimonthly).

Congress Watch (CW). 215 Pennsylvania Avenue SE, Washington, DC 20003. Tel: (202) 546-4996 Fax: (202) 547-7392. Director: Frank Clemente; f. 1971; Congressional lobby for consumer interests, citizen access to government decision making, campaign finance reform, trade, product safety, healthcare, product liability, and medical malpractice issues; Publications: *Congressional Voting Index* (annual).

Conservative Alliance (CALL). 2900 Eisenhower Avenue, Suite 200-C, Alexandria, VA 22314. Fax: (703) 329-2411. Executive Director: J. Barry Bitzer; f. 1977; Promotes strong national defense, private enterprise and less government intervention, regulation, and spending; Publications: *Call for Action* (quarterly); *Congressional Scorecard* (annual).

Consortium for the Study of Intelligence (CSI). 1730 Rhode Island Avenue NW, Suite 500, Washington, DC 20036. Tel: (202) 429-0129 Fax: (202) 659-5429. Coordinator: Roy Godson; f. 1979; Promotes research and education on intelligence; Publications: *Comparing Foreign Intelligence: The US, The USSR, UK, and the Third World*; *Intelligence Requirement for the 1980s*; *Intelligence Requirements for the 1990s*.

Constitutional Rights Foundation (CRF). 601 South Kingsley Drive, Los Angeles, CA 90005.

Tel: (213) 487-5590 Fax: (213) 386-0459. Executive Director: Todd Clark; f. 1963; Seeks to encourage youth to become active and responsible participants in society by emphasizing the values expressed in the Constitution, especially the Bill of Rights; Publications: *Bill of Rights in Action* (quarterly).

Consumer Alert (CA). 1001 Connecticut Avenue NW, Suite 1128, Washington, DC 20036. Tel: (202) 467-5809 Fax: (202) 467-5814 E-mail: calert@his.com. Website: http://www.his.com/~calert. Executive Director: Frances B. Smith; f. 1977; Consumer interest group opposed to excessive regulation, and supporting free enterprise, consumer rights and freedom of choice; Publications: *Consumer Alerts Comments* (bimonthly); *New Releases* (periodic); *Testimony* (periodic).

Consumer Information Center (CIC). 18 F Street NW, Room G-142, Washington, DC 20405. Tel: (202) 501-1794 Fax: (202) 501-4281. Website: http://www.pueblo.gsa.gov. Director: Teresa Nasif; f. 1970; Established by Presidential Order to promote information of interest to consumers; Publications: *Consumer Information Catalog* (quarterly).

Consumer Union of United States (CU). 101 Truman Avenue, Yonkers, NY 10703. Tel: (914) 378-2000. President: Rhoda H. Karpatkin; f. 1936; Provides consumers with information and advice on consumer goods and services; Publications: *Consumer Reports* (monthly); *On Health* (monthly); *Travel Letters* (monthly); *Zillions* (6/year).

Council for a Livable World (CLW). 110 Maryland Avenue NE, Suite 409, Washington, DC 20002. Tel: (202) 543-4100 Fax: (202) 543-6297 E-mail: clw@clw.org. Website: http://www.cofcc.org. Executive Director: John Isaacs; f. 1962; Concerned about the course of the arms race and issues of foreign and defense policies; Publications: *Candidate Profiles* (monthly); *Factsheets* (periodic); *Nuclear Arms Control Voting Record* (annual); *Reports (*periodic).

Council for Conservative Citizens (CofCC). PO Box 9683, St Louis, MO 63122. Tel: (314) 291-8474 E-mail: c.of.cc@juno.com, Website: http://www.cofcc.org. CEO: Gordon Lee Baum; f. 1985; Dedicated to states' rights, supports conservative principles, and rejects affirmative action programs; Publications: *Citizens' Informer* (quarterly); *Council Reporter* (semiannual).

Council for Responsible Genetics (CRG). 5 Upland Road, Suite 3, Cambridge, MA 02140. Tel: (617) 868-0870 Fax: (617) 491-5344. Executive Director: Wendy McGoodwin; f. 1983; Interested in the social impact of new genetic technologies, including their military and genetic engineering uses; Publications: *GeneWatch* (bimonthly).

Council of Better Business Bureaus (CBBB). 4200 Wilson Boulevard, Suite 800, Arlington, VA 22203-1804. Tel: (703) 276-0100 Fax: (703) 525-8277. Website: http://www.bbb.org/bbb/. President and CEO: James L. Bast; f. 1970; Seeks to promote and foster the highest ethical business relationship between business and the consumer community; Publications: *Advertising Topics Newsletter* (quarterly); *Annual Charity Index* (annual); *Do's and Don'ts in Advertising* (monthly); *Give, But Give Wisely* (bimonthly).

Council of Development Finance Agencies (CDFA). 1200 19th Street NW, Suite 300, Washington, DC 20036-2401. Tel: (202) 857-1162 Fax: (202) 429-5113 E-mail: aaron_mandel@SBA.com. Website: http://www.history.rochester.edu/edfat. Executive Director: Aaron Mindel; f. 1984; Seeks to encourage economic development financing programs; Publications: *CDFA Review* (bimonthly).

Council of Presidents (CP). c/o Susan Bianchi-Sand, Chair, National Committee on Pay Equity, 1126 16th Street NW, Suite 411, Washington, DC 20036. Tel: (202) 331-7343 Fax: (202) 331-7406. Addresses women's rights issues before the government, including worker training for women and the Equal Rights Amendment; Publications: *CCWH Newsletter* (5/year).

Disarm Education Fund (DEF). 36 East 12th Street, 6th Floor, New York, NY 10003. Tel: (212) 475-3232 Fax: (212) 979-1583 E-mail: disarm@igc.apc.org. Executive Director: Robert Schwartz; f. 1976; Promotes demilitarized foreign policy, international peace, social justice, and self-determination through opposition to military intervention and nuclear arms.

Drug Policy Foundation (DPF). 4455 Connecticut Avenue NW, Suite B-500, Washington, DC 20008. Tel: (202) 537-5005 Toll-Free: (800) 388-DRUG Fax: (202) 537-3007. President: Arnold S. Trebach; Seeks to protect individual rights by promoting alternative methods such as legalization, decriminalization, and medicalization of currently illegal substances; Publications: *Drug Policy Action* (bimonthly); *Drug Policy Collection* (annual); *Drug Policy Letter* (quarterly).

Eagle Forum (EF). PO Box 618, Alton, IL 62002. Tel: (618) 462-5415 or (202) 544-0353 Fax: (618) 462-8909 E-mail: eagle@eagleforum.org. Website: http://www.eagleforum.org. President: Phyllis Schlafly; f. 1975; Supports pro-family and conservative issues involving family, education, and national defense; Publications: *Phyllis Schlafly Report* (monthly).

Eternal Life. PO Box 787, Bardstown, KY 40004. Tel: (502) 348-3963 Fax: (502) 348-2224. Contact: William J. Smith; f. 1991; Promotes Catholic-inspired, family-centered sexuality and seeks to end abortion, fetal experimentation, euthanasia, etc.

Ethics Resource Center (ERC). 1747 Pennsylvania Avenue NW, Suite 400, Washington, DC 20007. Tel: (202) 737-2258 Toll-Free: (800) 777-1285 Fax: (202) 737-2258 E-mail: ethicsdc@aol.com. President: Michael G. Dhignealut; f. 1922; Works to strengthen the ethical foundations of America's institutions; Publications: *Ethics Journal* (quarterly); *Charter Education* (video); *Ethics at Work* (video).

Evangelicals for Social Action (ESA). 10 Lancaster Avenue, Wynnewood, PA 19096. Tel:

(215) 645-9390 Toll-Free: (800) 650-6600 Fax: (215) 649-8090 E-mail: esa@esa.mhs.compuserve.com. Website: http://www.libertynet.org/esa/. President: Ron Sider; f. 1978; Christian social action group seeking to serve the poor and powerless, and witness for Jesus Christ; Publications: *Christian Monographs on Public Policy* (bimonthly); *Green Cross Magazine* (quarterly); *Prism Magazine* (bimonthly).

Fairness and Accuracy in Reporting (FAIR). 130 West 25th Street, New York, NY 10001. Tel: (212) 633-6700 Fax: (212) 727-7668 E-mail: fair@fair.org. Website: http://www.fair.org/fair. Executive Director: Jeff Cohen; f. 1986; Promotes free press and free speech and encourages pluralism in the media; Publications: *Extra!* (6/year).

False Memory Syndrome Foundation. 3401 Market Street, Suite 130, Philadelphia, PA 19104-3315. Tel: (215) 387-1865 Toll-Free: (800) 568-8882 Fax: (215) 387-1917. Executive Director: Pamela Freyd; f. 1992; Researches the validity and effects of claims of the recovery of long-repressed memories; Publications: *The False Memory Syndrome Phenomenon* (booklet); *FMSF* (10/year).

Family Research Institute (FRI). PO Box 62640, Colorado Springs, CO 80962-2640. Tel: (303) 681-3113 Fax: (303) 681-3427. Executive Officer: Paul Cameron; f. 1982; Seeks to promote information about sexual, family, and substance abuse issues; Publications: *Family Research Report* (bimonthly).

Farm Aid. 334 Broadway, Suite 5, Cambridge, MA 02139. Tel: (617) 354-2922 Toll Free: (800) FARM-AID Fax: (617) 354-6992 E-mail: farmaid1@aol.com. Executive Director: Carolyn G. Mugar; f. 1985; Concerned with promoting public awareness of the plight of the American farmer and providing aid to agriculture-dependent families; Publications: *Farm Aid Update* (quarterly).

Federation for American Immigration Reform (FAIR). 1666 Connecticut Avenue NW, Suite 400, Washington, DC 20009. Tel: (202) 328-7004 Toll-Free: (800) 395-0890 Fax: (202) 387-3447 E-mail: fair@fairus.org. Website: http://www.fairus.org. Executive Director: Daniel Stein; f. 1979; Seeks to implement a 5-year moratorium on legal immigration, promote laws against illegal immigration, and reform other immigration policies; Publications: *Fair Immigration Report* (monthly); *Information Exchange* (quarterly).

Fellowship of Reconciliation (FOR). PO Box 271, Nyack, NY 10960. Tel: (914) 358-4601 Fax: (914) 358-4924 E-mail: fornatl@igcapc.org. Website: http://www.nonviolence.org/~nvweb/for. Executive Officer: Jo Becker; f. 1915; Religious pacifists seeking to substitute nonviolence and reconciliation for violence in international relations; Publications: *Fellowship* (6/year).

Feminists for Life of America (FFL). 733 15th Street NW, Suite 1100, Washington, DC 20005. Tel: (202) 737-3352 Fax: (202) 737-0414. Website: http://www.serve.com/fem4life. Executive Director: Serrin M. Foster; f. 1972; Seeks legal and social equality for all, from conception to natural death; Publications: *Profile Feminism: Different Voices*; *Sisterlife* (quarterly).

Forum International: International Ecosystems University (IEU). 91 Gregory Lane, Suite 21, Pleasant Hill, CA 94523. Tel: (510) 671-2900 Fax: (510) 946-1500 E-mail: forum@ix.netcom.com. Director: Nicolas D. Hetzer; f. 1965; Seeks to study and educate about environmental and social problems and how they are related ecosystemically; Publications: *Ecosphere* (bimonthly).

Foundation for American Communications (FACS). 3800 Barham Boulevard, Suite 409, Los Angeles, CA 90068. Tel: (213) 851-7372 Fax: (213) 851-9186. President: John E. Cox Jr.; f. 1976; Seeks to improve mutual understanding between major American institutions and the news media; Publications: *Communications Conference Workbook*; *FACS Report; Media Resource Guide*.

Foundation for Global Community (FGC). 222 High Street, Palo Alto, CA 94301. Tel: (415) 328-7756 Fax: (415) 328-7785. Website: http://www.globalcommunity.org. Executive Director: Richard Rathbun; f. 1982; Seeks to transform cultural values through personal mastery, education, and social action; Publications: *Timeline* (bimonthly).

Foundation to Improve Television (FIT). 50 Congress Street, Suite 925, Boston, MA 02109. Tel: (617) 523-5520 Fax: (617) 523-4619. President: William S. Abbott; f. 1969; Works to reduce the amount of violence depicted on television.

Free the Eagle (FTE). 666 Pennsylvania Avenue SE, Suite 402, Washington, DC 20003. Tel: (202) 543-6090 Fax: (202) 546-0029. Director: Tammy J. Lyles; f. 1980; Lobbies to encourage legislation maintaining free enterprise and individual freedom; Publications: *Eye on Washington* (periodic).

Free World Government, Earthbank. PO Box 332146, Coconut Grove, FL 33233-2146. Tel: (305) 368-0337 E-mail: do17629c@dcfreenet.seflinilib.us. Global Facilitator: Wendell Sharman Phillips; f. 1981; Seeks to promote international peace through the creation of a global democratic government.

Freedom House (FH). 120 Wall Street, New York, NY 10005. Tel: (212) 514-8040 Toll-Free: (800) 289-8880 Fax: (212) 514-8050. President: Adrian Karatnycky; f. 1941; Promotes political rights and civil liberties worldwide; Publications: *Freedom in the World: Political Rights and Civil Liberties* (annual); *Freedom Monitor* (semiannual); *Freedom Review* (bimonthly); *Survey of Press Freedom*.

Freedoms Foundation at Valley Forge (FFVF). PO Box 706, Valley Forge, PA 19482-0706. Tel: (610) 933-8825 Fax: (610) 935-0522 E-mail: ffvf@ffvf.org. Website: http://www.nef.org/ff/index.htm. Contact: Richard C.

Ustick; f. 1949; Seeks to promote responsible citizenship and the preservation of rights; Publications: *Freedoms Foundation Focus* (quarterly).

Friends of the United Nations. 1507 Stanford, Suite 5, Santa Monica, CA 90404. Tel: (310) 453-8489 Fax: (310) 453-8489. Executive Officer: Irving Sarnoff; f. 1986; Seeks to support the functions of the United Nations; Publications: *UN Information Update* (biweekly).

Frontlash. 815 16th Street NW, Washington, DC 20006. Tel: (202) 783-3993 Fax: (202) 783-3591. Executive Director: Cheryl Graeve; f. 1968; Seeks to increase the political participation of young people, minorities, senior citizens and workers; Publications: *Frontlash Update* (quarterly).

Fund for a Conservative Majority (FCM). PO Box 6829, Arlington, VA 22206. Tel: (703) 820-3830 Fax: (703) 820-4081. Chair: Robert C. Heckman; f. 1969; Seeks to create a conservative majority in Congress; Publications: *FCM Report.*

Fund for an Open Society (OPEN). 311 South Juniper Street, Suite 400, Philadelphia, PA 19107. Tel: (215) 735-6915 Fax: (215) 735-2507 E-mail: 102400.733@compuserve.com. Executive Director: Don DeMarco; f. 1975; Provide loans to persons making housing moves that decrease segregation; Publications: *OPEN Forum* (annual).

Fund for Stockowners Rights (FFSR). PO Box 65563, Washington, DC 20035. Tel: (703) 241-3700 or (818) 223-8080. Chair: Carl Olson; f. 1984; Seeks to unite stockholders in improving election methods and preventing anti-takeover abuses.

Gay and Lesbian Alliance Against Defamation/ New York (GLAAD/NY). 150 West 26th Street, Suite 503, New York, NY 10001. Tel: (212) 807-1700 Fax: (212) 807-1806. Director of Special Projects: Jason Huffner; f. 1985; Opposes bigotry and defamation of gays and lesbians through education; Publications: *Glaad Bulletin* (bimonthly); *Glaad Tidings* (weekly); *Media Guide to the Lesbian and Gay Community.*

Global Fund for Women. 425 Sherman Avenue, Suite 300, Palto Alto, CA 94306. Tel: (415) 853-8305 Fax: (415) 328-0384 E-mail: gfw@ globalfundforwomen.org. Website: http:// www.globalfundforwomen.org. Executive Director: Kavita N. Ramdas; f. 1987; Gives support to women's groups working on emerging, controversial, or difficult issues.

Green Seal. 1730 Rhode Island Avenue NW, Suite 1050, Washington, DC 20036. Tel: (202) 331-7337 Fax: (202) 331-7533 E-mail: greenseal @grnseal.com. Website: http://ww.greenseal.org. President: Dr. Arthur Weissman; f. 1990; Environmental certification and consumer education organization.

Ground Zero (GZ). 7135 SW 36th Street, Portland, OR 97219. Tel: (503) 245-3403 E-mail: emolander@aol.com. President: Roger Molander; f. 1981; Concerned with educating the public on nuclear war issues and issues of national security; Publications: *Firebreaks: War/Peace Game*; *Nuclear War: What's In It For You?*; *What About the Russians And Nuclear War.*

Groundwork for a Just World (GW). 11224 Kercheval, Detroit, MI 48214. Tel: (313) 822-2055 Fax: (313) 822-5197. Contact: Paula Cathcart; f. 1976; Catholic women seeking understanding and involvement with global and domestic issues of peace and justice; Publications: *Groundwork* (8/year); *Political Action Guide* (biennial).

Gun Owners Incorporated (GOI). 10100 Fair Oaks Boulevard, Suite I, Fair Oaks, CA 95628. Tel: (916) 967-4970 Fax: (916) 967-4974. Carolyn Herbertson; f. 1975; Seeks to defend the right to own firearms, while advocating harsh punishment for criminals who misuse firearms.

HALT -- Americans for Legal Reform (HALT-ALR). 1319 F Street NW, Suite 300, Washington, DC 20004. Tel: (202) 347-9600 Toll-Free: (888) FOR-HALT Fax: (202) 347-9606 E-mail: altfry@aol.com. Website: http:// www.halt.org. Executive Director: William Fry; f. 1977; Seeks to reform the legal system and educate the public in its effective use; Publications: *The Legal Reformer* (quarterly).

Handgun Control, Inc. (HCI). 1225 I Street NW, Suite 1100, Washington, DC 20005. Tel: (202) 898-0792 Fax: (202) 371-9615. Chair: Sarah Brady; f. 1974; Lobbies for legislative controls and governmental regulations on guns; Publications: *The American Handgun War* (film); *Guns Don't Die, People Do*; *Handgun Control-Progress Report* (quarterly).

Health and Energy Institute (HEI). 615 Kennebec Avenue, Takoma Park, MD 20912. Tel: (301) 585-5831. President: Kathleen M. Tucker; f. 1978; Concerned with the impact of nuclear energy on health and the environment; Publications: *Bubble, Bubble, Toil and Trouble: Reprocessing Nuclear Spent Fuel*; *Food Irradiation: Who Wants It?*; *Heat, High Water, and Rock Instability at Hanford*; *Radiation Victims Organization Directory* (periodic); *Uranium and the Nuclear Cycle*.

Honest Ballot Association (HBA). North Shore Towers, Building 3 Arcade, 272-30 Grand Central Parkway, Floral Park, NY 11005. Tel: (516) 466-4100 Fax: (718) 279-0873. President: Murray Schwartz; f. 1909; Union of citizens seeking to ensure clean elections.

Human Rights Campaign. 1101 14th Street NW, Washington, DC 20005. Tel: (202) 628-4160 Fax: (202) 347-5323. Website: http://www.hrcusa.org. Executive Director: Elizabeth Birch; f. 1980; Lobbies to advance the cause of gay and lesbian civil rights and promote responsible AIDS policy and research; Publications: *Capitol Hill Update* (bimonthly); *Momentum* (quarterly).

Human Rights Watch (HRW). 485 5th Avenue, 3rd Floor, New York, NY 10017. Tel: (212) 972-8400 Fax: (212) 972-0905. Executive Director: Kenneth Roth; f. 1987; Evaluates and monitors human rights worldwide; Publications: *Human Rights Watch Publications Catalog* (semiannual); *Human Rights Watch Quarterly Newsletter*; *Human Rights Watch World Report*.

Infact. 256 Hanover Street, 3rd Floor, Boston, MA 02113. Tel: (617) 742-4583 Fax: (617) 367-0191. Director: Kathryn Mulvey; f. 1977; Works to increase the public accountability of transnational corporations and to bring about change through strategic boycotts; Publications: *Bringing GE to Light: How General Electric Shapes Nuclear Weapons Policies for Profits*; *Deadly Deception: General Electric Nuclear Weapons and Our Environment* (video); *inFACT Update* (quarterly).

Inform. 120 Wall Street, 16th Floor, New York, NY 10005-4001. Tel: (212) 361-2400 Fax: (212) 361-2412 E-mail: inform@igc.apc.org. President: Joanna Underwood; f. 1974; Seeks to research and educate about business practices that damage the environment; Publications: *Inform Reports* (quarterly); *Toxics Watch* (book).

Initiative America (AI). 3115 N Street NW, Washington, DC 20007. Tel: (202) 333-4846. Director: Edward A. Dent; f. 1977; Seeks to support legislation permitting voter-initiated legislation at both the federal and state levels.

Institute for Democratic Socialism (IDS). 15 Dutch Street, Suite 500, New York, NY 10038. Executive Director: Alan Charney; f. 1977; Seeks to introduce alternative social and economic proposals into the public debate and to recognize socialist contributions to American society; Publications: *Socialist Forum* (3/year).

Institute for First Amendment Studies. PO Box 589, Great Barrington, MA 01230. Tel: (413) 528-3800 Fax: (413) 528-4466. President: Skipp Porteous; f. 1984; Ex-members of fundamentalist churches and others who are dedicated to the separation of church and state as provided for in the First Amendment; Publications: *The Freedom Writer* (bimonthly); *Walk Away* (quarterly).

Institute for Food and Development Policy (IFDP). 398 60th Street, Oakland, CA 94618. Tel: (510) 654-4400 Toll-Free: (800) 274-7826 Fax: (510) 654-4551 E-mail: foodfirst@ igc.apc.org. Website: http://netspace.org/ hungerweb/foodfirst/index.html. Executive

Director: Peter Rosset; f. 1975; Investigates and educates about the social and economic causes of world hunger; Publications: *Alternatives to the Peace Corps* (directory); *Food First Books* (catalog); *Food First News and Views* (quarterly).

Institute for Space and Security Studies (ISSS). c/o Robert Bowman, 5115 South Ala Highway, Melbourne Beach, FL 32951. Tel: (407) 952-0600. President: Robert Bowman; f. 1983; Works to prevent nuclear war and to educate the public and lawmakers regarding the weaponization of space; Publications: *ISSS Annual Report; Space and Security News* (quarterly).

Inter-American Commission of Women (CIM). c/o Organization of American States, 1889 F Street NW, Room 880, Washington, DC 20006. Tel: (202) 458-6084 Fax: (202) 458-6094. Executive Director: Margarita Roque; f. 1928; Agency of the OAS dealing with women's issues; Publications: *Final Report: Assembly of Delegates* (biennial); *Series: Studies* (periodic).

Inter-American Defense Board (IADB). 2600 16th Street NW, Washington, DC 20441. Tel: (202) 939-6600 or (202) 939-6602 Fax: (202) 939-6620 E-mail: name@menair-emhz.army.mil. Chair: John C. Ellerson; f. 1942; Studies and recommends measures concerning the collective self-defense of the American continent.

Intercollegiate Studies Institute (ISI). PO Box 4431, Wilmington, DE 19807-0431. Tel: (215) 525-7501 Toll-Free: (800) 526-7022 Fax: (215) 525-3315. President: T. Kenneth Cribb Jr.; f. 1953; Promotes scholarship and the conservative philosophy of individual liberty, limited government, free market economics, private property, and the moral and spiritual underpinnings of this philosophy; Publications: *Campus: America's Student Newspaper* (quarterly); *Continuity: a Journal of History* (semiannual); *The Intercollegiate Review: a Journal of Scholarship and Opinion* (2-4/year); *Modern Age* (quarterly); *The Political Science Reviewer* (annual).

Interfaith Center on Corporate Responsibility (ICCR). 475 Riverside Drive, Room 550, New York, NY 10115. Tel: (212) 870-2293 Fax: (212) 870-2023. Executive Director: Timothy H. Smith; f. 1974; Assists members in coordinating their corporate responsibility programs and expressing social responsibility with their investments by exchanging information and development strategies; Publications: *Corporate Examiner* (10/year).

Intergovernmental Health Policy Project (IHPP). 444 North Capitol Street, Suite 515, Washington, DC 20001. Tel: (202) 872-1445 Fax: (202) 785-0114 E-mail: icrw@igc.apc.org. Director: Dr. Geeta Rao Gupta; f. 1979; Serves as a clearinghouse for information on state health legislation; Publications: *Primary Care News* (bimonthly); *State ADM Report* (10/year).

International Black Women's Congress (IBWC). 1081 Bergen Street, Newark, NJ 07112. Tel: (201) 926-0570 Fax: (201) 926-0818. President: La Francis Rodgers-Rose; f. 1983; Seeks to unite members for mutual support and socioeconomic development; Publications: *Black Women's Health and Social Policy; International Black Women's Directory* (periodic); *Oni Newsletter* (quarterly).

International Center for Research on Women (ICRW). 1717 Massachusetts Avenue NW, Suite 302, Washington, DC 20036. Tel: (202) 797-0007 Fax: (202) 797-0020 E-mail: icrw@igc.apc.org. President: Mayra Buvinic; f. 1976; Seeks to promote social and economic development with women's full participation; Publications: *International Center for Research on Women Papers* (periodic).

International Committee Against Racism (INCAR). 150 West 28th Street, Room 301, New York, NY 10001. Tel: (212) 255-3959 Fax: (312) 663-9742. Executive Director: Carol Deak; f. 1973; Dedicated to fighting racism and building a multi-racial society; Publications: *Arrow* (bimonthly).

International Foundation for Election Systems (IFES). 1101 15th Street NW, 3rd Floor, Washington, DC 20005. Tel: (202) 828-8507 Fax: (202) 452-0804. Website: http://www.ifes.org. Chair: Charles T. Manatt; f. 1987; Dedicated to supporting and improving the election process to assure free, fair, and credible elections in countries that request such assistance; Publications: *Elections Today* (quarterly); *Technical Assessment Country Reports*.

International Peace Academy (IPA). 777 United Nations Plaza, 4th Floor, New York, NY 10017. Tel: (212) 687-4300 Fax: (212) 983-8246. President: Clara A Otunnu; f. 1970; Postgraduate educational institution specializing in training in the skill of conflict management; Publications: *International Peacekeeping* (quarterly); *Occasional Papers* (periodic); *Peacekeeper's Handbook*.

International Physicians for the Prevention of Nuclear War (IPPNW). 126 Rogers Street, Cambridge, MA 02142. Tel: (617) 868-5050 Fax: (617) 868-2560 E-mail: ippmwbos@igc.apc.org. Website: http://www.healthnet.org/ippnw/. Chair: Lachlan Forrow; f. 1980; Physicians seeking to focus international attention on the medical consequences of nuclear and conventional war; Publications: *Vital Signs* (quarterly); *Affiliate Directory* (semiannual); *Nuclear Wastelands*; *Opportunities for International Control of Weapons-Usable Fissile Materials*; *Effects of Low-Intensity Conflict on an Underdeveloped Country*.

International Religious Liberty Association (IRLA). c/o Bert B. Beach, 12501 Old Columbia Pike, Siver Spring, MD 20904-6600. Tel: (301) 680-6680 Fax: (301) 680-6695. Secretary General: Bert B. Beach; f. 1888; Promotes religious liberty, the respect for religious rights, and the human right to freedom and conscience and belief; Publications: *Conscience et Liberte* (semiannual); *Liberty* (bimonthly).

International Republican Institute (IRI). 1212 New York Avenue NW, Suite 900, Washington, DC 20005. Tel: (202) 408-9450 Fax: (202) 408-9462. President: Lorne Craner; f. 1983; Nongovernmental political development organization supporting and administering democratic education projects worldwide; Publications: *Country Specific Reports* (periodic); *IRI Newsletter* (quarterly).

Jewish Institute for National Security Affairs (JINSA). 1717 K Street NW, Suite 800, Washington, DC 20006. Tel: (202) 833-0020 Fax: (202) 296-6452 E-mail: jinsa@infi.net. Executive Director: Thomas Neumann; f. 1976; Seeks to inform the Jewish community of the necessity of an American defense program and inform the defense community of the value of a strategic partnership between the US and Israel; Publications: *Middle East Terrorism Selected Group Profiles*; *Security Affairs* (bimonthly).

John Birch Society (JBS). PO Box 8040, Appleton, WI 54913-8040. Tel: (414) 749-3780 Fax: (414) 749-3785. Website: http://www.jbs.org. President: John F. McManus; f. 1958; Conservative, anti-Communist, educational group with the goal of less government, more responsibility, and with God's help, a better world; Publications: *JBS Bulletin* (monthly); *The New America* (biweekly).

Justice Now (JN). PO Box 72304, Charleston, SC 29415-2304. Director: Douglas Wendell Raynor Jr.; f. 1991; Supports the death penalty as a solution to crime and prison overcrowding; Publications: *Justice Now Newsletter* (periodic).

Kach International (KI). PO Box 425, Midwood Station, Brooklyn, NY 11230. Tel: (718) 646-7301 Fax: (718) 761-0148. f. 1985; Concerned with the problems facing Israel and Jewish communities throughout the world and with bringing the KACH party to power in Israel; Publications: *KACH Newsletter* (bimonthly); *Only Thus* (monthly).

KlanWatch. 400 Washington Avenue, Montgomery, AL 36104. Tel: (334) 264-0286 Fax: (334) 264-0629. Contact: Joe Roy; f. 1980; Seeks to gather information about the Ku Klux Klan and to create laws to protect the rights of those the Klan is attacking; Publications: *Klanwatch Intelligence*

Report (bimonthly); *Klanwatch Law Report* (quarterly); *Hate, Violence, and White Supremacy: A Decade of Review 1980-1990.*

Knights of the Ku Klux Klan (KKK). PO Box 2222, Harrison, AR 72601. Tel: (501) 427-3414 Fax: (501) 427-3414. Director: Thom Robb; f. 1956; Seeks to end discrimination against the oppressed white majority; Publications: *Membership Internal Bulletin* (monthly); *White Patriot: Worldwide Voice of the Aryan People* (monthly).

Laborers Political League (LPL). 905 16th Street NW, Washington, DC 20006. Tel: (202) 638-5753 Fax: (202) 737-2754. Director: Donald Kaniewski; f. 1964; Supports candidates who demonstrate concern for the working person and seeks to inform workers of the need to exercise the right to vote.

Leadership Conference on Civil Rights (LCCR). 1629 K Street NW, Suite 1010, Washington, DC 20006. Tel: (202) 466-3311 Fax: (202) 466-3435. Executive Director: Ralph G. Neas; f. 1950; Coalition of national organizations working to promote passage of civil rights, social and economic legislation and enforcement of laws that already exist; Publications: *LCCR Memo.*

League of Conservative Voters (LCV). 1707 L Street NW, Suite 750, Washington, DC 20036. Tel: (202) 785-8683 Fax: (202) 835-0491 E-mail: icv.org. Website: http://www.icv.org. President: Debra Callahan; f. 1970; Supports environmentalists running in House, Senate, and gubernatorial elections; Publications: *The National Environmental Scorecard* (annual); *Presidential Profiles.*

League of Private Property Owners. PO Box 400, Battle Ground, WA 98604. Tel: (206) 687-2471 Fax: (206) 687-2973 E-mail: ccushman@pacifier.com. Executive Director: Charles S. Cushman; f. 1988; Seeks to defeat legislation limiting public access to federal lands and defend private property rights; Publications: *Congressional Directory* (periodic); *Land Rights* (biennial); *Land Rights Advocate.*

Liberty Federation (LF). PO Box 2000, Lynchburg, VA 24506. President: P. Gilamen; f. 1979; Dedicated to convincing morally conservative Americans that it is their duty to register and vote for candidates who agree with traditional moral values.

Made in the USA Foundation. 1925 K Street, Suite 100, Washington, DC 20006. Tel: (202) 822-6060 Fax: (202) 822-6062. Executive Director: Joel Joseph; f. 1989; Committed to preserving American competitiveness by promoting American products at home and abroad; Publications: *Made in the USA: a Catalog of the Best American Products* (annual); *Made in the USA Reports* (quarterly).

Media Watch (MW). PO Box 618, Santa Cruz, CA 95061. Tel: (408) 423-6355 Toll-Free: (800) 631-6353 Fax: (408) 423-6355 E-mail: mediawok @aol.com. Director: Ann Simonton; f. 1984; Seeks to improve the image of women in the media; Publications: *Action Agenda* (quarterly); *Don't be a TV: Television Victim* (video); *The Media May be Hazardous to Your Health* (video).

Men's Defense Association (MDA). 17854 Lyons, Forest Lake, MN 55025. Tel: (612) 464-7887 Fax: (612) 464-7135 E-mail: mensdefense@ aol.com. Website: http://www.mensdefense.org. President: Richard F. Doyle; f. 1972; Seeks to restore dignity to the male, prevent sexual discrimination against males, and engage in activities that strengthen the marriage relationship and the family; Publications: *The Liberator* (newsletter); *The Men's Manifesto*; *Divorce: What Everyone Should Know to Beat the Racket.*

Mexican American Legal Defense and Educational Fund (MALDEF). 634 South Spring Street, 11th Floor, Los Angeles, CA 90014. Tel: (213) 629-2512 Fax: (213) 629-0266. President: Antonia Hernandez; f. 1968; Seeks to protect the civil rights of Hispanics in the US; Publications: *Leadership Program Newsletter* (3/ year).

Millennium Institute. 1117 19th Street North, Suite 900, Arlington, VA 22209-1708. Tel: (703) 841-0048 Fax: (703) 841-0050 E-mail: millennium @igc.org. Website: http://www.igc.apc.org/ millenium. President: Gerald O. Barney; f. 1983; Promotes long-term, integrated global thinking; Publications: *Global 2000 Revisited: What Shall We Do?*; *Handbook: Preparing a 21st Century Study; Managing a Nation: The Microcomputer Software Catalog*; *Studies for the 21st Century*.

Moral Re-Armament (MRA). 1156 15th Street NW, Suite 910, Washington, DC 20005-1704. Tel: (202) 872-9077 Fax: (202) 872-9137 E-mail: 73414.62@compuserve.com. Website: http:// www.mra.org. Executive Director: Richard W.B. Ruffin; f. 1941; Desires to advance the Christian religion by transforming the character and motives of people and nations; Publications: *Breakthroughs* (monthly); *For a Change* (bimonthly).

Morality in Media (MIM). 475 Riverside Drive, Suite 239, New York, NY 10115. Tel: (212) 870-3210 Fax: (212) 870-2765. President: Robert W. Peters; f. 1962; Works to prevent the illegal traffic of hard-core pornography; Publications: *Morality in Media Newsletter* (bimonthly).

Ms. Foundation for Women (MFW). 120 Wall Street, 33rd Floor, New York, NY 10005. Tel: (212) 742-2300 Fax: (212) 742-1653 E-mail: info@ms.foundation.org. Website: http:// www.ms.foundation.org. President: Marie C. Wilson; f. 1972; Funds and assists women's self-help organizing efforts and pursues changes in public consciousness, law, and social policy.

NAACP Legal Defense and Education Fund (LDF). 99 Hudson Street, 16th Floor, New York, NY 10013. Tel: (212) 219-1900 Fax: (212) 226-7592. Director-Counsel: Elaine R. Jones; f. 1940; Works to provide support and litigation on the behalf of blacks and other minorities; Publications: *Annual Report; Equal Justice* (quarterly).

National Abortion and Reproduction Action League (NARAL). 1156 15th Street NW, Suite 700, Washington, DC 20005. Tel: (202) 973-3000

Fax: (202) 973-3096 E-mail: naral@naral.org. Website: http://www.naral.org. President: Kate Michelman; f. 1969; Seeks to maintain the right to legal abortion for all women; Publications: *NARAL Newsletter* (quarterly).

National Alliance of Black Organizations (NABO). 3724 Airport Boulevard, Austin, TX 78722. Tel: (512) 478-9802 Fax: (512) 478-9804. President: M.J. Anderson Sr.; f. 1976; Coordinates voter registration efforts among member organizations and serves as a forum for the exchange of ideas and experiences.

National Alliance of Supermarket Shoppers (NASS). c/o Martin Sloane, 2 Broadlawn Avenue, Great Neck, NY 11024. Tel: (516) 466-5142 Fax: (516) 487-9750. Executive Officer: Martin Sloane; f. 1980; Monitors government protection agencies and takes part in legislative activities concerning consumer issues; Publications: *Membership Quarterly* (newsletter).

National Arbor Day Foundation (NADF). 100 Arbor Avenue, Nebraska City, NE 68410. Tel: (402) 474-5655 Fax: (402) 474-0820. Website: http://www.arborday.org. President: John Rosenow; f. 1972; Dedicated to tree planting and environmental stewardship; Publications: *Arbor Day* (bimonthly); *Tree City USA Bulletin* (bimonthly).

National Association for Neighborhood Schools (NANS). c/o Joyce Haws, Communications Office, 3905 Muriel Avenue, Cleveland, OH 44109. Tel: (216) 749-0389 or (216) 398-4667 E-mail: rhaws@aol.com. Website: http:// www.member.aol.com/rhaws/nansofohio.html. President: William D'Onofrio; f. 1976; Seeks to end busing and eliminate racial quotas from schools; Publications: *NANS Bulletin* (bimonthly).

National Association for the Advancement of Colored People (NAACP). 4805 Mount Hope Drive, Baltimore, MD 21215. Tel: (410) 358-8900 Fax: (410) 358-3818. Executive Director: Earl Shinhosper; f. 1909; Seeks to achieve equal rights through the democratic process and eliminate racial prejudice by removing racial discrimination in housing, employment, voting, schools, the courts, transportation, recreation, and business; Publications: *Annual Report*; *Crisis* (10/year).

National Association of Cuban-American Women of the USA (NACAW-USA). 2513 South Calhoun Street, Fort Wayne, IN 46807-1305. Tel: (219) 745-5421 Fax: (219) 744-1363. President: G.F. del Cueto Beecher; f. 1972; Addresses issues affecting Hispanic and minority women to achieve goals such as equal education, training, and compensation.

National Association of Latino Elected and Appointed Officials (NALEO). NALEO Educational Fund, 3409 Garnet Street, Los Angeles, CA 90023. Tel: (213) 262-8503 Fax: (213) 262-9823. Executive Director: Aturo Vagas; f. 1975; Advocacy group dedicated to the advancement of Hispanic people.

National Association to Protect Individual Rights. c/o Karen Morison, 5015 Gadsen, Fairfax, VA 22032-3411. Tel: (703) 425-5347. President: Karen Morison; f. 1991; Conducts research on issues including information privacy and government budgeting.

National Black Media Coalition (NBMC). 11120 New Hampshire Avenue, Silver Springs, MD 20904. Tel: (301) 593-3600 Fax: (301) 593-3604. Executive Director: Carmen Marshall; f. 1973; Seeks to increase media access for blacks and other minorities; Publications: *Action Bulletin* (periodic); *For the Record* (semiannual); *Media Line* (monthly); *Reading List* (periodic).

National Campaign for Freedom of Expression (NCFE). 918 F Street NW, Suite 609, Washington, DC 20004. Tel: (202) 393-2787 Toll-Free (800) 477-6233 Fax: (202) 347-7376. Executive Director: David Mendoza; f. 1990; Concerned with fighting censorship of visual and performance arts; Publications: *NCFE Bulletin*.

National Center for Constitutional Studies (NCCS). HC-61 Box 1056, Malta, ID 83342. Tel: (208) 645-2625 Toll-Free: (800) 388-4512 Fax: (208) 645-2667. President: Zeldon Nelson; f.

1971; Seeks to promote programs that teach constitutional principles in the tradition of America's founding fathers; Publications: *Behind the Scenes in Washington* (monthly); *The Constitution: Special Reports* (periodic).

National Center for Neighborhood Enterprise (NCNE). 1424 16th Street NW, 3rd Floor, Washington, DC 20036. Tel: (202) 518-6500 Fax: (202) 588-0314. President: Robert L. Woodson; f. 1981; Supports community self-sufficiency and effective mediating structures in low-income communities; Publications: *In the News* (periodic); *Policy Dispatch* (periodic); *On the Road to Economic Freedom: An Agenda for Black Progress*.

National Coalition Against Censorship (NCAC). 275 7th Avenue, 20th Floor, New York, NY 10001. Tel: (212) 807-6222 Fax: (212) 807-6245 E-mail: ncac@netcom.com. Website: http://www.ncadp.com. Executive Director: Joan Burton; f. 1974; Concerned with fighting censorship to preserve the freedoms of thought, inquiry and expression. Helps organize state and local anti-censorship groups; Publications: *Censorship News* (newsletter), *Conference Report* (report), *Meese Commission Exposed* (report), *The Sex Panic: Women, Censorship, and Pornography* (report).

National Coalition for Black Voter Participation (NCBVP). 1629 K Street NW, Suite 801, Washington, DC 20006. Tel: (202) 659-4929 Fax: (202) 659-5025. Executive Director: Sonia R. Jarvis; f. 1976; Seeks to increase registration and participation of black voters.

National Coalition to Abolish the Death Penalty (NCADP). 918 F Street NW, Suite 601, Washington, DC 20004. Tel: (202) 347-2411 Fax: (202) 347-2510 E-mail: ncadp1@nicam.com. Website:http://www.ncadp.com. Executive Director: Steven Hawkins; f. 1976; Works to abolish the death penalty in the US and end all executions; Publications: *The Abolitionists Directory* (directory); *The Death Penalty Exchange* (periodic), *Execution Alert* (periodic).

National Committee for Independent Political Action (NCIPA). PO Box 170610, Brooklyn, NY 11217. Tel: (718) 643-9603. Coordinator: Ted Glick; f. 1984; Seeks to bring together progressive political organizations to change society and bring about political and economic change.

National Committee to Preserve Social Security and Medicare (NCPSSM). 2000 K Street NW, Suite 800, Washington, DC 20006. Tel: (202) 822-9459 Toll-Free: (800) 966-1935 Fax: (202) 822-9612. President: Martha A. McSteen; f. 1982; Seeks to preserve federal support programs through grassroots advocacy and education of senior citizens; Publications: *Secure Retirement, the NewsMagazine for Mature Americans* (bimonthly).

National Congress for Community Economic Development (NCCED). 11 Dupont Circle NW, Suite 325, Washington, DC 20036-1207. Tel: (202) 234-5009 Fax: (202) 234-4510. President and CEO: Steve Glaude; f. 1967; Provides assistance for organizations in community-based economic development; Publications: *Community Development Corporate Profile Book*; *Development Times* (8/year); *National Directory of Corporate and Foundation Support*; *Economic Development* (periodic); *Resources* (quarterly).

National Congress of American Indians (NCAI). 2010 Massachusetts Avenue NW, 2nd Floor, Washington, DC 20036. Tel: (202) 466-7767 Fax: (202) 466-7797 E-mail: nclncl@aol.com Website: http://www.fraud.org/. Executive Director: JoAnn K. Chase; f. 1944; Advocates interests of the American Indians; Publications: *Sentinel* (periodic).

National Consumers League (NCL). 1701 K Street NW, Suite 1200, Washington, DC 20006. Tel: (202) 835-3323 Fax: (202) 835-0747 E-mail: nclncl@aol.com. Website: http://www.fraud.org/. Executive Director and President: Linda Golodner; f. 1899; Encourages consumer participation in government and industrial decision-making and consumer issues; Publications: *AAFT Quarterly; Child Labor Monitor* (quarterly); *NCL Bulletin* (bimonthly).

National Corporation for the Protection of Children and Families (NCPCF). 800 Compton Road, Suite 9224, Cincinnati, OH 45231. Tel: (513) 521-6227 Fax: (513) 521-6337. Website: http://www.nationalcoalition.org. President: Jerry R. Kirk; f. 1983; Seeks to eliminate obscenity, child pornography, and material that is harmful to minors; Publications: *Standing Together* (periodic).

National Council for Families and Television (NCFT). c/o Leo Burnett Advertising, 10900 Wilshire Boulevard, Suite 700, Los Angles, CA 90024. Tel: (310) 443-2000 Fax: (310) 208-5984. President: Tricia McLeod Robin; f. 1977; Seeks to promote the creation of positive prime time television entertainment for children; Publications: *NCFT Information Service Bulletin* (monthly); *Television and Families* (quarterly).

National Council for Urban Economic Development (CUED). 1730 K Street NW, Suite 915, Washington, DC 20006. Tel: (202) 223-4735 Fax: (202) 223-4745. Executive Director: Jeff Finkle; f. 1967; Works for public and private participants in global economic development; Publications: *Commentary* (quarterly); *Economic Developments* (semimonthly); *Economic Developments Abroad* (bimonthly); *Legislative Report* (3/year).

National Council of Negro Women (NCNW). 633 Pennsylvania Avenue NW, Washington, DC 20004-2605. Tel: (202) 628-0015 Fax: (202) 785-8733. President: Dorothy I. Height; f. 1935; Seeks to develop the leadership of women in community, national, and international life; Publications: *Black Women's Voice* (periodic); *Sisters Magazine* (quarterly).

National Development Council (NDC). 51 East 42nd Street, Suite 300, New York, NY 10017. Tel: (212) 682-1106 Fax: (212) 573-6118. President: Robert Davenport; f. 1972; Brings innovative economic development programs to urban and rural communities interested in local business and industrial growth; Publications: *Developments Newsletter* (quarterly).

National Endowment for Democracy (NED). 1101 15th Street NW, Suite 700, Washington, DC 20005. Tel: (202) 293-9072. President: Carl Gershman; f. 1983; A private, grant-making, government-financed effort promoting worldwide development of democratic values and human rights and freedoms through private sector initiatives; Publications: *Journal of Democracy* (quarterly); *National Endowment for Democracy Newsletter* (annual).

National Energy Education Development Project (NEED). 102 Elden Street, Suite 15, Herndon, VA 20170. Tel: (703) 471-6263 Fax: (703) 471-6302 E-mail: need@erols.com. Website: http://www.energyconnect.com/nect. Chair: Robert Stuart; f. 1980; Seeks to educate individuals to make informed decisions regarding energy use and policy through a grassroots energy education network.

National Federation of Business and Professional Women's Clubs, Inc of the USA (BPW/USA). 2012 Massachusetts Avenue NW, Washington, DC 20036. Tel: (202) 293-1100 Fax: (202) 861-0298. Executive Director: Cynthia Gady; f. 1919; Seeks equality for women in the workplace through advocacy, information, and education; Publications: *Making Workplaces Work: Quality Work Policies for Small Businesses*; *National Business Woman* (quarterly).

National Forum Foundation (NFF). 511 C Street NE, Washington, DC 20002. Tel: (202) 543-3515 Fax: (202) 547-4101 E-mail: nff@nff.org. Website: http://www.eunet.hu/nff/. President: James Denton; f. 1977; Dedicated to promoting political and economic freedom.

National Health Policy Forum (NHPF). 2021 K Street NW, Suite 800, Washington, DC 20052. Tel: (202) 872-1390 Fax: (202) 862-9837. Director: Judith Miller Jones; f. 1971; Seeks to improve the process of federal decision-making in health policy through education; Publications: *Issue Briefs* (25-30/year).

National Immigration Forum. 220 I Street NE, Suite 220, Washington, DC 20002. Tel: (202) 544-0004 Fax: (202) 544-1905. Executive Director: Frank Sharry; f. 1982; Seeks to defend the rights of immigrants and help the communities where they settle; Publications: *A Guide to Immigration Facts and Issues: Action Alerts* (periodic); *The Golden Door* (quarterly); *Immigration Policy Matters* (bimonthly); *Together in our Differences: How Newcomers and Established Residents are Rebuilding America's Communities.*

National Institute for Work and Learning (NIWL). 1875 Connecticut Avenue NW, 9th Floor, Washington, DC 20009. Tel: (202) 884-8187 Tel: (202) 884-8186 Fax: (202) 884-8422. Website: http://www.stw.ed.gov or Website: htpp://www.aed.org. Director: Ivan Charner; f. 1971; Seeks to promote people's fullest potential by better integrating work and education.

National Latino Communications Center. 3171 Los Feliz Boulevard, Suite 200, Los Angeles, CA 90039. Tel: (213) 663-8294 Fax: (213) 663-5606 E-mail: kathernLLca@aol.com. Website: http://latino.sscnet.ucla.edu/community/nlcc. Executive Director: Jose-Luis Ruiz; f. 1971; Promotes Hispanic-oriented media productions; Publications: *National Latino Communications* (periodic).

National Leadership Coalition on AIDS (NLCA). 1730 M Street NW, Suite 905, Washington, DC 20036. Tel: (202) 429-0930 Fax: (202) 872-1977 E-mail: 76142.611@compuserve.com. President: B.J. Stiles; f. 1987;Provides information about AIDS to the business and labor community.

National League of Families of American Prisoners and Missing in Southeast Asia. 1001 Connecticut Avenue NW, Suite 919, Washington, DC 20036. Tel: (202) 223-6846 Fax: (202) 785-9410 E-mail: 76142.611@compuserve.com. Executive Director: Ann Mills Griffiths; f. 1970; Works for the return of all American POWs and the remains of those who died during the Vietnam War; Publications: *National League of Families* *of American Prisoners and Missing in Southeast Asia-Newsletter* (bimonthly).

National Legal and Policy Center. 1309 Vincent Place. McLean, VA 22101. Tel: (703) 847-3088 Fax: (703) 847-6969. Chairman: Ken Boehm; f. 1991; Promotes ethics in government.

National Organization for Men (NOM). 11 Park Place, New York, NY 10007. Tel: (212) 686-6253 or (212) 766-4030 Fax: (212) 791-3056. Website: http://www.tnom.com. Founder and President: Sidney Siller; f. 1983; Seeks equal rights for men in affirmative action programs, alimony, child custody, men's health, etc.; Publications: *The Quest* (bimonthly).

National Organization for the Reform of Marijuana Laws (NORMAL). 1001 Connecticut Avenue NW, Suite 1010, Washington, DC 20036. Tel: (202) 483-5500 Fax: (202) 483-0057 E-mail: natlnorml@aol.com. Website: http://www.norml.org. Deputy Director: Allen F. Street Pierre; f. 1970; Promotes the legalization of marijuana; Publications: *Citizen's Guide to Marijuana Laws* (annual); *NORMAL Reports* (periodic); *NORMAL's Active Resistance* (quarterly); *Ongoing Briefing* (monthly); *Potpourri* (monthly).

National Organization for Women (NOW). 1000 16th Street NW, Suite 700, Washington, DC 20036. Tel: (202) 331-0066 Fax: (202) 785-8576 E-mail: now@now.org. Website: http://www.now.org. President: Patricia Ireland; f. 1966; Seeks equality for women in government, industry, the professions, churches, and every other field of importance in American society; Publications: *National NOW Times* (bimonthly).

National Organization on Disability (NOD). 910 16th Street NW, Suite 600, Washington, DC 20006. Tel: (202) 293-5960 Fax: (202) 293-7999. Website: http://www.nod.org. President: Mary E. Dolan; f. 1982; Promotes the participation of disabled people in all aspects of life and seeks to improve the public attitude toward people with disabilities; Publications: *NOD Report* (quarterly).

National Peace Corps Association (NPCA). 1900 L Street, Suite 205, Washington, DC 20036. Tel: (202) 293-7728 Fax: (202) 293-7554. Website: http://www.rpcv.org. President: Charles F. Dambach; f. 1979; Former Peace Corps staff and volunteers seeking to further international understanding and the goals of the Peace Corps; Publications: *Constituent of Sustainable Development* (monthly); *Group Leaders Digest* (semimonthly); *Hot Line* (biweekly); *3/1/61* (quarterly); *World View Magazine* (quarterly).

National Pro-Life Democrats (NPLD). 4249 Nicollet Avenue, Minneapolis, MN 55409-2014. Executive Director: Mary Jo Cooley; Seeks to encourage the involvement of pro-lifers in Democratic Party politics.

National Resource Center of Women and AIDS (NRCWA). Center for Women Policy Studies, 1211 Connecticut Avenue NW, Suite 312, Washington, DC 20036. Tel: (202) 872-1770 Fax: (202) 296-8962. President Leslie R. Wolfe; f. 1987; Provides information of issues involving women and AIDS; Publications: *Guide to Resources on Women and AIDS* (annual directory); *Fighting for Our Lives: Women Confronting AIDS* (video); *Policy Papers* (periodic).

National Right to Work Committee (NRTWC). 8001 Braddock Road, Suite 500, Springfield, VA 22160. Tel: (703) 321-9820 Toll-Free: (800) 325-7892 Fax: (703) 321-7342. President: Reed E. Larson; f. 1955; Promotes the principle that everyone should have the right, but not be compelled, to join labor unions; Publications: *Insiders Report* (quarterly); *National Right to Work Newsletter* (monthly).

National Security Caucus Institute. 1155 15th Street NW, Suite 1101, Washington, DC 20005. Tel: (202) 484-1676. Executive Director: Gregg Hilton; f. 1979; Works to promote a strong defense by bringing together congressmen, businessmen, and others for policy discussions; Publications: *International Security Review* (periodic); *National Security Report* (periodic).

National Strategy Information Center (NSIC). 1730 Rhode Island Avenue NW, Suite 500, Washington, DC 20036. Tel: (202) 429-0129 Fax: (202) 659-5429 E-mail: nsic@ix.netcom.com. President: Roy Godson; f. 1962; Seeks to educate leaders of public opinion about national defense and emerging security challenges.

National Tax Limitation Committee (NTLC). 151 North Sunrise Avenue, Suite 901, Roseville, CA 95661. Tel: (916) 786-9400. President: Lewis K. Uhler; f. 1975; Seeks constitutional amendments to limit government spending and taxation; Publications: *Tax Limitation News* (quarterly); *Tax Watch* (monthly).

National Taxpayers Union (NTU). 108 North Alfred Street, Washington, DC 22314. Tel: (202) 683-5700 Toll-Free: (800) 829-4258 Fax: (202) 683-5722. Chair: James D. Davidson; f. 1969; Seeks to reduce public spending, cut taxes, and protect and inform the taxpayer; Publications: *Congressional Spending Analysis* (bimonthly); *Dollars and Sense* (6/year); *Tax Savings Report* (10/year); *Taxpayers Resource Book*.

National Urban League (NUL). 120 Wall Street, New York, NY 10021. Tel: (212) 310-9000 Fax: (212) 344-5332. CEO and President: Hugh Price; f. 1910; Seeks to eliminate racial segregation and discrimination in the U.S. and achieve equality for blacks and other minorities in every aspect of American life; Publications: *BEEP Newsletter* (quarterly); *Community Surveys and Reports* (periodic); *The Urban League News* (quarterly); *The Urban League Review* (semiannual).

National Urban/Rural Fellows (NU/RF). 55 West 44th Street, Suite 600, New York, NW 10036. Tel: (212) 921-9400 Fax: (212) 921-9572. Director: Edwin D. Acevedo; f. 1969; Seeks to bring opportunities in government and rural development to minorities; Publications: *Annual Report*; *Bio/Directory of Class* (annual).

National Women's Conference Center. c/o Gene Boyer, 46 Waterford Circle, Suite 202, Madison, WI 53719. Tel: (414) 887-1078 Fax:

(414) 885-3720. President: Gene Boyer; f. 1980; Promotes equality for women by providing information and leadership development; Publications: *Network Exchange* (newsletter).

National Women's Law Center (NWLC). 11 Dupont Circle NW, Suite 800, Washington, DC 20036. Tel: (608) 273-9760 or (954) 389-1879 Fax: (608) 273-9760. Co-President: Nancy Duff Campbell; f. 1972; Works for the advancement of the legal rights of women; Publications: *Update* (quarterly).

National Women's Political Caucus (NWPC). 1275 K Street NW, Suite 750, Washington, DC 20005. Tel: (202) 898-1100 Fax: (202) 898-0458. Executive Director: Jody Newman; f. 1971; Seeks to increase the influence of women in the political process; Publications: *Women's Political Times* (quarterly); *National Directory of Women Elected Officials*; *Fact Sheet on Women's Political Progress*.

National Write Your Congressman (NWYC). 9696 Skillman, Suite 170, Dallas, TX 75243-8253. Tel: (214) 342-0299 Fax: (214) 342-9186. President and CEO: Roger L. Adamson; f. 1958; Encourages and assists individuals in writing their public officials; Publications: *Congressman's Voting Records* (annual); *Legislative Update* (monthly); *Opinion Ballot* (monthly); *Voters Voice* (monthly).

Native American Rights Fund (NARF). 1506 Broadway, Boulder, CO 80302. Tel: (303) 447-8760 Fax: (303) 443-7776. Director: John E. Echohawk; f. 1970; Provides legal assistance to American Indians; Publications: *NARF Legal Review* (semiannual); *National Indian Law Library Catalog* (quarterly).

Network. 801 Pennsylvania Avenue SE, Suite 460, Washington, DC 20003-2167. Tel: (202) 547-5556 Fax: (202) 547-5510 E-mail: network@ igc.apc.org. Coordinator: Kathy Thornton; f. 1971; Seeks social justice and participation of citizens in the issues that affect their lives; Publications: *NETWORK Connection* (bimonthly); *NETWORKer* (bimonthly).

New Israel Fund (NIF). 1625 K Street NW, Suite 500, Washington, DC 20006. Tel: (202) 223-3333 Fax: (202) 659-2789 E-mail: info@nif.org. Website: http://www.nif.org. Executive Director: Norman S. Rosenberg; f. 1979; Promotes civil and human rights in Israel, Jewish-Arab equality, tolerance, and the reduction of social and economic gaps; Publications: *Alon Ha Keren Ha Hadasha LeYisrael* (periodic); *NIF Report* (quarterly); *Strengthening Democracy.*

North American Conference on Ethiopian Jewry (NACOEJ). 165 East 56th Street, New York, NY 10022. Tel: (212) 752-6340 Fax: (212) 980-5294 E-mail: nacoej@aol.com. Website: http://www.cais.com/nacoej. Executive Director: Barbara Ribakove Gordon; f. 1982; Works to advance the Ethiopian Jewish community in Israel; Publications: *Lifeline* (quarterly).

Operation Rescue (OR). PO Box 740066, Dallas, TX 75374. Tel: (214) 348-8866 Fax: (214) 348-7172. Website: http://www.orn.org.; f. 1987; Seeks to end abortion by organizing sit-ins and protests at abortion clinics to stop patient entries.

Pacifica Foundation (PF). 3729 Cahuenga Boulevard West, North Hollywood, CA 91604. Tel: (818) 985-8800 E-mail: srosas@aol.com. Acting Executive Director: Patricia Scott; f. 1946; Operates radio stations that seek to improve understanding between nations and between individuals; Publications: *Program Folio* (monthly); *Tape Brochures (*monthly); *Tape Catalog* (semiannual).

Parents' Music Resource Center (PMRC). 1500 Arlington Boulevard, Arlington, VA 22209. Tel: (703) 527-9466 Fax: (703) 527-9468. President: Barbara P. Wyatt; f. 1985; Works for ethical boundaries in the production of recorded music; Publications: *The Influence of the Media on Adolescents* (video*); Let's Talk Rock: A Parent's Primer* (video); *Music: a Health Issue* (video); *Raised on Rock 'n Roll: A Guide to Community Action* (video).

Pax Christi -- USA (PC-USA). 532 West 8th Street, Erie, PA 16502. Tel: (814) 453-4955 Fax:

(814) 452-4784. f. 1972; Works for justice, disarmament, human rights, and the Christian ideal of nonviolence; Publications: *Catholic Peace Voice* (quarterly).

Peace Action. 1819 H Street NW, Suite 420, Washington, DC 20006-3603. Tel: (202) 862-9740 Fax: (202) 862-9762. Executive Director: Gordon S. Clark; f. 1957; Seeks to end the global arms trade, enact a comprehensive nuclear test ban treaty, and reduce the number of nuclear weapons and US interventions abroad; Publications: *Grassroots Organizer* (monthly); *Peace Action.*

Peace Development Fund (PDF). PO Box 1280, Amherst, MA 01004. Tel: (413) 256-8306 Fax: (413) 256-8871. Executive Director: Linda Stout; f. 1981; Awards grants to peace and justice groups that seek to educate the public about the economic and social costs of the arms race and military spending, US policy, and racism.

People for the American Way (PFAW). 2000 M Street NW, Suite 400, Washington, DC 20036. Tel: (202) 467-4999 Fax: (202) 293-2672. President: Arthur J. Kropp; f. 1980; a nonpartisan constitutional liberties organization that seeks to reaffirm the traditional American values of pluralism, diversity, and freedom of expression and religion; Publications: *Attacks on the Freedom to Learn* (annual).

People's Medical Society (PMS). 462 Walnut Street, Allentown, PA 18102. Tel: (610) 770-1670 Toll-Free: (800) 624-8773 Fax: (610) 770-0607 E-mail: peoplesmed@compuserve.com. President: Charles B. Inlander; f. 1982; Seeks to promote citizen involvement in healthcare policy-making; Publications: *People's Medical Society Newsletter* (bimonthly).

Physicians for Human Rights (PHR). 100 Boylston Street, Suite 702, Boston, MA 02116. Tel: (617) 695-0041 Fax: (617) 695-0307 E-mail: pnphrusa@ige.apc.org. Executive Director: Leonard Rubenstein; f. 1986; Works to bring the skills of medical professionals to the protection of human rights; Publications: *Medical Action Alert* (monthly); *Medical Testimony on Victims of*

Torture: a Physician's Guide to Political Asylum Cases; *Record* (3/year).

Physicians for Social Responsibility (PSR). 1101 14th Street, 7th Floor, Washington, DC 20005. Tel: (202) 898-0150 Fax: (202) 898-0172. Executive Director: Robert M. Muril; f. 1961; Physicians concerned with the threat of nuclear war, environmental degradation, and violence; Publications: *Briefing Papers* (periodic); *PSR Annual Report*; *PSR Report* (quarterly).

Planetary Citizens (PC). PO Box 1045, Mount Shasta, CA 96067. Tel: (916) 926-3244 Fax: (916) 926-1245. President: Donald Keys; f. 1971; Advocates expanding the authority of the United Nations to a world government, seeks global oneness and interdependence; Publications: *Planet Earth* (quarterly).

Project Vote! 1511 K Street NW, Suite 326, Washington, DC 20005. Tel: (202) 638-9016 Fax: (202) 383-5900. Executive Director: Sanford A. Newman; f. 1982; Seeks to increase electoral participation among low-income, minority, and unemployed citizens; Publications: *How to Develop a Voter Registration Plan* (video); *How to Register Voters at a Central Site* (video).

Public Advocate of the US (PAUS). 5613 Leesburg Pike, Suite 9 ENCYC, Falls Church, VA 22041. Tel: (202) 546-3224. Executive Director: Eugene Delgaudio; f. 1978; Advocates limiting the federal government and returning powers to the state and local level; Publications: *Impact Reports* (periodic); *Register of Opinion* (periodic); *Report to Congress* (semiannual).

Public Citizen (PC). East 1600 20th Street, NW, Washington, DC 20009. Tel: (202) 588-1000. President: Joan Claybrook; f. 1971; Supports the work of citizen advocates focusing on consumer rights issues; Publications: *Buyers Up News*; *Health Letter* (monthly); *Public Citizen* (bimonthly).

Public Service Research Council (PSRC). 527 Maple Avenue, Vienna, VA 22180. Tel: (703) 242-3575 Fax: (703) 242-3579. President: David

Y. Denholm; f. 1973; Assists in strikes, unionization, and legislation for public sector employees; Publications: *Forewarned* (monthly).

Quixote Center (QC). PO Box 5206, Hyattsville, MD 20782. Tel: (301) 699-0042 Fax: (301) 864-2182. Co-Director: Dolores Pomerleau; f. 1975; Catholic organization engaged in funding and humanitarian aid, education, and the promotion of democracy.

Reagan Alumni Association (RAA). 122 South Royal Street, Suite A, Alexandria, VA 22314-3328. Tel: (703) 768-3111 Fax: (703) 768-2156. Executive Director: Louis J. Cordia; f. 1987; Staff and political appointees from the Reagan and Bush administrations seeking to advance the economic and social agenda of Ronald Reagan; Publications: *Reagan Alumni Directory* (annual); *Reagan Alumni Newsletter*.

Refugee Policy Group (RPG). 1424 16th Street NW, Suite 401, Washington, DC 20036. Tel: (202) 387-3015 Fax: (202) 667-5034. Executive Director: Dennis Gallagher; f. 1982; Seeks to increase public awareness of refugee issues and engage in analysis and research; Publications: *RPG Review* (periodic).

Religious Roundtable (RR). PO Box 11467, Memphis, TN 38111. Tel: (901) 458-3795 Fax: (901) 324-0265. President: Edward E. McAteer; f. 1978; Seeks the moral rebirth of America, based upon Judeo-Christian ethics.

Republicans for Choice (RFC). 2760 Eisenhower Avenue, Suite 260, Alexandria, VA 22314-5223. Tel: (703) 836-8907 or (703) 960-9882 Fax: (703) 519-8843. Chair: Ann Stone; f. 1990; Seeks to change the Republican Party's platform to reflect the views of pro-choice Republicans.

Results. 236 Massachusetts Avenue NE, Suite 300, Washington, DC 20002. Tel: (202) 543-9340 Toll-Free: (800) 900-LEAD Fax: (202) 543-7512 E-mail: results@action.org. Website:http://www.results.action.org. Executive Director: Lynn McMullen; f. 1980; Works to end world hunger by healing the break between people and government; Publications: *Entry Point* (quarterly); *Idea Letter* (monthly).

Robert A. Taft Institute of Government (TTI). Queens College Powdermaker, Suite 186, Flushing, NY 11367. Tel: (212) 682-1530 Fax: (212) 953-1927. President: Maryann M. Feeney; f. 1961; Promotes understanding of the basic principles of the American political system and encourages a more active citizen interest and participation in government at all levels.

Rutherford Institute (RI). PO Box 7482, Charlottesville, VA 22906-7482. Tel: (804) 978-3888 Fax: (804) 978-1789. Website: http://www.rutherford.org, President: John W. Whitehead; f. 1982; Provides legal services for persons whose First Amendment Rights are being threatened; Publications: *Rutherford Magazine* (monthly).

Search for Common Ground (SCG). 1601 Connecticut Avenue, Suite 200, Washington, DC 20009. Tel: (202) 265-4300 Toll-Free: (800) 426-4302 Fax: (202) 232-6718. Website: http://www.saf.org. President: John Marks; f. 1981; Seeks to ensure international security by finding a common ground and common understanding between people; Publications: *Bulletin of Regional Cooperation in the Middle East* (quarterly).

Second Amendment Foundation (SAF). James Madison Building, 12500 NE 10th Place, Bellevue, WA 98005. Tel: (206) 454-7012 Fax: (206) 451-3959. Website: http://www.saf.org. President: Joseph P. Tartaro; f. 1974; Dedicated to promoting understanding of the constitutional right to privacy and to bear firearms; Publications: *The Gottlieb-Tartaro Report* (monthly); *Gun News Digest* (quarterly); *Gun Week Newspaper* (periodic); *Second Amendment Reporter* (quarterly); *Women and Guns* (monthly).

Small Business Council of America (SBCA). 4800 Hampden Lane, 7th Floor, Bethesda, MD 20814. Tel: (301) 656-7603 Fax: (301) 654-7354. Chair: Paula Calimafde; f. 1979; Seeks to keep federal tax and employee benefit information from becoming burdensome and to create economic incentive for small business; Publications: *News Flashes* (periodic); *SBCA Member and Congressional Directory* (annual); *Tax Report* (monthly).

Smokers' Rights Alliance (SRA). PO Box 1169, Ridgefield, CT 06877. President: Dave W. Branton; f. 1987; Seeks to preserve the right to smoke without the unnecessary interference of the government; Publications: *Smoke Signals* (quarterly).

Social Justice for Women. 59 Temple Place, Suite 307, Boston, MA 02111. Tel: (617) 482-0747 Fax: (617) 695-2891. Associate Director: Phyllis Buccio-Nataro; f. 1986; Provides assistance to non-violent female offenders; Publications: *Social Justice for Women Newsletter* (quarterly).

Southern Christian Leadership Conference (SCLC). 334 Auburn Avenue NE, Atlanta, GA 30303. Tel: (404) 522-1420 Fax: (404) 659-7390. Website: http://sclcnational.com. President: Martin Luther King III; f. 1957; a nonsectarian coordinating agency for local organizations seeking full citizenship rights, equality, and the integration of African Americans.

Southern Poverty Law Center (SPLC). PO Box 2087, Montgomery, AL 36102. Tel: (334) 264-0286 Fax: (334) 264-0629. Executive Director: Edward Ashworth; f. 1971; Seeks to protect and advance the legal and civil rights of poor people; Publications: *Klanwatch Intelligence Report* (monthly).

Southwest Voter Registration Education Project (SVREP). 403 East Commerce, Suite 220, San Antonio, TX 78205. Tel: (210) 222-0224 Toll Free: (800) 404-VOTE Fax: (210) 222-8474. President: Antonio Gonzalez; f. 1975; Seeks to register minority voters in the West and Southwest; Publications: *National Hispanic Voter Registration Campaign* (bimonthly).

Starthrowers (SOS). PO Box 192, 615 Trowbridge Street, Franklin, LA 70538. Tel: (318) 828-2375 or (318) 828-5588 Fax: (318) 828-4039. Executive Officer: Bernard Broussard; f. 1965; Organizes boycotts and petitions to support peace, social justice, human rights, and anti-abortion, anti-euthanasia, anti-death penalty agenda; Publications: *Agape in New Testament* (bimonthly); *Starthrowers Magazine* (quarterly).

Students in Free Enterprise (SIFE). 1959 East Kerr, Springfield, MO 65803. Tel: (417) 831-9523 Fax: (471) 831-6165. CEO and President: Alvin Rohrs; f. 1975; Develops programs to teach free enterprise principles to students and citizens; Publications: *SIFE Lines Newsletter* (quarterly).

Tax Analysts. 6830 North Fairfax Drive, Arlington, VA 22213. Tel: (703) 533-4400 Toll-Free: (800) 955-3444 Fax: (703) 533-4444 Website: http://www.fax.org. Executive Director: Thomas F. Field; f. 1970; Reviews developments in federal tax law; Publications: *Exempt Organizations Tax Review* (monthly); *Highlights and Documents* (daily); *Index-Digest Bulletin of IRS Rulings* (semiannual); *Insurance Tax Review* (monthly); *Natural Resources Tax Review* (monthly); *State Tax Notes* (daily); *Tax Notes International* (weekly); *Tax Related Documents* (weekly).

The Fair Tax (TFT). 11015 Cumpston Street, North Hollywood, CA 91601. Tel: (818) 763-1000 Toll-Free: (800) FAIR-TAX Fax: (818) 769-7358. President and Founder: Boris Isaacson; f. 1986; Favors a proposal under which all federal, state, and local taxes would be replaced with a 1% trade charge on all purchases; Publications: *Tax Free America*.

The Fund for Peace (TFP). 823 United Nations Plaza, Suite 717, New York, NY 10017. Tel: (212) 661-5900 Fax: (212) 661-5904. Acting Executive Director: W. Howard Wriggins; f. 1957; Seeks to study problems that threaten human survival, such as poverty, the arms race, ethnicity, and nationalism; Publications: *ACCESS Resource Guide*; *Horn of Africa Reports* (periodic); *ACCESS Issue Briefs*.

TransAfrica. 1744 R Street NW, Washington, DC 20009. Tel: (202) 797-2301 Fax: (202) 547-7687. Executive Director: Randall Robinson; f. 1977; Concerned with political and human rights of the people of Africa and the Caribbean, as well as those of African descent throughout the world; Publications: *TransAfrica News* (semiannual).

Twentieth Century Fund (TCF). 41 East 70th Street, New York, NY 10021. Tel: (212) 535-4441 Fax: (212) 879-9197. Website: http://epn.org/tef.html. President: Richard C. Leone; f. 1919; Analyzes economic affairs, foreign affairs, and political, governance, and media issues.

US Institute of Peace (USIP). 1550 M Street NW, Suite 700, Washington, DC 20005. Tel: (202) 457-1700 Fax: (202) 429-6063. President: Richard H. Solomon; f. 1984; Created by Congress to promote and support peace scholarships and research; Publications: *Peace Watch* (bimonthly); *Peaceworks* (report); *Report* (biennial).

US Public Interest Research Group (USPIRG). 218 D Street SE, Washington, DC 20003. Tel: (202) 546-9707 Fax: (202) 546-2461 E-mail: uspirg@pirg.org. Website: http://www.pirg.org. Executive Director: Gene Karpinski; f. 1983; Supports public interest and advocacy issues; Publications: *Citizen Agenda* (quarterly).

Union of Concerned Scientists (UCS). 2 Brattle Square, Cambridge, MA 02238-9105. Tel: (617) 547-5552 Fax: (617) 864-9405. Executive Director: Howard C. Ris Jr.; f. 1969; Studies the societal impact of advanced technology; Publications: *Legislative Alert* (periodic); *Nucleus* (quarterly); *The Renewable Solution to Global Warming*; *Steering a New Course: Transportation, Energy and the Environment*.

United Black Church Appeal (UBCA). c/o Christ Church, 860 Forest Avenue, Bronx, NY 10456. Tel: (718) 665-6688. President: Wendell Foster; f. 1980; Objective is to organize the black clergy and black church as leaders in the liberation of the black community.

United Homeowners' Association (UHA).
1511 K Street NW, 3rd Floor, Washington, DC 20005. Tel: (202) 408-8842 Fax: (202) 408-8156 E-mail: a.clark@uha.org. Website: http://uha.org. President: Jordan Clark; f. 1990; Homeowner advocacy group that monitors legislation and policy changes; Publications: *The United Homeowners* (bimonthly).

United Indians of All Tribes Foundation (UIATF). Daybreak Star Arts Center, Discovery Park, PO Box 99100, Seattle, WA 98199. Tel: (206) 285-4425 Fax: (206) 282-3640. Executive Director: Bernie Whitebear; f. 1970; Provides social, cultural, and educational services to the urban Native American community; Publications: *Daybreak Star Press* (monthly).

United States Committee for Refugees (USCR). 1717 Massachusetts Avenue NW, Suite 701, Washington, DC 20036. Tel: (202) 347-3507 Fax: (202) 347-3418. Website: http://www.refugees.org. Director: Roger P. Winter; f. 1958; Seeks to educate the American public about the plight of the world's refugees and provide nongovernmental action to meet the needs of the world's refugee situation; Publications: *Issue Papers* (quarterly); *Refugee Reports* (monthly); *World Refugee Survey* (annual).

United States Defense Committee (USDC).
3238 Wynford Drive, Fairfax, VA 22031-2828. Tel: (703) 280-4226. President: Henry L. Walther; f. 1982; Promotes a strong foreign policy and national defense; Publications: *Defense Watch* (quarterly).

Urban Institute (UI). 2100 M Street NW, Washington, DC 20037. Tel: (202) 833-7200 Fax: (202) 429-0687. President: William Gorham; f. 1968; Works with government officials and administrators to find solutions to the nation's social and economic problems; Publications: *Annual Report*; *Policy and Research Report* (3/year); *Policy Bites (*bimonthly); *Update* (bimonthly).

Vietnam Veterans of America (VVA). 1224 M Street NW, Washington, DC 20005-5783. Tel: (202) 628-2700 Toll-Free: (800) VVA-1316 Fax: (202) 628-5880. President: George Duggins; f. 1978; Seeks to provide employment, education, psychological assistance and healthcare to the American veterans of the Vietnam War; Publications: *VVA Veteran* (monthly).

War Resisters League (WRL). 339 Lafayette Street, New York, NY 10012. Tel: (212) 228-0450 Fax: (212) 228-6193 E-mail: wrl@igc.apc.org. Website: http://www.nonviolence.org/~nvweb/wrl.; f. 1923; Pacifist organization seeking international economic and social cooperation and nonviolence; Publications: *Calendar* (annual); *Guide to War Tax Resistance*; *Literature List*; *Nonviolent Activist* (8/year); *Organizers Manual*.

Women Against Pornography (WAP). PO Box 845, Times Square Station, New York, NY 10108-0845. Tel: (212) 307-5055. Contact: Dorchen Leidholdt; f. 1979; Feminist organization which seeks to change public opinion of pornography to view it as a form of prostitution; Publications: *Women Against Pornography Newsreport* (2-4/year).

Women's Campaign Fund (WCF). 734 15th Street NW, Suite 500, Washington, DC 20005. Tel: (202) 393-8164 Fax: (202) 393-0649. Website: http://www.womenscampaignfund.org. Executive Director: Marjorie Margolies-Mezvinsky; f. 1974; Seeks to support the election of qualified, progressive women to public offices.

Women's International League for Peace and Freedom, US Section (WILPF-US). 1213 Race Street, Philadelphia, PA 19107-1691. Tel: (215) 563-7110 Fax: (215) 563-5527 E-mail: wilpfnatl@igc.org. President: Betty Burks; f. 1915; Women seeking to eliminate US military and economic intervention abroad, discrimination, and government surveillance and repression; Publications: *Building Peace* (quarterly); *Pax et Libertas* (quarterly); *Peace and Freedom* (bimonthly); *Program and Legislative Action* (bimonthly); *Woman for All Seasons*; *The Woman's Budget*.

Women's Legal Defense Fund (WLDF). 1875 Connecticut Avenue NW, Suite 710, Washington, DC 20009. Tel: (202) 986-2600 Fax: (202) 986-2539. President: Judith Lichtman; f. 1971; Works for women's rights in family law, employment, women's health, and other areas; Publications: *WLDF News* (semiannual).

World Federalist Association (WFA). PO Box 15250, Washington, DC 20003. Tel: (202) 546-3950 Toll-Free: (800) WFA-0123 Fax: (202) 546-3749. Executive Officer: Tim Barner; f. 1947; Seeks to promote a world order characterized as a democratic world federation; Publications: *World Federalist* (quarterly).

World Jewish Congress, American Section (WJC). 501 Madison Avenue, 17th Floor, New York, NY 10022. Tel: (212) 755-5770 Fax: (212) 755-5883. Executive Director: Alan Steinberg; f. 1936; Protects the rights, status, and interests of Jews and Jewish communities throughout the world; Publications: *Batefutsot* (monthly); *Boletin Informative OJI* (biweekly); *Christian-Jewish Relations* (quarterly); *Coloquio* (quarterly); *Gesher* (quarterly); *News and Views From the WJC* (6-8/year); *Patterns and Prejudices* (quarterly); *Soviet Jewish Affairs* (annual).

World Organization for Jews From Arab Countries (WOJAC). 1125 Park Avenue, New York, NY 10128. Tel: (212) 427-1246. President: Heskel M. Haddad; f. 1975; Defends the rights of Jews in Arab countries.

World Peace Prayer Society (WPPS). 800 3rd Avenue, 37th Floor, New York, NY 10022. Tel: (212) 755-4755 Fax: (212) 935-1389 E-mail: peacepal@worldpeace.org. Chair: Masami Saionji; f. 1955; Seeking to spread world peace through prayer; Publications: *Global Link Newsletter* (3-4/year).

Worldwatch Institute (WI). 1776 Massachusetts Avenue NW, Washington, DC 20036. Tel: (202) 452-1999 Fax: (202) 296-7365 E-mail: wwpub@igc.apc.org. President: Lester R. Brown; f. 1974; Seeks to anticipate global problems and social trends and to focus attention on emerging social issues; Publications: *State of the World* (annual); *World Watch* (bimonthly); *Worldwatch Papers* (6-8/year).

Young America's Foundation (YAF). 110 Elden Street, Herndon, VA 22070. Tel: (703) 318-9608 Toll-Free: (800) 292-9231 Fax: (703) 318-9122. President: Ron Robinson; f. 1969; Service organization for politically-conservative high school and college students; Publications: *Campus Leader* (10/year); *Continuity* (semiannual); *Libertas* (bimonthly).

Political Action Committees (PACs)

A political action committee (PAC) is the political arm of a business, labor union, professional association or any other interest group that is legally able to raise money on a voluntary basis from its constituents in order to donate funds to preferred candidates or political parties.

Established in 1971 as part of the Federal Elections Campaign Act of that year, PACs have had growing impact in the funding of American political campaigns. The more than 4,000 PACs registered with the Federal Elections Commission account for nearly 40 percent of all funds spent on elections.

This list contains the 200 largest PACs based upon the election cycle, including the 1996 presidential election.

Action Committee for Rural Electrification (ACRE)
4301 Wilson Boulevard
Arlington, VA 22203
Treasurer: Patrick E. Gioffre
FEC ID#: C00002972
Total Disbursements: $1,168,748.

Active Ballot Club (United Food and Commerical Workers International Union)
1775 K Street NW
Washington, DC 20006
Treasurer: Jerry Menapace
FEC ID#: C00002766
Total Disbursements: $3,167,640.

AFL-CIO Committee on Political Education/Political Contributions Committee
815 16th Street NW
Washington, DC 20006
(202) 637-5101
(202) 637-5107 (Fax)
Treasurer: Richard L. Trumka
FEC ID#: C00003806
Total Disbursements: $1,720,161.

AFLAC Incorporated Political Action Committee (AFLACPAC)
Worldwide Headquarters
Columbus, GA 31999
Treasurer: Joey M. Loudermilk
FEC ID#: C00034157
Total Disbursements: $697,559.

Aircraft Owners and Pilots Association Political Action Committee
421 Aviation Way
Frederick, MD 21701
Treasurer: Roger Myers
FEC ID#: C00131185
Total Disbursements: $892,545.

Airline Pilots Association Political Action Committee
1625 Massachusetts Avenue NW
Washington, DC 20036
Treasurer: Duane E. Woerth
FEC ID#: C00035451
Total Disbursements: $1,089,607.

Akin, Gump, Strauss, Hauer, & Feld LLP Civic Action Committee
1333 New Hampshire Avenue NW, Suite 400
Washington, DC 20036
Treasurer: Joel Janowsky
FEC ID#: C00104901
Total Disbursements: $459,975.

Amalgamated Transit Union - COPE
5025 Wisconsin Avenue NW
Washington, DC 20016
(202) 537-1645
(202) 244-7824 (Fax)
Treasurer: Oliver W. Green
FEC ID#: C00032995
Total Disbursements: $957,981.

American Academy of Ophthalmology Inc Political Committee (OPHTHPAC)
655 Beach Street
San Francisco, CA 94109
Treasurer: Paula E. Lent
FEC ID#: C00196246
Total Disbursements: $942,958.

American AIDS Political Action Committee
1808 Swann Street NW
Washington, DC 20009
Treasurer: Thomas F. Sheridan
FEC ID#: C00283101
Total Disbursements: $601,786.

American Airlines Political Action Committee
1101 17th Street NW
Washington, DC 20036
Treasurer: Julie L. Nichols
FEC ID#: C00107300
Total Disbursements: $475,808.

American Association of Nurse Anesthetists Separate Segregated Fund (CRNA-PAC)

222 South Prospect Avenue
c/o Finance Department
Park Ridge, IL 60068.
Treasurer: Mark Krzmarzick
FEC ID#: C00173153
Total Disbursements: $785,958.

American Bankers Association Bank PAC
1120 Connecticut Avenue NW, Suite 851
Washington, DC 20036
(202) 663-5115/5075
(202) 663-7544 (Fax)
Treasurer: Gary W. Fields
FEC ID#: C00004275
Total Disbursements: $1,529,576.

American Chiropractic Association Political Action Committee
1701 Clarendon Boulevard
Arlington, VA 22209
(703) 276-8800
(703) 243-2593 (Fax)
Treasurer: Dr. James Edwards
FEC ID#: C00102764
Total Disbursements: $475,808.

American Council of Life Insurance, Life Insurance PAC
1001 Pennsylania Avenue NW
Washington, DC 20004
(202) 624-2000
(202) 624-2319 (Fax)
Treasurer: Richard Gunderson
FEC ID#: C00147066
Total Disbursements: $760,936.

American Crystal Sugar Political Action Committee
101 North 3rd Street
Moorhead, MN 56560
Treasurer: Samual S. M. Wai
FEC ID#: C00110338
Total Disbursements: $660,072.

American Dental Political Action Committee
1111 14th Street NW, 11th Floor
Washington, DC 20005
(202) 898-2400
(202) 898-2437 (Fax)
Treasurer: Dr. Lewis Earle
FEC ID#: C00000729
Total Disbursements: $1,488,290.

American Federation of State, County, and Municipal Employees - People Qualified
1625 L Street NW
Washington, DC 20036
(202) 452-4800
(202) 429-1197 (Fax)
Treasurer: William Lucy
FEC ID#: C00011114
Total Disbursements: $4,307,997.

American Federation of Teachers Committee on Political Education
555 New Jersey Avenue NW
Washington, DC 20001
(202) 879-4436
(202) 393-6375 (Fax)
Treasurer: Edward J. McElroy
FEC ID#: C00028860
Total Disbursements: $2,655,527.

American Health Care Association Political Action Committee (AHCA-PAC)
1201 L Street NW
Washington, DC 20005
(202) 842-4444
(202) 842-3860 (Fax)
Treasurer: Gerald L. Baker
FEC ID#: C00006080
Total Disbursements: $754,401.

American Hospital Association Political Action Committee (AHAPAC)
325 7th Street NW
Washington, DC 20007
Treasurer: Al Jackson

FEC ID#: C00106146
Total Disbursements: $1,129,589.00

American Institute of Certified Public Accountants Effective Legislation Committee (AICPA)
Harborside Financial Center
201 Plaza 3
Jersey City, NJ 07311
Treasurer: Donna G. Borowicz
FEC ID#: C00077321
Total Disbursements: $1,848,826.

American Maritime Officers
AFL-CIO Voluntary Political Action Fund
650 4th Avenue
Brooklyn, NY 11232
Treasurer: Edward V. Kelly
FEC ID#: C00027532
Total Disbursements: $1,176,327.

American Medical Association Political Action Committee
1101 Vermont Avenue NW
Washington, DC 20005
(202) 789-7400
(202) 789-7469 (Fax)
Treasurer: Kevin Walker
FEC ID#: C00000422
Total Disbursements: $4,133,528.

American Nurses' Association PAC (ANA-PAC) (N-CAP)
600 Maryland Avenue SW, Suite 100W
Washington, DC 20024
Treasurer: Rebecca M. Patton
FEC ID#: C00017525
Total Disbursements: $967,707.

American Occupational Therapy Association Inc Political Action Committee
4720 Montgomery Lane
PO Box 31220
Bethesda, MD 20824

Treasurer: Chris Bluhm
FEC ID#: C00089086
Total Disbursements: $678,341.

American Optometric Association Political Action Committee
1505 Prince Street, Suite 300
Alexandria, VA 22314
(703) 739-9200
(703) 739-9497 (Fax)
Treasurer: Roger Pabstod
FEC ID#: C00024968
Total Disbursements: $968,683.

American Society of Anesthesiologists Incorporated Political Action Committee (ASAPAC)
520 North Northwest Highway
Park Ridge, IL 60068
Treasurer: Roger A. Moore, MD
FEC ID#: C00255752
Total Disbursements: $779,655.

American Telephone & Telegraph Company Political Action Committee (AT&T PAC)
1 Oak Way
Berkeley Heights, NJ 07922
Treasurer: S. L. Prendergast
FEC ID#: C00185124
Total Disbursements: $2,746,738.

Americans for Free International Trade Political Action Committee Inc
112 S West Street, Suite 310
Alexandria, VA 22314
(703) 684-8880
(703) 836-5256 (Fax)
Treasurer: David Conant
FEC ID#: C00250399
Total Disbursements: $1,851,113.

Americans for a Republican Majority (ARMPAC)

1155 21st Street NW, Suite 300
Washington, DC 20036
Treasurer: Corwin Teltschik
FEC ID#: C00292946
Total Disbursements: $701,335.

Arthur Andersen PAC (AKA Arthur Andersen/Andersen Consulting PAC)
1666 K Street NW
Washington, DC 20006
Treasurer: Jeffrey J. Peck
FEC ID#: C00221168
Total Disbursements: $713,678.

Associated Builders and Contractors Political Action Committee (ABC/PAC)
1300 North 17th Street
Rosslyn, VA 22209
Treasurer: Charles E. Hawlins III
FEC ID#: C00010421
Total Disbursements: $549,746.

Associated General Contractors Political Action Committee
1957 East Street NW
Washington, DC 20006
(202) 393-2040
(202) 347-5412 (Fax)
Treasurer: Stephen E. Sandherr
FEC ID#: C00082917
Total Disbursements: $804,375.

Association of Trial Lawyers of America Political Action Committee
1050 31st Street NW
Washington, DC 20007
(202) 965-3500
(202) 338-8709 (Fax)
Treasurer: Carmen Belefonte
Total Disbursements: $5,084,785.

BANC ONE PAC
100 East Broad Street
Columbus, OH 43271

Treasurer: Robert E. Wahlman
FEC ID#: C00128512
Total Disbursements: $1,330,484.

**BankAmerica Corporation Political Action
Committee (BACPAC)**
(Successor of BankAmerica Election Fund,
Government Relations Unit #13117)
PO Box 37000
San Francisco, CA 94137
Treasurer: Gregory E. Swanson
FEC ID#: C00147702
Total Disbursements: $535,516.

**Barnett People for Better Government Inc
- Federal A PAC of Barnett Banks Inc**
50 North Laura Street (1114)
PO Box 40789
Jacksonville, FL 32203
Treasurer: Brian A. Babcock
FEC ID#: C00094656
Total Disbursements: $588,399.

**Bellsouth Corporation Employees' Federal
Political Action Committee**
1155 Peachtree Street NE, Suite 1925
Atlanta, GA 30309
Treasurer: Gary L. Walton
FEC ID#: C00174060
Total Disbursements: $552,696.

**BellSouth Telecommunications Inc
Employees Federal Political Action
Committee**
1155 Peachtree Street NE, Suite 1925
Atlanta, GA 30309
Treasurer: Arlen G. Yokley
FEC ID#: C00099655
Total Disbursements: $892,547.

**Beneficial Management Corporation and
Affiliated Corporations Political Action
Committee**
453 New Jersey Avenue SE

Washington, DC 20003
Treasurer: Lisa Perez
FEC ID#: C00043711
Total Disbursements: $459,832.

**Black America's Political Action
Committee**
2029 P Street NW, Suite 302
Washington, DC 20036
Treasurer: Douglas White
FEC ID#: C00300921
Total Disbursements: $1,899,486.

**Brotherhood of Locomotive Engineers
PAC Fund**
1370 Ontario Street, Standard Building
Cleveland, OH 44113
Treasurer: Russell W. Bennett
FEC ID#: C00099234
Total Disbursements: $630,197.

**Brown & Williamson Tobacco Corporation
Employee Political Action Committee
(EMPAC)**
PO Box 35090
Louisville, KY 40232
Treasurer: Michael J. Shannon
FEC ID#: C00087791
Total Disbursements: $492,012.

**Build Political Action Committee of the
National Association of Home Builders**
1201 15th Street NW
Washington, DC 20005
Treasurer: Phillip L. Blair
FEC ID#: C00000901
Total Disbursements: $1,886,424.

**California Medical Political Action
Committee**
221 Main Street, 2nd Floor
San Francisco, CA 94105
Treasurer: J. Brennan Cassidy, MD

FEC ID#: C00003194
Total Disbursements: $701,810.

Campaign America
1 Indiana Square, Suite 2800
Indianapolis, IN 46204
Treasurer: William R. Neale
FEC ID#: C00088369
Total Disbursements: $4,859,674.

**Campaign for a New American Century
(Republican Fund for the 90s)**
1114 17th Avenue South, Suite 103
Nashville, TN 37212
Treasurer: Stacey R. Lukens
FEC ID#: C00281923
Total Disbursements: $683,844.

Capitol Committee
257 East 200 South, Suite 950
Salt Lake City, UT 84111
Treasurer: Stanley R. DeWaal
FEC ID#: C00235572
Total Disbursements: $440,749.

**Carpenters Legislative Improvement
Committee/United Brotherhood of
Carpenters & Joiners of AME**
101 Constitution Avenue NW
Washington, DC 20001
(202) 546-6206
(202) 546-3873 (Fax)
Treasurer: Douglas J. McCarron
FEC ID#: C00001016
Total Disbursements: $1,774,193.

**Chase Manhattan Corporation Fund for
Good Government**
270 Park Avenue, 44th Floor
New York, NY 10017
Treasurer: Bridget A. Filippon
FEC ID#: C00003830
Total Disbursements: $682,116.

**Chrysler Corporation Political Support
Committee (Chrysler Political Support)**
1000 Chrysler Drive
Auburn Hills, MI 48326
Treasurer: Thomas P. Capo
FEC ID#: C00043687
Total Disbursements: $659,369.

Citicorp Voluntary Political Fund Federal
1101 Pennsylvania Avenue NW, Suite 1000
Washington, DC 20004
Treasurer: Martha A. Golden
FEC ID#: C00088088
Total Disbursements: $521,079.

**Civic Involvement Program/General
Motors Corporation**
3044 West Grand Boulevard, MC 482 111 143
Detroit, MI 48202
Treasurer: Kimber Lee Franz
FEC ID#: C00076810
Total Disbursements: $777,521.

Credit Union Legislative Action Council
805 15th Street NW, Suite 300
Washington, DC 20005
Treasurer: Thomas J. Griffiths
FEC ID#: C00007880
Total disbursements: $778,647.

**Coastal Corporation Employee Action
Fund**
9 Greenway Plaza
Houston, TX 77046
Treasurer: Ronald D. Matthews
FEC ID#: C00091702
Total Disbursements: $623,842.

Committee for a Democratic Majority
307 5th Street NE, 2nd Floor
Washington, DC 20002
Treasurer: William C. Oldaker
FEC ID#: C00302067
Total Disbursements: $686,883.

Committee on Letter Carriers Political Education (Letter Carriers Political Action Fund)
100 Indiana Avenue NW
Washington, DC 20001
Treasurer: Florence Johnson
FEC ID#: C00023580
Total Disbursements: $1,689,071.

Committee on Political Action of the American Postal Workers Union AFL-CIO
1300 L Street NW
Washington, DC 20005
Treasurer: Douglas C. Holbrook
FEC ID#: C00010322
Total Disbursements: $1,179,368.

Committee for Thorough Agricultural Political Education of Associated Milk Producers Inc
PO Box 5288
Arlington, TX 76005
Treasurer: J. S. Stone
FEC ID#: 00001594
Total Disbursements: $1,079,069.

Commodity Futures Political Fund of the Chicago Mercantile Exchange
30 South Wacker Drive
Chicago, IL 60606
Treasurer: M. Scott Gordon
FEC ID#: C00076299
Total Disbursements: $560,082.

Compass Bancshares Inc Political Action Committee (COMPASS BANCPAC)
PO Box 10566
Birmingham, AL 35296
Treasurer: Sue L. Brewis
FEC ID#: C00142596
Total Disbursements: $729,612.

Coopers & Lybrand PAC
1900 K Street NW

Washington, DC 20006
Treasurer: Allen J. Weltmann
FEC ID#: C00107235
Total Disbursements: $575,690.

Council for a Livable World
110 Maryland Avenue NE
Washington, DC 20002
Treasurer: Philip Schrag
FEC ID#: C00029165
Total Disbursements: $657,086.

Credit Union Legislative Action Council
805 15th Street NW, Suite 300
Washington, DC 20005
(202) 628-2862
Treasurer: Thomas J. Griffiths
FEC ID#: C00007880
Total disbursements: $778,647.

CWA-COPE Political Contributions Committee
501 3rd Street NW
Washington, DC 20001
Treasurer: Barbara J. Easterling
FEC ID#: C00002089
Total Disbursements: $2,321,469.

Dealers Election Action Committee of the National Automobile Dealers Association
400 Westpark Drive
McLean, VA 22102
Treasurer: Leonard Fichtner
FEC ID#: C00040998
Total Disbursements: $3,248,147.

Deloitte and Touche LLP Federal Political Action Committee
1001 Pennsylvania Avenue NW, Suite 350N
Washington, DC 20004
Treasurer: Wade S. Williams
FEC ID#: C00211318
Total Disbursements: $754,684.

Democratic Republican Independent Voter Education Committee
25 Louisiana Avenue NW
Washington, DC 20001
Treasurer: William W. Hamilton Jr
FEC ID#: C00032979
Total Disbursements: $9,931,244.

Democrats 2000
1311 L Street NW, Suite 300
Washington, DC 20005
Treasurer: Ethan Strimling
FEC ID#: C00230342
Total Disbursements: $1,236,047.

District Council 37 AFSCME Public Employees Organized for Political and Legislative Equality (DC37PEOPLE)
PO Box 2882
Church Street Station
New York, NY 10008
Treasurer: Arthur Tibaldi
FEC ID#: C00149211
Total Disbursements: $1,177,420.

District No. 1 - PCD MEBA Political Action Fund (MEBA-PAF)
444 North Capitol Street NW, Suite 800
Washington, DC 20001
Treasurer: Paul Krupa
FEC ID#: C00279380
Total Disbursements: $700,303.

Effective Government Committee
607 14th Street NW, Suite 800
Washington, DC 20005
Treasurer: David Jones
FEC ID#: C00190876
Total Disbursements: $1,152,356.

Elect-The Political Action Committee of the Alabama Farmers Federation
PO Box 11023
Montgomery, AL 36111

Treasurer: John H. Dorrill Jr.
FEC ID#: C00094573
Total Disbursements: $1,066,209.

EMILY's List
805 15th Street NW, Suite 400
Washington, DC 20005
(202) 326-1400
(202) 547-1415 (Fax)
Treasurer: Ellen R. Malcom
FEC ID#: C00193433
Total Disbursements: $13,660,696 .

Empire Dental Political Action Committee
7 5th Avenue
Fairport, NY 14450
Treasurer: Dr. Warren M. Shaddock
FEC ID#: C00006296
Total Disbursements: $436,697.

Employees of Northrop Grumman Corporation Political Action Committee
1234 6th Street, Suite 204
Santa Monica, CA 90401
Treasurer: Daralyne Reed
FEC ID#: C00088591
Total Disbursements: $794,880.

Engineers Political Education Committee/ International Union of Operating Engineers
1125 17th Street NW
Washington, DC 20036
Treasurer: Michael J. Murphy
FEC ID#: C00029504
Total Disbursements: $1,420,967.

English Language Political Action Committee
PO Box 9558
Washington, DC 20016
Treasurer: Jan C. Zall
FEC ID#: C00199802
Total Disbursements: $471,636.

Enron Corporation Political Action Committee
PO Box 1188, EB 4520
Houston, TX 77251
Treasurer: Robert H. Butts
FEC ID#: C00104810
Total Disbursements: $462,892.

Ernst & Young Political Action Committee
1225 Connecticut Avenue NW, Suite 800
Washington, DC 20036
Treasurer: John E. Toole
FEC ID#: C00227744
Total Disbursements: $1,068,091.

EXXON Corporation Political Action Committee (EXPAC)
PO Box 2180
Houston, TX 77252
Treasurer: Karen M. Kresta
FEC ID#: C00121368
Total Disbursements: $621,886.

Federal Express Corporation Political Action Committee (FEPAC)
1980 Nonconnah Boulevard
Memphis, TN 38132
Treasurer: A. Doyle Cloud Jr.
FEC ID#: C00068692
Total Disbursements: $1,594,191.

Florida Medical Political Action Committee
PO Box 10269
Tallahassee, FL 32302
Treasurer: James Dolan, MD
FEC ID#: C00007484
Total Disbursements: $757,685.

FLUOR Corporation Public Affairs Committee (FLUOR PAC)
3333 Michelson Drive
Irvine, CA 92730
Treasurer: Andrew M. Schwartz

FEC ID#: C00034132
Total Disbursements: $602,873.

Food Marketing Institute Political Action Committee (FOOD PAC)
800 Connecticut Avenue NW, Suite 500
Washington, DC 20006
Treasurer: Harry R. Sullivan
FEC ID#: C00014555
Total Disbursements: $456,865.

Ford Motor Company Civic Action Fund
c/o Corporate Cash Management - PAC
Detroit, MI 48275
Treasurer: Kimber Lee Franz
FEC ID#: C00046474
Total Disbursements: $884,214.

Gay and Lesbian Victory Fund
1012 14th Street NW, Suite 1000
Washington, DC 20005
Treasurer: David Clarenbach
FEC ID#: C00251835
Total Disbursements: $1,053,979.

General Electric Company Political Action Committee
1299 Pennsylvania Avenue NW, Suite 1100
Washington, DC 20004
(202) 637-4455
(202) 637-4006 (Fax)
Treasurer: Blaine Barron
FEC ID#: C00024869
Total Disbursements: $841,570.

Glaxo Wellcome Inc Political Action Committee
5 Moore Drive
PO Box 13358
Research Triangle Park, NC 27709
Treasurer: B. Michael Gipson
FEC ID#: C00199703
Total Disbursements: $651,979.

GOPAC Incorporated
440 1st Street NW, Suite 400
Washington, DC 20001
Treasurer: Lisa B. Nelson
FEC ID#: C00251801
Total Disbursements: $4,654,338.

GTE Corporation Political Action Club (GTE PAC)
1850 M Street NW, Suite 1200
Washington, DC 20036
Treasurer: Jennifer A. Minarczik
FEC ID#: C00025163
Total Disbursements: $639,666.

Harrah's Entertainment Inc Employee's Political Action Committee (Promus/ Harrah's PAC)
1023 Cherry Road
Memphis, TN 38117
Treasurer: Gary L. Burhop
FEC ID#: C00239947
Total Disbursements: $584,172.

Hollywood Women's Political Committee
3679 Motor Avenue, Suite 302
Los Angeles, CA 90034
Treasurer: Judith Dornstein
FEC ID#: C00188979
Total Disbursements: $1,402,269.

Household International Inc & Subsidiary Companies Political Action Committee (HOUSEPAC)
2700 Sanders Road
Prospect Heights, IL 60070
Treasurer: Robert C. Sekany
FEC ID#: C00033423
Total Disbursements: $545,626.

Houston Industries Political Action Committee
PO Box 4567
Houston, TX 77210

Treasurer: Dan Cromack
FEC ID#: C00081455
Total Disbursements: $470,646.

Human Rights Campaign Fund Politcal Action Committee
1101 14th Street NW, 2nd Floor
Washington, DC 20005
Treasurer: Elizabeth Birch
FEC ID#: C00235853
Total Disbursements: $1,137,121.

Illinois State Medical Society Political Action Committee (IMPAC)
20 North Michigan Avenue, Suite 700
Chicago, IL 60602
Treasurer: Paul F. Mahon MD.
FEC ID#: C00005488
Total Disbursements: $512,424.

Independent Action Inc.
645 Pennsylvania Avenue SE, 2nd Floor
Washington, DC 20003
Treasurer: Mark Ingram
FEC ID#: C00139741
Total Disbursements: $478,605.

Independent Bankers Association of America Political Action Committee (IBAA PAC)
1 Thomas Circle NW, Suite 950
Washington, DC 20005
(202) 659-8111
(202) 659-9216 (Fax)
Treasurer: Ronald K. Ence
FEC ID#: C00032698
Total Disbursements: $519,707.

Independent Insurance Agents of America Inc Political Action Committee (INSURPAC)
412 1st Street SE, Suite 300
Washington, DC 20003
(202) 863-7000

(202) 863-7015 (Fax)
Treasurer: Paul A. Equale
FEC ID#: C00022343
Total Disbursements: $722,850.

International Association of Firefighters Interested in Registration and Education PAC
1750 New York Avenue NW
Washington, DC 20006
Treasurer: Vincent J. Bollon
FEC ID#: C00029447
Total Disbursements: $791,393.

International Brotherhood of Boilermakers (IN SP BLDRS, BKMTHS, FRGRS & HLPRS-LEG ED) FUND
753 State Avenue, Suite 565
Kansas City, KS 66101
Treasurer: Jerry Willburn
FEC ID#: C00005157
Total Disbursements: $446,060.

International Brotherhood of Electrical Workers Committee on Political Education
1125 15th Street NW
Washington, DC 20005
(202) 833-7000
(202) 467-6316 (Fax)
Treasurer: Jack F. Moore
FEC ID#: C00027342
Total Disbursements: $3,413,113.

International Brotherhood of Painters & Allied Trades Political Action Together Political CMTE
1750 New York Avenue NW
Washington, DC 20006
Treasurer: James A. Williams
FEC ID#: C00000885
Total Disbursements: $584,027.

International Longshoresmen's Association AFL-CIO Committee on

Political Education ILA-COPE
17 Battery Place
New York, NY 10004
Treasurer: Robert E. Gleason
FEC ID#: C00158576
Total Disbursements: $1,396,226.

Investment Management Political Action CMTE of the Investment Company Institute (IMPAC)
1401 H Street NW, Suite 1200
Washington, DC 20005
Treasurer: C. Richard Pogue
FEC ID#: C00105981
Total Disbursements: $582,245.

Ironworkers Political Action League
1750 New York Avenue NW, Suite 400
Washington, DC 20006
Treasurer: James E. Cole
FEC ID#: C00027359
Total Disbursements: $1,458,226.

ISSUES '96 (ISSUES '94)
2800 1 Indiana Square
Indianapolis, IN 46204
Treasurer: William R. Neale
FEC ID#: C00109744
Total Disbursements: $444,076.

IUE CMTE on Political Education International Union/Electronic Electrical Tech Salaried Mach Workers AFL-CIO
1126 16th Street NW
Washington, DC 20036
Treasurer: Edward Fire
FEC ID#: C00006247
Total Disbursements: $502,896.

Joint Action Committee for Political Affairs
PO Box 105
Highland Park, IL 60035
Treasurer: Joan Canel

FEC ID#: C00139659
Total Disbursements: $468,396.

Justice-PAC
2091 East Valley Parkway, Suite 1C
Escondido, CA 92027
Treasurer: Randy J. Goodwin
FEC ID#: C00159319
Total Disbursements: $534,254.

Laborers' Political League
905 16th Street NW
Washington, DC 20006
Treasurer: R. P. Vinall
FEC ID#: C00007922
Total Disbursements: $2,392,101.

**League of Conservative Voters Inc
Political Action Committee**
1707 L Street NW
Washington, DC 20036
Treasurer: Sydney Butler
FEC ID#: C00252940
Total Disbursements: $1,289,716.

Lincoln Club of Orange County
950 South Coast Drive, Suite 195
Costa Mesa, CA 92626
Treasurer: Frank H. Greinke
FEC ID#: C00035246
Total Disbursements: $492,156.

**Lockheed Employees' Political Action
Committee**
4500 Park Granada Boulevard, Building 9
Calabasas, CA 91399
Treasurer: Scott Hallman
FEC ID#: C00030783
Total Disbursements: $486,548.

**Lockheed Martin Employees' Political
Action Committee**
1725 Jefferson Davis Highway

Crystal Square 2, Suite 300
Arlington, VA 22202
Treasurer: Stephen E. Chaudet
FEC ID#: C00303024
Total Disbursements: $1,222,149.

Machinists Non-Partisan Political League
9000 Machinists Place
Upper Marlboro, MD 20772
Treasurer: Donald E. Wharton
FEC ID#: C00002469
Total Disbursements: $3,615,292.

Majority Leader's Fund
4451 Brookfield Corporate Drive, Suite 200
Chantilly, VA 20151
Treasurer: Robert Morgan
FEC ID#: C00301366
Total Disbursements: $1,574,332.

**Massachusetts Mutual Life Insurance
Company Political Action Committee**
1295 State Street
Springfield, MA 01111
Treasurer: Allan B. Bixby
FEC ID#: C00118943
Total Disbursements: $511,628.

**MBNA Corporation Federal Political
Committee**
MBNA Corporation
Wilmington, DE 19884
Treasurer: John W. Scheflen
FEC ID#: C00252866
Total Disbursements: $825,974.

**Mid-America Conservative Political
Action Committee**
2507 Loma
Cedar Falls, IA 50613
Treasurer: Leroy Dale Corey
FEC ID#: C00139972
Total Disbursements: $459,147.

Mid-America Dairymen Inc - Dairy Educational Political Action Committee (MID-AM/DEPAC)
3253 East Chestnut Expressway
Springfield, MO 65802
(417) 865-9641
Treasurer: Roger Eldridge
FEC ID#: C00001388
Total Disbursements: $820,813.

Monday Morning Political Action Committee
PO Box 10097
Arlington, VA 22210
Treasurer: Trudy Matthes Barksdale
FEC ID#: C00304022
Total Disbursements: $1,297,721.

Morgan Companies Political Action Committee (MORGANPAC)
60 Wall Street
New York, NY 10260
(212) 483-2323
(212) 648-5116 (Fax)
Treasurer: Cory N. Strupp
FEC ID#: C00104299
Total Disbursements: $754,237.

Morgan Stanley & Company Incorporated Better Government Fund
1221 Avenue of the Americas, 34th Floor
New York, NY 10020
Treasurer: James A. Runde
FEC ID#: C00067215
Total Disbursements: $543,809.

NAPUS PAC for Postmasters (Political Education for Postmasters)
8 Herbert Street
Alexandria, VA 22305
Treasurer: Teena Cregan
FEC ID#: C00100404
Total Disbursements: $540,003

National Abortion and Reproductive Rights Action League PAC
1156 15th Street NW, 7th Floor
Washington, DC 20005
(202) 973-3000
Treasurer: Evan J. Goldman
FEC ID#: C00079541
Total Disbursements: $589,302.

National Air Traffic Controllers Association Political Action Committee
1150 17th Street NW, Suite 701
Washington, DC 20036
Treasurer: Barry Krasner
FEC ID#: C00238725
Total Disbursements: $439,594.

National Association of Broadcasters Television and Radio Political Action Committee
1771 North Street NW
Washington, DC 20036
(202) 429-5300
(202) 775-2157 (Fax)
Treasurer: James C. May
FEC ID#: C00009985
Total Disbursements: $664,204.

National Association of Convenience Stores Political Action Committee
1605 King Street
Alexandria, VA 22314
Treasurer: Marc N. Katz
FEC ID#: C00126763
Total Disbursements: $451,287.

National Association of Life Underwriters Political Action Committee
1922 F Street NW
Washington, DC 20006
(202) 331-6000
(202) 331-2163 (Fax)
Treasurer: Paul M. Smith Sr
FEC ID#: C00005249
Total Disbursements: $1,894,532.

National Association of Retired Federal Employees Political Action Committee (NARFE-PAC)
1533 New Hampshire Avenue NW
Washington, DC 20036.
(202) 234-0832
(202) 797-9697 (Fax)
Treasurer: Frank G. Atwater
FEC ID#: C00091561
Total Disbursements: $1,673,758.

National Association of Social Workers Political Action for Candidate Election
750 1st Street NE, Suite 700
Washington, DC 20002
Treasurer: Kathy Woods-Dobbins
FEC ID#: C00060707
Total Disbursements: $914,494.

National Beer Wholesalers' Association Political Action Committee (NBWA PAC)
1100 South Washington Street
Alexandria, VA 22314
Treasurer: Ronald A. Sarasin
FEC ID#: C00144766
Total Disbursements: $1,541,939.

National Cable Television Association's Political Action Committee (CABLE PAC)
1724 Massachusetts Avenue NW
Washington, DC 20036
(202) 775-3550
(202) 775-3671(Fax)
Treasurer: Kenneth A. Gross
FEC ID#: C00010082
Total Disbursements: $641,640.

National Cattlemen's Beef Association Political Action Committee (NCBA-PAC)
5420 South Quebec Street
PO Box 3469
Englewood, CO 80155
Treasurer: Lori Pitts
FEC ID#: C00028787
Total Disbursements: $442,655.

National City Corporation PAC (National City PAC/NC PAC)
1900 East 9th Street
National City Center
Cleveland, OH 44114
Treasurer: Allen C. Waddle
FEC ID#: C00141036
Total Disbursements: $464,083.

National Committee for an Effective Congress
122 C Street NW, Suite 650
Washington, DC 20001
Treasurer: James F. Byron
FEC ID#: C00003558
Total Disbursements: $2,341,074.

National Committee to Preserve Social Security and Medicare - PAC
2000 K Street NW, 8th Floor
Washington, DC 20006
Treasurer: Shelly C. Shulman
FEC ID#: C00172296
Total Disbursements: $2,277,182.

National Conservative Club (National Congressional Club)
100-C Hunter Place
PO Box 18848
Youngsville, NC 27596
Treasurer: Carter Wrenn
FEC ID#: C00119370
Total Disbursements: $914,912.

National Educational Association Political Action Committee
1201 16th Street NW
Washington, DC 20036
(202) 833-4000
(202) 822-7741 (Fax)
Treasurer: Ken Melley
FEC ID#: C00003251
Total Disbursements: $5,031,657.

National Federation of Independent Business/Save America's Free Enterprise Trust
600 Maryland Avenue SW, Suite 700
Washington, DC 20024
Treasurer: Fred Holladay
FEC ID#: C00101105
Total Disbursements: $1,111,102.

National PAC
600 Pennsylvania Avenue SE, Suite 207
Washington, DC 20003
Treasurer: Marvin Josephson
FEC ID#: C00150995
Total Disbursements: $1,441,207.

National Restaurant Association Political Action Committee
1200 17th Street NW
Washington, DC 20036
Treasurer: Elaine Z. Graham
FEC ID#: C00003764
Total Disbursements: $950,845.

National Right to Life Political Action Committee
419 7th Street NW, Suite 500
Washington, DC 20004
Treasurer: Amarie Natividad
FEC ID#: C00111278
Total Disbursements: $2,230,796.

National Rural Letter Carriers' Association Political Action Committee
1630 Duke Street, 4th Floor
Alexandria, VA 22314
Treasurer: Ruth C. Pugh
FEC ID#: C00072025
Total Disbursements: $693,806.

NationsBank Corporation PAC
600 Peachtree Street NE, Suite 1500
Atlanta, GA 30308
Treasurer: J. Mark Leggett

FEC ID#: C00043489
Total Disbursements: $700,663.

New Jersey State Laborers' Political Action Committee/Laborers' Political League
104 Interchange Plaza, Suite 301
PO Box 554
Cranbury, NJ 08512
Treasurer: Frank Sorge
FEC ID#: C00214643
Total Disbursements: $1,459,125.

New Republican Majority Fund
228 South Washington Street, Suite 200
Alexandria, VA 22314
Treasurer: J. Stanley Huckaby
FEC ID#: C00300483
Total Disbursements: $1,386,087.

New York State Laborers Political Action Committee
1828 2nd Avenue
New York, NY 10128
Treasurer: Salvatore Lanza
FEC ID#: C00220566
Total Disbursements: $1,774,930.

NRA Political Victory Fund
11250 Waples Mill Road
Fairfax, VA 22030
(703) 267-1000
(703) 267-3925 (Fax)
Treasurer: Mary Rose Jennison
FEC ID#: C00053553
Total Disbursements: $6,642,888.

Ohio Medical Political Action Committee (OMPAC)
1500 Lake Shore Drive
Columbus, OH 43204
Treasurer: Tim Maglione
FEC ID#: C00003327
Total Disbursements: $429,676.

Oregon Education Association People for Improvement of Education
6900 SW Haines Road
Tigard, OR 97223
Treasurer: Robert G. Crumpton
FEC ID#: C00017343
Total Disbursements: $902,590.

Outback Steakhouse Inc Political Action Committee
550 North Reo Street, Suite 204
Tampa, FL 33609
Treasurer: Joseph J. Kadow
FEC ID#: C00253153
Total Disbursements: $606,582.

Peat Marwick Partners/Principals & Employees Political Action Committee (Peat Marwick/PAC)
PO Box 18254
Washington, DC 20036
Treasurer: Stephen E. Allis
FEC ID#: C00280222
Total Disbursements: $494,160.

Pennsylvania Medical Political Action Committee
PO Box 8820
Harrisburg, PA 17105
Treasurer: Jerry L. Rothenberger
FEC ID#: C00004929
Total Disbursements: $534,063.

Pfizer Inc PAC
235 East 42nd Street
New York, NY 10017
Treasurer: Alan G. Levin
FEC ID#: C00016683
Total Disbursements: $457,531.

Philip Morris Companies Inc Political Action Committee (PHIL-PAC)
120 Park Avenue
New York, NY 10017

Treasurer: George R. Lewis
FEC ID#: C00089136
Total Disbursements: $1,321,849.

Physical Therapy Political Action Committee (PT-PAC)
1111 North Fairfax Street
Alexandria, VA 22314
Treasurer: Pamela Phillips
FEC ID#: C00012880
Total Disbursements: $1,306,049.

Podiatry Political Action Committee
9312 Old Georgetown Road
Bethesda, MD 20814
(301) 571-9200
(301) 530-2752 (Fax)
Treasurer: Gerald D. Peterson
FEC ID#: C00008839
Total Disbursements: $527,363.

Price Waterhouse Partners' Political Action Committee
1301 K Street NW, Suite 800W
Washington, DC 20005
Treasurer: Gilbert Simonetti Jr.
FEC ID#: C00232173
Total Disbursements: $474,555.

Public Affairs PAC
6734 Westcott Road
Falls Church, VA 22042
Treasurer: Eugene A. Delgaudio
FEC ID#: C00224493
Total Disbursements: $569,548.

Realtors Political Action Committee
430 North Michigan Avenue
Chicago, IL 60611
(312) 329-8200
Treasurer: Martin Edwards Jr.
FEC ID#: C00030718
Total Disbursements: $2,269,891.

Republican Majority Fund
PO Box 19897
Alexandria, VA 22320
Treasurer: Rachel Pearson
FEC ID#: C00296640
Total Disbursements: $646,208.

Republican Network to Elect Women (RENEW)
1555 King Street, Suite 300
PO Box 507
Alexandria, VA 22313
Treasurer: Yolanda Esham
FEC ID#: C00280339
Total Disbursements: $640,195.

Republicans for Choice
2760 Eisenhower Avenue
Alexandria, VA 22314
Treasurer: Ann Stone
FEC ID#: C00241083
Total Disbursements: $992,863.

Responsible Citizens Political League - A Project of the Trans Committee International Union (TCU)
3 Research Place
Rockville, MD 20850
Treasurer: Frank Ferlin Jr
FEC ID#: C00006338
Total Disbursements: $610,458.

RJR Political Action Committee (RJR PAC)
PO Box 718
Winston-Salem, NC 27102
Treasurer: Janis M. Krebs
FEC ID#: C00042002
Total Disbursements: $963,958.

SBC Communications Inc Employee Federal Political Action Committee (SBC EMPAC)
175 East Houston, Room 7-A-50

San Antonio, TX 78205
Treasurer: Donald E. Kiernan
FEC ID#: C00109017
Total Disbursements: $674,857.

Seafarers Political Activity Donation - Seafarers International Union of NA- AGLIWD DIST (SPAD)
5201 Auth Way
Camp Springs, MD 20746
(301) 899-0675
(301) 899-7355 (Fax)
Treasurer: Michael Neuman
FEC ID#: C00004325
Total Disbursements: $1,608,582.

Service Employees International Union Political Campaign Committee
1313 L Street NW
Washington, DC 20005
(202) 628-0384
Treasurer: Betty Bednarczyk
FEC ID#: C00004036
Total Disbursements: $1,291,615.

Sheet Metal Workers International Association Political Action League (PAL)
1750 New York Avenue NW
Washington, DC 20006
(202) 783-5880
(202) 662-0893 (Fax)
Treasurer: Michael J. Sullivan
FEC ID#: C00007542
Total Disbursements: $1,477,632.

Sierra Club Political Committee
85 2nd Street, 2nd Floor
San Francisco, CA 94105
Treasurer: Daniel Weiss
FEC ID#: C00135368
Total Disbursements: $677,883.

Team Ameritech Political Action Committee
30 South Wacker Drive, 35th Floor

Chicago, IL 60606
Treasurer: Robert J. Kolbe
FEC ID#: C00174763
Total Disbursements: $1,496,159.

Tenneco Inc Employees Good Government Fund
701 Pennsylvania Avenue NW, Suite 710
Washington, DC 20004
Treasurer: Robert T. Blakely
FEC ID#: C00089961
Total Disbursements: $860,515.

Texas Medical Association Political Action Committee
401 West 15th Street
Austin, TX 78701
Treasurer: David A. Marwitz
FEC ID#: C00001214
Total Disbursements: $1,360,707.

Time Future Inc (Successor to Bill Bradley for US Senate)
4 Hawthorne Avenue
Princeton, NJ 08540
Treasurer: John V. Roos
FEC ID#: C00270736
Total Disbursements: $878,251.

Transport Workers Union - Local 100 Political Contributors Committee
80 West End Avenue, 6th Floor
New York, NY 10023
Treasurer: Dennis Calhoun
FEC ID#: C00135475
Total Disbursements: $982,943.

Transport Workers Union Political Contributions Committee
80 West End Avenue
New York, NY 10023
Treasurer: John J. Kerrigan
FEC ID#: C00008268
Total Disbursements: $938,012.

Transportation Political Education League
14600 Detroit Avenue
Cleveland, OH 44107
Treasurer: Roger D. Griffeth
FEC ID#: C00001636
Total Disbursements: $2,510,748.

Trucking Political Action Committee of the American Trucking Associations Inc
430 1st Street SE
Washington, DC 20003
Treasurer: Donna Weinrich
FEC ID#: C00002881
Total Disbursements: $464,369.

UAW-V-CAP (UAW Voluntary Community Action Program)
8000 East Jefferson
Detroit, MI 48214
(313) 926-5531
(313) 824-5750 (Fax)
Treasurer: Roy O. Wyse
FEC ID#: C00002840
Total Disbursements: $3,955,068.

Union of Needletrades Industrial & Textile Employees Campaign Committee (UNITE CAMP COMM)
1710 Broadway
New York, NY 10019
Treasurer: Arthur Loevy
FEC ID#: C00004861
Total Disbursements: $879,467.

Union Pacific Fund for Effective Government
555 13th Street NW, Suite 450 West
Washington, DC 20004
(202) 662-0100
(202) 662-0199 (Fax)
Treasurer: Mary McAuliffe
FEC ID#: C00010470
Total Disbursements: $1,335,754.

United Association Political Education Committee
901 Massachusetts Avenue NW
Washington, DC 20001
Treasurer: Marion A. Lee
FEC ID#: C00012476
Total Disbursements: $1,209,040.

United Mine Workers of America - Coal Miners Political Action Committee
900 15th Street NW
Washington, DC 20005
(202) 842-7200
(202) 842-7227 (Fax)
Treasurer: Carlos Tarley
FEC ID#: C00013342
Total Disbursements: $952,986.

United Parcel Service of America Inc Political Action Committee (UPSPAC)
55 Glenlake Parkway NE
Atlanta, GA 30328
Treasurer: D. Scott Davis
FEC ID#: C00064766
Total Disbursements: $2,957,935.

United Services Automobile Association Group Political Action Committee (USAA GROUP PAC)
9800 Fredericksburg Road
San Antonio, TX 78288
Treasurer: Jose Robles Jr
FEC ID#: C00164145
Total Disbursements: $470,868.

United Steel Workers of America Political Action Fund
5 Gateway Center
Pittsburgh, PA 15222
Treasurer: Leo W. Gerard
FEC ID#: C00003590
Total Disbursements: $1,915,676.

United Technologies Corporation Political Action Committee
1401 I Street NW, Suite 600
Washington, DC 20005
Treasurer: Wade H. Robert
FEC ID#: C00035683
Total Disbursements: $450,078.

US West Inc Political Action Committee (USWest PAC)
5325 Zuni, Room 630
Denver, CO 80221
Treasurer: Debra Pestana
FEC ID#: C00184374
Total Disbursements: $452,396.

UST Executives, Administrators, and Managers Political Action Committee (USTEAM PAC)
100 West Putnam Avenue
Greenwich, CT 06830
(203) 661-1100
(203) 622-3315 (Fax)
Treasurer: Wendy B. Grammas
FEC ID#: C00104851
Total Disbursements: $816,725.

Veterans of Foreign Wars Political Action Commitee Inc
200 Maryland Avenue NE, Suite 506
Washington, DC 20002
Treasurer: Gerald E. Jonas
FEC ID#: C00113001
Total Disbursements: $545,161.

Voice of Teachers for Education/ Committee on Political Education of New York State United Teachers (VOTE/Cope) of NYSUT
159 Wolf Road, Box 15-008
Albany, NY 12212
Treasurer: Alan B. Lubin
FEC ID#: C00021121
Total Disbursements: $2,904,037.

Voluntary Contributors for Better Government: A Program of Employees International Paper
1101 Pennsylvania Avenue NW, Suite 200
Washington, DC 20004
Treasurer: Arthur W. Brownell
FEC ID#: C00034405
Total Disbursements: $477,020.

Voters for Choice/Friends of Family Planning
PO Box 53301, Suite 201
Washington, DC 20009
Treasurer: Mary Jean Collins
FEC ID#: C00109355
Total Disbursements: $1,178,929.

Wish List
3205 North Street NW
Washington, DC 20007
Treasurer: Kendall Wilson
FEC ID#: C00258277
Total Disbursements: $505,812.

WMX Technologies Inc Employees' Better Government Fund (WMX PAC)
601 Pennsylvania Avenue NW
North Building, Suite 300
Washington, DC 20004
Treasurer: James L. Elitzak
FEC ID#: C00119008
Total Disbursements: $775,394.

Women's Campaign Fund Inc
734 15th Street NW, Suite 500
Washington, DC 20005
(202) 393-8164
(202) 393-0649 (Fax)
Treasurer: Doreen Frasca
FEC ID#: C00015024
Total Disbursements: $2,771,841.

Your Pro-Choice Voter Guide
1592 Union Street, Suite 477

San Francisco, CA 94123
Treasurer: Philip Muller
FEC ID#: C00270439
Total Disbursements: $465,384.

Political Science Research Institutes

Political science research institutes (PSRI) are organizations affiliated with a college or university that engage in the study of politics and policy. PSRIs are distinct from think tanks, which are independent organizations that study politics and policy. However, like think tanks, PSRIs often reflect a particular political bias.

Institutes are listed alphabetically by their college or university affiliation.

Arizona State University -- *Center for Urban Studies*. College of Public Programs, PO Box 870803, Tempe, AZ 85287-0803. Tel: (602) 965-9216 Fax: (602)) 965-8530. Director: Dr. Ann Schneider; f. 1969; Publications: *Center for Urban Studies Report Series* (occasional).

Arizona State University -- *Media Research Program*. Cronkite School of Journalism, Tempe, AZ 85287-1305. Tel: (602) 965-7051 Fax: (602) 965-7041. Director: Dr. Bruce D. Merrill; f. 1989; Publications: *Arizona Speaks: Cactus State Poll*.

Arizona State University -- *Morrison Institute for Public Policy*. School of Public Affairs, Tempe, AZ 85287-4405. Tel: (602) 965-7424 Fax: (602) 965-9219 Website: http://www.asu.edu/copd. Director: Dr. Rob Melnick; f. 1982.

Ashland University -- *John M. Ashbrook Center for Public Affairs*. Ashland, OH 44805. Tel: (419) 289-5411 Fax: (419) 289-5425 E-mail: troepke@ashland.edu. Website: http://www.ashland.edu/ashb.html. Director: Peter W. Schramm; f. 1983.

Auburn University -- *Center for Governmental Services*. 2236 Haley Center, Auburn University, AL 36849-5225. Tel: (334) 844-4781 Fax: (334) 844-1919 E-mail: cgs@cgs.auburn.edu. Website: http://www.auburn.edu/~outrace/egs.html. Director: Dr. Keith J. Ward; f. 1976.

Ball State University -- *Office of Politics and Public Policy*. Department of Political Science, North Quadrangle 264, Muncie, IN 47306. Tel: (317) 285-8780 Fax: (317) 285-8980 E-mail: 00rhscheele@bsu.edu. Director: Dr. Raymond H. Scheele; f. 1970.

Bernard Baruch College of City University of New York -- *Center for the Study of Business and Government*. 17 Lexington Avenue, PO Box E1300, New York, NY 10010. Tel: (212) 802-5720 Fax: (212) 802-5722. Director: Dr. M. Anne Hill; f. 1978.

Brooklyn College of City University of New York -- *Urban Studies Program*. 99 Hudson Street, Brooklyn, NY 10013. Tel: (718) 966-4038 Fax: (718) 966-4014. Director: Professor Edward T. Rogowsky; f. 1981.

Brown University -- *A. Alfred Taubman Center for Public Policy and American Institutions*. 67 George Street, Box 1977, Providence, RI 02912. Tel: (401) 863-2201

Fax: (401) 863-2452 E-mail: thomasanton @brown.edu. Website: http://www.brown.edu/ departments/taubmancenter. Director: Professor Thomas J. Anton; f. 1977; Publications: *Policy Advisor*; *Public Policy Report*; *Public Opinion of Public Policy*.

California State University, Dominguez Hills -- *Center for Policy Research and Evaluation (CPRE)*. SBS F 117, 1000 East Victoria Street, Carson, CA 90747. Tel: (310) 516-3436 Fax: (310) 516-3547. Director: Dr. Edith F. Neumann; f. 1994; Publications: *CPRE Reports*.

California State University, Fullerton -- *Center for Governmental Studies*. Division of Political Science and Criminal Justice, PO Box 6848, Fullerton, CA 92634-6848. Tel: (714) 278-3521 Fax: (714) 278-3524 E-mail: Kboyum@FULLERTON.EDU. Chair: Sandra Sutphen; f. 1972.

California State University, Long Beach -- *Bureau of Governmental Research and Services*. 1250 Bellflower Boulevard, Long Beach, CA 90840. Tel: (526) 985-5418 Fax: (562) 985-4672 Website: http://www. beachmpa.csulb.edu. Director: Dr. Michelle Saint-Germain; f. 1974.

California State University, Long Beach -- *Graduate Center for Public Policy and Administration*. 1250 Bellflower Boulevard, Long Beach, CA 90840-4602. Tel: (562) 985-4177 Fax: (562) 985-4672. Director: Dr. Daniel M. Barber; f. 1973.

California State University, Los Angeles -- *Edmund G. "Pat" Brown Institute of Public Affairs*. 5151 State University, Los Angeles, CA 90032-8261. Tel: (213) 343-3770 Fax: (213) 343-3774. Executive Director: Dr. Jaime Regalado; f. 1980.

Claremont Graduate University -- *Claremont Institute for Economic Policy Studies*. McManus Hall 225, 170 East 10th Street, Claremont, CA 91711-6163. Tel: (909)

621-8074 Fax: (909) 621-8545 E-mail: willettd@cgu.edu. Director: Thomas D. Willett.

Claremont McKenna College -- *Rose Institute of State and Local Government*. 340 East 9th Street, Claremont, CA 91711. Tel: (909) 621-8159 Fax: (909) 607-4288 E-mail: alanheslop@mckenna.edu. Website: http:// www.mckenna.edu/rose. Director: Dr. Alan Heslop; f. 1973; Publications: *Atlas of South Central Los Angeles*.

Clark Atlanta University -- *Southern Center for Studies in Public Policy*. 223 James P. Brawley Drive SW, Atlanta, GA 30314. Tel: (404) 880-8085 Fax: (404) 880-8090 E-mail: scspp@cau.edu. Website: http://www.cau.edu. Director: Dr. Robert A. Holmes; f. 1968.

Clemson University -- *Strom Thurmond Institute of Government and Public Affairs*. PO Box 345130, Clemson, SC 29634-5203. Tel: (864) 656-4700 Fax: (864) 656-4780 E-mail: beck@clemson. edu. Website: http:// www.strom. clemson.edu. Director: Dr. Robert H. Becker; f. 1981.

Cleveland State University -- *The Urban Center*. College of Urban Affairs, Cleveland, OH 44115. Tel: (216) 687-2134 Fax: (216) 687-9277. Director: Larry Ledebur; f. 1979.

Duke University -- *Center for Health Policy Research and Education*. 125 Old Chemistry Building, Box 90253, Durham, NC 27708. Tel: (919) 684-3023 Fax: (919) 684-6246 E-mail: match001@ mc.duke.edu. Director: David B. Matchar, M.D.; f. 1981.

Duke University -- *The Governors Center*. Box 90246, Durham, NC 27708-0246. Tel: (919) 613-7374 Fax: (919) 681-8288 E-mail: gov-ctr@pps.duke.edu. Website: http:// www.pubpol,duke.edu/centers/govctr. Director: Vicky Patton; f. 1981.

Duke University -- *Terry Sanford Institute of Public Policy*. PO Box 90239, Durham,

NC 27708-0239. Tel: (919) 613-7309 Fax: (919) 681-8288 E-mail: cook@pps.duke.edu. Website: http://www. pubpol.duke.edu. Director: Philip Cook; f. 1971; Publications: *Duke Policy News* (semiannually).

Eastern Washington University -- *Institute for Urban & Local Studies.* West 421 Riverside, Suite 902, Spokane, WA 99201. Tel: (509) 359-6200 Fax: (509) 359-4230. Director: Dr. Anthony H. Anderson; f. 1984.

Emory Universiry -- *Carter Center.* 453 Freed Parkway, Atlanta, GA 30307. Tel: (404) 331-3900 Fax: (404) 331-0283. Website: http://www.emory.edu/cartercenter. Executive Director: Dr. John B. Hardman; f. 1982; Publications: *Carter Center News* (biennially); *Conference Report Series.*

Evergreen State College -- *Washington State Institute for Public Policy.* Seminar 3162, Mail Stop TA-00, Olympia, WA 98505. Tel: (360) 866-6000 Fax: (360) 866-6825. Director: Roxanne Lieb; f. 1983.

Florida International University -- *Institute for Public Opinion Research.* ACII-301, North Campus, Miami, FL 33181. Tel: (305) 919-5778 Fax: (305) 919-5242. Website: http://www.fiu.edu/orgs/ipor. Director: Dr. Hugh Gladwin; f. 1983; Publications: *FIU/Florida Poll* (annually).

Florida State University -- *Florida Center for Public Management.* 118 North Woodward Avenue, Tallahassee, FL 32306-2670. Tel: (850) 644-6460 Fax: (850) 644-0152 E-mail: aeinbind@mailer.fsu.edu. Website: http://www.fgtc.com. Director: Larry K. Gross.

Florida State University -- *Institute for Health and Human Services Research.* Morgan Building, 2035 East Paul Dirac Drive, Suite 236, Tallahassee, FL 32310-4086. Tel: (904) 644-2710 Fax: (904) 644-8331 E-mail: amcneece@garnet.fsu.edu.Website: http://

www.IHHSR.FSU.GOV. Director: Dr. A. McNeece; f. 1986.

Florida State University -- *Pepper Institute on Aging and Public Policy.* 651 Bellamy, Tallahassee, FL 32306-2290. Tel: (904) 644-2831 Fax: (904) 644-2304 E-mail: mhardy@garnet.acns.fsu.edu. Contact: Melissa Hardy; f. 1976.

Fordham University -- *Institute for Urban Studies.* 441 East Fordham, Bronx, NY 10458. Tel: (718) 817-1000. f. 1963.

George Mason University -- *Public Choice Center.* Carow, M5N 1D3, Fairfax, VA 22030. Tel: (703) 323-3774 Fax: (703) 323-3772 E-mail: CRBERT@UMS1.GMU.EDU. Director: Dr. Robert D. Tollison; f. 1969; Publications: *Public Choice* (9/year).

George Washington University -- *Intergovernmental Health Policy Project.* 2021 K Street NW, Suite 800, Washington, DC 20006. Tel: (202) 872-1445 Fax: (202) 785-0114 E-mail: ihpp@gwisz.circ.gwu.edu. Website: http://www.gwu.edu/-ihpp. Director: Richard E. Merritt; f. 1978; Publications: *State Health Notes* (semimonthly); *State Health Reports on Mental Health*; *Alcoholism & Drug Abuse* (10/year); *Primary Care News.*

Georgia State University -- *School of Policy Studies.* 35 Broad Street, Atlanta, GA 30329. Tel: (404) 651-3993 Fax: (404) 651-3996 E-mail: prcbam@langate.gsu.edu. Website: http://www.prcueb,gsu.edu. Director: Dr. Roy Bahl; f. 1988.

Goucher College -- *Sarah T. Hughes Field Politics Center.* Baltimore, MD 21204. Tel: (410) 337-6256 Fax: (410) 337-6405 E-mail: mmarshal@goucher.edu. Director: Marcia Marshall.

Harvard University -- *A. Alfred Taubman Center for State and Local Government.* John F. Kennedy School of Government, 79 John F. Kennedy Street, Cambridge, MA

02138. Tel: (617) 495-2199 Fax: (617) 496-1722 E-mail: alanaltschuler@ harvard.edu.Website:http://www.KSG.harvard.edu/taubman/. Director: Alan Altshuler; f. 1988; Publications: *Annual Report*; *The Public's Capital* (quarterly).

Harvard University -- *Center for Business and Government*. 79 John F. Kennedy Street, Cambridge, MA 02138. Tel: (617) 495-1446 Fax: (617) 496-0063.

Harvard University -- *Malcolm Wiener Center for Social Policy*. John F. Kennedy School of Government, 79 John F. Kennedy Street, Cambridge, MA 02138. Tel: (617) 495-1461 Fax: (617) 496-9053 E-mail: juliewilson@ harvard.edu. Website: http://www.ksg.harvard.edu/socpol. Director: Julie Wilson; f. 1987.

Harvard University -- *Program on Information Resources Policy*. 65 Rear Mount Auburn Street, Cambridge, MA 02138. Tel: (617) 495-4114 Fax: (617) 495-3338 E-mail: pirp@ fas.harvard.edu. Website: http://www.pirp.harvard.edu. Chair: Anthony G. Oettinger; f. 1972.

Hillside College -- *Center for Constructive Alternatives/The Shavano Institute*. 33 East College Street, Hillsdale, MI 49242. Tel: (517) 437-7341 or (800) 437-2268 Fax: (517) 437-0654. Vice President: Ronald L. Trowbridge; f. 1972.

Hunter College of City University of New York -- *Urban Research Center*. Department of Urban Affairs & Planning, 695 Park Avenue, New York, NY 10021. Tel: (212) 772-5519 Fax: (212) 772-5593 E-mail: urban@ hunter.cuny.edu. Chair: Eugene L. Birch; f. 1962.

Illinois State University -- *Census and Data Users Services*. Res. Services Building, Suite A, Normal, IL 61761. Tel: (309) 438-5946 Fax: (309) 438-2898 E-mail: treadway@ rs6000cmp.ilstu.edu. Director: Dr. Roy C. Treadway; f. 1979.

Indiana State University -- *Center for Governmental Services*. Holmstedt Hall, Room 315, Terre Haute, IN 47809. Tel: (812) 237-2436 Fax: (812) 237-3445 E-mail: psmohad@scifac. indstate.edu. Director Dr. Manindra K. Mohapatra; f. 1966; Publications: *Public Policy Research Newsletter* (quarterly); *Lake County Government Study Lecture Series*; *Bibliography on Indiana Public Policy*.

Indiana State University -- *Center for Urban-Regional Studies*. Department of Geography, Geology, and Anthropology. Sci. 122, Terre Haute, IN 47809. Tel: (812) 237-2289 Fax: (812) 237-8029 E-mail: gejones@ scifac.instate.edu. Director: Dr. Robert C. Larson; f. 1972.

Indiana University, Bloomington -- *Workshop in Political Theory and Policy Analysis*. 513 North Park Avenue, Bloomington, IN 47408-3895. Tel: (812) 855-0441 Fax: (812) 855-3150 E-mail: workshop@indiana.edu. Co-Director: Vincent Ostrom; f. 1973; Publications: *Workshop Reprint Series*.

Johns Hopkins University -- *Institute for Policy Studies*. 3400 North Charles Street, Wyman Park Center, Baltimore, MD 21218-2668. Tel: (410) 516-7174 Fax: (410) 516-8233 E-mail: lsalamon@jnunix.hcs.jhu.edu. Website: http://www.jhu.edu/~ips/naps/tester.html. Director Dr. Lester M. Salamon; f. 1972.

Kennesaw State College -- *Hewlett Packard Telephone Survey Research Laboratory*. PO Box 444, Marietta, GA 30061. Tel: (770) 423-6464 Fax: (770) 423-6395, E-mail: hmcginni@kscmail.kennesaw.edu. Director: Dr. Harry McGinnis.

Kent State University -- *Institute for African American Affairs*. Department of Pan-African Studies, Kent, OH 44242-0001. Tel: (216) 672-2300 Fax: (216) 672-4837. Director: Edward W. Crosby; f. 1969; Publications: *Kitabu Newsletter*.

Louisiana State University -- *Office of Government Programs*. 379 Pleasant Hall, Baton Rouge, LA 70803. Tel: (504) 388-6746 Fax: (504) 388-6200 E-mail: ogp@ lanmail.ocs.lsu.edu. Director: Dr. Brooke Allphin; f. 1972.

Louisiana State University -- *Public Administration Institute*. 3200 CEBA Building, Baton Rouge, LA 70803. Tel: (504) 388-6743 Fax: (504) 334-1719 E-mail: parich@ unix1.sncc.lsu.edu. Director: James A. Richardson.

Loyola University, Chicago -- *Institute of Urban Life*. 10 East Pearson, 1st Floor, Room 101, Chicago, IL 60611. Tel: (312) 915-6666 Fax: (312) 915-6433. President: Ed Marciniak; f. 1962.

Maharishi University of Management -- *Institute of Science, Technology and Public Policy*. 1000 North 4th Street, DB 1137, Fairfield, IA 52557-1137. Tel: (515) 472-1200 Fax: (515) 472-1165 E-mail: istpp@mum.edu. Website: http://www.mum.bdu. Director: Dr. John S. Hagelin.

Marist College -- *Marist Institute for Public Opinion*. 290 North Road, Poughkeepsie, NY 12601. Tel: (914) 575-5050 Fax: (914) 575-5111. Director: Dr. Lee M. Miringoff; f. 1978; Publications: *The Polling Place* (annually).

Marshall University -- *The John Deaver Drinko Academy for American Political Institutions and Civic Culture*. 400 Hal Greer Boulevard, Huntington, WV 25755-2014. Tel: (304) 696-3183 Fax: (304) 696-3197 E-mail: neal@marshall.edu. Executive Director: Dr. Alan B. Gould.

Massachusetts Institute of Technology -- *Center for Energy and Environmental Policy Research*. E40-279, Cambridge, MA 02139-4307. Tel: (617) 253-3551 Fax: (617) 253-9845 E-mail: ellerman@ mit.edu. Website: http://www.web.mit.edu/ceepr/. Executive Director: A. Denny Ellerman; f. 1977.

Massachusetts Institute of Technology -- *Center for Technology, Policy and Industrial Development*. 77 Massachusetts Avenue, E40-209, Cambridge, MA 02139. Tel: (617) 253-1661 Fax: (617) 258-7733 E-mail: drdr@ mit.edu. Website: http://www.mit.edu. Director: Daniel Roos; f. 1985.

Massachusetts Institute of Technology -- *Defense and Arms Control Studies Program*. 292 Main Street, 6th Floor, Room E38-64, Cambridge, MA 02139. Tel: (617) 253-5265 Fax: (617) 258-7858. Director: Professor Harvey M. Sapolsky; f. 1974; Publications: *DACS Facts Newsletter* (monthly); *Breakthroughs* (biennially); *Post-Soviet Defense Notes* (quarterly).

Michigan State University -- *Center for Urban Affairs*. East Lansing, MI 48824. Tel: (517) 353-9533 Fax: (517) 355-1772 E-mail: dwthornt@msu.edu. Website: http://UAP.MSU.EDU/. Director: Dr. Dozier Thornton; f. 1968.

Mississippi State University -- *Center for Small Town Research and Design*. PO Box AQ, Mississippi State, MS 39762. Tel: (601) 325-2207 Fax: (601) 325-8872 E-mail: shannon@sarc.msstate. edu. Website: http://www.misstate.edu. Director: Shannon Crisis; f. 1979.

Mississippi State University -- *Social Science Research Center (SSRC)*. 103 Res. Boulevard, PO Box 5287, Mississippi State, MS 39762. Tel: (601) 325-7127 Fax: (601) 325-7966 E-mail: acosby@lan.ssrc.msstate.edu. Website: http://www.ssrc.msstate.edu. Director: Dr. Arthur G. Cosby; f. 1950; Publications: *Social Research Report Series*.

Morgan State University -- *Institute for Urban Research*. Cold Spring Lane & Hillen Road, Armory 204, Baltimore, MD 21239. Tel: (410) 319-3004 Fax: (410) 319-3718 E-mail: rhill@ moac.morgan.edu. Director: Dr. Robert B. Hill; f. 1979; Publications: *IUR Research Notes*.

New York University -- *Taub Urban Research Center.* 4 Washington Square North, New York, NY 10003. Tel: (212) 998-7500 Fax: (212) 995-3890. Director: Dr. Mitchell L. Moss; f. 1981; Publications: *Working Paper Series.*

North Carolina State University -- *Center for Urban Affairs and Community Services.* PO Box 7401, Raleigh, NC 27695-7401. Tel: (919) 515-3211 Fax: (919) 515-3642 E-mail: yevonebranon@ncsu.edu. Director: Dr. Yevonne S. Brannon; f. 1966.

Northern Illinois University -- *Center for Governmental Studies.* Dekalb, IL 60115-2854. Tel: (815) 753-1907 Fax: (815) 753-2305. Director: Charles E. Trott; f. 1969; Publications: *City Management in Illinois* (monthly); *Evaluation Forum* (Semiannually); *Illinois GIS and Mapnotes* (annually).

Northwestern University -- *Center for Urban Affairs and Policy Research.* 2040 Sheridan Road, Evanston, IL 60208-4100. Tel: (847) 491-3395 Fax: (846) 491-9916 E-mail: b_weisbrod@nwu.edu. Director: Burton A. Weisbrod; f. 1968; Publications: *Working Paper Series*; *Center Research & Policy Reports*; *Urban Affairs News* (periodically).

Ohio State University -- *National Regulatory Research Institute.* 1080 Carmack Road, Columbus, OH 43210. Tel: (614) 292-9404 Fax: (614) 292-7196 E-mail: jones.1@osu.edu. Website: http://www.nrri,ohio-state.edu. Director: Dr. Douglas N. Jones; f. 1976; Publications: *NRRI Quarterly Bulletin.*

Ohio University -- *Institute for Local Government Administration and Rural Development.* 143 Tech. and Enterprise Building, Athens, OH 45701-2979. Tel: (614) 593-4388 Fax: (614) 593-4398 E-mail: weinberg@ilgard.ilgard. ohiou.edu. Website: http://www.ilgard.ohio.edu. Director: Mark L. Weinberg; f. 1981; Publications: *W.K. Kellogg Training Manuals*; *Employment and Business Opportunities for Low Income Popula-*

tions in SE Ohio; *Educational Access*; *Environmental Regulation.*

Ohio Wesleyan University -- *Ben A. Arneson Institute of Practical Politics & Public Affairs.* Elliot Hall, Delaware, OH 43015. Tel: (614) 368-3934 Fax: (614) 368-3644 E-mail: cfpinkele@ou.edu. Website: http://www.ou.edu. Director: Dr. Carl F. Pinkele; f. 1947.

Oklahoma State University -- *Center for Local Government Technology.* 308 CITD, Stillwater, OK 74078. Tel: (405) 744-6049 Fax: (405) 744-7268. Director: Dr. Michael Hughes; f. 1974.

Pennsylvania State University -- *Institute for Policy Research and Evaluation.* N253 Burrowes Building, University Park, PA 16802. Tel: (814) 865-9561 Fax: (814) 865-3098 E-mail: iqf@psu.edu. Website: http://cac.psu.du/s9c/ipre.html. Director: Dr. Irwin Feller; f. 1964.

Pennsylvania State University at Harrisburg -- *Institute of State and Regional Affairs.* 777 West Harrisburg Pike, Room 310, Middletown, PA 17057-4898. Tel: (717) 948-6178 Fax: (717) 948-6306 E-mail: xvc@psu.edu. Website: http:// www.hbg.psu.edu/PSDC/. Director: Michael T. Behney; f. 1973; Publications: *Pennsylvania Statistical Abstract.*

Portland State University -- *Center for Urban Studies.* PO Box 751-CUS, Portland, OR 97207. Tel: (503) 725-4042 Fax: (503) 725-8480 E-mail: ken@upa .pdx.edu or cus@upa.pdx/edu. Website: http://www.upa.pdx.edu/cus/. President: Kenneth J. Dueker; f. 1966.

Princeton University -- *Center of Domestic and Comparative Policy Studies.* Wilson School of Public and International Affairs, Robertson Hall, Princeton, NJ 08544-1013. Tel: (609) 258-4778 Fax: (609) 258-2649 E-mail: mnd@pucc. Website: http://

www.princeton.edu. Director: Michael N. Danielson; f. 1990.

Providence College -- *Feinstein Institute for Public Service.* Feinstein Academic Center, Providence, RI 02918. Tel: (401) 865-2786 Fax: (401) 865-1206 E-mail: rickbatt@ providence.edu. Website: http:// www.providence.edu/psp/. Director: Dr. Richard M. Battistoni.

Rutgers University -- *Center for Government Service (CGS).* 33 Livingston Avenue, Suite 200, New Brunswick, NJ 08901-1979. Tel: (732) 932-3640 Fax: (732) 932-3586 E-mail: hcoleman@rci.rutgers.edu. Director: Henry A. Coleman; f. 1950; Publications: *The Legislative District Data Book*; *New Jersey Legislative District Data Book.*

Rutgers University -- *Center for Public Interest Polling.* Eagleton Institute of Politics, New Brunswick, NJ 08901. Tel: (908) 828-2210 Fax: (908) 932-1551 E-mail: jballou@ rci.rutgers.edu. Website: http:// www.rci.rutgers.edu/~eaglepol. Director: Janice Ballou; f. 1971.

Rutgers University -- *Center for the American Woman and Politics.* Eagleton Institute of Politics, New Brunswick, NJ 08901. Tel: (908) 932-9384 Fax: (908) 932-6778. Website: http://www.rci.rutgers.edu/~cawp. Acting Director: Debbie Walsh; f. 1971; Publications: *News & Notes.*

Rutgers University -- *Center for Urban Policy Research.* 33 Livingston Avenue, Suite 400, Civic Square, New Brunswick, NJ 08901. Tel: (732) 932-3134 Fax: (732) 932-2363 E-mail: glickman@ ric.rutgers.edu. Website: http://www.policy.rutgers.edu. Director: Norman Glickman; f. 1969; Publications: *Subdivision & Site Plan Handbook*; *America's New Market Geography*; *Microcomputers in Urban Planning & Management.*

Rutgers University -- *Eagleton Institute of Politics.* 90 Clifton Avenue, New Brunswick, NJ 08901. Tel: (908) 828-2210 Fax: (908) 932-6778 E-mail: eagleton@ rci.rutgers.edu. Website: http://www.rcl.rutgers.edu/~eagleton. Director: Ruth Mandel; f. 1956.

Rutgers University -- *Forum for Policy Research.* 401 Cooper Street, Camden, NJ 08102. Tel: (609) 225-6311 Fax: (609) 225-6559 E-mail: ccq@clam.rutgers.edu or fpr@ clam.rutgers.edu. Director: Jay A. Sagler; f. 1979; Publications: *Forum Research Reports.*

St Louis University -- *Center for Urban Programs and Research.* 221 North Grand Boulevard, St Louis, MO 63103. Tel: (314) 977-3934 Fax: (314) 977-3874. Director: Dr. George Dorian Wendel; f. 1968.

San Diego State University -- *Institute of Public and Urban Affairs.*San Diego, CA 92182-4505. Tel: (619) 594-6084 Fax: (619) 594-1165. Director: Louis M. Rea; f. 1957.

San Diego State University -- *Public Administration Center.* PSFA-100, San Diego, CA 92182-0367. Tel: (619) 594-6084 Fax: (619) 594-1165. Operations Manager: Polly S. Von Richeter; f. 1957.

Seton Hall University -- *Center for Public Service.* 400 South Orange Avenue, South Orange, NJ 07079. Tel: (201) 761-9510; Fax: (201) 761-2463 E-mail: melesha@ shu.edu. Director: Dr. Naomi Bailin Wish.

Shippensburg University of Pennsylvania -- *Center for Local and State Government.* Horton Hall - 05, Shippensburg, PA 17257. Tel: (717) 532-1502 Fax: (717) 532-1273 E-mail: mclehm@ark.ship.edu. Director: Mary C. Lehman; f. 1974.

State University of New York -- *Nelson A. Rockefeller Institute of Government.* 411 State Street, Albany, NY 12203. Tel: (518) 443-5522 Fax: (518) 443-5788 E-mail: cooperm @rockinst.org. Website: http://rockinst.org.

Director: Dr. Richard P. Nathan; f. 1982; Publications: *New York State Statistical Yearbook* (annually); *Rockefeller Institute of Government Bulletin* (annually); *Governing the Empire State*; *Modern Governorship Series*.

Syracuse University -- *Center for Policy Research*. 426 Eggers Hall, Syracuse, NY 13244-1090. Tel: (315) 443-3114 Fax: (315) 443-1081 E-mail: tmsmeeding@ maxwell.syr.edu. Website: http:// www.cpr.maxwell.syr.edu. Director: Timothy M. Smeeding; f. 1961; Publications: *Aging Studies Program Series*; *Metropolitan Studies Program Series*; *Income Security Policy Series*; *Cross-National Studies in Aging Series*.

Temple University -- *Center for Study of Federalism*. 1616 Walnut Street, Room 507, Philadelphia, PA 19103. Tel: (215) 204-1480 Fax: (215) 204-7784 E-mail: v2026R@ vm.temple.edu. Director: Daniel J. Elazar; f. 1967; Publications: *Publius*; *The Journal of Federalism* (quarterly); *Covenant Letter*; *Federalism Report*.

Temple University -- *Center for Public Policy*. Gladfelter Hall, 10th Floor, 12th Street and Brooks Mall, Philadelphia, PA 19122. Tel: (215) 204-5156 Fax: (215) 204-7779. Director: Jack Greene; f. 1984; Publications: *IPPS Research Reports* (occasional).

Texas A&M University -- *Center for Presidential Studies*. College Station, TX 77843-4348. Tel: (409) 845-9764 Fax: (409) 862-7953 E-mail:gedwards@tamu.edu. Director: George C. Edwards III; f. 1991.

Texas A&M University -- *Center for Public Leadership Studies*. College Station, TX 77843-4348. Tel: (409) 845-3038 Fax: (409) 847-8924 E-mail: e399av@ polisci.tamu.edu. Director: Dr. Arnold Vedlitz; f. 1993.

Texas A&M University -- *Military Studies Institute*. College Station, TX 77843-4236.

Tel: (409) 845-5336 Fax: (409) 862-4314 E-mail: msi@tamu.edu. Website: http:// www.tamu.edu. Director: Joseph G. Dawson III; f. 1984; Publications: *The Great War 1914-18*; *Commanders in Chief*.

Texas A&M University -- *Public Policy Research Institute*. 314 Bell Building, College Station, TX 77843-4476. Tel: (409) 845-8800 Fax: (409) 845-0249 E-mail: ppri@ tamu.edu. Website: http://www.priweb.tamured. Director: Charles Johnson; f. 1983.

Tufts University -- *Lincoln Filene Center*. Upper Campus Road, Medford, MA 02155. Tel: (617) 627-3453 Fax: (617) 627-3401. Website: http://www.tufts.edu/as/lfc. Director: Patricia M. Barnicle; Publications: *Quest for Funds*.

University at Albany, State University of New York -- *Center for Legislative Development*. 423 State Street, Albany, NY 12203. Tel: (518) 434-0472 Fax: (518) 434-0394 E-mail: cld@cnsvax. albany.edu. Website: http:// www.albany.edu/cld. Director: Dr. Abdo Baaklini; f. 1970.

University at Albany, State University of New York -- *Center for Policy Research*. 300 Milne Hall, 135 Western Avenue, Albany, NY 12222. Tel: (518) 442-3850 Fax: (518) 442-3398 E-mail: jeryl.mumpower@albany.edu. Website: http://www.albany.edu/cpr/. Director: Jeryl L. Mumpower; f. 1986.

University at Albany, State University of New York -- *Center for Technology in Government*. 1400 Washington Avenue, PAC 264, Albany, NY 12222. Tel: (518) 442-3892 Fax: (518) 442-3886 E-mail: info@ ctg.albany.edu. Website: http://www.@ctg. albany.edu. Contact: Dr. Sharon Dawes; f. 1993.

University at Albany, State University of New York -- *Center for the Study of the States*. Nelson A. Rockefeller Institute of Government, 411 State Street, Albany, NY

12203. Tel: (518) 443-5285 Fax: (518) 443-5274 E-mail:boydd@rockinst.org. Website: http://rockinst.org. Contact: Donald J. Boyd; f. 1990; Publications: *State Revenue Reports* (quarterly).

University at Albany, State University of New York -- *Center for Women in Government.* Draper 302 4 DR-302, 135 Western Avenue, Albany, NY 12203. Tel: (518) 442-3896 Fax: (518) 442-3877 E-mail: saidel@cmsibm.albany.edu. Executive Director: Judith R. Saidel; f. 1978; Publications: *Women in Public Service Bulletin*; *News on Women in Government.*

University of Akron -- *Center for Urban Studies.* 225 South Main Street, Polsky Building, Akron, OH 44325-7903. Tel: (330) 972-7616 Fax: (330) 972-6376. Acting Director: Dr. Terry Buss; f. 1965; Publications: *AAJEC Quarterly Reports.*

University of Akron -- *Ray C. Bliss Institute of Applied Politics.* 302 East Buchtel, Akron, OH 44325-1904. Tel: (330) 972-5182 Fax: (330) 972-9579 E-mail: jgreen@ uakemr.edu. Director: John C. Green; f. 1986.

University of Alabama -- *Capstone Poll.* PO Box 870216, Tuscaloosa, AL 35487-0216. Tel: (205) 348-3820 Fax: (205) 348-2849 E-mail: dmcallu@ua1vm.ua.edu. Director: Debra Moehle McCallum; f. 1980.

University of Alabama at Birmingham -- *Center for Urban Affairs.* 901 15th Street South Suite 141, Birmingham, AL 35294-2060. Tel: (205) 934-3500 Fax: (205) 934-0662 E-mail: ucua007@uabdpo.dpo. uab.edu. Website: http://www.uab.edu/cua/. Director: Dr. Robert G. Corley; f. 1969.

University of Arizona -- *Udall Center for Studies in Public Policy.* 803/811 East 1st Street, Tucson, AZ 85719. Tel: (520) 621-7189 Fax: (520) 621-9234 E-mail: udallctr@ ccit.arizona.edu.Website: http://upr.admin.edu/ udalcenter/udallcntr.htm. Director: Robert G.

Varady; Publications: *Initiative*; *Policy Currents* (quarterly).

University of Arkansas at Little Rock -- *UALR Institute of Government.* 2801 South University, Library 502, Little Rock, AR 72204. Tel: (501) 569-8572 Fax: (501) 569-8538 E-mail: rdrobert son@ualr.edu. Director: Dr. Roby Robertson; Publications: *Fiscal Policy in Arkansas.*

University of California at Berkeley -- *Institute of Governmental Studies.* 109 Moses Hall, MC 2370, Berkeley, CA 94720-2370. Tel: (510) 642-1474 Fax: (510) 642-3020. Website: http://www.igs.berkeley.edu: 880801. Director: Professor Nelson W. Polsby; f. 1919; Publications: *Public Affairs Report* (bimonthly).

University of California at Berkeley -- *Institute of Urban and Regional Development (IURD).* 316 Wurster Hall, Berkeley, CA 94720-1870. Tel: (510) 642-4874 Fax: (510) 643-9576 E-mail: jurd@ uclink.berkeley.edu. Website: http://www.ced.berkeley.edu/iurd.edu/ iurd. Director: Judith Innes; f. 1963; Publications: *IURD Universe.*

University of California, Davis -- *Institute of Governmental Affairs.* Davis, CA 95616-8617. Tel: (916) 752-2042 Fax: (916) 752-2835 E-mail: alolmstead@ucdavis.edu. Website: http://polar.ucdavis.edu/igahome.html. Director: Dr. Alan L. Olmstead; f. 1962.

University of Charleston -- *Institute for Public Affairs and Policy Studies.* 66 George Street, Charleston, SC 29424. Tel: (803) 953-5737 Fax: (803) 953-8140 E-mail: felts@cofc.edu. Director: Dr. Arthur A. Felts; f. 1977.

University of Chicago -- *Center for Urban Research and Policy Studies.* 969 East 60th Street, Chicago, IL 60637. Tel: (773) 702-1431 Fax: (773) 702-0874. Director: Professor Lawrence E. Lynn, Jr.; f. 1965; Publications: *CURPS Working Paper Series.*

University of Chicago -- *George J. Stigler Center for the Study of the Economy and the State*. 1101 East 58th Street, Chicago, IL 60637. Tel: (703) 702-7457 Fax: (703) 702-0458 E-mail: fac169@gsbvax.uchicago.edu. Director: Professor Sam Peltzman; f. 1977.

University of Cincinnati -- *Institute for Policy Research*. ML 0132, Cincinnati, OH 45221. Tel: (513) 556-5028 Fax: (513) 556-9023 E-mail: alfred.tuchfarber @uc.edu. Website: http://www.ipr.uc.edu. Director: Dr. Alfred J. Tuchfarber; f. 1971.

University of Colorado at Boulder -- *American Politics Research Center*. 130 Ketchum Building, CB 333, Boulder, CO 80309-033. Tel: (303) 492-2680 Fax: (303) 492-0978. Director: Walter Stone.

University of Colorado at Boulder -- *Colorado Center for Public Policy Research*. 126 Ketchum Building, CB 333, Boulder, CO 80309-0330. Tel: (303) 492-2953 Fax: (303) 492-0978 E-mail: susan.clarke@colorado.edu. Director: Sam Fitch; f. 1960.

University of Colorado at Boulder -- *Program on Political and Economic Change*. Institute of Behavioral Science, CB 487, Boulder, CO 80309. Tel: (303) 492-6404 Fax: (303) 492-3609 E-mail: wonda.umbreit @colorado.edu. Director: Dr. Edward S. Greenberg; f. 1967.

University of Connecticut -- *Institute of Public and Urban Affairs*. Storrs, CT 06269-1106. Tel: (860) 486-4518 Fax: (860) 486-3109 E-mail: mpa@uconnum.uconn.edu. Director: Richard C. Kearney; f. 1963.

University of Connecticut -- *Institute of Public Service*. Bishop Center, U-14, Storrs, CT 06269-4014. Tel: (860) 486-2828 Fax: (860) 486-5221 E-mail: ghill@ irismonarch.ced.uconn.edu. Director: George E. Hill; f. 1944; Publications: *Connecticut Government* (biennially).

University of Delaware -- *Center for Energy and Environmental Policy*. College of Urban Affairs and Public Policy, Newark, DE 19716. Tel: (302) 831-8405 Fax: (302) 831-3098 E-mail: jbbyrne@udel.edu. Website: http://www.ceep. udel.edu. Director: Dr. John M. Byrne; f. 1984.

University of Delaware -- *Delaware Public Administration Institute*. College of Urban Affairs and Public Policy, Graham Hall, Room 180, Newark, DE 19716. Tel: (302) 831-8971 Fax: (302) 831-3587. Director: Jerome R. Lewis; f. 1973; Publications: *Survey of Pay Policies*; *A Guide for Delaware Governments* (biennially).

University of Denver -- *Center for Public Policy and Contemporary Issues*. 2050 East Iliff, Denver CO 80208. Tel: 303 871 3400 Fax: 303 871 3066. Director: Richard D. Lamm; f. 1987.

University of Florida -- *Center for Governmental Responsibility*. College of Law, 230 Bruton-Geer, PO Box 117629, Gainesville, FL 32611-7629. Tel: (352) 392-2237 Fax: (352) 392-1457 E-mail: jlmills@nervm.nerdc. ufl.edu. Website: http://nersp.nerdc.ufl.edu/~lawinfo/ college/cgr/. Director: Jon Mills; f. 1973.

University of Georgia -- *Carl Vinson Institute of Government*. 201 North Milledge, Athens, GA 30602-5482. Tel: (706) 542-2736 Fax: (706) 542-9301 E-mail: mitchell@ igs.cviog.uga.edu. Website: http://www.cviog. uga.edu. Director: Sam Mitchell Jr; f. 1965; Publications: *State and Local Government Review* (3/year); *Teaching Georgia Government Newsletter* (quarterly).

University of Georgia -- *Survey Research Center*. 114 Barrow Hall, Athens, GA 30602. Tel: (706) 542-6110 Fax: (706) 542-4057 E-mail: lwhite@uga.cc.uga.edu. Website: http://www.uga.edu. Director: Dr. Jack K. Martin; f. 1981; Publications: *Handbook of Survey Research Actively Involved in Academic Grant Activities*.

University of Houston: -- *Center for Public Policy*. College of Social Science, Houston, TX 77204-5341. Tel: (713) 743-1000 Fax: (713) 743-3978 E-mail: thorc@uh.edu. Website: http://www.crystal.cpp.uh.edu. Assistant Director: Thor Christensen; f. 1980; Publications: *Houston Economics* (quarterly); *Databook Houston* (monthly).

University of Houston -- *Public Affairs Research Center*. Department of Political Science, 4004 PGH, 4800 Calhoun, Houston, TX 77204-3474. Tel: (713) 743-3909 Fax: (713) 743-3927. Director: Professor Richard Murray; f. 1967.

University of Idaho -- *Bureau of Public Affairs Research*. 202 Administration Building, Moscow, ID 83844-3164. Tel: (208) 885-6563 Fax: (208) 885-8964. Director: Dr. Florence Heffron; f. 1960.

University of Illinois -- *Institute of Government and Public Affairs.* 1007 West Nevada Street, University of Illinois at Urbana-Champaign, Urbana, IL 61801. Tel: (217) 333-3340 Fax: (217) 244-4817 E-mail: j-knott@ igpa.uiuc.edu. Website: http:// www.igpa.uiuc.edu/igpa.htm. Director: Robert F. Rich; f. 1947; Publications: *Policy Forum* (occasionally); *IGPA Working Papers Series* (occasionally); *IGPA Newsletter*.

University of Illinois at Springfield -- *Illinois Legislative Studies Center*. PAC 466, Springfield, IL 62794-9243. Tel: (217) 786-6574 Fax: (217) 786-6542 Free: (800) 252-8533 E-mail: vanderslick.jack@uis.edu. Director: Dr. Jack Van Der Slick; f. 1973; Publications: *Almanac of Illinois Politics*; *Comparative State Politics* (bimonthly); *Illinois Issues*.

University of Illinois at Springfield -- *Institute for Public Affairs*. Springfield, IL 62794-9243. Tel: (217) 786-6576 Fax: (217) 786-6542 E-mail: ford.nancy@uis.edu. Website: http://www.uis.edu/~ipa/ipa. html. Executive Director: Nancy L. Ford; Publications: *Illinois Issues*; *Psychohistory Review*; *Comparative State Politics* (bimonthly).

University of Illinois at Urbana-Champaign -- *Merriam Laboratory for Analytic Political Research*. 512 East Chalmers Street, Champaign, IL 61820. Tel: (217) 244-0739 Fax: (217) 333-4369 E-mail: d-zinnes@ uiuc.edu. Website: http://www.merriam.uius.ed. Director: Dina A. Zinnes; f. 1985; Publications: *Merriam Series in Analytic Political Research*.

University of Iowa -- *Comparative Legislative Research Center*. 334 Schaeffer Hall, Iowa City, IA 52242-1409. Tel: (319) 335-2361 Fax: (319) 335-3211 E-mail: lsq@uiowa.edu. Director: Gerhard Loewenberg; f. 1971; Publications: *Legislative Studies Quarterly*.

University of Kentucky -- *Survey Research Center*. 403 Breckinridge Hall, Lexington, KY 40506. Tel: (606) 257-4684 Fax: (606) 323-1972 E-mail: srcl0l@ukcc.uky.edu. Director: Teri Wood; f. 1979.

University of Louisville -- *Urban Studies Institute* -- Center for Urban and Economic Research. 426 West Bloom Street, Louisville, KY 40208. Tel: (502) 852-6626 Fax: (502) 852-4558 E-mail: usi01@ulky.edu. Director: Dr. John P. Nelson; f. 1966; Publications: *Annual Housing Report for Kentucky*; *Kentucky Elderly Needs Assessment*; *How Many Kentuckians: Population Forecasts*; *Annual Estimates of Poverty for Kentucky Counties*; *Kentucky Household Forecasts*.

University of Louisville -- *Urban Studies Institute* -- Survey and Evaluation Research Unit. 426 West Bloom Street, Louisville, KY 40292. Tel: (502) 852-7952 Fax: (502) 852-4558 E-mail: sjclea01@ulk.edu. Director: John Nelson; f. 1966.

University of Maine -- *Margaret Chase Smith Center for Public Policy*. 5715 Coburn Hall, Orono, ME 04469-5715. Tel: (207) 581-

1645 Fax: (207) 581-1266 E-mail: steve_ballard @voyager. umeres.maine.edu. Contact: Dr. Steve Ballard; Publications: *Maine Policy Review*; *Focus on Public Policy*.

University of Maryland -- *Bureau of Governmental Research.* School of Public Affairs, 2101 Van Munching Hall, College Park, MD 20742. Tel: (301) 405-6330 Fax: (301) 403-4675 E-mail: wbroadnax@puafmail.umd.edu. Director: Walter D. Broadnax; f. 1947; Publications: *Maryland Policy Studies*; *Maryland Profiles*.

University of Maryland -- *Center for Political Leadership and Participation.* 1126 Taliaferro Hall, College Park, MD 20742-6111. Tel: (301) 405-5751 Fax: (301) 405-6402 E-mail: gs4l@umail. umd.edu. Director: Georgia Sorenson; f. 1989; Publications: *Cicicas*; *International Directory of Women Political Leaders*.

University of Maryland at College Park -- *Institute for Governmental Service.* College Park, MD 20742. Tel: (301) 403-4610 Fax: (301) 403-4222 E-mail: bh34@ umail.umd.edu. Director: Barbara S. Hawk; f. 1959; Publications: *Outreach* (5/year); *Maryland Government Report* (annually); *Did You Know?* (occasional).

University of Massachusetts, Boston -- *John W. McCormack Institute of Public Affairs.* 100 Morrissey Boulevard, Boston, MA 02125-3393. Tel: (617) 287-5550 Fax: (617) 287-5544 E-mail: woodbury@ umbsky.cc.umb.edu. Director: Robert L. Woodbury; f. 1983; Publications: *New England Journal of Public Policy* (semiannually).

University of Michigan -- *Center for Political Studies.* 426 Thompson, Ann Arbor, MI 48106-1248. Tel: (313) 763-1347 Fax: (313) 764-3341. Website: http://www.isr.umich.edu/ cps/. Director: Dr. William Zimmerman.

University of Michigan -- *Inter-University Consortium for Political and Social Re-search (ICPSR).* PO Box 1248, Ann Arbor, MI 48106. Tel: (313) 764-2570 Fax: (313) 764-8041 E-mail: icpsrnetmail@um.cc.umich.edu. Website: http://www.icpsr.umich.edu. Executive Director: Dr. Richard D. Rockwell; f. 1962; Publications: *Guide to Resources and Services* (annually); *ICPSR's Bulletin* (quarterly).

University of Michigan -- *Office of Tax Policy Research.* School of Business Administration, 701 Tappan Street, Ann Arbor, MI 48109-1234. Tel: (313) 936-0765 Fax: (313) 763-4032 E-mail: jslemrod@umich.edu. Website: http://www.bus. umich.edu/faculty/ jslemrod.html. Director: Joel Slemrod; Publications: *Tax Research News* (semiannually).

University of Minnesota -- *Center for Urban and Regional Affairs (CURA).* 330 Humphrey Center, 301 19th Avenue South, Minneapolis, MN 55455. Tel: (612) 625-1551 Fax: (612) 626-0273 E-mail: wcraig@atlas.socsci. umn.edu. Website: http:// www. umn.edu/cura. Director: Thomas M. Scott; f. 1968; Publications: *CURA Reporter* (5/year).

University of Minnesota -- *Center on Women and Public Policy.* 301 19th Avenue South, Minneapolis, MN 55455. Tel: (612) 625-3409 Fax: (612) 625-3513 E-mail: skenny@hhh.wmn.edu.Website: http:// www.hhh.umn.edu/centers/wpp/. Director: Sally J. Kenney; Publications: *Women's Watch* (quarterly).

University of Minnesota -- *Hubert H. Humphrey Institute of Public Affairs.* 300 Humphrey Center, 301 19th Avenue South, Minneapolis, MN 55455. Tel: (612) 625-0669 Fax: (612) 625-6351 E-mail: geschuh@ hhh.umn.edu. Website: http:// www.hhh.umn.edu. Dean: G. Edward Schuh; f. 1936.

University of Minnesota -- *Reflective Leadership Center.* Humphrey Institute, Room 55, 301 19th Avenue South, Minneapolis,

MN 55455. Tel: (612) 625-7377 Fax: (612) 625-6351. Director: Sharon Anderson; f. 1981.

University of Nebraska at Omaha -- *Center for Public Affairs Research.* Peter Kiewit Conference Center, Omaha, NE 68182. Tel: (402) 595-2311 Fax: (402) 595-2366 E-mail: rsmith@fa-cpacs.unomaha.edu. Director: Dr. Russell Smith; f. 1966.

University of Nevada, Reno -- *Center for Applied Research.* Reno, NV 89557. Tel: (702) 784-6718 Fax: (702) 784-4506 E-mail: calder@scs. unr.edu. Website: http://www.sab.car.unr.edu. Director: Dr. Judy Calder; f. 1959; Publications: *Nevada Public Affairs Review* (semiannually).

University of New Mexico -- *Division of Government Research (DGR).* 1920 Lomas Boulevard SW, Room 116, Albuquerque, NM 87131-6025. Tel: (505) 277-3305 Fax: (505) 277-6540 E-mail: dgrint@unm.edu.Website: http://www/unm. edu/~dgrint/dgr.html. Director: James W. Davis; f. 1945; Publications: *DGR Review* (occasionally).

University of New Mexico -- *Institute for Applied Research Services.* 1920 Lomas Boulevard NE, Albuquerque, NM 87131. Tel: (505) 277-5934 Fax: (505) 277-7008 E-mail: leezink@unm.edu.Website: http://www.unm.edu/~buslink. Assoc. Vice President: Lee B. Zink; f. 1968; Publications: *NM Business*; *Current Economic Report*; *FOR-UNM*.

University of New Orleans -- *Survey Research Center.* Department of Political Science, New Orleans, LA 70148-2340. Tel: (504) 280-6467 Fax: (504) 280-3838 E-mail: sehpo@uno.edu. Director: Dr. Susan Howell; f. 1985.

University of North Carolina at Chapel Hill -- *Center for Urban and Regional Studies.* Hickerson House, CB 3410, Chapel Hill, NC 27599-3410. Tel: (919) 962-3074 Fax: (919) 962-2518 E-mail: rohe.curs@mhs.unc.edu.

Website: http://www.unc.edu/deptslcurs. Director: William M. Rohe; f. 1957.

University of North Carolina at Chapel Hill -- *Institute of Government.* CB 3330, Knapp Building UNC-CH, Chapel Hill, NC 27599-3330. Tel: (919) 966-5381 Fax: (919) 962-0654. Director: Michael R. Smith; f. 1931; Publications: *Popular Government* (quarterly); *School Law Bulletin* (quarterly).

University of North Carolina at Charlotte -- *Urban Institute.* 9201 University City Boulevard. Charlotte, NC 28223-0001. Tel: (704) 547-2307 Fax: (704) 547-3178 E-mail: wjmccoy@ email.uncc.edu. Website: http://www.coe.uncc.edu/urbinst. Director: William McCoy; f. 1969; Publications: *Research & News.*

University of North Dakota -- *Bureau of Governmental Affairs.* PO Box 7167, Grand Forks, ND 58202-7167. Tel: (701) 777-3041 Fax: (701) 777-3555 E-mail: pynn@ badlands.nodak.edu. Director: Dr. Ronald E. Pynn; f. 1960.

University of North Florida -- *Center for Public Leadership.* 4567 St Johns Bluff Road South, Jacksonville, FL 32224. Tel: (904) 646-2463 Fax: (904) 646-2979 E-mail: jseroka@ gw.unf.edu. Director: Dr. Jim Seroka.

University of Notre Dame -- *Thomas J. White Center on Law and Government.* Notre Dame Law School, Notre Dame, IN 46556. Tel: (219) 631-5913 Fax: (219) 631-6371 E-mail: john.h.robinson.1 @nd.edu. Director: Professor John Robinson; f. 1978; Publications: *Notre Dame Journal of Law, Ethics and Public Policy.*

University of Oklahoma -- *Carl Albert Congressional Research and Studies Center.* 630 Parrington Oval, Room 101, Norman, OK 73019-0375. Tel: (405) 325-6372 Fax: (405) 325-6419 E-mail: rpeters@ou.edu. Website: http://www.ou.edu/special/albertctr/. Director

& Curator: Ronald M. Peters Jr; f. 1979; Publications: *Extensions* (semiannually).

University of Pennsylvania -- *Fels Center of Government.* 3814 Walnut Street, Philadelphia, PA 19104-6197. Tel: (215) 898-8216 Fax: (215) 898-8604 E-mail: johnjm@ upenn.edu. Director: Dr. John J. Mulhern; f. 1954.

University of Rochester -- *Public Policy Analysis Program.* Department of Political Science, Harkness Building 334, Rochester, NY 14627. Tel: (716) 275-2611 Fax: (716) 271-1616 E-mail: dewr@troi.cc.rochester.edu. Website: http://www.rochester.edu/college/ppa. Director: Professor David Weiner; f. 1976; Publications: *Public Policy Analysis Working Papers*.

University of South Carolina at Columbia -- *Institute of Public Affairs.* 1508 Carolina Plaza, Columbia, SC 29208. Tel: (803) 777-8157 Fax: (803) 777-4575 E-mail: dobson@ iopa.sc.edu. Website: http://www.iopa.sc.edu. Director: L. Douglas Dobson; f. 1945; Publications: *South Carolina Policy Forum* (quarterly); *Review of Public Personnel Administration* (ROPPA) (quarterly); *South Carolina Pollution Prevention* (quarterly).

University of South Dakota -- *Governmental Research Bureau.* Vermillion, SD 57069. Tel: (605) 677-5702 Fax: (605) 677-5116 E-mail: sfeimer@sunbird.usd.edu. Website: http://www.usd.edu. Director: Sr. Steven H. Feimer; f. 1939; Publications: *Public Affairs*.

University of Tennessee Knoxville -- *Center for the Study of War and Society.* 220 Hoskins Library, Knoxville, TN 37996-0411. Tel: (423) 974-0128 E-mail: cwjohnso@utk.edu. Director: Dr. Charles Johnson; f. 1987.

University of Texas at Austin -- *Policy Research Institute.* LBJ School of Public Affairs, Drawer Y, University Station, Austin, TX 78713-8925. Tel: (512) 471-4697. Director: Max Sherman; f. 1982.

University of Utah -- *Center for Public Policy and Administration.* 2120 Annex Building, Salt Lake City, UT 84112. Tel: (801) 581-6491 Fax: (801) 585-5489 E-mail: fthebert @cppa.utah.edu. Director: Dr. James J. Gosling; f. 1979.

University of Utah -- *Hinckley Institute of Politics.* 253 Orson Spencer Hall, Salt Lake City, UT 84112. Tel: (801) 581-8501 Fax: (801) 581-6277 E-mail: gadems@ hick.ley.utah.edu. Director: Ted Wilson; f. 1965.

University of Virginia -- *Welden Cooper Center for Public Service.* 918 Emmet Street North, Suite 300, Charlottesville, VA 22903. Tel: (804) 982-5522 Fax: (804) 982-5524 E-mail: ccpsuva@virginia.edu. Website: http://www.virginia.edu/~cpserv. Director: John P. Thomas; f. 1987; Publications: *University of Virginia News Letter* (10/year); *Virginia Statistical Abstract* (biennially).

University of Virginia -- *EARTH 2020: Center for Environmental Policy.* 2020 UVA, 104 Midmont Lane, Charlottesville, VA 22903. Tel: (804) 982-5273 Fax: (804) 982-5297 E-mail: unis@sysm.acs .virginia.edu or gim4f@virginia.edu. Director: George Moein.

University of Virginia -- *Thomas Jefferson Center for Political Economy.* 114 Rouss Hall, Charlottesville, VA 22903. Tel: (804) 924-3179 Fax: (804) 982-2904 E-mail: cah2k@ virginia.edu. Director: Professor Charles Holt; f. 1957.

University of Virginia -- *White Burkett Miller Center of Public Affairs.* PO Box 5106, Charlottesville, VA 22905. Tel: (804) 924-7235 Fax: (804) 982-2739 E-mail: kwt8b@ virginia.edu. Website: http://www.virginia.edu/ ~miller. Director: Dr. Kenneth W. Thompson; f. 1975; Publications: *Miller Center Journal*; *Miller Center Report* (quarterly); *Imprimatur*.

University of Washington -- *Institute for Public Policy and Management.* Parrington Hall, PO Box 353060, Seattle, WA 98195-3060.

Tel: (206) 543-0190 Fax: (206) 616-5764 E-mail: bjnarver@ uwashington.edu. Website: http://www.gspa. washington.edu/ippm/ippmgeneral.html. Director: Betty Jane Narver; f. 1969; Publications: *Washington Policy Choices* (quarterly).

University of Washington -- *Northwest Policy Center.* PO Box 353060, Seattle, WA 98195-3060. Tel: (206) 543-7900 Fax: (206) 616-5769 E-mail: npchox@u.washington.edu. Website: http://weber.u.washington.edu/~npcweb/. Executive Director: Paul Sommers; Publications: *Changing Northwest Newsletter* (quarterly); *Northwest Portrait* (annually).

University of Washington -- *Treaty Research Center.* PO Box 352930, Seattle, WA 98195. Tel: (206) 685-2875 Fax: (206) 616-3152. Director: Professor Edmond Mignon; Publications: *Five-volume World Treaty Index by ABC-Clio Press.*

University of West Florida -- *Whitman Center for Public Service.* Building 50, Room 139, Pensacola, FL 32514. Tel: (904) 474-2367 Fax: (904) 474-2373 E-mail: whitcntr@ uwf.cc.uwf.edu. Website: http://www.uwf.edu/~whitcntr. Director: Dr. C. E. Teasley III; f. 1978.

University of Wisconsin at Madison -- *Institute for Research on Poverty.* Social Science Building, Room 3412, 1180 Observatory Drive, Madison, WI 53706. Tel: (608) 262-6358 Fax: (608) 265-3119. Website: http://www.ssc. wisc.edu/irpl. Director: Professor Barbara L. Wolfe; f. 1966; Publications: *Focus* (3/year).

University of Wisconsin at Madison -- *Robert M. LaFollette Institute of Public Affairs.* 1225 Observatory Drive, Madison, WI 53706. Tel: (608) 262-3581 Fax: (608) 265-3233 Free: (800) 462-7403 E-mail: brcleary@ facstaff.wic.edu. Website: http://www. lafollette.wisc.edu. Contact: Alice Honeywell; f. 1983; Publications: *Policy Report* (biennially); *Public Policy Book Series.*

University of Wisconsin at Madison -- *Urban and Regional Planning Graduate Research Center.* Music Hall, 925 Bascom Mall, Madison, WI 53706. Tel: (608) 262-6851 E-mail: urpllib@ macc.wisc.edu. Librarian: Samina Raja; f. 1965.

University of Wisconsin at Milwaukee -- *Urban Research Center.* Physics Building, Room 450, PO Box 413, Milwaukee, WI 53201. Tel: (414) 229-5916 Fax: (414) 229-3884. Director: Dr. Stephen L. Percy; f. 1974.

University of Wyoming -- *Government Research Bureau.* PO Box 3197, University Station, Laramie, WY 82071. Tel: (307) 766-6484 Fax: (307) 766-6671 E-mail: jking@ uwyo.edu. Director: Professor James King; f. 1970.

Utah State University -- *Institute of Political Economy.* Logan, UT 84322-1597. Tel: (801) 797-2064 Fax: (801) 797-3751 E-mail: cneilsen@hass.usu.edu. Administrative Director: Dr. Roberta Herzberg; f. 1983; Publications: *The Institute Perspective*; *Annual Report.*

Vanderbilt University -- *Center for Health Policy.* 1207 18th Avenue South, Nashville, TN 37212. Tel: (615) 322-0045 Fax: (615) 322-8081. Acting Director: James Blumstein.

Vanderbilt University -- *Center for State and Local Policy.* 1207 18th Avenue South, Nashville, TN 37212. Tel: (615) 322-8524 Fax: (615) 322-8081. Director: May W. Shayne.

Vanderbilt University -- *Institute for Public Policy Studies.* 1207 18th Avenue South, Nashville, TN 37212. Tel: (615) 322-8505 Fax: (615) 322-8081 E-mail: russell@uansvs. vanderbilt. edu. Website: http://www.vanderbilt. edu. Director: Dr. Clifford S. Russell; f. 1975.

Virginia Commonwealth University -- *Center for Public Policy.* 901 West Franklin Street, Box 843016, Richmond, VA 23284-2508. Tel: (804) 828-6837 Fax: (804) 828-6838

E-mail: rholsworth wr@campbell.vcu.edu. Website: http://www.vcu.edu/cppweb/ cpphome.htm/. Executive Director: Dr. Robert Holsworth; f. 1978.

Virginia Commonwealth University -- *Survey Research Laboratory.* 901 West Franklin, Box 3016, Richmond, VA 23284-3016. Tel: (804) 828-8813 Fax: (804) 828-6133 E-mail: jbradfor@saturn.vcu.edu.Website: http://www.vcu.edu/srt. Contact; Dr. Judith Bradford Jr; f. 1982.

Virginia Polytechnic Institute and State University -- *Center for Public Administration and Policy.* The Thomas-Conner House, 104 Draper Road, Mail Stop 0520, Blacksburg, VA 24061. Tel: (540) 231-5133 Fax: (540) 231-7067 E-mail: humpty@ vtvm1.cc.vt.edu; cpcp@vt.edu. Website: http://www.arch.vt.edu/ CAUS/PAintro.html; Director: Dr. James F. Wolf; f. 1977; Publications: *Administration and Society.*

Virginia Polytechnic Institute and State University -- *Center for Urban and Regional Studies.* Architecture Annex, Blacksburg, VA 24061-0113. Tel: (540) 231-5485 Fax: (540) 231-3367 E-mail: knox@ vt.edu. Website: http://www.arch.vt.edu/. Director: Dr. Paul Knox; f. 1966; Publications: *Research Digest Series.*

Washington State University -- *Division of Governmental Studies and Services.* Pullman, WA 99164-4870. Tel: (509) 335-3329 Fax: (509) 335-2362 E-mail: faclovri@ mail.wsu.edu. Website: http://www.wsu.edu: 8080/~Politics/writeups/dgss.htm. Director: Professor Nicholas Lovich Jr; f. 1964.

Wayne State University -- *Center for Arts and Public Policy.* College of Fine, Performing and Communication Arts, 542 Manoogian Hall, Detroit, MI 48202. Tel: (313) 577-2952 Fax: (313) 577-6300 E-mail: bbrock@ cms.cc.wayne.edu. Director: Dr. Bernard L. Brock; f. 1993; Publications: *Journal for the Arts and Public Policy.*

Wayne State University -- *Center for Urban Studies.* Faculty/Administration Building, Room 3040, 656 West Kirby, Detroit, MI 48202. Tel: (313) 577-2208 Fax: (313) 577-1274 E-mail: alobsig@cms.cc.wayne.edu. Website: http://www.cus. wayne.edu. Director: Dr. Diane Brown; f. 1967; Publications: *Detroit Metropolitan Area Public Policy Survey* (DMAPPS); *Special Research Series*; *Urban Centerpiece.*

Western Michigan University -- *Institute of Government and Politics.* Department of Political Science, Kalamazoo, MI 49008-5012. Tel: (616) 387-5696 Fax: (616) 387-3999 E-mail: butterfield@wmich.edu. Website: http://www.wmich.edu /igp. Director: Dr. Jim Butterfield; f. 1979; Publications: *The New Europe and the World*; *Changing Asia*; *Asia Security Issues.*

Williams College -- *Center for Environmental Studies.* Kellogg House, PO Box 632, Williamstown, MA 01267. Tel: (413) 597-2346 Fax: (413) 597-3489 E-mail: kai.n.lee@ williams.edu. Website: http://www.williams.edu: 03/CES/. Director: Dr. Kai N. Lee; f. 1967; Publications: *Journal* (annually).

Think Tanks

Think tanks are independent organizations that engage in politics and public policy. They are distinct from political associations because they are generally not membership organizations and from political science research institutes that are administered under the guidance of a college or university.

Listed below are the most active and influential think tanks in American politics. Where possible, the editors have identified the political leanings of the organization, publications, and current concerns as well as contact information.

Advocacy Institute
1707 L Street NW, Suite 400
Washington, DC 20036
(202) 659-8475
(202) 659-8484 (Fax)
E-mail: ai0001@advinst.org
Co-Directors: David Cohen, Michael Pertschuk and Kathleen Sheekey

f. 1985; a liberal institute that works with domestic and international groups fighting for social and economic justice so that they have the tools they need to develop strong and independent voices.

Publications: *Comprehensive Framework and Analysis of Tobacco Industry Strategies and Tactics*; *Freebates: An Action Guide for States*; *Leadership for a Living Democracy*; and *Toward a Gun-Safe Society: Movement Building Strategies*.

Current Concerns: Campaign finance reform, Challenging free-market Libertarian ideology-Certain Trumpet Program, Civil and human rights, Civil Society: Promoting public interest advocacy, Environment and energy efficiency-Gas Guzzler Campaign; Network for Efficient, Safe and Sustainable Transportation, Gun violence prevention and Smoking Control-Smoking Control Advocacy Resource Center.

American Conservative Union
1007 Cameron Street
Alexandria, VA 22314
(703) 836-8602
(703) 836-8606 (Fax)
E-mail: amconun@itx.netcom.com
Director: Jeff Hollingsworth

f. 1964; directed by a hard-line conservative who engages in lobbying, public education and related activites to advance conservative political ideas and principles.

Publication: *Battle Line* (newsletter).

Current Concerns: Federal Budget and Implementation of the Contract with America.

American Enterprise Institute for Public Policy Research
1150 17th Street NW
Washington, DC 20036
(202) 862-5800

(202) 862-7177
President: Christopher C. DeMuth

f. 1943; less conservative than Heritage with a constellation of big names who seek to preserve the foundations of a free society, limited government, competitive private enterprise, vital cultural and political institutions, and a vigilant defense through vigorous inquiry, debate and writing.

Publications: *The American Enterprise* (bimonthly); *AEI Newsletter* (monthly); *Economic Outlook* (monthly); *Latin American Outlook* (monthly); *On the Issues* (biweekly); *Agricultural Policy Reform in the United States*; *Agricultural Trade Policy: Letting Markets Work*; *American Trade Policy: A Tragedy in the Making*; *The Antitrust Laws*; *Assessing the Enviromental Impact of Farm Policies*; *Attitudes Toward the Environment: Twenty-Five Years After Earth Day*; *Choice and Efficiency in Food Safety Policy*; *CIA Estimates of Soviet Military Expenditures: Errors and Waste*; *The Corporation and the Constitution*; *The Dangerous Drift to Preferential Trade Agreements*; *Deregulating Freight Transportation*; *Distributional Analysis of Tax Policy*; *The Economics of Crop Insurance and Disaster Aid*; *The Effects of Credit Policies on US Agricultural*; *The Fiscal Revolution in America: Hoover to Clinton*; *The Foreign Investment Debate: Opening Markets Abroad or Closing Markets at Home?*; *The Germans: Portrait of a New Nation*; *Health Care Choices*; *Private Contracts as Instruments of Health Reform*; *Industrial Policy and Semiconductors: Missing the Target*; *Making Science Pay: The Economics of Agricultural R & D Policy*; *The Neoconservative Imagination: Essays in Honor of Irving Kristol*; *The New Illustrated Guide to the American Economy*; *On Character*; *On the Other Hand...Essays on Economics*; *Economists and Politics*; *Reforming Agricultural Commodity Policy*; *Toward a More Perfect Union: Writings of Herbert J. Storing*; *Transmission Prising and Stranded Costs in Electric Power Industry*; *The Tyranny of Numbers: Mismeasurement and Misrule*; and *The Vaccines for Children Program: A Critique*.

Current Concerns: Economic policy studies: Financial markets, Fiscal and monetary policy, Health policy, International trade and finance, Regulation, Telecommunications policy, Foreign and Defense policy: Area studies, Asian studies, Defense and arms control, US foreign policy, Social and political studies: Education, Culture and Religion, Law and Constitution, Politics, Social and individual responsibility.

American Legislative Exchange Council
910 17th Street NW, 5th Floor
Washington, DC 20006
(202) 466-3800
(202) 466-3801 (Fax)
Director: Daniel B. Denning

f. 1973; a conservative institute which seeks to develop dynamic partnerships between state legislators and the private sector in order to advance a public policy agenda based on the Jeffersonian principles of free markets, limited government, individuals liberties and traditional family values...To help members create effective, innovative public policies which promote free enterprise, spur economic growth, encourage individual responsibility and independence and enhance the nation's competitiveness in the global marketplace.

Publications: *ALEC Forum* (occasional); *FYI* (biweekly); *The State Factor* (occasional); *Issue Analysis* (occasional); *Legislative Issue Briefs* (occasional); *Breaking the Chain: From Dependency to Opportunity*; *The Crisis in America's State Budgets*; *Environmental Partners*; *Evidence of a Failed System: A Study of Pretrial Release Agreements in California*; *Expanding Transit Service through Regulatory Mechanisms*; *Keeping the Promise: A Comprehensive Health Care Plan for the States*; *People*;

Markets and Government: How Economic Policy Creates Wealth Reform and Workers' Compensation; Public-Private Partnerships in Transportation Infrastructure; Report Card on American Education; Report Card on Crime and Punishment; The Sourcebook of American State Legislation and Sovereignty of the People and Devolution: An Agenda for the Restoration of the Tenth Amendment.

Current Concerns: Bail reform, Balanced budget amendment, Capital gains tax, Clean air and water strategies, Curriculum reform, Education finance, Enterprise zones, Environment regulations, Free-market health care, Insurance fraud, International competitiveness, Interstate banking, Job training, Labor market reform, Low-Income housing, Medicare reform, Prison privatization, Privatization of public housing, Product liability, Punitive damages, Rent control, State rights, School vouchers, Striker replacement, Regulations and taxes on business, Telecommunications regulations, Tourism, Trade, tariffs and quotas, Transportation, Truth in sentencing, Tort reform, Victims' rights, Welfare reform and Workers' compensation.

Americans Back in Charge Foundation/ Term Limits Legal Institute

900 Second Street NE, Suite 200A
Washington, DC 20002
(202) 371-0450
(202) 371-0210
E-mail: 72242.651@compuserve.com
Director: Cleta Deatherage Mitchell

f. 1991; a right of center institute which seeks to provide research, education and legal services in the effort to limit terms for all members of Congress.

Publications: *A Survey of Voter Attitudes: Term Limits and Taking Congress off Welfare: The Perks, Pay and Pensions of the Welfare System for Congress.*

Current Concerns: Term limits for members of Congress.

Americans for Democratic Action

1625 K Street NW, Suite 210
Washington, DC 20006
(202) 785-5980
(202) 785-5969
E-mail: adaction@ix.netcom.com
Director: Amy Isaacs

f. 1947; has been called the "Conscience of the Democratic Party" which reflects the New Deal legacy as well as the insurgent liberalism of Robert F. Kennedy Jr. seeking to promote liberal domestic and foreign policy to serve the real and changing needs of American Democracy.

Publications: *Annual Voting Record; a Ratings of Members of Congress on a Liberal Scale; ADA Today* and *ADAction News and Notes* (weekly when Congress is in session).

Current Concerns: Foreign policy, Health care, Military policy, Minimum wage and Women's issues.

The Brookings Institution

1775 Massachusetts Avenue NW
Washington, DC 20036
(202) 797-6000
(202) 797-2604 (Fax)
E-mail: in%"brookinfo@brook.edu
Director: Michael H. Armacost

f. 1916; the granddaddy of all think tanks with a reputation for being a liberal institution but which is actually moderate, seeking to improve the performance of American institutions, the effectiveness of government programs and the quality of US public policies.

Publications: *The Brookings Review* (quarterly); *Brookings Papers on Economic Activity* (semiannual); *Microeconomics* (annual); *The Brookings Newsletter* (quarterly); *The Disappearing American Voter; Ethics in Congress: From Individual to Institutional Corruption; The Federal Budget: Politics; Policy; Process; Fine Print: The Contract with America; Devolution; and Administrative Realities of American Federalism; Inside the Reinvention Machine: Appraising Government Reform; Media Polls in American Politics; The Presidency in a Separate System and Reviving the American Dream.*

Current Concerns: Arms control, Balanced budget amendments, Campaigns and elections, Conflict resolution, Congressional reform, Corporate governance, Crime, Defense spending, Education reforms, Environmental sustainability, Federal tax policy, Federalism and devolution, Global economic integration, Government downsizing, Health care, Housing, Income distribution, Infrastructure, International trade, Latin America, Middle East, National security, Politics and the media, Productivity, Regulatory policy, Telecommunications reform, Urban social policy, US-China relations, US living standards and Welfare reform.

Cato Institute
1000 Massachusetts Avenue NW
Washington, DC 20001
(202) 842-0200
(202) 842-3490 (Fax)
E-mail: cato@cato.org
President: Edward H. Crane

f. 1977; roots are solidly libertarian, an outgrowth of Ayn Rand's philosophy which is too radical for Republicans, seeking to increase the understanding of public policies based on the principles of limited government, free markets, individual liberty and peace.

Publications: *Briefing Papers* (3 issues a year); *Cato Journal* (3 issues a year); *Foreign Policy Briefings* (5 issues a year); *Policy Analysis* (12-15 issues a year); *Regulation* (4 issues a year); *Cato Policy Report* (bimonthly); *Cato Handbook for Congress; The Government Factor: Undermining Journalistic Ethics in the Information Age and The Politics and Law of Term Limits.*

Current Concerns: Corporate welfare, Defense spending, Deregulation, Regulatory reform, Environmental reform, Health care reform, Income tax abolition, Privatization, Social Security reform and Term limits.

Center for National Policy
1 Massachusetts Avenue NW, Suite 333
Washington, DC 20001
(202) 682-1800
(202) 682-1818 (Fax)
E-mail: cnp@access.digex.net
President: Maureen S. Steinbruner

f. 1981; a Democratic Hamiltonian institute dedicated to developing better understanding about major issues confronting the nation.

Publications: *Center for National Policy* (quarterly); *America Tomorrow: The Choices We Make; Giving Children A Chance: The Case for More Effective National Policies; Montana: Steady State in Transition; Regulating for the Future: The Creative Balance; Regulating the New Financial Services Industry and US Agriculture: Myth, Reality and National Policy;*

Current Concerns: Domestic and foreign policy, Foreign assistance, Political process, US economy.

Center for Policy Alternatives
1875 Connecticut Avenue NW, Suite 710
Washington, DC 20009

(202) 387-6030
(202) 986-2539 (Fax)
E-mail: cfpa@capaccess.org
President: Linda Tarr-Whelan

f. 1975; US counterpart to the Fabian Society exposing the left-of-center Social Democratic philosophy which promotes pragmatic public policy change that supports families, strengthens communities, conserves resources for future generations and enhances participation by every citizen.

Publications: *Alternatives* (10 issues yearly); *State Reports on Citizen Participation* (biannual); *Alternative Balloting Strategies; Environmental Justice: Legislation in the States; Freebates: An Action Guide for States; Implementation of the National Voter Registration Act: A Status Report; Law-Making under the GATT: A Guide to Help Legislators Cope with Trade Agreements; Motor Voter: An Overview of its Implementation and Impact on Registration; State Progress Toward Sustainable Development; State Report on Reproductive Choice; Telecommunications Ideas that Work and Women and Political Vitality Map.*

Current Concerns: Citizen participation, Community development, Economic development, Election law reform, Employment policy, Environmental awareness, Family and work, Financial deregulation, Government reform, Health care, Housing, Impact of GATT and NAFTA on states, Investment of employment pension funds, Leadership development, Reproductive rights, Resource conservation, Rural development, Waste prevention, Sustainable development, Tax reform, Telecommunications, Trade issues, Unemployment and underemployment, Voter registration andWomen's economic issues.

Center for Public Integrity
1634 I Street NW, Suite 902
Washington, DC 20006

(202) 783-3900
(202) 783-3906 (Fax)
E-mail: ctrforpi@essential.org
Director: Charles Lewis

f. 1989; non-partisan institute seeking to make certain that issues become known to the public and to journalists, resulting in informed, educated discourse on policy decisions and American public holding officials on all levels accountable for their actions.

Publications: *The Public i* (occasional); *Beyond the Hill: Where Have all the Members Gone?; For Their Eyes Only: How Presidential Appointees Treat Public Documents as Their Personal Property; Private Parties: Political Party Leadership in Washington's Mercenary Culture; Saving for a Rainy Day II: How Congress Spends Leftover Campaign Cash; Short Changed: How Congress and Special Interest Benefit at the Expense of American People; Under the Influence: Presidential Candidates and their Campaign Advisors and Well-Healed: Lobbying for the Health Care Reform.*

Current Concern: Influence of special interests on decision-making process and in election of public officials.

Center for Responsive Politics
1320 19th Street NW
Washington, DC 20036
(202) 857-0044
(202) 857-7809 (Fax)
E-mail: info@crp.org
Director: Ellen S. Miller

f. 1983; officially nonpartisan (espouses liberal causes) institution seeking to study Congress, particularly the role money plays in its elections and actions, aimed at creating a more involved citizenry and more responsive Congress.

Publications: *Capital Eye* (bimonthly); *Beyond the 30-Seond Spot: Enhancing the Media's Role in Congressional Campaigns; Campaign Spending Out of Control; Follow the Money Handbook; Open Secrets: The Encyclopedia of Congressional Money and Politics; PACs in Profile; PACs on PACs: The View from the Inside; The Role of Mail in Decision Making in Congress; The Role of Politicians in Public Charities; Spending in Congressional Elections: A Never-Ending Spiral and The Wealth Primary: Campaign Fundraising and the Constitution.*

Current Concerns: Campaign finance, Congressional ethics, Congressional structure and operations and Effect of political money on public policy.

Center on Budget and Policy Priorities
777 North Capitol Street NW, Suite 705
Washington, DC 20002
(202) 408-1080
(202) 408-1056 (Fax)
President: Robert Greenstein

f. 1981; a liberal institution seeking to analyze the impact of fiscal policy and programs on the welfare of low- and middle-income families and to assess budgetary priorities.

Publication: *WIC Newsletter.*

Current Concerns: Federal and state fiscal and tax policies, Defense budgets, Tax benefits and entitlements, Food and nutrition, Housing , Welfare reform and Income distribution.

Christian Coalition
1801 Sara Drive, Suite L
Chesapeake, VA 23320
(804) 424-2630
(804) 420-1077 (Fax)
or
227 Massachusetts Avenue NE, Suite 1001

Washington, DC 20002
(202) 547-3600
(202) 543-2978 (Fax)
Director: Randy Tate

f. 1989; the most articulate institute for the Religious Right which seeks to educate people of faith about issues that impact families.

Publications: *Christian American* (10 issues yearly); *Religious Rights Watch* (monthly); *Christian Coalition Congressional Scorecard and Contract with the American Family.*

Current Concerns: Choice in education, Defending the unborn, Family tax relief, Freedom of religious expression, Term limits and Voluntary prayer in schools.

Citizens' Research Foundation
3716 South Hope Street
Los Angeles, CA 90007
(213) 743-2303
(213) 743-2110 (Fax)
Director: Herbert E. Alexander

f. 1958; a nonpartisan institution seeking to study the role of money in the political process, serving as a nonpartisan observer and interpreter of trends in political finance and election reform.

Publications: *Political Moneyline* (quarterly); *Financing the 1996 Election and Political Orientation: Nonpartisan.*

Current Concern: Campaign finance reform.

Common Cause
2030 M Street NW
Washington, DC 20036
(202) 833-1200
(202) 659-3716 (Fax)
President: Ann McBride

f. 1970; a liberal citizens' lobby dedicated to increasing government accountability and improving government performance.

Publications: *Common Cause Magazine* (quarterly); *Assembly-Line Approval: A Common Cause Study of Senate Confirmation of Federal Judges; Campaign Finance Reform: The Unfinished Agenda; Common Cause Manual of Money and Politics; The Failure-To-Enforce Commission: A Common Cause Study of the FEC; Missing Money: A Common Cause Study of Federal Tax Expenditures; A Plague on Both their Houses and Robber Barons of the 90s: A Study of Political Contributions from the Telecommunications Industry.*

Current Concerns: Term-limits, Campaign Finance Reform, Tax Collection and IRS Reform.

Concord Coalition
Washington, DC 20036
(202) 467-6222
(202) 467-6333 (Fax)
E-mail: debthawk@ix.netcom.com
Director: Martha Phillips

f. 1992; a nonpartisan institute seeking to eliminate chronic federal budget deficits and build a sound economy for current and future generations.

Publications: *The Concord Courier* (quarterly); *Debt Busters; Facing Facts Fax Alert; The Fact About Pensions and Zero Deficit Plan.*

Current Concerns: Creating a strong economy, Eliminating chronic federal budget deficits and Reforming entitlement spending.

Congressional Management Foundation
513 Capitol Court NE, Suite 100
Washington, DC 20002
(202) 546-0100
(202) 547-0936 (Fax)
Director: Richard Shapiro

f. 1977; a nonpartisan institute seeking to enhance the efficiency and effectiveness of Congress by improving its management practices.

Publications: *Congressional Intern Handbook; House of Representatives Employment Practices; US Senate Employment Practices; Politicians and their Spouses' Careers; Setting Course: A Congressional Management Guide* and *Working in Congress: The Staff Perspective.*

Current Concerns: Congressional ethics, Congressional staff employment trends, Management training of congressional staff and Strategic planning.

Empower America
1776 I Street NW, Suite 890
Washington, DC 20006
(202) 452-8200
(202) 296-8679 (Fax)
Director: Charles M. Kupperman

f. 1993; a Republican institute seeking to promote progressive conservative public policies at both the state and national level, based on the principles of economic growth, international leadership and cultural renewal.

Publications: *EA Ideas* (bimonthly); *Highlights* (quarterly); and *Policy Papers.*

Current Concerns: Abolition of the Department of Education, Crime, Drug policy, Illegitimacy, Legal reform, Immigration, Popular culture, School choice and Flat Tax.

Ethics and Public Policy Center

1015 15th Street NW, Suite 900
Washington, DC 20005
(202) 682-1200
(202) 408-0682 (Fax)
E-mail: eppc@aol.com
President: George Weigel

f. 1976; a religious conservative institute (not part of religious right) seeking to clarify and to reinforce the bond between the Judeo-Christian moral tradition and the public debate over domestic and foreign policy issues.

Publications: *American Character* (quarterly); *American Purpose* (quarterly); *American Jews and the Separationist Faith: The New Debate on Religion in Public Life; Benchmarks: Great Constitutional Controversies in the Supreme Court; Building the Free Society; Democracy; Capitalism and Catholic Social Teaching; Capturing the Culture: Film; Art and Politics; Creation at Risk? Religion; Science and Environmentalism; Disciples and Democracy: Religious Conservatives and the Future of American Politics; 1492 and All That: Political Manipulations of History; The Nine Lives of Population Control; Reinventing the American People; Unity and Diversity Today and Religious Liberty in the Supreme Court.*

Current Concerns: Abortion, American citizenship and identity, Catholic social doctrine, Euthanasia, First Amendment religion clause, Religious right and Human rights with special reference to religious freedom.

Free Congress Foundation

717 2nd Street NE
Washington, DC 20002
(202) 546-3000
(202) 543-8425 (Fax)
E-mail: http://www.net.fcref.org
President: Paul M.Weyrich

f. 1977; a coalition of grassroots conservative groups which are dedicated to conservative governance, traditional values and institutional reform.

Publications: *Empowerment* (occasional); *Essays on Our Times* (occasional); *Judicial Selection Monitor* (monthly); *New Electric Railway Journal* (quarterly); *Policy Insights* (occasional); *The Anti-Defamation League's Campaign of Defamation; Beyond Judicial Activism and Judge Stephen Breyer and the Search for Judicial Philosophy.*

Current Concerns: Conservative governance, Cultural conservatism, Law and democracy, Social policy, State policy and Runs National Empowerment Television, a 24-hour cable network.

The Heritage Foundation

214 Massachusetts Avenue SE
Washington, DC 20002
(202) 546-4400
(202) 546-8328 (fax)
Website: http://www.heritage.org
President: Edwin J. Feulner, Jr.

f. 1973; a bastion of conservative thought seeking to formulate and promote public policies based on the conservative principles of free enterprise, limited government, individual freedom, traditional American values and a strong national defense.

Publications: *Heritage Members News* (bimonthly); *Heritage Today* (bimonthly); *Reforming Congress* (monthly); *Policy Review* (bimonthly); *Guide to Public Policy Experts* (annual); *Backgrounder* (occasional); *Backgrounder Update* (occasional); *Committee Briefs* (occasional transcripts when Congress is in session); *Critical Issues* (short monographs); *Executive Memorandum; Talking Points; Issue Bulletin; America's Failed $4 Trillion War on Poverty; Freeing America's Farmers: The Heritage Plan for*

Rural Prosperity; The Index of Economic Freedom; Rolling Back Government: A Budget Plan to Rebuild America and The Ruling Class; Inside the Imperial Congress.

Current Concerns: Asia, Budget and tax policies, Deregulation, Education reform, Entitlements , Federalism, Foreign aid, Health care, Missile defenses, National security budget, Post-Cold War strategy, Russia, Tele-communications reform, Trade, United Nations and Welfare reform.

Hoover Institution on War, Revolution and Peace
Stanford, CA 94305
(415) 723-1754
(415) 723-1687 (Fax)
President: John Raisian

f. 1919; a conservative institute seeking to impact knowledge and understanding of the complex and evolving world, and to offer one of the principal archival and library holdings on social, economic and political change in the 20th century.

Publications: *The Hoover Letter* (quarterly); *Hoover Series on Public Policy; Can Congress be Fixed?; Economics in Action; The Flat Tax and How Republicans Captured the House.*

Current Concerns: Democracy and free markets, American institutions and economic performance and International rivalries and global cooperation.

The Independent Institute
134 98th Avenue
Oakland, CA 94603
(510) 632-1366
(510) 568-6040 (Fax)
E-mail: Independ@dnai.com
President: David J. Theroux

f. 1986; a nonpartisan institute with heavy conservative overtones that seeks to produce and widely disseminate comprehensive, nonpoliticized studies of the origins and solutions to critical economic and social problems, and conduct numerous conferences and media programs based on this work.

Publications: *The Independent* (quarterly); *The Independent Review* (quarterly); *Independent Policy Reports* (quarterly); *Independent Briefings* (occasional); *The Academy in Crisis; Agriculture and the State; American Health Care; Antitrust and Monopoly; Arms; Politics and the Economy; Beyond Politics; The Diversity Myth; Freedom; Feminism and the State; The Melting Pot: Immigration Myths and Realities; Money and the Nation State; Out of Work: Unemployment and Government; Private Prisons; Private Rights and Public Illusions; Regulation and the Reagan Era; Taxing Liberty: Predatory Politics and Taxation; That Every Man Be Armed; Toxic Liability; The Voluntary City and Writing Off Ideas: Taxation and Philanthropy.*

Current Concerns: Agriculture, Antitrust competition, Banking/Finance regulation, Civil liberties, Constitutional law and federalism, Criminal justice, Defense spending and procurement, Drugs, Economic development, Education, Energy, Environment and natural resources, Family and children, Government spending, Healthcare, Immigration, Insurance regulation, International trade, Land use, Legal liability, Privatization, Regulation and deregulation, Taxation, Telecommunications, Transportation, Unemployment and labor, Urban issues and Women's rights.

Institute for Policy Studies
1601 Connecticut Avenue NW, 5th Floor
Washington, DC 20009
(202) 234-9382
(202) 387-7915 (Fax)

E-mail: irss@apc.org
Co-Directors: John Cavanagh and Michael Shuman

f. 1963; the liberal counterpart to Cato Institute which seeks to serve as an independent center of thought, action and social invention in the exploration of alternate directions to achieving real security, economic justice and grassroots political participation of citizens in the life of the nation.

Publications: *Counterpunch* (22 issues yearly); *FASTNet; Sustainable Communities Journal* (quarterly); *State of the Union* (annual); *Trading Freedom: How Free Trade Affects Our Lives, Work and Environment* and *Who Pays? Who Profits? The Truth About the American Tax System.*

Current Concerns: National security, Political reform to curb the influence of money, Sustainable communities, Sustainable jobs and Technology policy.

Joint Center for Political and Economic Studies
1090 Vermont Avenue NW, Suite 1100
Washington, DC 20005
(202) 789-3500
(202) 789-6390 (Fax)
E-mail: jointctr@capcon.net
President: Eddie N. Williams

f. 1970; a liberal institute seeking to improve the socioeconomic status of black Americans by expanding their effective participation in the political and public policy arenas, and promote communications and relationships across racial and ethnic lines to strengthen the nation's pluralistic society.

Publications: *Focus* (monthly); *Black Elected Officials: A National Roster; The Declining Economic Status of Black Children; Economic Perspectives on Affirmative Action;*

Minorities and Privatization: Economic Mobility at Risk; Poverty; Inequality and the Crisis of Social Policy; Visions of a Better Way: A Black Appraisal of Public Schooling; Voting Rights in America: Continuing the Quest for Full Participation and *Who Defends America? Race, Sex and Class in the Armed Forces.*

Current Concerns: Africa, Black economic status , Black family issues, Black voter participation and registration, Civil rights, Drug abuse, Education, Employment, Minority set-asides and Welfare and poverty.

The League of Women Voters of the United States
1730 M Street NW, 10th Floor
Washington, DC 20036
(202) 429-1965
(202) 429-0854 (Fax)
E-mail: lwv@lwv.org
President: Carolyn Jefferson-Jenkins

f. 1920; officially a nonpartisan institute encouraging the informed and active participation of citizens in government and influencing public policy through education and advocacy.

Publications: *The National Voter* (quarterly); *CARE Package: Tools for Citizen Action on Health Care; Focus on the Voter: Lessons from the 1992 Election; Expanding School-Age Child Care: A Community Action Guide; Fighting Hunger: A Guide to Development of Community Actions Projects; Getting the Most out of Debates; Impact on Congress; A Grassroots Lobbying Handbook for Local League Activists; Impact on Issues; Public Policy on Reproductive Choice: A Community Action Guide; Reaching for the American Dream: Economic Policy for the Future; Talking Trash: A Citizen Education Guide; Tell it to Washington; 10 Steps to a Successful Registration Drive* and *Understanding Economic Policy: A Citizen's Handbook.*

Current Concerns: Campaign finance reform, Children's welfare, Environmental issues, Gun control, Health care and Voter registration and participation.

Manhattan Institute for Policy Research

52 Vanderbilt Avenue
New York, NY 10017
(212) 599-7000
(212) 599-3494 (Fax)
President: Lawrence Mone

f. 1977; a conservative institute seeking to develop and encourage public policies at all levels of government, which will allow individuals the greatest scope for achieving their potential, both as participants in a productive economy and as members of a functioning society.

Publication: *City Journal* (quarterly).

Current Concerns: Civil justice reform, Education, Immigration, Social welfare policy, Tax policy, Telecommunications and Urban policy.

National Center for Policy Analysis

North Central Plaza, 12655 North Central Expressway, Suite 720
Dallas, TX 75243
(214) 386-6272
(214) 386-0924 (Fax)
President: John C. Goodman

f. 1983; a libertarian institute seeking to discover and promote private alternatives to government regulation and control, solving problems by relying on the strengths of the competitive, entrepreneurial private sector.

Publications: *Executive Alert* (bimonthly) and 10 to 12 reports per year.

Current Concerns: Health care, Tax policy and Environment.

National Women's Political Caucus

1211 Connecticut Avenue NW, Suite 425
Washington, DC 20036
(202) 785-1100
(202) 785-3605 (Fax)
Director: Ruth Pagani

f. 1971; officially nonpartisan institute dedicated to increasing the number of women in elected and appointed office at all levels of government, regardless of party affiliation.

Publications: *Women's Political Times* (quarterly); *Candidate Lists; Directory of Women Elected Officials* (biennial); *Factsheet on Women's Political Progress* (biennial) and *Special Election Reports.*

Current Concern: Number of women in elective office.

Pacific Research Institute for Public Policy

755 Sansome Street, Suite 450
San Francisco, CA 94111
(415) 989-0833
(415) 989-2411 (Fax)
E-mail: PRIPP@aol.com
President: Sally C. Pipes

f. 1979; a conservative institute seeking to promote the principles of individual freedom and personal responsibility which are best encouraged through policies that emphasize a free economy, private initiative and limited government.

Publications: *A Message from the President* (quarterly); *Angry Classrooms; Vacant Minds: What's Happened to our High Schools; Crisis and Leviathan: Critical Episodes in the Growth of American Government; Environmental Gore: A Constructive Response to Earth in the Balance; Freedom; Technology and the First Amendment; Free Market Environmentalism; Grand Theft and Petit Larceny: Property Rights in America; How to Start a Charter School; Index of*

Leading Environmental Indicators; Privatization and Local Government; Sovereign Nations or Reservations: An Economic History of American Indians; Unfinished Business: A Civil Rights Strategy for America's Third Century and What Everyone Should Know About Economics and Prosperity.

Current Concerns: Civil rights, Education, Environment, Health care reform, Legal reform, Privatization and Urban studies.

Political Economy Research Center
502 South 19th Avenue, Suite 211
Bozeman, MT 59715
(406) 587-9591
(406) 586-7555 (Fax)
E-mail: perc@perc.org
Director: Terry L. Anderson

f. 1980; a conservative opposition to environmentalism which seeks to promote a realistic alternative approach to solve environmental and resource allocation problems, one characterized by less government and more reliance on private property rights and individual incentives.

Publications: *PERC Reports* (quarterly); *PERC Policy Series* (quarterly); *The Political Economy Forum series; Enviro-capitalists and Eco-sanity: A Commonsense Guide to Environmentalism.*

Current Concerns: Free-market environmentalism, Global warming, Hazardous waste, Indian Reservation economies, Land use, Privatization and Water marketing.

Progress and Freedom Foundation
1301 K Street West, Suite 650
Washington, DC 20005
(202) 289-8928
(202) 289-6079 (Fax)

E-mail: mail@pff.org
President: Jeffrey A. Eisenach

f. 1993; a futuristic conservative organization dedicated to creating a positive vision of the future founded in the historical principles of the American Ideal.

Publications: none.

Current Concerns: American Politics, Energy, Federal budget, Government reform, Housing and urban issues, Medical innovation, Telecommunications and Welfare reform.

Progressive Policy Institute
318 C Street NE
Washington, DC 20002
(202) 547-0001
(202) 544-5014 (Fax)
E-mail: inmfo@dlcppi.org
President: William Marshall III

f. 1989; a centrist think tank formerly associated with President Clinton which seeks to adapt America's progressive tradition of individual liberty, equal opportunity and civic enterprise to the challenges of the post-industrial era.

Publication: *The New Democrat* (bimonthly).

Current Concerns: Affirmative Action, Economic/Budgetary issues, Political reform and Welfare reform.

Project Vote Smart/Center for National Independence in Politics
129 NW 4th Street, Suite 204
Corvallis, OR 97330
(541) 754-2746
(541) 754-2747 (Fax)
E-mail: commments@vote-smart.org
Director: Richard Kimball

f. 1988; a nonpartisan institute seeking to give all citizens free, instant access to abundant factual information about candidates and elected officials.

Publications: *Tomorrow's News* (quarterly); *The Reporter's Sourcebook; US Government: Owner's Manual* and *Voter's Self-Defense Manual.*

Current Concern: Elections and candidates.

Public Citizen, Inc
1600 20th Street NW
Washington, DC 20009
(202) 588-1000
E-mail: http://www.esential.org
President: John B. Claybrook

f. 1971; a liberal institute which seeks to fight for government and corporate accountability, consumer rights in the marketplace, safe products, a healthy environment, fair trade, and clean and safe energy sources through lobbying, research, public outreach and litigation.

Publications: *Health Letter; Public Citizen Magazine; Worst Pills, Best Pills News; The Green Buyer's Car Guide; Questionable Doctors* and *Women's Health Alert.*

Current Concerns: Auto safety, Campaign finance reform, Citizen empowerment, Clean and safe energy sources, Consumer rights, Corporate and government accountability, Drug and food safety, Environment, Fair trade practices, Freedom of information, Health care delivery, Healthful environment and workplace, Insurance reform, Nuclear safety, Occupational health, Pesticide regulatory reform, Product liability, Regulatory reform and Safe products.

Reason Foundation
3415 South Sepulveda Boulevard, Suite 400
Los Angeles, CA 90034

(310) 391-2245
(310) 391-4395 (Fax)
E-mail: reason-r@netcom.com
President: Robert W. Poole Jr.

f. 1978; a libertarian institute seeking to support the rule of law, private property and limited government protecting prosperity and act as a check against encroachments on liberty.

Publications: *Reason* (monthly); *Privatization Watch* (monthly); *Guidelines for Airport Privatization; Health and Social Service in the Post-Welfare State: Are Vouchers the Answer?; Intergovernmental Contracting for Public Services; Revolution at the Roots: Making our Government Smaller; Better and Closer to Home; Rightsizing Government: Lessons from America's Public Sector Innovators; State Voucher Programs in the United States* and *State Privatization Handbook.*

Current Concerns: Devolution, Education, Environment, Infrastructure and Privatization.

The Rockford Institute
934 North Main Street
Rockford, IL 61072
(815) 964-5053
(815) 965-1826 (Fax)
E-mail: therockfordinstitute@bossnt.com
President: Allan C. Carlson

f. 1976; a far-right conservative institute seeking the promotion of liberty, the defense of natural family, the affirmation of Scriptural truth, the promotion of self-reliance and decentralization in politics and economics striving for the renewal of Christendom in this time and place.

Publications: *Chronicles: A Magazine of American Culture* (monthly); *The Family in America* (monthly); *The Religion & Society Report* (monthy); *Main Street Memorandum* (quarterly); *The Conservative Movement;*

Family Questions; From Cottage to Work Station: The Family's Search for Social Harmony in the Industrial Age; The Homestead; Immigration and the American Identity; In Search of a National Morality; The Politics of Human Nature; The Retreat from Marriage and *Utopia Against the Family.*

Current Concerns: Authentic Federalism, Classics-based education, Family autonomy, Home schooling, Immigration, Religion in society, Integrity at the academy, Limited central government, Stewardship of creation, Strong local government and Welfare state.

Alexis de Tocqueville Institution
1611 North Kent Street
Arlington, VA 22554
(703) 351-4969
(703) 351-0090
President: Merrick Carey

f. 1987; a libertarian institute that studies, promotes and extends the principles of classical liberalism: political equality, civil liberty and economic freedom.

Publications: op-ed pieces in major newspapers.

Current Concerns: African Development Project, The American Immigration Institute, Center on Regulation and Economic Growth, Committee for the Common Defense, IMF Assessment Project and Value Added Tax Project.

US Term Limits
1511 K Street NW, Suite 450
Washington, DC 20005
(202) 393-6440
(202) 393-6434 (Fax)
E-mail: ustl@ibm.net
Director: Paul Jacob

f. 1992; a bipartisan institute seeking to restore citizen control of government through the enactment of national, state and local level term limits.

Publications: *No Uncertain Terms* (10 issues yearly) and *The Constitutional Case for Term Limits.*

Current Concern: Term limits for elected officials.

Urban Institute
2100 M Street NW
Washington, DC 20037
(202) 833-7200
(202) 429-0687 (Fax)
E-mail: paffairs@ui.urban.org
President: William Gorham

f. 1968; a liberal institute seeking to sharpen thinking about society's problems and efforts to solve them, improve government decisions and their implementation, and increase citizens' awareness about important public choices.

Publications: *Briefing Highlights* (occasional); *Policy and Research Report* (3 issues yearly); *Policy Bites* (bimonthly); *Sourcebook for Reporters* (biennial); *UPDATE Newsletter* (monthly); *Entitlements and the Elderly: Protecting Promises; Recognizing Realities; Medicaid Since 1980: Cost; Coverage and the Shifting Alliance Between the Federal Government and the States; Organizing to Count: Change in the Federal Statistical System; Reality and Research: Social Science and US Urban Policy Since 1960; State-Level Databook on Health-Care Access and Financing; Urban Consumer Theory and The Work Alternative: Welfare Reform* and *Realities of the Job Market.*

Current Concerns: Health, Human resources, Income and benefits, Population, Public finance and Housing.

Overview: Elections
and the Political Market Place

Legislatures in democratic countries are the embodiments of what is called, for the lack of a better term, the people's will. Most constitutions describe them as sovereign bodies, or bodies wherein the sovereignty of the people resides. This sovereignty is transferred from the voters to the members of legislatures, vesting them with the quality of representation, more commonly known as mandate.

Representation is a mystical concept that defies definition, yet is cardinal to the functioning of a democracy. Members of a legislature may represent geographical districts delimited, in the case of lower houses, by the size of the population or, as in the case of upper houses, on the basis of different criteria. In any case, it is the delegated power that gives legislators their special cachet. However, the two mechanisms--elections and political parties--by which the collective will of the people is transferred to the representatives are deeply flawed.

Edmund Burke tried to overcome this problem by calling members of legislatures trustees who do not simply represent voters but act as custodians of the national interest. In a classic passage from *The Reflections on the Revolution in France*, he said that a legislator should use "his unbiased opinion, mature judgment and enlightened conscience" to formulate the political agenda and propose alternative solutions.

Geographic units were the primary constituencies of premodern legislatures because their members were expected to champion parochial interests. But geography has become irrelevant in the 20th century because communications technology has shortened distances and brought broader national interests into play. The idea of

representation has therefore receded into the background, especially in the context of newly emerging social divisions. Newly assertive minorities are struggling to establish their identities and are clamoring for more representation according to their numbers. Women, substantially underrepresented until recently, are also pressing for more representation. Voter expectations regarding the representativeness of representative institutions are thus vastly different from actual electoral outcomes.

The strengths and weaknesses of legislatures are directly related to the strengths and weaknesses of the electoral mechanism that drives them. The electoral system determines how representatives are chosen. Two main types of electoral systems exist. One is the continental model of proportional representation (PR) in which seats are divided up among the lists or parties in proportion to the number of votes obtained by each.

The second, known as "first past the post," is the system that prevails in the United States and in countries following the Westminster model. It is associated with the existence of two powerful parties and it strongly discourages third or independent parties. Under this system, most winning candidates enjoy only a plurality of votes, not a majority. Further, because nonvoters make up between 40 and 60 percent of the electorate in any but the most important elections, a representative may be chosen by between 20 and 26 percent of the total electorate. Nevertheless, he or she claims to represent the 40 to 60 percent who never voted as well as the 20 to 24 percent who voted for opposing candidates. This remains one of the inexplicable conundrums of democracy. Voter apathy is so widespread in the United States that it vitiates the electoral connection between the winning candidate and the electorate.

Despite these shortcomings, elections play a vital role in democracy. They serve to galvanize the interests of voters, dramatize the personalities and issues, and test the mettle of political leaders. Elections bring out whatever excitement and glamor there is to politics. They are the closest to a Roman holiday that politics has to offer. Party conventions with their screaming delegates and banners, colors and pageantry, are a cross between a carnival and a cheerleading rally, but they also reveal the earthy side of politics.

Political campaigns are generally described in military terms, such as strategy, tactics and headquarters. They also use the language of trials. The electorate tends to be likened to a jury deciding between the submissions of the rival parties. But this analogy is somewhat misleading. Voters are not jurors. At least a good percentage of voters are partisan supporters of one or the other party. And the contestants are not lawyers advancing rational arguments.

Although campaigning in the early days meant only speechmaking and canvassing (with an occasional parade), political campaigning has become in the 20th century an extension of advertising. The effort is to sell candidates or programs or issues that they represent. From the 1950s onward, campaign techniques have become an elaborate science, and campaign consulting has developed as a profession. New devices like private polling, staged press conferences, one liners and sound bites, photo-ops and pseudo events have become part of the armory of electoral campaigning. Computers enable candidates to use direct mail to target individual voters. Sometimes candidates are only performers acting under the direction of their "handlers." Increasing sophistication has also led to the growth of negative campaigning.

Media coverage has also changed in quality and content. Much of the effort goes into providing materials neatly timed for the television news bulletins. The media have become more and more driven by the horse-race element in elections, providing shifting polls that sometimes turn out to be self-fulfilling. In elections, as in sports, winning is not merely everything, it is the only thing.

Electoral campaign strategies are only one of several factors that affect electoral outcomes. Access to money and access to media are among the others. There are few elections in which the playing field is level for all contestants. Campaign financing is an issue that has been dogging both Democrats and Republicans for years. Attempts to control campaign outlays have been foiled by the independent political action committees. Although there are clear rules on financial disclosure, they are often evaded.

Campaign money is a sensitive political subject, as are all issues affecting elections. Reforms are achieved only slowly over the course of several decades. Since 1971 there have been four Federal Elections Campaign Acts (1971, 1974, 1976 and 1979) passed by Congress to redress the more glaring inequities of the system. These efforts have significantly improved the administration and enforcement of campaign finance regulations, but they have not eliminated all possible abuses.

Federal Election Commission
and
State Election Bodies

FEDERAL ELECTION COMMISSION
99 E Street NW
Washington, DC 20463
(202) 219-3420
(800) 219-3420
Website: http://www.fec.gov

The Federal Election Commission (FEC) is an independent regulatory agency. It administers and enforces the provisions of the Federal Election Campaign Act of 1971, as amended. The act requires the disclosure of sources and uses of funds in campaigns for any federal office, limits the size of individual contributions, and provides for partial public financing of presidential elections. Partial funding is available to candidates on a matching basis if they meet certain requirements. Full funding for the general election is available to qualified candidates.

The commission is composed of six members appointed by the president and confirmed by the Senate. The commissioners serve staggered six-year terms, and no more than three commissioners may be members of the same political party. The chairman and vice chairman must be members of different political parties; they are elected annually by their fellow commissioners.

The commission staff is headed by a staff director. Other senior staff members include a general counsel, the secretary of the commis-

sion, and assistant staff directors for audit, reports analysis, public disclosure, information, and administration.

The Presidential Election Campaign Fund Act of 1971 authorized the commission to certify payments to presidential campaigns from the Presidential Election Campaign Fund. (This money comes from taxpayers who have indicated on their federal tax returns that they wish $3.00 of their taxes to be contributed to the fund.)

The act, as amended, requires campaign committees to file periodic financial reports. It also establishes limits on the size and type of contributions a candidate may receive. Contributions from national banks, corporations, labor organizations, government contractors, and nonresident foreign nationals are prohibited. Also prohibited are contributions of cash (currency) in excess of $100, contributions from one person given in the name of another and contributions exceeding legal limits.

Any candidate for federal office and any political group or committee formed to support a candidate must register with the FEC; the committee treasurer must periodically file reports on campaign finances with the clerk of the House of Representatives (candidates for House seats), the secretary of the Senate (candidates for Senate seats), or the FEC. Individuals and committees making independent expenditures on behalf of or against a candidate also must file reports. In addition, campaign reports must be submitted to the secretary of state (or equivalent office) in the state where the nomination or election is sought or where the political committee's headquarters is located. Reports are made available to the public within 48 hours of their receipt.

To register with the FEC, candidates and committees must submit a statement of candidacy that designates a principal campaign committee. (This committee must be registered by filing a statement of organization within 19 days.) Other financial disclosure documents submitted include the candidate's authorization of a political committee, a report of receipts and expenditures, a statement of independent expenditures on behalf of or against a candidate, and a statement of any debt settlements. Disclosure statements must also be filed showing costs incurred on behalf of candidates by corporations, labor organizations, membership organizations, and trade associations for certain partisan communication, conducted within their own particular organization.

Independent expenditures are payments for communications that advocate the election or defeat of a candidate, but made without the cooperation of the particular candidate or campaign committee. Independent expenditures over $250 per calendar year must be reported to the FEC. Independent expenditures may not be regulated except for disclosure.

FEC staff members review the reports for errors or omissions; if any are found, the campaign or committee is requested to provide additional information. If this information is not supplied, the FEC has the authority to begin a formal investigation. If, after the investigation, the commission decides that violations of the law did occur, it has the authority to negotiate a conciliation agreement with the party in question. Failure to negotiate an agreement within legal parameters allows the FEC to seek enforcement of the law and the imposition of civil penalties in U.S. District Court.

These procedures to enforce compliance also apply to cases in which the FEC discovers a violation of campaign finance law. FEC investigations of alleged violations can spring from a routine review or audit of a report or from a complaint sent to the FEC from another group or individual.

If candidates or committees have questions concerning the finance laws as they relate to specific campaigns, they may request an advisory opinion from the commission. Advisory opinion requests and advisory opinions are available for public inspection at the Public Records Office.

The commission also administers provisions of the law covering the public financing of presidential primaries and general elections. Public funds are also made available to national party committees for their nominating conventions. Candidates who accept public campaign funds must adhere to spending limits imposed by the Federal Election Campaign Act Amendments of 1976 (FECA). The limits are adjusted each campaign season to account for inflation. The commission provides matching grants to presidential primary candidates who have raised more than $5,000 in individual contributions of less than $250 from individuals in 20 different states and who agree to limit expenditures.

FECA sets a limit for primary and general elections. The candidates agree to limit expenditures and cannot accept any private contributions for the general election campaign. Candidates are allowed to accept private contributions to pay for certain legal and accounting fees. Candidates may reject public funds entirely, freeing them to spend as much as they like. The limits on the size of contributions remain the same, however.

The FEC determines a candidate's eligibility for public funds. If eligible, the candidate or committee is certified by the commission to the Treasury Department. After receiving subsequent submissions for matching funds, the commission certifies specific amounts to be paid from the fund. The Treasury is responsible for the actual disbursement of money.

The FEC also operates the National Clearinghouse for Election Administration. The clearinghouse collects information on election procedures and makes it available to federal, state, and local election officials.

The Public Records Office maintains and

makes available to the public all campaign finance reports filed by federal candidates and committees since 1972. Copies of campaign reports may be requested in person, by mail, or by phone. There is a charge for this service. The office is open to the public from 9:00 a.m. to 5:00 p.m. During reporting deadline periods and at certain other times the Public Records Office is open during extended hours in the evening and on weekends; check with the office to determine its schedule. Copy machines are available.

The Public Records Office also makes available the following reference materials:

— Statistical summaries of campaign finance reports.

— Computer indexes and cross-indexes to help locate documents.

— Advisory opinion requests and texts of advisory opinions.

— Audit reports.

— Press releases.

— Copies of court cases filed by the FEC.

— The Multi-Candidate Committee Index (MCC), which lists political action committees (PACs) that may make contributions at the highest level.

— Commission memoranda, agendas of all commission meetings, agenda items, and minutes.

Campaign finance reports may also be inspected at the following locations:

Clerk of the House of Representatives
Office of Records and Registration
1036 LHOB
Washington, DC 20515
(202) 225-1300

The clerk's office maintains for public inspection microfilm copies of original reports filed by candidates for the U.S. House of Representatives and their committees.

Secretary of the Senate
Office of Public Records
SH-232
Washington, DC 20510
(202) 224-0329

The secretary's office maintains for public inspection microfilm copies of original reports filed by candidates for the U.S. Senate and their committees.

Copies of campaign records may also be inspected at the office of the secretary of state (or the equivalent office) in the state where a candidate is seeking nomination or election, or where the campaign headquarters is located.

A list of state offices is available from the FEC.

Complaints alleging violations of the Federal Election Campaign Act, as amended, or FEC regulations should be sent to this office. Complaints must be in writing, sworn to and notarized, and must contain the name, address, and telephone number of the person making the complaint; a statement of the facts and evidence concerning the complaint should also be included. Complaints must be signed by the person making the complaint and must include a statement indicating whether the complaint is made at the suggestion of or on the behalf of any other person. For information on complaint procedure, call Public Information Services, (202) 219-3420 or the toll-free number, (800) 424-9530.

FEDERAL GOVERNMENT AGENCIES

Federal Election Commission
Office of Election Administration
999 E Street NW
Washington, DC 20463
(800) 424-9530
(202) 219-3670

(202) 219-8500 (Fax)
Director: Penelope Bonsall

Department Of Justice
Voting Section, Civil Rights Division
PO Box 66128
Washington, DC 20035-6128
(202) 307-3266
(202) 307-3961 (Fax)
Deputy Chief: Barry Weinberg

Federal Voting Assistance Program
Pentagon, Room 1B-457
Washington, DC 20301
(800) 438-VOTE
(703) 695-0633
(703) 693-5507 (Fax)
Director: Phyllis Taylor

VOTING SYSTEMS
INDEPENDENT TEST AUTHORITY
ACCREDITATION BOARD

Thomas R. Wilkey, Chair
Executive Director
New York State Board of Elections

Yvonne Smith, Vice Chair
Assistant to the Executive Director
Illinois State Board of Elections

Marie Brewer, Executive Assistant
Office of the Commissioner of Elections
Baton Rouge, Louisiana

Paul Craft, Computer Audit Analyst
Division of Elections
Tallahassee, Florida

Lisa Daniel, Director of Elections
Arizona Department of State
Phoenix, Arizona

Steve Freeman, Software Consultant
League City, Texas

Tom Harrison, Executive Director
Texas Ethics Commission
Austin, Texas

Denise Lamb, Director of Elections
New Mexico Secretary of State
Santa Fe, New Mexico

Robert Naegele, President
Granite Creek Technology
Pacific Grove, California

Brit Williams, Professor
CSIS Department
Kennesaw State College
Marietta, Georgia

Ex Officio:

Penelope Bonsall, Director
Office of Election Administration
Federal Election Commission
Washington, DC

Joe Hazeltine
Director of Commercial Operations
Wyle Laboratories
Huntsville, Alabama

Jennifer Price
Director of Software Engineering
Nicholas Research
Huntsville, Alabama

STATE ELECTION BODIES

Alabama

Office of Secretary of State
PO Box 5616
Montgomery, AL 36130-5616
(334) 242-7210
(334) 242-4993 (Fax)
E-mail: vicki.balogh@alalinc.net
Website: www.alalinc.net/alsecst.htm
Director: Vicki Balogh

Anita Tatum, Director of Voter Registration
Alabama State House, Room 236
Montgomery, AL 36130
(334) 242-4337
(334) 242-2940 (Fax)

Alaska

Division of Elections
PO Box 110017
Juneau, AK 99811-0017
(907) 465-4611
(907) 465-3203 (Fax)
E-mail: sandi_stout@gov.state.ak.us
Website: www.gov.state.ak.us/ltgov/elections/
homepage.html
Director: Sandra Stout

Gail Fenumiai, Election Programs Specialist
PO Box 110017
Juneau, AK 99811 0017
(907) 465-4611
(907) 465-3203 (Fax)

American Samoa

Board of Elections
PO Box 3790
Pago Pago, AS 96799
(011) (684) 633-1632
(011) (684) 633-7118 (Fax)
Chief Election Officer: Soliai T. Fuimaono

Arizona

Department of State
1700 West Washington, 7th Floor
Phoenix, AZ 85007
(602) 542-8683
(602) 542-6172 (Fax)
E-mail: idaniel@mail.sosaz.com
Deputy Secretary: Lisa K. Daniel
Website: www.sosaz.com

Arkansas

Elections Board
State Capitol, Room 206
Little Rock, AR 72209
(501) 682-3471
(501) 682-3408 (Fax)
Director: Jacque Alexander

California

Elections Division
1230 J Street, Room 232
Sacramento, CA 95814
(916) 653-3228
(916) 653-5634 (Fax)
E-mail: ssjm%tsla@ts9.teale.ca.gov
Chief: John Mott-Smith
Website: vote96.ss.ca.gov/

Colorado

Department of State
1560 Broadway, Suite 200
Denver, CO 80202
(303) 894-2680
(303) 894-2242 (Fax)
E-mail: billcompton<sos.elect1@state.co.us
Director: Bill Compton

Connecticut

State Board of Elections
30 Trinity Street

Hartford, CT 06106
(860) 566-3106
(860) 566-3221 (Fax)
Director: Thomas Ferguson

Delaware

Department of Elections
32 Loockerman Square, Suite M-107
Dover, DE 19904
(302) 739-4277
(302) 739-6794 (Fax)
E-mail: tcook@bdsnet.com
Director: Thomas J. Cooke
Website: www.state.de.us/agencies/election

District of Columbia

Board of Elections & Ethics
441 4th Street NW, Suite 250
Washington, DC 20001
(202) 727-6511
(202) 347-2648 (Fax)
Director: Alice P. Miller

Florida

Division of Elections, Department Of State
Capitol 1801
Tallahassee, FL 32399-0250
(904) 488-7690
(904) 488-1768 (Fax)
E-mail: drancourt@mail.dos.state.fl.us
Director: David Rancourt
Website: www.election.dos.state.fl.us

Georgia

Georgia Elections Division
Suite 1104, West Tower
2 Martin Luther King Jr Drive SE
Atlanta, GA 30334-1505
(404) 656-2871
(404) 651-9536 (Fax)
Director: Linda Beazley

Guam

Election Commission
PO Box BG
Agana, GU 96910
Director: Henry Torres

Hawaii

Office of Elections
802 Lehua Avenue
Pearl City, Hawaii 96782
(808) 453-8683
(808) 453-6006 (Fax)
E-mail: elections@aloha.net
Chief Officer: Dwayne Yoshina
Website: www.hawaii.gov/elections

Idaho

Chief Deputy Secretary of State for Elections
203 State House
Boise, ID 83720
(208) 334-2300
(208) 334-2282 (Fax)
Director: Ben Ysura

Illinois

State Board of Elections
1020 South Spring Street
PO Box 4187
Springfield, IL 52708
(217) 782-4141
(217) 782-5959 (Fax)
Director: Ron Michaelson

Yvonne Smith, Assist. to the Exec. Director
State Board of Elections
State of Illinois Center
100 West Randolph, Suite 14-100
Chicago, IL 60601
(312) 814-6440
(312) 814-6485 (Fax)

Indiana

Election Commission
302 West Washington, Room E032
Indianapolis, IN 46204
(317) 232-3930
(317) 233-6793 (Fax)
E-mail: laurie_christie_at_seb@
ima.isd.state.in.us
Co-Directors: Laurie Christie and Mary Ann
    Tippett
Website: www.ai.org/seb/index.html

Iowa

Department of State
Hoover State Office Building, 2nd Floor
Des Moines, IA 50319
(515) 281-6598
(515) 242-5953 (Fax)
E-mail: carol@sos.state.is.us
Deputy Secretary: Carl Olsen
Website: www.sos.state.ia.us/election/
    elecmain.htm

Kansas

Department of State
300 SW 10th Avenue
Capitol Building, 2nd Floor
Topeka, KS 66612-1594
(913) 296-4559
(913) 291-3051 (Fax)
E-mail: bradb@ssmail.wpo.state.ks.us
Assistant: Brad Bryant
Website: www.ink.org/public/sos/elewelc.html

Kentucky

State Board of Elections
140 Walnut Street
Frankfort, KY 40601
(502) 573-7100
(502) 573-4369 (Fax)
E-mail: grussell@mail.state.ky.us
Director: George Russell

Website: www.state.ky.us/agencies/sbe/
    sbehome.htm

Louisiana

State Elections Commission
4888 Constitution Avenue
PO Box 14179
Baton Rouge, LA 70898-4179
(504) 925-7885
(504) 925-1841 (Fax)
Commissioner: Jerry Fowler

Wade Martin II, Administrator
Election Division
State Capitol, 19th Floor
PO Box 94125
Baton Rouge, LA 70804-9125
(504) 342-4972
(504) 342-2066 (Fax)

Maine

Bureau of Corporations, Elections, and
    Commissions
101 State House Station
Augusta, ME 04101
(207) 287-6308
(207) 287-5874 (Fax)
E-mail: ssjflyn@smtp.state.me.us
Director: Julie Flynn
Website: www.state.me.us/sos/cec/elec/
    elec.htm#gen96

Maryland

State Administrative Board of Election Laws
Old Armory Building, 11 Bladen Street
PO Box 231
Annapolis, MD 21404-0231
(410) 974-3711
(410) 974-2019 (Fax)
Deputy Administrator: Julian Manelli

Massachusetts

Election Division
One Ashburton Place, Room 1705
Boston, MA 02133
(617) 727-2828
(617) 742-3238 (Fax)
Director: John Cloonan

Michigan

Bureau of Elections
Mutual Building, 4th Floor
208 North Capitol Avenue
Lansing, MI 48918
(517) 373-2540
(517) 373-0941 (Fax)
E-mail: christopherT@sosmail.state.mi.us
Director: Christopher M. Thomas
Website: www.sos.state.mi.us/election/
elect.html

Minnesota

Election Division
180 State Office Building
100 Constitution Avenue
St Paul, MN 55155-1299
(612) 215-1440
(612) 296-9073 (Fax)
Director: Joseph Mansky

Mississippi

State Board of Elections
PO Box 136
Jackson, MS 39205
(601) 359-6359
(601) 359-1607 (Fax)
Director: Bryant Bell

Missouri

State of Missouri
PO Box 778

Jefferson City, MO 65102
(573) 751-4875
(573) 526-3242 (Fax)
E-mail: dcheshir@mail.sos.state.mo.us
Director: Debbie Cheshire
Website: www.mosl.sos.state.mo.us/

Jim McAdams, Deputy Secretary of State for
Elections
State Information Center
Jefferson City, MO 65102
(573) 751-4875
(573) 526-3242 (Fax)

Montana

State Board of Elections
State Capitol, Room 225
Helena, MT 59620
(406) 444-4732
(406) 444-3976 (Fax)
E-mail: ct1158%zip003@email.mt.gov
Director: Joe Kerwin
Website: www.mt.gov/sos/123456

Nebraska

State Board of Elections
State Capitol, Suite 2300
Lincoln, NE 68502
(402) 471-3229
(402) 471-3237 (Fax)
Assistant Secretary: Neal Erickson

Nevada

State Board of Elections
Capitol Complex
Carson City, NV 89710
(702) 687-3176
(702) 687-6913 (Fax)
Deputy Secretary: Pamela Crowell

New Hampshire

Secretary of State
State House, Room 204
Concord, NH 03301
(603) 271-3242
(603) 271-2361 (Fax)
Director: Honorable William M. Gardner

New Jersey

State Board of Elections
20 West State Street (CN304)
Trenton, NJ 08625
(609) 292-3760
(609) 777-1280 (Fax)
Director: Joe Britt

New Mexico

Department of State
State Capitol Building, Room 420
Santa Fe, NM 87503
(505) 827-3621
(505) 827-3634 (Fax)
E-mail: 73160.1711@compuserve.com
Director: Denise Lamb
Website: www.web.state.nm.us/elect.htm

New York

State Board of Elections
Swan Street Building, Core 1
6 Empire Street Plaza, Suite 201
Albany, NY 12223-1650
(518) 474-8100
(518) 486-4068 (Fax)
E-mail: twilkey@elections.state.ny.us
Director: Thomas R. Wilkey
Website: www.elections.state.ny.us

North Carolina

State Board of Elections
133 Fayetteville Street Mall, Suite 100

Raleigh, NC 27602-2169
(919) 733-7173
(919) 715-0135 (Fax)
E-mail: gbartlett@sboe.state.nc.us
Director: Gary Bartlett

North Dakota

Department of State
600 East Boulevard Avenue
Bismarck, ND 58505
(701) 328-4146
(701) 328-2992 (Fax)
E-mail: msmail.sccory@ranch.state.nd.us
Administrator: Cory Fong

Ohio

Elections Division
30 East Broad Street, 14th Floor
Columbus, OH 43266-0418
(614) 466-2585
(614) 752-4360 (Fax)
Administrator: Patricia Wolfe

Gretchen A. Quinn, Assist. Elections Counsel
Elections Division
30 East Broad Street, 14th Floor
Columbus, OH 43266-0418
(614) 466-2585
(614) 752-4360 (Fax)

Oklahoma

State Elections Board
Room 6, State Capitol
Oklahoma City, OK 73105
(405) 521-2391
(405) 521-6457 (Fax)
E-mail: ward@lsb.lsb.state.ok.us
Secretary: Lance Ward
Website: www.state.ok.us/-elections/

Oregon

Office of Secretary of State
141 State Capitol
Salem, OR 97310
(503) 986-1500
(503) 373-7414 (Fax)
Director: Colleen Sealock

Pennsylvania

Commissioner of Elections
304 North Office Building
Harrisburg, PA 17120
(717) 787-5280
(717) 787-2854 (Fax)
Director: Dick Filling

Puerto Rico

Puerto Rico State Election Commission
PO Box 9066525
San Juan, PR 00906-6525
(787) 723-1006
(787) 721-7940 (Fax)
President: Juan R. Melecio

Rhode Island

State Board of Elections
50 Branch Avenue
Providence, RI 02904
(401) 277-2345
(401) 621-3255 (Fax)
Director: Robert J. Fontaine

South Carolina

Ethics Commission
PO Box 5987
Columbia, SC 29250
(803) 734-9060
(803) 734-9366 (Fax)
Director: Jim F. Hendrix

South Dakota

Department of State
500 East Capitol Avenue
Pierre, SD 57501
(605) 773-3537
(605) 773-6580 (Fax)
E-mail: chrisn@sos.state.sd.us
Supervisor: Chris Nelson
Website: www.state.sd.us/state/executive/sos/
sos.htm

Tennessee

Tennessee Secretary of State's Office
James K. Polk Building, Suite 500
Nashville, TN 37243
(615) 741-7956
(615) 741-1278 (Fax)
E-mail: bkthompson@mail.state.tn.us
Coordinator: Brook Thompson
Website: www.state.tn.us/sos/election.htm

Texas

Department of State
PO Box 12060
Austin, TX 78711-2060
(512) 463-9873
(512) 475-2811 (Fax)
E-mail: amcgeehan@sos.state.tx.us
Deputy Assistant: Ann McGeehan
Website: www.sos.state.tx.us/elec96/index.htm

Utah

State Board of Elections
State Capitol, Room 203
Salt Lake City, UT 84114
(801) 538-1522
(801) 538-1557 (Fax)
E-mail: gvpbmain.kpotter@state.ut.us
Director: Kelleen Potter
Website: www.gvnfo.state.ut.us/lt_gover/
election.htm

Vermont

Office of Secretary of State
109 State Street
Montpelier, VT 05609-1101
(802) 828-2231
(802) 828-2496 (Fax)
Director: Ellen Tofferi

Virgin Islands

Virgin Islands Board of Elections
PO Box 6038
St Thomas, VI 00801
(809) 774-3107
(809) 776-2391 (Fax)
Director: John Abramson

Virginia

State Board of Elections
200 North 9th Street, Room 101
Richmond, VA 23219
(804) 786-6551
(804) 371-0194 (Fax)
Secretary: M. Bruce Meadows

Washington

Office of Secretary Of State
Elections Division
Legislative Office Building
PO Box 40220
Olympia, WA 98504-0220
(360) 902-4151
(360) 586-5629 (Fax)
E-mail: 103176.2773@compuserv.com
Director: Gary McIntosh

West Virginia

State Board of Elections
State Capitol, Room 157-K
Charleston, WV 25305-0770

(304) 558-6000
(304) 558-0900 (Fax)
Assistant Secretary: Jan Castro

Wisconsin

State Elections Board
132 East Wilson Street, Suite 300
PO Box 2973
Madison, WI 53702
(608) 266-8004
(608) 267-0500 (Fax)
Director: Kevin Kennedy

Wyoming

State Board of Elections
Wyoming State Capitol, Room B38
Cheyenne, WY 82002-0020
(307) 777-7186
(307) 777-5988 (Fax)
E-mail: elections@missc.state.wy.us
Officer: Peggy Nighswonger

Leagues of Women Voters

The League of Women Voters of the United States
1730 M Street NW
Washington, DC 20036-4508
(202) 429-1965
(202) 429-0854 (Fax)
E-mail: lwv@lwv.org
Website: http://www.lwv.org
President: Carolyn Jefferson-Jenkins

Founded in 1920, the League of Women Voters is a nonpartisan political organization that encourages the informed and active participation of citizens in government, and it influences public policy through education and advocacy. It is a unique activist network that derives its strength from the energy and commitment of more than a hundred thousand members and supporters nationwide. The League knows first-hand the value of citizens organized for change.

The League ambitiously pursues its dual mission: (1) to encourage the active and informed participation of citizens in government and to increase understanding of major public policy issues; (2) to secure public policies that promote League goals reached through member participation and agreement.

The League is strictly nonpartisan; it neither supports nor opposes candidates for office at any level of government. At the same time, the League is wholeheartedly political—working to influence public policy through education and advocacy. It is the original grassroots citizen network, directed by the consensus of its members across the country.

LWV of Alabama
637 Horseshoe Curve
Pike Road, AL 36064-3409
(334) 270-0539
(334) 277-1220 (Fax)
E-mail: lwvalabama@classic.msn.com
Co-Presidents: Dr. Anne Permaloff and Andrea
    G. Summer

LWV of Alaska
1542 East 27th Avenue
Anchorage, AK 99508-3922
(907) 272-0366
(907) 272-0366 (Fax)
President: Wilda Hudson

LWV of Arizona
20003 146th Drive
Sun City West, AZ 85375-5735
(602) 997-5218
(602) 997-5218 (Fax)
E mail: lwvmp@aol.com
President: Lila J. Schwartz
Website: http://www.primenet.com/~lwvazlil/

LWV of Arkansas
The Executive Building
2020 West 3rd, Suite 504
Little Rock, AR 72205
(501) 376-7760
(501) 376-7760 (Fax)
E-mail:_ lwvar@aristole.net
President: Bobbie E. Hill

LWV of California
926 J Street, Suite 515
Sacramento, CA 95814
(916) 442-7215
(916) 442-7362 (Fax)
President: Karyn Gill
Website: http://ca.lwv.org

LWV of Colorado
3022 South Josephine Street
Denver, CO 80210-6046
(303) 863-0437
(303) 863-0437 (Fax)
President: Marilyn Shuey
Website: http://www.sni.net/lwvco

LWV of Connecticut
3 Meadow Road
Darien, CT 06820-6112
(203) 288-7996
(203) 288-7998 (Fax)
E-mail: lwvct@ct2.nai.net
President: Kristin Karpen
Website: http://www.lwvct.org

LWV of Delaware
333 Hampton Road
Wilmington, DE 19803-2425
(302) 571-8948
(302) 571-8948 (Fax)
E-mail: jacharris@aol.com
President: Jacqueline Harris

LWV of District of Columbia
2025 I Street NW, Suite 916

Washington, DC 20006-2000
(202) 331-4122
(202) 331-4196 (Fax)
E-mail: voters1@capaccess.org
President: Luci Murphy
Website: http://www.capaccess/lwvdc

LWV of Florida
624 Orange Street
Palm Harbor, FL 34683-5219
(850) 224-2545
(850) 222-4485 (Fax)
E-mail: xwqq10a@prodigy.com
President: Fay P. Law
Website: http://www.cs.uwf.edu/~lwhite/lwvf/
lwvf.htm

LWV of Georgia
1776 Peachtree Street NW, Suite 533N
Atlanta, GA 30309-2307
(404) 874-7352
(404) 874-7353 (Fax)
E-mail: lwvofga@atlanta.com
President: Sara S. Clark
Website: http://www.ga.lwv.org

LWV of Hawaii
49 South Hotel Street, Suite 314
Honolulu, HI 96813
(808) 531-7448
(808) 599-5669 (Fax)
E-mail: krplan@hgea.org
President: Jean Y. Aoki
Website: http://www.hi.lwv.org

LWV of Idaho
2449 Moscow Mountain Road
Moscow, ID 83843
(208) 883-5362
E-mail: cwoodall@turbonet.com
Copresidents: Carol Woodall and Shirley E. Zeller

LWV of Illinois
332 South Michigan Avenue, Suite1050
Chicago, IL 60604-4301

(312) 939-5935
(312) 939-6887 (Fax)
E-mail: lwvil@aol.com
President: Jan Flapan
Website: http://www.il.lwv.org

LWV of Indiana
11908 Hoster Road
Carmel IN 46033-9779
(317) 241-8683
(317) 241-8740 (Fax)
E-mail: lwvin@earthlink.net
President: Dalyte E. Hartsough

LWV of Iowa
PO Box 41037
Des Moines, IA 50311
(515) 277-0814
(515) 277-6793 (Fax)
E-mail: mdlange@commonlink.com
President: Mary Lange
Website: http://lwvia.cornell-iowa.edu

LWV of Kansas
2661 East Ray Avenue
Salina, KS 67401-7680
(913) 234-5152
(913) 234-0818 (Fax)
Copresidents: Susan Holmes and Kaye Cleaver

LWV of Kentucky
605 Foxfire Road
Elizabethtown, KY 42701-9412
(502) 875-6481
(502) 875-6481 (Fax)
E-mail: hilliard@kvnet.org
President: Betty Hillard
Website: http://1999.76.161.101/organizations/
    lwvky/

LWV of Louisiana
21 Dauterive Court
Kenner, LA 70065
(504) 344-3326

(504) 344-3326 (Fax)
President: Malinda Hill Holmes

LWV of Maine
18 Birch Meadow Road
Brunswick, ME 04011-2955
(207) 622-0256
(207) 729-8292 (Fax)
Copresidents: Sally Bryant and Sarah Walton
Website: http://www.curt.slibrary.com/
    lwvmaine.htm

LWV of Maryland
7009 Woodscape Drive
Clarksville, MD 21029-1635
(410) 269-0232
(410) 268-7301 (Fax)
E-mail: lwvmd@aol.com
President: Joan Paik
Website: http://www.bepl.lib.md.us/~lwv/

LWV of Massachusetts
133 Portland Street, Lower Level
Boston, MA 02114
(617) 523-2999
(617) 248-0881 (Fax)
E-mail: lwvma@ma.lwv.org
President: Nancy Carapezza

LWV of Michigan
11528 Plymouth Woods Drive, Building 2
Livonia, MI 48150-4500
(517) 484-5383
(517) 484-3086 (Fax)
E-mail: lwvmi@mlc.lib.mi.us
President: Flora McRae
Website: http://www.mic.lib.mi.us/~lwvmi/

LWV of Minnesota
505 Lake Avenue
White Bear Lake, MN 55110-1631
(612) 224-5445
(612) 292-9417 (Fax)
E-mail: lwvmn@mtn.org

President: Judy Duffy
Website: http://freenet.msp.mn.us/ipl/pol/lwvmn/

LWV of Mississippi
PO Box 55505
Jackson, MS 39216-5505
(601) 352-4616
President: Kay Higginbotham

LWV of Missouri
7245 Cornell Avenue
St Louis, MO 63130-3025
(314) 961-6869
(314) 961-8393 (Fax)
E-mail: lwv@jinx.umsl.edu
President: Carol Portman
Website: http://www.umsl.edu/~lwv

LWV of Montana
493 Roaring Lion Road
Hamilton, MT 59840-8909
(406) 363-3734
President: Ruth Centers
Website: http://www.marsweb.com/~lwvmt/

LWV of Nebraska
6908 Northland Drive
Omaha, NE 68152-1019
(402) 475-1411
(402) 475-1411 (Fax)
E-mail: lwvne@binary.net
President: Deanna Frisk
Website: http://www.binary.net/lwvne/

LWV of Nevada
PO Box 1194
Carson City, NV 89702
(702) 884-2659
E-mail: celiah@compuserve.com_
Copresidents: Celia Hildebrand and Deann D.
   Stout

LWV of New Hampshire
164 Federal Hill Road
Milford, NH 03055-3518
(603) 225-5344
President: Lillian M. Nelligan

LWV of New Jersey
517 Arthur Drive
Cherry Hill, NJ 08003-3005
(609) 394-3303
(609) 599-3993 (Fax)
E-mail: lwvnj@eclipse.org
President: Dorothy Dunfee
Website: http://www.lwvnj.org

LWV of New Mexico
2526 Tramway Terrace Court NE
Albuquerque, NM 87122
(505) 856-7757
E-mail: lwvabc@nmia.com
Copresidents: Charlotte Serof and Barbara
   Robinson
Website: http://www.nmia.com/lwvmn

LWV of New York
87 Catherine Road
Scarsdale, NY 10583-6918
(518) 465-4162
(518) 465-0812 (Fax)
E-mail: 75663.2743@compuserve.com
President: Evelyn Stock
Website: http://www.crisny.org/not-for.profit/
   lwvac.lwvnys/lwny.html

LWV of North Carolina
215 Pinecroft Drive
Raleigh, NC 27609-6614
(919) 783-5995
(919) 783-5995 (Fax)
President: Marian Dodd
Website: http://www.rtpnet.org/~lwvnc/

LWV of North Dakota
1146 5th Street North

Fargo, ND 58102-3713
(701) 772-7940
President: Lois Altenberg

LWV of Ohio
17 South High Street, Suite 650
Columbus, OH 43215-3413
(614) 469-1505
(614) 469-7918 (Fax)
E-mail: lwvoinfo@lwvohio.org
President: Anne Smead
Website: http://www.lwvohio.org

LWV of Oklahoma
525 NW 13th Street
Oklahoma City, OK 73103
(405) 232-8683
(405) 236-8683 (Fax)
President: Carol Woodward
Website: http://connections.oklahoman.net/lwvok

LWV of Oregon
3363 NW Crest Drive
Corvallis, OR 97330-1808
(503) 581-5722
(503) 581-9403 (Fax)
E-mail: lwvor@open.org
President: Paula Krane
Website: http://www.open.org/lwvor

LWV of Pennsylvania
226 Forster Street
Harrisburg, PA 17102-3220
(717) 234-1576
(717) 234-1576 (Fax)
E-mail: 73172.2754 @compuserve.com
President: Mary F. Etezady
Website: http://www.libertynet.org.pa

LWV of Rhode Island
437 Lloyd Avenue
Providence, RI 02906-4546
(401) 453-1111
President: Hollie Courage

LWV of South Carolina
PO Box 1264
Walterboro, SC 29488-1264
(803) 791-9044
(803) 791-9044 (Fax)
Copresidents: Mary Ann Burtt and Laurel Suggs

LWV of South Dakota
47133 69th Street
Sioux Falls, SD 57108-8106
(605) 338-5525
(605) 332-1333 (Fax)
E-mail: minahall@iw.net
President: Mina E Hall

LWV of Tennessee
1227 Toddington Drive
Murfreesboro, TN 37130-5629
(615) 297-7134
(615) 383-6504 (Fax)
E-mail: lwvtn@compuserve.com
President: Faye Johnson
Website: http://ourworld.compuserve.com/
  homepages/lwvtn/

LWV of Texas
5551 Montrose Drive
Dallas, TX 75209-6504
(512) 472-1100
(512) 472-4114 (Fax)
E-mail: lwvtx@aol.com
Copresidents: Julie Lowenberg and Nancy Wilson
Website: http://www.main.org/leguewv/home.html

LWV of Utah
11650 South Hidden Circle
Sandy, UT 84092
(801) 272-8683
(801) 272-5942 (Fax)
E-mail: lwvut@xmission.com
President: Janice Gygi
Website: http://www.xmission.com/~lwvut

LWV of Vermont
11 Fitzsimonds
Jericho, VT 05465-9711
(802) 657-0242
E-mail: yanas@together.net
President: Sonya Schuyler

LWV of Virgin Islands
PO Box 638
Saint Thomas, VI 00801
(809) 774-3106
President: Debra A. Roumu Brown

LWV of Virginia
10102 Nadine Drive
Vienna, VA 22181-4048
(804) 649-0333
(804) 649-0339 (Fax)
President: Connie Houston

LWV of Washington
9633 47th Avenue SW
Seattle, WA 98136-2715
(206) 622-8961
(206) 622-4908 (Fax)
E-mail: lwvwa@speakeasy.org
President: Elizabeth Pierini
Website: http://www.speakeasy.org/~lwvwa

LWV of West Virginia
2023 Huber Road
Charleston, WV 25314-2279
(304) 342-2706
(304) 342-1377 (Fax)
E-mail: emst@citynet.net
President: Ellender M. Stanchina
Website: http://web.mountain.net/~mhalley/
    lwvwv.htm

LWV of Wisconsin
5701 Anchorage Avenue
Madison, WI 53705-4401
(608) 256-0827
(608) 256-2853 (Fax)

E-mail: genfund@lwvwi.org
Copresidents: Kathryn Johnson and Ellen
    Sorenson

LWV of Wyoming
320 8th Street
Rawlins, WY 82301-5453
(307) 324-5460
Copresidents: Angeline Kinnaman and Janna
    Nordman

Campaign Managers
and
Political Consultants

Campaign managers and political consultants are the senior officials in most campaigns for public office. These experts provide technology solutions, critical services such as fundraising and volunteer coordination, and strategies for electoral success. Campaign consultants provide overall management of the campaign and often stay on after an election to provide continuing political strategy advice. In a presidential election, a campaign manager will direct a paid staff of as many as 300 individuals.

If a (D) follows the name of the organization, then the organization either primarily or exclusively assists Democratic candidates. If an (R) follows the name, then it assists primarily or exclusively Republican candidates. No (D) or (R) means the group will handle either party's candidates.

Abacus Assoc. (D). 52 School Street, Hatfield, MA 01038. Tel: (413) 247-9430 Fax: (413) 247-5813. Principal: Janet Grenzke.

Adams & Co. (R). PO Box 17727, Salem, OR 97305. Tel: (503) 585-2119 Fax: (503) 363-5814. E-mail: bullseye@ravicom.com. Principal: Chuck Adams.

Pat Adams & Assoc. (D). 810 G Street SE, Washington, DC 20003. Tel: (202) 544-8078 Fax: (202) 544-3041. Principal: Pat Adams.

Will Adams Assoc. PO Box 382, Liberty, MO 64068. Tel: (816) 781-7655 or (816) 781-6514 Fax: (816) 792-4743. Principal: Will Adams.

Agenda Setters. PO Box 9711, Madison, WI 53715. Tel: (608) 835-9772. Principal: John Lease.

Allegheny Political Resources (D). 308 The Highwood, 372 South Highland, Pittsburgh, PA 15206. Tel: (412) 363-1419 Fax: (412) 363-1419. Principal: William Peduto.

Richard V. Allen Co. 905 16th Street NW, Washington, DC 20006. Tel: (202) 737-2824. Principal: Richard V. Allen.

Alliance Pacific Inc. 608 Flour Mill, West 621 Mallon, Spokane, WA 99201. Tel: (509) 325-3220 Fax: (509) 326-5663. Principal: Kerry Lynch Johnson.

American Research Management (D). 3118 Juniper Lane, Falls Church, VA 22044. Tel: (703) 237-0104 Fax: (703) 237-0106. Principal: Jeffrey T. Browne.

Anderson & Kern (R). PO Box 2283, 15658 Viking Grove Lane, Valley Center, CA 92082. Tel: (760) 751-0910 Fax: (760) 751-0868. E-mail: jjkern@aol.com. Principal: John Kern.

Associated Writers Ink (D). PO Box 14787, Gainesville, FL 32604. Tel: (352) 591-1172.

Fax: (352) 591-1172. Principal: John J. Hotaling.

Avakian & Assoc. (D). 5868 Hallridge Circle, Columbus, OH 43232. Tel: (614) 863-1012 Fax: (614) 925-2957. E-mail: hullonian@aol.com. Principal: Steve Avakian.

Avenel Assoc., Inc. (D). 1300 Connecticut Avenue NW, Suite 650, Washington, DC 20036. Tel: (202) 328-0199 Fax: (202) 452-4175 E-mail: earl@avenel.com. Principal: Robert Earl Bender.

B.H.I. (D). 2600 Douglas Road, Suite 1007, Coral Gables, FL 33134. Tel: (305) 461-3873 Fax: (305) 461-3970. Principal: Jacqueline Basha.

Bailey Political Consulting (R). 1104 Country Hills Drive, Suite 304, Ogden, UT 84403. Tel: (801) 629-0057 Fax: (801) 629-0061. Principal: Charles R. Bailey.

John P. Bakke. 539 Melody Lane, Memphis, TN 38120. Tel: (901) 682-9509 Fax: (901) 685-2796. Principal: John P. Bakke.

Marlene Bane Assoc., Consultant (D). 5816 Etiwanda Avenue, Suite 1, Tarzana, CA 91356. Tel: (818) 757-3031 Fax: (818) 757-3175. Principal: Marlene Bane.

Bannon Research (D). 80 F Street NW, Suite 804, Washington, DC 20001. Tel: (202) 628-4809 Fax: (202) 628-3702. Principal: Brad Bannon.

Bass & Howes, Inc. (D). 1818 N Street NW, Suite 450, Washington, DC 20036. Tel: (202) 530-2900 Fax: (202) 590-2901. Principal: Marie Bass.

Bates Neimand (D). 1900 L Street NW, Suite 500, Washington, DC 20036. Tel: (202) 496-9238 Fax: (202) 496-9244 E-mail: info@batesneimand.com. Principal: Ross Bates.

Bay Communications (D). 6 Deepwater Court, Edgewater, MD 21037. Tel: (410) 224-1115 Fax: (410) 224-8305. Principal: Michael F. Ford.

Beck Company. 12862 Via Adventura, Santa Ana, CA 92705. Tel: (714) 730-0662 Fax: (714) 631-1845. Principal: Gary Beck.

Beckel Cowan, a Cassidy Company. 700 13th Street NW, Suite 1100, Washington, DC 20005. Tel: (202) 783-5600 Fax: (202) 783-1166. Principal: Bob Beckel.

Bendixon & Assoc., Inc. (D). 2405 Riverview Terrace, Alexandria, VA 22303. Tel: (703) 329-9581 Fax: (703) 329-9503. Principal: Sergio Bendixen.

Benesch, Friedlander, Oplan & Aronoff. 2300 BP America Building, 200 Public Square, Cleveland, OH 44114 2378. Tel: (216) 363-4663. Principal: James M. Friedman.

Berryhill Assoc. (R). 1629 K Street NW, Suite 1100, Washington, DC 20006. Tel: (202) 785-6711 Fax: (202) 331-4212. Principal: John Nicholson.

Blackwater Assoc. PO Box 5151, Columbia, SC 29250. Tel: (803) 771-7489. Principal: Karen Sundstrom.

Blakemore & Assoc. (R). 3323 Richmond Avenue, Suite C, Houston, TX 77098-3007. Tel: (713) 526-3399 Fax: (713) 526-4434. Principal: Allen Blakemore.

Blanford Communications (D). 611 Broadway, Suite 627, New York, NY 10012. Tel: (212) 260-9905 Fax: (212) 260-9908. Principal: Ernest Lendler.

Bonner & Assoc. 1101 17th Street NW, Suite 800, Washington, DC 20036. Tel: (202) 463-8880 Fax: (202) 833-3584. Principal: Jack Bonner.

John C. Bottenberg & Assoc. 800 Jackson, Suite 1120, Topeka, KS 66612. Tel: (913) 235-2324 Fax: (913) 357-3390. Principal: John C. Bottenberg.

Boyd Assoc., Inc. (R). PO Box 1317, Exton, PA 19341. Tel: (215) 942-4335 Fax: (215) 942-0258. Principal: Debra J. Boyd.

Bragg, Maddox & Taylor (D). 3250 Wilshire Boulevard, Suite 1505, Los Angeles, CA 90010. Tel: (213) 389-6123 Fax: (213) 389-5875. Principal: Felicia Bragg.

Howard A. Brock. PO Box 185, Altamont, NY 12009-0185. Tel: (518) 861-6467. Principal: Howard A. Brock.

Bronrott Communications (D). 4415 Rosedale Avenue, Bethesda, MD 20814. Tel: (301) 652-6016 Fax: (301) 656-0441. Principal: Bill Bronrott.

Brown Giorgetti Consultants (D). 3 Gateway Center, 22nd Floor, Pittsburgh, PA 15222. Tel: (412) 553-6343 Fax: (412) 642-2601. Principal: Nello Giorgetti.

Brown Inc. (D). 720 East Zia Road, Santa Fe, NM 87505. Tel: (505) 982-3410 Fax: (505) 983-1926. Principal: Chris Brown.

Lee Brown Company, Inc. (R). PO Box 1888, Sioux Falls, SD 57101. Tel: (605) 224-6373 Fax: (605) 224-1060. Principal: Lee Brown.

Michael Brown Assoc. 28 Potters Lane, New Rochelle, NY 10805-3307. Tel: (914) 636-3113 Fax: (914) 636-7146. Principal: Michael Brown.

Richard A. Brown (D). 2030 Allen Place NW, Washington, DC 20009. Tel: (202) 745-1987. Principal: Richard A. Brown.

Lynn Bryan & Assoc. (R). 115 West California Boulevard, Suite 419, Pasadena, CA 91105. Tel: (818) 577-7203 Fax: (818) 568-2983 E-mail: lbanda@aol.com. Principal: Lynn Bryan.

Business Industry Pol. Education Comm. PO Box 23021, Jackson, MS 39225. Tel: (601) 353-4941 Fax: (601) 353-5486. Principal: Richard Wilcox.

Cahill, Wolfgram & Assoc. PO Box 506, De Forest, WI 53532-0506. Tel: (608) 846-5358 Fax: (608) 251-7680. Principal: Jane Cahill.

Calabrese & Assoc. (R). 5100 Westheimer, Suite 200, Houston, TX 77056. Tel: (713) 968-6553 Fax: (713) 960-0142. Principal: Denis Calabrese.

California Communications Group (D). 1830 5th Avenue, Sacramento CA 95818-3826. Tel: (916) 556-1150 Fax: (916) 447-1998. Principal: Ron Grey

California Consulting & Management (R). PO Box 1622, Redlands, CA 92373. Tel: (909) 795-4359. Principal: Paul Woodruff.

Campaign Connection (D). 1809 7th Avenue, Suite 1610, Seattle, WA 98101-1313. Tel: (206) 443-1990 Fax: (206) 382-1338 E-mail: cconnex@ aa.net. Principal: Cathy Allen.

Campaign Consultants, Inc. (R). 50 Washington Street, Reno, NV 89503. Tel: (702) 786-7478. Principal: Bill Martin.

Campaign Consultants. PO Box 7281, Little Rock, AR 72217. Tel: (501) 225-3996 Fax: (501) 225-5167. E-mail: jlrussell@aristotle.net. Principal: Jerry L. Russell.

Campaign Design Group (D). 727 15th Street NW, 11th Floor, Washington, DC 20005. Tel: (202) 393-0404 Fax: (202) 347-4308. Principal: Elizabeth A. Sullivan.

The Campaign House (R). 334 Cooper Road, Suite D4, Berlin, NJ 08009. Tel: (609) 753-1234 Fax: (609) 753-0440. Principal: Greg Law.

Campaign Management Services, Inc. (R).
104 North Carolina Ave SE, Washington, DC
20003. Tel: (202) 547-7177 Fax: (202) 546-
3091. Principal: Ronald W. Pearson.

Campaign Services Group Inc. (CSG) (R).
8626 Tesoro Drive, Petroleum Tower, Suite
306, San Antonio, TX 78217. Tel: (210) 804-
0181. Fax: (210) 804-0503. E-mail: demkiller
@aol.com. Principal: John Weaver.

Campaign Services. 731 Pacific Avenue, San
Luis Obispo, CA 93401. Tel: (805) 549-8014.
Principal: Dan Pittaway.

Campaign Works, The (D). PO Box 2646,
West Palm Beach, FL 33402 2646. Tel: (407)
832-2853. Fax: (407) 832-5708. or 1400 20th
Street NW, Suite 513, Washington, DC 20036.
Tel: (202) 463-7691 Fax: (202) 463-8152.
Principal: Daryl Glenney.

Campaigns & Elections Inc. (R). 3311
North Sterling, Suite 10, Peoria, IL 61604-1837.
Tel: (309) 682-1054 Fax: (309) 682-0321.
Principal: Mary Alice Erickson.

Campbell Crane and Assoc., Inc. 1010
Pennsylvania Avenue SE, Washington, DC
20003. Tel: (202) 546-4991. Principal: Jeanne
Campbell.

Cannon & Eger (D). HCR 1, PO Box 5164,
Kea'au, HI 96749. Tel: (808) 966-8565 Fax:
(808) 966-7872 E-mail: billeger@gte.net.
Website: http://www.hawaii-island.com. Principal: Bill Eger.

Capitol Avenue Consulting. 425 West
Capitol, Suite 3300, Little Rock, AR 72201.
Tel: (501) 374-5505 Fax: (501) 374-5520.
Principal: David R. Martin.

Capitol Corporation (R). 1 Fawcett Place,
Suite 130, Greenwich, CT 06830-6581. Tel:
(203) 661-7962. Principal: Frank Trotta.

Carlyle Gregory Company (R). PO Box
2180, Falls Church, VA 22042. Tel: (703) 532-

1365 Fax: (703) 533-7614 E-mail: gopconsult@
aol.com. Principal: Carlyle Gregory.

The Carmen Group (R). 1401 I Street NW,
Suite 900, Washington, DC 20005. Tel: (202)
785-0500 Fax: (202) 785-5277. Principal:
David Carmen.

Thomas Carroll Campaigns. 128 Grant
Avenue, Suite 216, Sante Fe, NM 87501. Tel:
(505) 983-2203 Fax: (505) 982-2548. Principal:
Thomas Carroll.

Carville & Begala (D). 329 Maryland
Avenue NW, Washington, DC 20002. Tel:
(202) 543-1196 Fax: (202) 546-1490. Principal:
James Carville.

**Casey Communications Management, Inc.
(D).** 25800 NW Highway, Suite 800,
Southfield, MI 48075. Tel: (810) 746-6070 Fax:
(810) 746-6068. Principal: John Bailey.

Cavalier and Assoc. 1121 L Street, Suite
810, Sacramento, CA 95814. Tel: (916) 444-
8060 Fax: (916) 444-6544. Principal: Charles
Cavalier II.

Channell & Assoc. (D). 516 DeLeon Drive,
El Paso, TX 79912. Tel: (915) 833-0079 Fax:
(915) 585-2723. Principal: Tim Channell.

Charles, Tricot & Sullivan (D). PO Box
50228, Columbia, SC 29250. Tel: (803) 779-
9455. Principal: Chuck Sullivan.

Cherry Political & PR Consulting (R). 227
North Bronough Street, Suite 4100, Tallahassee, FL 32301. Tel: (850) 561-3600 Fax: (850)
561-1155. Principal: Linda Z. Cherry.

Chesapeake Media (R). 31830 Bittorf Lane,
Cordova, MD 21625. Tel: (410) 364-5009 Fax:
(410) 364-5971. or 1169 Washington Street,
Bath, ME 04530. Tel: (207) 443-9193 E-mail:
aray@skipjack.bluecral.org. Principal: Alex
Ray.

Christopherson & Co. 6143 South Willow Drive, Suite 430, Greenwood Village, CO 80111. Tel: (303) 779-4920 Fax: (303) 779-0165. Principal: Dan Christopherson.

Cire Advertising, Inc. (R). 2401 T Circle, Norman, OK 73069. Tel: (405) 236-0836 Fax: (405) 447-4848. Principal: Mike Hammer.

Civic Service, Inc. 1050 Connecticut Avenue NW, Suite 870, Washington, DC 20036. Tel: (202) 785-2070 Fax: (202) 785-1102. Principal: Roy Pfautch.

Clarke Communications Group, The. RD 4 PO Box 1215, Montpelier, VT 05602. Tel: (802) 456-1732 Fax: (802) 456-1732 E-mail: ccgroupinc@aol.com. Principal: Rod Clarke.

Paul Clarke & Assoc. 17052 Maiden Street, Northridge, CA 91325. Tel: (818) 993-9053 Fax: (818) 993-5109. Principal: Paul C. Clarke.

Cleary & Assoc. (R). 908 Dillon Drive, Omaha, NE 68132. Tel: (402) 397-9200 Fax: (402) 397-9384. Principal: Jim Cleary.

D. R. Clough & Co. PO Box 4629, Portland, ME 04112. Tel: (207) 772-9002. Principal: David R. Clough.

Coalitions Group, Inc. (R). 1300 Commonwealth Avenue, Alexandria, VA 22301. Tel: (703) 684-5750 Fax: (703) 584-0922 E-mail: 73277.332@compuserve. Principal: Bill Lee.

Cole, Hargrave, Snodgrass & Assoc. (R). 6218 North Western, Suite 201, Oklahoma City, OK 73118. Tel: (405) 848-1585 Fax: (405) 848-3915. or 512 North Washington Street, Alexandria, VA 22314. Tel: (703) 518-8927. Principal: Tom Cole.

Robert A. Collins (D). 4840 St Bernard Avenue, New Orleans, LA 70122. Tel: (504) 288-6890. Principal: Robert A. Collins.

Elizabeth Colton (D). 1848 Pine Street, San Francisco, CA 94109. Tel: (415) 775-0111 Fax: (415) 775-6198. Principal: Elizabeth Colton.

Communications Company, The (D). 511 2nd Street NE, Washington, DC 20002. Tel: (202) 547-4467 Fax: (202) 543-6911. Principal: Jay Reuse.

Congressional Mgt. Foundation. 513 Capitol Court NE, Suite 100, Washington, DC 20002. Tel: (202) 546-0100 Fax: (202) 547-0936. Principal: Richard H. Shapiro.

Conservative Solutions (R). 2305 Southlane Court, Irving, TX 75038-5652. Tel: (214) 255-7913. Principal: Brian Humek.

William Cook Public Relations. 225 Water Street, Suite 1600, Jacksonville, FL 32202. Tel: (800) 359-COOK or (904) 789-1610 Fax: (904) 353-1554. Principal: Leo Bottary.

Marguerite Cooper (D). 4301 47th Street NW, Washington, DC 20016. Tel: (202) 966-8203. Principal: Marguerite Cooper.

Coronado Communications (R). 109 Spanish Village, Dallas, TX 75248. Tel: (214) 386-7127. Principal: Dick Leggitt.

Cottington Marti Inc. (R). 2626 East 82nd Street, Suite 121, Minneapolis, MN 55425. Tel: (612) 853-2266 Fax: (612) 853-2262. Principal: Scott Cottington.

Pat Cotton Assoc. (R). 5646 Milton, Suite 409, Dallas, TX 75206. Tel: (214) 891-0110 or (214) 891-0117 Fax: (214) 891-0122 E-mail: patcotton@ibm.net. Principal: Pat Cotton.

Cox & Assoc. (D). 3625 Manchaca, Suite 302, Austin, TX 78704. Tel: (512) 444-2654 Fax: (512) 444-3533. Principal: Patrick Cox.

CPC Corporation (R). 9824 South Park Circle, Fairfax Station, VA 22039. Tel: (703) 451-1987 Fax: (703) 455-1986 E-mail: cpccmeb @mail.eroes.com. Principal: Michael Belefski.

Crow & Assoc. (R). 183 East Glenarm, Suite 103, Pasadena, CA 91105. Tel: (818) 441-0924 Fax: (818) 500-1768. Principal: Kathleen Crow.

Cypress Media Group. PO Box 53198, Atlanta, GA 30355. Tel: (770) 640-9918 Fax: (770) 640-9819. Principal: Randall P. Whatley.

Diana Daggett Consulting (R). 1800 Valdez Drive NE, Albuquerque, NM 87112. Tel: (505) 296-1878. Principal: Diana Daggett.

Darden Research Corporation. 1534 North Decatur Road, Atlanta, GA 30307. Tel: (404) 377-9294. Principal: Claibourne Darden.

Lea Lavole Davis Political Campaign Consultant (R). 865 Lake Lotela Drive, Avon Park, FL 33825. Tel: (813) 452-5282 Fax: (813) 452-1044. Principal: Lea Davis.

Mike Davis Public Relations, Inc. (D). 3716 National Drive, Suite 118, Raleigh, NC 27612. Tel: (919) 787-6411 Fax: (919) 787-6508 E-mail: 75443.61@compuserve.com. or Washington, DC Tel: (202) 986-1716. Principal: Mike Davis.

Susan Davis International. 1000 Vermont Avenue NW, Suite 700, Washington, DC 20005. Tel: (202) 408-0808 Fax: (202) 408-1231. Principal: Susan A. Davis.

db Consulting (D). 10308 Propps NE, Albuquerque, NM 87112. Tel: (505) 296-9214 Fax: (505) 296-9214. Principal: Don Brown.

DCM Group, The (R). 1320 Old Chain Bridge Road, Suite 220, McLean, VA 22101. Tel: (703) 883-1355 Fax: (703) 883-1850 E-mail: ed@dcm.com. Principal: Ed DeBolt.

Delta Design Group (D). 409 Washington Avenue, Greenville, MS 38701. Tel: (601) 335-6148 Fax: (601) 378-2836 E-mail: nworkman @tecinfo.com. Principal: Noel Workman.

Democratic Comm. Group, The. 135 Victoria Road, New Britain, CT 06052. Tel: (860) 827-0537 Fax: (860) 827-0537 E-mail: dmalin@courant.infi.net. Principal: David S. Malinowski.

Democratic Consulting Group, Inc. (D). PO Box 1488, Jackson, MS 39215. Tel: (601) 352-7037 Fax: (601) 949-8492 E-mail: nash@ metamall.com. Principal: Jere Nash.

Derish & Assoc., Inc. (D). 1701 Franklin Street, San Francisco, CA 94109. Tel: (415) 771-0551 Fax: (415) 647-1125. Principal: Seth Derish.

Donald Devine Co. (R). 919 Prince Street, Alexandria, VA 22314. Tel: (703) 683-6833 Fax: (703) 684-7642. Principal: Donald Devine.

Dillard Associates (D). 1100 North University, Suite 109, Little Rock, AR 72207. Tel: (501) 663-1202 Fax: (501) 663-1218 E-mail: dilnet@intellinet.com. Principal: Mary Frost Dillard.

Direct Impact Strategic Communications (D). 931 East 86th Street, Suite 111, Indianapolis, IN 46240. Tel: (317) 259-4700 Fax: (317) 475-0521 E-mail: gvigran@iquest.net. Principal: Gary H. Vigran.

Dittman Strategic Campaigns (R). 8115 Jewel Lake, DRC Building, Anchorage, AK 99502. Tel: (907) 243-3345 Fax: (907) 243-7172. Principal: David Lynn Dittman.

Doak Carrier & Assoc. (D). 1000 Thomas Jefferson Street NW, Suite 306, Washington, DC 20007. Tel: (202) 342-7700 Fax: (202) 342-2087 E-mail: doakca@aol.com. Principal: David Doak.

Dolphin Group, Inc. (R). 10866 Wilshire Boulevard, Suite 550, Los Angeles, CA 90024. Tel: (310) 446-4800 Fax: (310) 446-1896. Principal: Lee Stitzenberger.

James Doundoulakis. 11020 71st Avenue, Forest Hills, NY 11375. Tel (718) 575-0683. Principal: James Doundoulakis.

DPS Enterprises. PO Box 2104, Alexandria, VA 22301-0104. Tel: (703) 685-1188. Principal: Diane P. Scott.

Duberstein Group, The. 2100 Pennsylvania Avenue NW, Suite 350, Washington, DC 20037-3202. Tel: (202) 728-1100 Fax: (202) 728-1123. Principal: Kenneth Duberstein.

Eagle Consulting Group, Inc., The (R). 107 North 45th Street, Suite 114, Harrisburg, PA 17111. Tel: (717) 564-3202 Fax: (717) 564-3227 E-mail: 70670,20g@compuserve.com. Principal: Christopher Nicholas.

Ed Allison Inc. (R). 1341 G Street NW, 2nd Floor, Washington, DC 20005. Tel: (202) 783-1800 Fax: (202) 783-2913. Principal: Ed Allison.

Election Enterprises (R). PO Box 275, Billings, MT 59103. Tel: (406) 252-7424 Fax: (406) 252-7424. Principal: Elwood English.

Electoral Group, Inc./Attorney at Law. 50 Hillcrest Avenue, New Britain, CT 06053. Tel: (860) 224-4874 Fax: (860) 224-4436. Principal: Paul S. Vayer.

Ellis Hart Assoc., Inc. (R). 1301 Dove Street, Suite 710 Newport Beach, CA 92660-2470. Tel: (714) 675-0015 Fax: (714) 675-9417. Principal: David Ellis.

Emmons & Company, Inc. (D). 102 Kelsey Drive, Richmond, KY 40475 1171. Tel: (606) 624-9623 Fax: (606) 623-2666. Principal: Dale Emmons.

Engen & Assoc. (D). PO Box 2703, Sherman, TX 75091. Tel: (903) 892-4439. Principal: Erik O. Engen.

Epley Assoc. (D). 6302 Fairview Road, Suite 200, Charlotte, NC 28211. Tel: (704) 442-9100 Fax: (704) 442-9903 E-mail: epley@epley-pr.com. Principal: Joe Epley. Website: http://www.epley-pr.com.

Bryan Eppstein & Company, Inc. (R). 4055 International Plaza, Suite 520, Fort Worth, TX 76109-4800. Tel: (817) 737-3656 Fax: (817) 737-4245. Principal: Bryan Eppstein.

Evets Management Services, Inc. 844 Texas Avenue, Shreveport, LA 71101. Tel: (318) 424-1695. Principal: Elliot B. Stonecipher.

Fairbank, Maslin, Maullin & Assoc. (D). 2425 Colorado Avenue, Suite 180, Santa Monica, CA 90404. Tel: (310) 828-1183 Fax: (310) 453-6562 E-mail: fmma@crl.com. Principal: John Fairbank.

Federal & State Legislative Services, Inc. 2596 F, South Arlington Mill Drive, Arlington, VA 22206. Tel: (703) 845-9070 Fax: (703) 845-9070. Principal: Edmund C. Brickfield.

Randolph G. Flood. 422 1st Street SE, Suite 210, Washington, DC 20003. Tel: (202) 544-6675. Principal: Randolph Flood.

Foreman & Heidepriem, Inc. (D). 1100 New York Avenue NW, Suite 1030W, Washington, DC 20005. Tel: (202) 822-8060 Fax: (202) 822-9088. Principal: Nikki Heidepriem.

Forsythe, Francis, Erraut (R). 2685 South Rainbow, Suite 112, Las Vegas, NV 89102. Tel: (702) 362-5457 Fax: (702) 362-9960. Principal: Steve Forsythe.

Fowler Communications (D). PO Box 50627, Columbia, SC 29250. Tel: (803) 799-7550 Fax: (803) 771-7442. Principal: Donald Fowler.

Fraioli, Inc. (D). 80 F Street NW, Suite 804, Washington, DC 20001. Tel: (202) 347-3042 Fax: (202) 347-3046 E-mail: fraioli@aol.com. Principal: Michael Fraioli.

John Franzen Multimedia (D). 610 C Street NE, Washington, DC 20002. Tel: (202) 543-4430 Fax: (202) 543-8693 E-mail: jfranzen@ compuserve.com. Principal: John Franzen.

Douglas Fulmer & Assoc. (D). 14278 Bridgel Trail, Strongsville, OH 44136-8900. Tel: (440) 846-0308. Principal: Douglas Fulmer.

G.T. Long (D). PO Box 2156, Route 2, Horton Bay, MI 49712. Tel: (616) 582-7043. Principal: G.T. Long.

Garth Group, The. 505 Park Avenue, 8th Floor, New York, NY 10022-1106. Tel: (212) 838-8800 Fax: (212) 752-1838. Principal: David L. Garth.

Gerl, Scotti & Assoc. (D). PO Box 424, Lewisburg, WV 24901. Tel: (304) 645-7362 Fax: (304) 645-7362. Principal: Jim Gerl.

Gilliard Blanning & Assoc. (R). 921 11th Street, Suite 600, Sacramento, CA 95814. Tel: (916) 444-1502 Fax: (916) 444-0128 E-mail: 76746.2275@compuserve.com. Principal: Dave Gilliard.

Robert J. Giuffra, Jr. (R). 8 Hawthorne Road, Bronxville, NY 10708. Tel: (914) 793-5302. Principal: Robert J. Giuffra Jr.

Glazer & Assoc. (D). 30 Sleepy Hollow Lane, Orinda, CA 94563. Tel: (916) 781-7918 Fax: (916) 781-7943. Principal: Steve Glazer.

Glick Assoc. (D). 222 Park Avenue South, New York, NY 10003. Tel: (212) 353-9200 Fax: (212) 477-8235. Principal: Joseph Glick.

Goddard Claussen/First Tuesday. 3300 Douglas Boulevard, Suite 400, Roseville, CA 95661. Tel: (916) 774-0628 Fax: (916) 774-0640. or 1150 Connecticut Avenue NW, Washington, DC 20036. Tel: (202) 955-6200 Fax: (202) 342-4459. Principal: Richard Claussen.

Goldman Assoc. (D). 4 South Market Street, Boston, MA 02109. Tel: (617) 227-5073 Fax: (617) 227-2379. Principal: Michael Goldman.

Mark Goode Enterprises (R). 1120 Connecticut Avenue NW, Suite 270, Washington, DC 20036. Tel: (202) 466-2616 Fax: (202) 785-3162. Principal: Mark Goode.

Governmental Consultant Services, Inc. 530 West Ionia, Suite B, Lansing, MI 48933. Tel: (517) 484-6216 Fax: (517) 484-0140. Principal: Robert Vander Laan.

Grant, Inc. (R). PO Box 2688, Lynchburg, VA 24501. Tel: (804) 845-1323. Principal: Al Grant.

Grassroots Concepts. PO Box 68401 Seattle, WA 98168. Tel: (206) 382-0212. Principal: Robert Hoyden.

Grassroots Political Campaigns (D). 6310-305 Greenwood Parkway, Northfield, OH 44067. Tel: (216) 467-2915 Fax: (216) 467-9753. Principal: Murray Fishel.

Dan Greenblat, Consultant (R). 4182 Pallon Court, San Diego, CA 92124-2703. Tel: (619) 530-2368. Principal: Dan Greenblat.

Grossfeld/Severns (D). 350 South Mill Avenue, Tempe, AZ 85281. Tel: (602) 784-4890 Fax: (602) 784-4999 E-mail: grosssev@ goodnet.com. Principal: Bob Grossfeld.

S. J. Guzzetta & Assoc. PO Box 17274, Alexandria, VA 22302. Tel: (800) 562-6624 or (703) 549-7586 Fax: (703) 423-6613. Principal: Sal Guzzetta.

John D. Hamilton (D). 2110 Park Avenue, Lincoln, NE 68502. Tel: (402) 476-3198. Principal: John D. Hamilton.

Hamilton & Staff (D). 4201 Connecticut Avenue NW, Suite 212, Washington, DC 20008. Tel: (202) 686-5900 Fax: (202) 686-7080 E-mail: billham@dgsys.com. Principal: William R. Hamilton.

Hampton Enterprises (D). 1121 Arlington Boulevard, Suite 919, Arlington, VA 22209. Tel: (703) 522-3652 Fax: (703) 525-2373. Principal: Brian Hampton.

Hands On Campaign Consulting (D). 2665 Matheson Way, Sacramento, CA 95864. Tel: (916) 484-7895 Fax: (916) 444-1710. Principal: Chris M. Maupin.

Harrison & Goldberg Inc. (D). 2464 Massachusetts Avenue, Cambridge, MA 02141. Tel: (617) 864-1721 Fax: (617) 864-2919. Principal: Tubby Harrison.

Hebrock & Assoc. Inc. 253 East Virginia Street, Tallahassee, FL 32301. Tel: (904) 222-1988. Principal: Bill J. Hebrock.

Helsel Assoc. (R). PO Box 12088, Harrisburg, PA 17108. Tel: (717) 234-2989 Fax: (717) 234-4111. Principal: Thomas Helsel Jr.

Hickman Brown Research, Inc. (D). 1350 Connecticut Avenue NW, Suite 206, Washington, DC 20036. Tel: (202) 659-4000 Fax: (202) 659-1832. Principal: Harrison Hickman.

Holman Communication. 1667 K Street NW, Suite 390, Washington, DC 20006. Tel: (202) 822-6804. Principal: Diana L. Holman.

Hopcraft Communications (D). 3551 N Street, Sacramento, CA 95816. Tel: (916) 457-5546 Fax: (916) 456-6545. Principal: Stephen Hopcraft.

Hortos Advertising. PO Box 419, St Clair, MI 48079. Tel: (810) 329-1010 Fax: (810) 329-7100. Principal: Patrick Hortos.

Hoving Group, The. 4831 Albemarle Street NW, Washington, DC 20016. Tel: (202) 939-8980 Fax: (202) 939-8972 E-mail: hovings@ aol.com. Principal: Kate Hoving.

Huckaby & Assoc. (R). 641 Fulton Avenue, Suite 250, Sacramento, CA 95825. Tel: (916) 483-4995 Fax: (916) 483-4264. Principal: Gary C. Huckaby.

George Humphreys Assoc. (R). 304 Townsend Place, Atlanta, GA 30327. Tel: (404) 233-6704 Fax: (404) 365-0225. Principal: George Humphreys.

Dan Hunter Creative Services (D). 1101 Walnut, Des Moines, IA 50309. Tel: (515) 288-8908 Fax: (515) 243-4317 or (202) 483-7842. Principal: Dan Hunter.

Wayne Hurder/Public Relations (D). 615 Willard Place, Raleigh, NC 27603. Tel: (919) 828-3250. Principal: Wayne Hurder.

Image Works, The (R). Vandivort Center, 350 East Walnut 110LL, Springfield, MO 65806. Tel: (417) 831-0110 Fax: (417) 831-0288. Principal: Joseph H. Straughan.

Independent Opinion Research & Comm., Inc. (D). PO Box 501, Wrightsville Beach, NC 28480. Tel: (910) 799-9703 Fax: (910) 799-3891. Principal: Susan K. Bulluck.

Index Group/Miller Partners, Inc. (R). 102 18th Avenue East, Seattle, WA 98112. Tel: (206) 448-4972 Fax: (206) 328-6060 E-mail: indexteam@aol.com. Principal: Gloria Miller.

Integrated Marketing Communications. 241 West 30th Street, Suite 600, New York, NY 10001. Tel: (212) 643-1623. Principal: Menachem Lubinsky.

Integrated Strategies Group (D). 319 South 17th Street, Suite 232, Omaha, NE 68102-1911. Tel: (402) 345-2320. Principal: Michael O'Conner.

International Civics, Inc. 145 Park Avenue, Apt 4B, East Rutherford, NJ 07073-1824. Tel: (201) 768-0505 Fax: (201) 784-3992. Principal: Edward Grefe.

Isenson Assoc. (D). PO Box 564, Olympia, WA 98507. Tel: (206) 426-7115. Principal: Beverly P. Isenson.

J S R Consulting (D). PO Box 101, Port Jervis, NY 12771. Tel: (914) 858-8673 Fax: (914) 856-1361. Principal: Joseph S. Rifkin.

Jackson Communications (D). 6 Merrimack Place, Suite 3, Haverhill, MA 01830. Tel: (508) 469-9885 Fax: (508) 469-9881 E-mail: jaxoncomm@aol. com. Principal: Bud Jackson.

Johnson & Staff (D). 3385 Coastal Highway, Apt 5, St Augustine, FL 32045-1775. Tel: (904) 371-9871 Fax: (904) 371-9875. Principal: R.V. Johnson.

Bill Johnson Survey Research, Inc. (D). 850 Bronx River Road, Yonkers, NY 10478. Tel: (914) 776-0701. Principal: William G. Johnson.

Margaret Jones & Assoc. (D). 1081 New Gibraltar Square, Stone Mountain, GA 30083. Tel: (770) 469-8707 Fax: (770) 498-7695. Principal: Margaret Hylton Jones.

JRA Communications Group (D). 3101 Ocean Park Boulevard, Suite 304, Santa Monica, CA 90405. Tel: (310) 399-1219 Fax: (310) 392-6516 E-mail: jragroup@aol.com. Principal: Jeffrey Robinson.

Oscar F. Juarez & Assoc. (R). 105 East Robinson, Suite 300, Orlando, FL 32801. Tel: (407) 843-0013 Fax: (407) 872-8663. Principal: Oscar F. Juarez.

Kadas Assoc. (D). 105 Shepherd Street, Rockville Center, NY 11570. Tel: (516) 766-6235. Principal: James Levy.

Grace Kaminkowitz Enterprises. 1143 South Plymouth Court, Suite 501, Chicago, IL 60605. Tel: (312) 987-0038 Fax: (312) 987-1022. Principal: Grace Kaminkowitz.

Barry Kaplovitz Assoc. 60 Charlesgate West, Boston, MA 02215. Tel: (617) 437-0847. Principal: Barry Kaplovitz.

Katz & Assoc. (R). 4275 Executive Square 700, La Jolla, CA 92037. Tel: (619) 452-0031 Fax: (619) 546-0911. Principal: Sara M. Katz.

Kemet Group, The. PO Box 19302, Detroit, MI 48219. Tel: (313) 533-7874. Principal: Nabil Leach.

Kimball Petition Management, Inc. 31225 La Baya Drive, Suite 108, Westlake Village, CA 91362. Tel: (818) 597-7770 Fax: (818) 865-1315 E-mail: fred@kpm.com. Principal: Kelly Kimball.

Steve Kline Campaigns (D). 1095 Market Street, Suite 612, San Francisco, CA 94103. Tel: (415) 255-8673 Fax: (415) 255-2376. Principal: Steve Kline.

Knight Phillips Assoc., Inc. (D). PO Box 5128, Charleston, WV 25301. Tel: (304) 345-6046 Fax: (304) 345-1067. Principal: Thomas A. Knight.

Knox Group, The. RR 2, PO Box 1010, Waterbury, VT 05676. Tel: (802) 244-5906 Fax: (802) 244-5906. Principal: Toby Knox.

Christine D. Koerner Assoc. (D). 1706 Old Stage Road, Alexandria, VA 22308. Tel: (703) 780-9420 Fax: (703) 780-3286. Principal: Christine Koerner.

William Kostka & Assoc. 1407 Larimar Square, Denver, CO 80202. Tel: (303) 623-8421 Fax: (303) 573-5426. Principal: William Kostka.

Nicolas Kulibaba Assoc. 9807 Croom Road, Upper Marlboro, MD 20772. Tel: (301) 627-5589. Principal: Nicolas Kulibaba.

Lacy Communications (R). PO Box 3489, Hamilton, NJ 08619. Tel: (609) 587-7830. Principal: John J. Lacy Jr.

Paul Laxalt Group, The. 801 Pennsylvania Avenue NW, Suite 750, Washington, DC 20004. Tel: (202) 624-0640. Principal: Paul Laxalt.

Lee Assoc. 1305 Franklin Street, Oakland, CA 94612. Tel: (415) 893-6383. Principal: Barbara Lee.

Legislative Performance Group. 9 Monroe Parkway, Suite 120, Lake Oswego, OR 97035. Tel: (503) 635-5864. Principal: Jack Kane.

Levins Group, The. 265 North Hibiscus Drive, Hibiscus Island, Miami Beach, FL 33139. Tel: (305) 532-7603 Fax: (305) 532-7603. Principal: Linda Levins.

Robert M. Levy & Assoc. 708 NE 69th Street, Suite 1730, Miami, FL 33138. Tel: (305) 758-1194 Fax: (305) 758-4294. or 216 South Adams Street, Tallahassee, FL 32301. Tel: (904) 681-0254 Fax: (904) 681-0295. Principal: Robert M. Levy.

Allan J. Lichtman (D). 9219 Villa Drive, Bethesda, MD 20817. Tel: (301) 530-8262. Principal: Allan J. Lichtman.

Lunde & Burger. 1101 King Street, Suite 601, Alexandria, VA 22314. Tel: (703) 838-5511 Fax: (703) 838-9249. Principal: Brian Lunde.

Luntz Research Companies, The (R). 1000 Wilson Boulevard, Suite 950, Arlington, VA 22209. Tel: (703) 358-0080 Fax: (703) 358-0089. Principal: Frank I. Luntz.

Main Street Media (D). PO Box 381, Mocksville, NC 27028. Tel: (704) 634-3118. Principal: Wanda R. Edwards.

Joel R. Maliniak Political Communications (D). 308 North Arden Boulevard, Los Angeles, CA 90004. Tel: (213) 464-3080. Principal: Joel Maliniak.

Mallard Group, Inc., The (R). 2861 Executive Drive, Suite 100, Clearwater, FL 34622.

Tel: (813) 572-4665 Fax: (813) 572-1828 E-mail: Mallardgrp@aol.com. Principal: John T. Hebert.

Malloy & Assoc. (D). 372 Central Park West, Suite 3M, New York, NY 10025. Tel: (212) 666-8674 Fax: (212) 749-8387. Principal: Patrick J. Malloy.

Management Services. 4109 Nicklaus, Corpus Christi, TX 78413. Tel: (512) 854-0045. Principal: Mary Salisbury.

Mandate: Campaign Media (D). PO Box 2124, Woodbridge, VA 22193. Tel: (703) 583-6277 Fax: (703) 583-8504 E-mail: 76046.723@ compuserve.com. Principal: Michael Shannnon.

Marathon Communications (D). 8436 West 3rd Street, Suite 700, Los Angeles, CA 90048. Tel: (213) 655-4660 Fax: (213) 655-6478 E-mail: 74722.353@ compuserve.com. Principal: Richard Lichtenstein.

Market Strategies Inc. (R). 2000 Town Center, Suite 2600, Southfield, MI 48075. Tel: (810) 350-3020 Fax: (810) 350-3023. or 1301 Pennsylvania Avenue NW, Suite 703, Washington, DC 20004. Tel: (212) 393-2800 Fax: (212) 393-2805. Principal: Alexander Gage.

Marketing Campaign Strategies, Inc. (D). 1609 Nueces, Austin, TX 78701. Tel: (512) 476-7797. Principal: Richard Jenson.

Marlowe & Company (D). 1667 K Street NW, Suite 480, Washington, DC 20006. Tel: (202) 775-1796 Fax: (202) 775-0214. Principal: Howard Marlowe.

Martin & Brown (R). 2300 Paseo Del Prado, Suite 202, Las Vegas, NV 89102. Tel: (702) 362-7700. Principal: Mark Brown.

Martin Assoc. (R). 9725 Cinnamon Creek Drive, Vienna, VA 22180. Tel: (703) 759-4890. Principal: J. Allen Martin.

Martin Corporation. 6803 Cantrell, Suite 364, Little Rock, AR 72207. Tel: (501) 329-9426 Fax: (501) 329-9427. Principal: David F. Martin.

Mortimer Matz Assoc. (D). 321 Broadway, 2nd Floor, New York, NY 10007. Tel: (212) 385-3800 Fax: (212) 385-3804. Principal: Mortimer Matz.

Kevin M. McAuliffe Commun. & Editorial Svcs. (D). 451 East 14th Street, Apt 3D, New York, NY 10009. Tel: (212) 677-0921 Fax: (212) 777-5688. Principal: Kevin McAuliffe.

Vern McCarthy, Ltd. (R). 8 Brighton Lane, Oak Brook, IL 60521-2324. Tel: (708) 954-2850 Fax: (708) 954-2851. Principal: Vern I. McCarthy.

William McClintock Assoc. (R). 269 Sheffield Street, Mountainside, NJ 07092. Tel: (908) 232-0968 Fax: (908) 232-2285. Principal: William F. McClintock.

McElroy Communications. 2410 K Street, Suite C, Sacramento, CA 95816. Tel: (916) 447-7415 Fax: (916) 447-4944. Principal: Leo McElroy.

McFadden and Assoc. 3426 West 66th Street, Chicago, IL 60629. Tel: (312) 434-4295. Principal: Monica E. McFadden.

McGuire & Company (D). 2962 Fillmore Street, San Francisco, CA 94123. Tel: (415) 775-1931 Fax: (415) 775-4159. Principal: Scott McGuire.

Hank McManus Assoc., Inc. (D). 127 East 59th Street, New York, NY 10022. Tel: (212) 755-7730. Principal: Hank McManus.

MD2 Strategic Campaigns. 2190 South Ashland Avenue, Green Bay, WI 54304. Tel: (414) 498-1000 Fax: (414) 498 -871. Principal: Craig S. Dickman.

Mica, Dudinsky & Assoc. 305 East Capitol Street SE, Washington, DC 20003. Tel: (202) 543-2143 Fax: (202) 543-3992. or PO Box 756, Winter Park, FL 32790. Tel: (305) 628-3688. Principal: John L. Mica.

Nicholas J. Miglino. 217 Broadway, New York, NY 10007. Tel: (212) 513-1616. Principal: Nicholas J. Miglino.

Miles & Assoc. (R). 1045 Teviot Place NW, Salem, OR 97304. Tel: (503) 585-0123 Fax: (503) 363-8898 E-mail: dmiles@milesnet.com. Principal: Denny Miles.

Bill Miles Assoc., Inc. (D). PO Box 748, Tupelo, MS 38802. Tel: (601) 842-5040. Principal: William T. Miles.

Miller Legislative Services. PO Box 10024, Arlington, VA 22210. Tel: (703) 527-6146 Fax: (703) 527-6272. Principal: William Miller.

Mitchell Research & Communications, Inc. (R). 211 Evergreen, PO Box 4066, East Lansing, MI 48823. Tel: (517) 351-4111 Fax: (517) 351-1265. Principal: Steve Mitchell.

MLB Research Assoc. (D). 1 Cross Path Road, Hadley, MA 01035. Tel: (413) 582-0165 Fax: (413) 582-7013. Principal: Matt L. Barron.

Morris Carick, Inc. (D). 432 Park Avenue South, Suite 1206, New York, NY 10016. Tel: (212) 696-9308 Fax: (212) 696-9147. or 3190 Beachwood Drive, Los Angeles, CA 90034. Tel: (213) 469-1592. Principal: Hank Morris.

Dick Morris (R). 20 Beeholm Road, West Redding, CT 06896. Tel: (203) 938-2535 Fax: (203) 938-4055. Principal: Dick Morris.

Murphine Group, The (D). 1350 Connecticut Avenue NW, Suite 1102, Washington, DC 20036. Tel: (202) 488-4873 Fax: (202) 488-4873. Principal: Ralph Murphine.

James S. Nathanson & Assoc. (R). 317 Talbott Tower, 131 North Ludlow Street, Dayton, OH 45402. Tel: (513) 222-0131 Fax: (513) 223-0423. Principal: James S. Nathanson.

National Media Inc. (R). 211 North Union Street, Suite 200, Alexandria, VA 22314. Tel: (703) 683-4877 Fax: (703) 683-3579. Principal: Robin D. Roberts.

National Political Services, Inc. 308 East 30th Street, Suite 4 New York, NY 10016. Tel: (212) 689-7683 Fax: (212) 685-6618. Principal: Joseph Mercurio.

Jack Neil & Assoc. PO Box 864, 1 Church Circle, Annapolis, MD 21404. Tel: (410) 269-0380. Principal: Jack Neil.

Christopher Nelson & Assoc. (R). PO Box 1228, Sugarloaf, CA 92386. Tel: (909) 585-2676. Principal: Chris Nelson.

New Mexico Consultants (D). 1104 Chama Street NE, Albuquerque, NM 87110-7116. Tel: (505) 266-1998 Fax: (505) 888-4101. Principal: Richard Kennedy.

New West Communications (D). PO Box 3142, Kearney, NE 68848. Tel: (308) 234-6381. Principal: Gary Goldberg.

New West Policy Group L.L.C. 223 East Union Street, Prescott, AZ 86303. Tel: (602) 776-7200 Fax: (602) 776-0146. Principal: Richard T. Mayol.

New York Consultancy (R). 42 North Avenue, New Rochelle, NY 10805. Tel: (914) 632-7000. Principal: Frank Trotta.

Phil Noble & Assoc. (D). 32 Bull Street, Charleston, SC 29401. Tel: (803) 853-8190 Fax: (803) 722-4283. or 313 East Capitol Street SE, Washington, DC 20003. Tel: (202) 546-3550 Fax: (202) 544-0863. Principal: Phil Noble.

Nofziger Communications (R). 1225 I Street NW, Suite 300, Washington, DC 20005. Tel: (202) 785-0500. Principal: Lyn Nofziger.

Norway Hill Assoc. (R). Norway Hill, Hancock, NH 03449. Tel: (603) 525-3818. Principal: David M. Carney.

Numbercrunchers, Inc. (R). 42 North Avenue, New Rochelle, NY 10805. Tel: (914) 235-0800. Principal: Richard J. Behn.

Mary Rose Oakar & Assoc., Inc. (D). 2621 Lorain Avenue, Cleveland, OH 44113. Tel: (216) 522-0550 Fax: (216) 522-0552. or PO Box 25577, Georgetown Station, Washington, DC 20007. Principal: Mary Rose Oakar.

One Acorn Management. 4845 Highway 1675, Somerset, KY 42501. Tel: (606) 274-4685 Fax: (606) 274-4126. Principal: Doris G. Petercheff.

Oram Ingram & Zurawski, Inc. 2290 South Jones, Suite 100, Las Vegas, NV 89102. Tel: (702) 878-9750. Principal: Kent Oram.

O'Grady and Assoc. (D). 16 East Broad Street, Suite 310, Columbus, OH 43215. Tel: (614) 464-3640 Fax: (614) 464-9371. Principal: Pete O'Grady.

Pacific Gateway Group (R). 450 A Street, Suite 400, San Diego, CA 92101. Tel: (619) 234-3491 Fax: (619) 234-1712. Principal: Doug Perkins.

Pacific Islands Washington Office (R). PO Box 26142, Alexandria, VA 22313. Tel: (703) 519-7757 Fax: (703) 548-0633 E-mail: piwowpr @erols.com. Principal: Fred Radewagen.

Pacwest Consultants (R). 21651 SE Edwards Drive, Clackamas, OR 97015. Tel: (503) 658-2841 Fax: (503) 658-7835. Principal: Dick Younts.

Eileen E. Padberg Consulting (R). 2801 Business Center Drive, Suite 125, Irvine, CA

92715. Tel: (714) 756-8477 Fax: (714) 756-2215. Principal: Eileen E. Padberg.

Paramount Communications (R). PO Box 215452, Sacramento, CA 95825. Tel: (916) 481-9451 Fax: (916) 481-9451 or PO Box 2123, Salinas, CA 93901. Tel: (408) 753-1499 E-mail: paracom@juno.com. Principal: Andrew Russo.

Dale Parker. PO Box 246, Boone, NC 28607. Tel: (704) 264-1052 Fax: (704) 264-4529. Principal: Dale Parker.

Patterson & McLaughlin Communications. 36 West 44th Street, New York, NY 10036. Tel: (212) 302-0400. Principal: Martin J. McLaughlin.

Tony Payton & Assoc. (R). 2638 South Lynn Street, Arlington, VA 22202. Tel: (703) 836-3051 Fax: (703) 836-3267 E-mail: tpawins@erols.com. Principal: Tony Payton.

Pearson & Pipkin, Inc. (R). 104 North Carolina Avenue SE, Washington, DC 20003-1841. Tel: (202) 547-7177 E-mail: govtrel@aol.com. Principal: Ronald W. Pearson.

Pelleran & Assoc. (D). PO Box 10135, Lansing, MI 48901. Tel: (517) 371-5410. Principal: K.P. Pelleran.

Stanton Phillips & Assoc. (D). 2009 North 14th Street, Suite 510, Arlington, VA 22201. Tel: (703) 522-8800 Fax: (703) 841-0845. Principal: Stanton Phillips.

PlanGraphics. 202 West Main Street, Suite 200, Frankfort, KY 40601. Tel: (502) 223-1501 Fax: (502) 223-1235. Principal: Tracy Morris.

Polisci (D). 501 Wellington Avenue, Seattle, WA 98122. Tel: (206) 328-4423 Fax: (206) 322-5680. Principal: Rudi Bertschi.

Political Advertising & Consulting (R). 115 Shepardson Lane, Alameda, CA 94502. Tel: (510) 814-6195 Fax: (510) 814-6966 E-mail: mbarnespac@aol.com. Principal: Mark Barnes.

Political Affairs, Inc. 343 3rd Street, Suite 203, Baton Rouge, LA 70802. Tel: (504) 346-6767 Fax: (504) 346-8878. Principal: James Burland.

Political Communications (D). 10530 Tanwood, Baton Rouge, LA 70809. Tel: (504) 293-7001 Fax: (504) 293-7758 E-mail: mbeychok@aol.com. Principal: Michael Beychok.

Political Communications (R). 2235 Webster Street, San Francisco, CA 94115. Tel: (415) 567-6301 Fax: (415) 929-0937 E-mail: harlowell@aol.com. Principal: Harvey Hukari.

Political Designs (D). 231 Market Place, Suite 235, San Ramon, CA 94583. Tel: (800) 827-1466 Fax: (510) 551-7633. Principal: J. Bradford Senden.

Political Issues Management. 136 East 57th Street, New York, NY 10022. Tel: (212) 759-9155 Fax: (212) 308-7243. Principal: Tanya Melich.

Political Strategy. 8391 Beverly Boulevard, Suite 321, Los Angeles, CA 90048. Tel: (213) 655-4968. Principal: Richard Baer.

Gary L. Prange (R). 1030 South 1st Street, Suite 8, Springfield, IL 62704. Tel: (217) 528-7315 Fax: (217) 528-7315. Principal: Gary L. Prange.

Primacy Group, The (D). 3609 4th Avenue, San Diego, CA 92103. Tel: (619) 295-6923 Fax: (619) 295-0487. Principal: Larry Remer.

Victor L. Profughi. Rhode Island College, 600 Mount Pleasant, Providence, RI 02908. Tel: (401) 456-8056 Fax: (401) 456-8379. Principal: Victor L. Profughi.

Public Concepts Inc. 5730 Corporate Way, Suite 214, West Palm Beach, FL 33407. Tel:

(561) 688-0061 Fax: (561) 688-0471. Principal: Randy Nielsen.

Public Policy Communications (D). 73 Trowbridge Street, Belmont, MA 02178. Tel: (617) 489-0461 Fax: (617) 489-6841 E-mail: bobschaeffer@igc.apc.org. Principal: Robert A. Schaeffer.

Public Policy Systems (D). 130 Bowdoin Street, Suite 1109, Boston, MA 02108. Tel: (617) 523-0050 Fax: (617) 523-8510. Principal: Bill Carito.

Public Strategies Inc. (D). 98 San Jacinto Boulevard, Suite 900, Austin, TX 78701-4039. Tel: (512) 478-1676. Principal: Jack Martin.

Quest Opinion Research. 23 Randall Street, Providence, RI 02904. Tel: (401) 949-1384 Fax: (401) 456-8379. Principal: Victor Profughi.

Larry Quinn, Political Consultant (D). 49 Pointview Drive, Troy, NY 12180. Tel: 518 274 3249 Fax: 518 274 3249. Principal: Larry Quinn.

R*M*M Consulting National Fundraising (D). 332 1/2 Maryland Avenue NE, Washington, DC 20002. Tel: (202) 543-8880 Fax: (202) 543-9829 E-mail: rmmconsult@aol.com. Principal: Kenneth S. Christensen.

R&R Advertising. PO Box 80130, Las Vegas, NV 89180-0103. Tel: (702) 794-0222 Fax: (702) 794-0208. Principal: Sig Rogich.

Ranagan Agency, The (R). 5 East San Luis Street, Suite 201, Salinas, CA 93901. Tel: (408) 758-2133 Fax: (408) 758-2150. Principal: Ron Ranagan.

Raritan Assoc., Inc. (R). 16 Woodcrest Drive, Morristown, NJ 07960. Tel: (908) 828-5896 Fax: (908) 846-0372. Principal: Stephen A. Salmore.

Reese & Assoc. (D). 1040 Bellview Place, McLean, VA 22102. Tel: (703) 893-3967 Fax: (703) 893-3421. Principal: Matt Reese.

H & G Reich. 127 Mount Hope Boulevard, Hastings on Hudson, NY 10706. Tel: (914) 478-4464. Principal: Gerri Reich.

Reid Strategies. 655 Riverside Drive, Suite 209N, Memphis, TN 38103. Tel: (901) 522-9934 Fax: (901) 529-9413. Principal: Steven Reid.

Research & Polling, Inc. 7500 Jefferson NE, Courtyard 2, Albuquerque, NM 87109. Tel: (505) 821-5454 Fax: (505) 821-5474. Principal: Brian Sanderoff.

Resource Management Assoc. 3934 Bel Aire Road, Des Moines, IA 50310. Tel: (515) 278-2283. Principal: Jane E. Magers.

Resource Team, The (R). PO Box 418, Warren, IN 46792. Tel: (219) 375-2652. Principal: David L. Daugherty.

Rich & Assoc. (D). 124 East High Street, Jefferson City, MO 65101. Tel: (314) 635-6362. Principal: Pam Schantz Rich.

Ridder/Braden, Inc. (D). 1776 Lincoln Street, Union Station 1318, Denver, CO 80203. Tel: (303) 832-2444 Fax: (303) 832-2555 E-mail: rbider@aol.com. Principal: Rick Ridder.

RKS Strategies (D). 800 North 2nd Avenue, Arcadia, CA 91006. Tel: (818) 357-9362 Fax: (818) 357-1103 E-mail: rksstrat@earthlink.net. Principal: Robert K. Stiens.

Mary Rose & Assoc. (D). PO Box 91840, Santa Barbara, CA 93109. Tel: (805) 965-3952 Fax: (805) 966-1306. Principal: Mary R. Rose.

Rothstein & Co. (D). 2101 Connecticut Avenue, Suite 32, Washington, DC 20008. Tel: (202) 232-9096 Fax: (202) 328-9064. Principal: Joe Rothstein.

RWD Assoc. (R). PO Box 44, Dunellen, NJ 08812-0044. Tel: (908) 968-5032 Fax: (908) 752-2876. Principal: Roger Dornbierer.

San Diego Poll. 5409 Hewlett Drive, San Diego, CA 92115. Tel: (619) 582-0080. Principal: Oscar J. Kaplan.

Sautter Communications (D). 3623 Everett Street NW, Washington DC 20008. Tel: (202) 244-3111 Fax: (202) 244-4220 E-mail: sauttercom@aol.com. Principal: Chris Sautter.

Schanzel & Assoc. (R). 10983 Mayfield Road, Chardon, OH 44024. Tel: (216) 285-2566 Fax: (216) 285-2566 E-mail: shanz@en.com. Principal: Dean J. Schanzel.

Christian Schock & Assoc. (D). 1079 Paradise Acres, Galesburg, IL 61401. Tel: (708) 741-1753. Principal: Christian Schock.

SDC Consulting (R). RR 1, PO Box 1798, Holts Summit, MO 65043. Tel: (314) 295-4830. Principal: Shannon D. Cavenue

Shafto & Assoc. 515 Post Oak Boulevard, Suite 120, Houston, TX 77027. Tel: (713) 840-1221. Principal: Sandra Shafto.

Shipley & Assoc., Inc. (D). 919 Congress Avenue, Austin, TX 78701. Tel: (512) 474-7514 Fax: (512) 472-2802. Principal: George C. Shipley.

Craig Shirley & Assoc. (R). 1225 Patrick Street, Alexandria, VA 22314. Tel: (703) 739-5920 Fax: (703) 739-5924 E-mail: csa@townhall.com. Principal: Craig Shirley.

Paul Shone & Assoc, Inc. (D). 141 Putnam Avenue, Cambridge, MA 02139. Tel: (617) 492-3736 Fax: (617) 834-1004. Principal: Paul Shone.

Shortt Comm. Group, Ltd. PO Box 14120, Savannah, GA 31416. Tel: (912) 232-9390 Fax: (912) 232-8213. Principal: Michael L. Shortt.

Randy Siefkin Campaigns (R). PO Box 4402, Modesto, CA 95352. Tel: (209) 521-8772 Fax: (209) 521-6772. Principal: Randy Siefkin.

Mark Siegel & Assoc. 1030 15th Street NW, Suite 408, Washington, DC 20005. Tel: (202) 371-5600 Fax: (202) 371-5608. Principal: Mark Siegel.

Siegel & Nicholl Company (D). 5750 Wilshire Boulevard, Suite 561, Los Angeles, CA 90036. Tel: (213) 937-5706 Fax: (213) 937-9613 E-mail: msiegel@pacificnet.net. Principal: Jack Nicholl.

Richard L. Silver (D). 824 Winslow Street, Suite 214, Redwood City, CA 94063. Tel: (415) 368-7112. Principal: Richard L. Silver.

Simons & Assoc. (R). 55 East Deerwood Road, Suite 157, Savannah, GA 31410. Tel: (912) 897-6185 Fax: (912) 898-1725. Principal: David C. Simons.

Smith & Assoc. (R). 807 Brazos Street, Suite 408, Austin, TX 78701. Tel: (512) 499-0601 Fax: (512) 499-0640. or 3740 North Josey, Suite 210, Carolton, TX 75007. Tel: (214) 395-2241 Fax: (214) 395-2230. Principal: Todd M. Smith.

Smith & Harroff, Inc. (R). 11 Canal Center Plaza, Suite 104, Alexandria, VA 22314. Tel: (703) 683-8512 Fax: (703) 683-4622 E-mail: eblakely@mindspring.com. Principal: J. Brian Smith.

L. Garry Smith & Assoc. 311 East Park Avenue, Tallahassee, FL 32301. Tel: (904) 224-5081 Fax: (904) 222-6800. Principal: Matt Bryan.

Ronald Smith Company (R). 1548 North Kings Road, Los Angeles, CA 90069. Tel: (213) 656-6204 Fax: (213) 650-8239. Principal: Ronald Smith.

Carl O. Snowdon & Assoc. PO Box 371, Annapolis, MD 21404. Tel: (410) 269-1524. Principal: Carl O. Snowden.

Solem & Assoc. (D). 550 Kearny Street, Suite 110, San Francisco, CA 94108. Tel: (415) 788-7788 Fax: (415) 788-7858 E-mail: solem @solem.com. Principal: Don Solem.

Southern Assoc. (D). RR 1, PO Box 15, Belden, MS 38826-9706. Tel: (601) 256-2711 Fax: (601) 256-2120. Principal: Danny Golding.

Special Forces Communications (R). 2100 Susquehanna Road, Abington, PA 19001. Tel: (215) 572-0717. Principal: Mark R. Weaver.

Squier/Knapp Ochs Communications (D). 511 2nd Street NE, Washington, DC 20002. Tel: (202) 547-4970. Principal: Robert D. Squier.

Howard N. Stark (R). 88 South Willard Street, Burlington, VT 05401. Tel: (802) 863-1708. Principal: Howard N. Stark.

Staton, Hughes & Shafer (D). 530 Howard, Suite 200, San Francisco, CA 94105. Tel: (415) 495-4910 Fax: (415) 495-5733 E-mail: info@ statonhughes.com. Principal: Mary Hughes.

Strategic Campaign Initiatives (D). 12608 Safety Turn, Bowie, MD 20715. Tel: (301) 464-5988 Fax: (301) 464-3040. Principal: Brenda L. Beitzell.

Strategic Communications (R). 124 Rivoli Street, Suite 1, San Francisco, CA 94117-4363. Tel: (415) 664-9685 Fax: (415) 664-9358 E-mail: ammcomm@worldnet.att.net. Principal: Anthony M. Malandra.

Strategy Group For Republican Politics, The (R). 8202 Glencullen Court, Dublin, OH 43017. Tel: (614) 717-0842 Fax: (614) 717-0547. or 10707 Bull Ridge Drive, Austin, TX 78759. Tel: (512) 338-4068 Fax: (512) 338-4069. or 419 South Perry Street, Know House, Montgomery, AL 36104. Tel: (334) 263-7812

E-mail: rexelsass@aol.com. Principal: Rex Elsass. Website: http://www.strategy-group.com.

Strategy Group, Inc., The (D). 730 North Franklin, Suite 601, Chicago, IL 60610. Tel: (312) 944-7737 Fax: (312) 944-8699. or 1901 L Street NW, 3rd Floor, Washington, DC 20036. Tel: (202) 452-9418 Fax: (202) 296-7532 E-mail: stratgrp@aol.com. Principal: Liz Sears.

Strother/Duffy/Strother (D). 1400 I Street NW, Suite 450, Washington, DC 20005. Tel: (202) 626-5650 Fax: (202) 639-8974 E-mail: rdsfilms@ aol.com. Principal: Raymond D. Strother.

Sunwood Assoc. (D). 1741 Lanier Place NW, Suite 24, Washington, DC 20009. Tel: (202) 387-5233. Principal: Susan Bonfield Herschkowitz.

Sutherland MultiMedia (D). 7750 Broadway, San Antonio, TX 78209. Tel: (210) 820-3278 Fax: (210) 820-3375. Principal: Tucker Sutherland.

Talmey Research & Strategy, Inc. (D). PO Box 1070, Boulder, CO 80306. Tel: (303) 443-5300 Fax: (303) 447-9386. Principal: Paul Talmey.

Tammany Hall. 916 Seagirl Boulevard, Far Rockaway, NY 11691-5632. Tel: (718) 329-0310 Fax: (718) 327-2857. Principal: Bill Mark.

Target Enterprises (R). 16501 Ventura Boulevard, Suite 515, Encino, CA 90068. Tel: (818) 905-0005 Fax: (818) 905-1444. Principal: David Bienstock.

Targeted Creative Communications (R). 1000 Duke Street, Alexandria, VA 22314. Tel: (703) 684-1987 Fax: (703) 684-3948. Principal: Dan Hazelwood.

Terris & Jaye (D). 400 Montgomery Street, Suite 900, San Francisco, CA 94104-1223. Tel:

(415) 291-0679 Fax: (415) 291-0724. Principal: Michael Terris.

THC Consulting (R). 1949 Chestnut Street, Suite 101, San Francisco, CA 94123. Tel: (415) 576-2552 Fax: (415) 421-1480. Principal: Mark P. Harner.

Thompson Communications, Inc. (R). PO Box 5, 200 West Jefferson Street, Marshfield, MO 65706. Tel: (417) 859-5428 Fax: (417) 468-7577. Principal: John P. Thompson.

Thomson Mgt. Group, Inc., The (D). 2108 North Military Road, Arlington, VA 22207. Tel: (703) 524-1595 Fax: (703) 524-9855 E-mail: thomsonmgt@aol.com. Principal: Alexander B. Thomson.

Thornbrugh & Assoc. (R). 11435 East 5th Street, Tulsa, OK 74128. Tel: (918) 437-1466. Principal: Paul E. Thornbrugh.

Nancy Todd, Inc. (D). 853 Vanderbilt Beach Road, Suite 331, Naples, FL 34108. Tel: (941) 592-9130 Fax: (941) 592-9133 E-mail: ntodd@aol.com. Principal: Nancy Todd.

Tompkison Group, The (D). 2059 Camden Avenue, Suite 300, San Jose, CA 95124. Tel: (408) 978-2866 Fax: (408) 448-4777. Principal: Catherine Matsuyo Tompkison.

Torok Group, The. 1901 US Highway 130, North Brunswick, NJ 08902. Tel: (908) 940-9484 Fax: (908) 821-1082. Principal: Enid R. Torok.

Trudell Political Consultants (D). 4432 East Viking Road, Las Vegas, NV 89121. Tel: (702) 451-3631. Principal: Harriet Trudell.

Tyson Organization, The (D). 5016 Fall River Drive, Fort Worth, TX 76103. Tel: (817) 451-3944 E-mail: tysorg@ltw.com. Principal: Gerald S. Tyson.

Voter Contact Services (D). PO Box 43, Amherst, MA 01004. Tel: (800) VCS-File Fax: (413) 256-8886 E-mail: mihann@javanet.com. Principal: Mike Hannahan. Website: http://bbs.vcsnet.com.

Walker, Bush & Co. (R). 429 Brattle Road, Syracuse, NY 13203. Tel: (315) 426-0637. Principal: William Bartlett Bush.

Wallace Assoc. (D). PO Box 1836, Little Rock, AR 72203. Tel: (501) 376-3880. Principal: Douglas Wallace.

Jack Walsh & Assoc., Inc. (D). 22 Richmond Street, West Boxbury, MA 02132. Tel: (617) 325-1050 Fax: (617) 325-0387. Principal: Jack Walsh.

David J. Warager, Esq. (R). 2 Overlook Road, Suite S9, White Plains, NY 10605. Tel: (914) 761-3332. Principal: David J. Warager.

Arthur Weber & Assoc. (R). 1140 23rd Street NW, Washington, DC 20037. Tel: (202) 293-7187 Fax: (202) 872-1150. Principal: Joseph A. Weber.

Welchert Company, The (D). 1525 Market Street, Suite 200, Denver, CO 80202. Tel: (303) 615-9725 Fax: (303) 615-9735. Principal: Steve Welchert.

Western Advocates Inc. 1234 Court Street NE, Salem, OR 97223. Tel: (503) 620-3356 Fax: (503) 598-0298 E-mail: westernadv@aol.com. Principal: Burton Weast.

Western Pacific Research, Inc. (R). 4100 Truxton Avenue, Suite 210, Bakersfield, CA 93309. Tel: (805) 327-4141 Fax: (805) 327-3672. or 6735 Fair Oaks Boulevard, Suite 8, Carmichael, CA 95608. Tel: (916) 483-8111 Fax: (916) 483-8137. Principal: Mark Abernathy.

Whistlestop Communications, Inc. (R). 1810 Broad Ripple Avenue, Suite13, PO Box 802, Indianapolis, IN 46206-0802. Tel: (317) 259-0781 Fax: (317) 259-0754 E-mail: whistle@

whistlestopgop.com. Principal: Keith L. Shallenberger.

Whitesides Stonecipher & Assoc. 509 Marshall Street, Suite 716, Shreveport, LA 71101. Tel: (318) 424-8198. Principal: Alan Stonecipher.

Whitney & Assoc. (R). 722 Gibbon Street, Alexandria, VA 22314-1408. Tel: (703) 836-1003 Fax: (703) 836-1004 E-mail: p447@ erols.com. Principal: Carol A. Whitney.

Whouley & Assoc. (D). 1 Beacon Street, Suite 1320, Boston, MA 02108. Tel: (617) 268-9263 Fax: (617) 742-6880. Principal: Michael J. Whouley.

Wild Goat Campaigns (D). 6198 Marteney Avenue, Kent, OH 44240. Tel: (216) 677-1155 Fax: (216) 677-1155 E-mail: politx@aol.com. Principal: Scott Walker.

Wilkes Company, The. PO Box 6933, Lubbock, TX 79493-6933. Tel: (806) 765-5298 Fax: (806) 744-4902 E-mail: 74167.177@ compuserve.com. Principal: Morris Wilkes.

Williams & Assoc. (R). 6 Riptide Court, Newport Beach, CA 92663. Tel: (714) 631-1911 Fax: (714) 631-7232. Principal: Michael R. Williams.

Williams & Assoc. (R). 342 Essex Street, Salem, MA 01970. Tel: (508) 744-3771 Fax: (508) 744-7042. Principal: David E. Williams.

John L. Williams Productions (R). Route 1, PO Box 178, Lapine, AL 36046. Tel: (334) 277-9069 Fax: (334) 224-5063. Principal: Johnny Williams.

Wills Thompson Paschall (D). 100 Morgan Keegan Drive, Suite 410, Little Rock, AR 72201. Tel: (501) 666-8200 Fax: (501) 666-8214 E-mail: paschall.wtp@ltw.com. Principal: Bill Paschall.

Wilson, Grand Communications (R). 407 North Washington Street, Alexandria, VA 22314. Tel: (800) 678-9276 or (703) 739-0330 Fax: (703) 739-0332 E-mail: winelects@ aol.com. Principal: Paul O. Wilson.

Windsor Group, The (R). 1401 West Paces Ferry Road, Suite 1403, Atlanta, GA 30327. Tel: (404) 261-4444 Fax: (404) 455-4355. Principal: Tom Perdue.

Winner/Wagner & Mandabach Campaigns. 100 Wilshire Boulevard, Suite 1950, Santa Monica, CA 90407-1110. Tel: (310) 576-4800 Fax: (310) 576-4811 E-mail: wwm1@aol.com. Principal: Paul Mandabach.

Winner/Wagner & Francis (D). 1000 Potomac Street NW, Suite 401, Washington, DC 20007. Tel: (202) 333-2533 Fax: (202) 342-0763. or 152 West 57th Street, 18th Floor, New York, NY 10019. Tel: (212) 765-6767 Fax: (212) 765-5843. Principal: Leslie C. Francis.

Winning Strategies (D). 2621 Palisade Avenue, New York, NY 10463. Tel: (718) 824-5060. Principal: Joseph A. Lucchese.

Wirthlin Group, The (R). 1363 Beverly Road, McLean, VA 22101. Tel: (703) 556-0001 Fax: (703) 506-1071. Principal: Richard B. Wirthlin.

Wisdom Organization Inc., The (R). 517 South Ramona Street, Suite 301, Corona, CA 91719. Tel: (909) 340-1505 Fax: (909) 340-9905. Principal: Gordon Williams.

Scott Wolf & Assoc. (D). 70 President Avenue, Providence, RI 02906. Tel: (401) 831-6787. Principal: Scott Wolf.

Words That Work. 8302 West Ashford Lane, Muncie, IN 47304-9501. Tel: (765) 759-7421 Fax: (765) 759-7421 E-mail: mhmasse@ bsu.edu. Principal: Mark H. Masse.

Yankee Communications (R). 240 Bonita Drive, Bakersfield, CA 93305. Tel: (805) 334-1776 Fax: (805) 326-1997. Principal: Jimmy Yee.

D. Yoakam, Political Consultant (R). 1735 Urbana Way, Sacramento, CA 95833. Tel: (916) 929-8616. Principal: Doug Yoakam.

George Young & Assoc., Inc. (R). 520 Washington Boulevard, Suite 816, Marina Del Rey, CA 90292. Tel: (310) 822-0370 Fax: (310) 822-5613 E-mail: shine32875@aol.com. Principal: George Young.

Zimmerman & Markman (D). 1250 6th Street, Santa Monica, CA 90401. Tel: (310) 451-2522 Fax: (310) 451-7494. Principal: Bill Zimmerman.

Public Opinion and Campaign Pollsters

Pollsters provide public opinion surveys that guide political campaigns as well as the development of policy and other strategies. Additionally, pollsters often conduct surveys for the news media and for research purposes.

In most political campaigns, pollsters play a critical role in helping to define strategy, test policy positions, and highlight potential strengths and weaknesses in their candidate's or parties' issues or electoral base as well as assessing the strengths and weaknesses of the opposition's campaign.

If a (D) follows the name of the organization, then the organization either primarily or exclusively assists Democratic candidates. If a (R) follows the name, then it assists primarily or exclusively Republican candidates. No (D) or (R) means the group will handle either party's candidates.

Abacus Assoc. (D). 52 School Street, Hatfield, MA 01038. Tel: (413) 247-9430 Fax: (413) 247-5813. President: Janet Grenzke.

Accurus Systems, Inc (D). PO Box 2213, Burlington, NC 27216. Tel: (910) 226-2385 Fax: (919) 222-1314 E-mail: accurus@aol.com. Principal: Douglas Cox.

Will Adams Assoc. PO Box 382, Liberty, MO 64068. Tel: (816) 781-7655 or (816) 781-6514 Fax: (816) 792-4743. President: Will Adams.

Alabama Business Consultants. 8423 Enterprise Avenue, Tuscaloosa, AL 35406. Tel: (205) 345-2877. President: Robert Robicheaux.

Altamira Communications Group. 9457 Las Vegas Boulevard South, Suite G, Las Vegas, NV 89123-3352. Tel: (702) 263-0333. President: Bob Patrick.

American Campaign Management. 1552 Garland Avenue, Tustin, CA 92680. Tel: (714) 544-3298 Fax: (714) 544-3298. Principal: Mark Ferguson.

American Strategies. 210 Bretano Way, Greenbrae, CA 94904-1304. Tel: (415) 825-3962 Fax: (415) 687-1275. President: Kevin J. O'Donnell.

American Viewpoint (R). 300 North Washington Street, Suite 505, Alexandria, VA 22314. Tel: (703) 684-3325 or (800) 684-4410 Fax: (703) 684-9295. President: Linda A. DiVall.

Anzalone Research, Inc. (D). 4001 Carmichael Road, Suite 540, Montgomery, AL 36106. Tel: (334) 277-3121 Fax: (334) 277-4656. or 412 1st Street SE, Suite 100, Washington, DC 20003. Tel: (202) 484-2151 E-mail: anzalone@mont.mindspring.com. Principal: John Anzalone.

Ask America Market Research. 1932 Stockton Boulevard, Sacramento, CA 95816. Tel: (916) 452-3300 Fax: (916) 452-3547 E-mail: askamerica@aol.com. President: Michael K. Pettengill.

Atlantic Research Company. 109 State Street, Boston, MA 02109. Tel: (617) 720-0174 Fax: (617) 589-3731. President: Peter Hooper.

Attitude Measurement. 1310 Industrial Highway, Southampton, PA 18966. Tel: (215) 364-1440 Fax: (215) 364-3912. Principal: Ray Roshkoff.

Ayres & Associates. (R). 875 Old Roswell Road, Suite E 500, Roswell, GA 30076. Tel: (770) 594-7898 Fax: (770) 594-0107 E-mail: qwayres@aol.com. President: Q. W. Ayres.

John P. Bakke. 539 Melody Lane, Memphis, TN 38120. Tel: (901) 682-9509 Fax: (901) 685-2796. Principal: John P. Bakke.

Bannon Research (D). 80 F Street NW, Suite 804, Washington, DC 20001. Tel: (202) 628-4809 Fax: (202) 628-3702. President: Brad Bannon.

Behavior Research Center. 1101 North First Street, Phoenix, AZ 85004. Tel: (602) 258-4554 or (800) 279-1212 Fax: (602) 252-2729. Resident Director: Earl de Berge.

Bendixon & Associates, Inc (D). 2405 Riverview Terrace, Alexandria, VA 22303. Tel: (703) 329-9581 Fax: (703) 329-9503. Owner: Sergio Bendixon.

Bennett, Petts & Associates (D). 1875 Connecticut Avenue NW, Suite 630, Washington, DC 20009. Tel: (202) 332-1100 Fax: (202) 332-1809 E-mail: bpbpolls@aol.com. Principal: Anna Bennett.

Bigham Consulting. 409 Channel Drive, Island Lake, IL 60042. Tel: (841) 526-3736 or (708) 999-5252 Fax: (841) 526-3736 E-mail: 71760. 2520@compuserve.com. Principal: Fred Bigham.

Blackwater Assoc. PO Box 5151, Columbia, SC 29250. Tel: (803) 771-7489. Associate: Karen Sundstrom.

Boyd Assoc., Inc (R). PO Box 1317, Exton, PA 19341. Tel: (215) 942-4335 Fax: (215) 942-0258. President: Debra J. Boyd.

Gene Bregman and Associates (D). 5 3rd Street, Suite 328, San Francisco, CA 94103. Tel: (415) 957-9700 Fax: (415) 957-9723. Principal: Gene Bregman.

Bruskin/Goldring Research (R). 100 Metroplex Drive, Edison, NJ 08817. Tel: (908) 572-7300 or (800) 634-5773 Fax: (908) 572-7980. Political Director: David Kamioner.

Cambridge Reports/Research International. 955 Massachusetts Avenue, Cambridge, MA 02139. Tel: (617) 661-0110 Fax: (617) 661-3575. Principal: Michael Malinoski.

Campaign & Opinion Research Analysts. 110 East Cornerview Road, Gonzales, LA 70737. Tel: (504) 647-1767 Fax: (504) 647-6600. President: Ronald E. Weber, Ph.D.

Capitol Avenue Consulting. 425 West Capitol, Suite 3300, Little Rock, AR 72201. Tel: (501) 374-5505 Fax: (501) 374-5520. President: David F. Martin.

Carolina Report, The. PO Box 12074, Rock Hills, SC 29731. Tel: (803) 329-5449 Fax: (803) 323-2347. Principal: Glen Broach.

Center for Research and Public Policy, The (R). 35 Elm Street, 3rd Floor, New Haven, CT 06510. Tel: (203) 776-9222 Fax: (203) 777-1807. President: Jerry C. Lindsley.

Century Research Corporation. 37 Walnut Hill Road, Ridgefield, CT 06877. Tel: (203) 438-4959 Fax: (203) 431-6980. President: Albert J. Ungar.

Chamberlain Research Consultants. 4801 Forest Run Road, Suite 101, Madison, WI

53704. Tel: (608) 246-3010 Fax: (608) 246-3019. Principal: Sharon R. Chamberlain.

Charlton Research Co. (R). 44 Montgomery Street, Suite 1710, San Francisco, CA 94104. Tel: (415) 981-2343 Fax: (415) 981-4850 E-mail: charltonsf@aol.com. President: Charles F. Rund.

CIAC Election Services. 15 Wildbrook, Irvine, CA 92714. Tel: (714) 786-5671 Fax: (714) 786-8721. Principal: Kay McNally.

Civic Service, Inc. 1050 Connecticut Avenue NW, Suite 870, Washington, DC 20036. Tel: (202) 785-2070 Fax: (202) 785-1102. Principal: Roy Pfautch.

CM Research (R). 1555 King Street, Suite 200, Alexandria, VA 22314. Tel: (703) 519-7797 Fax: (703) 519-8523 E-mail: 75713.2261@compuserve. com. President: Christine Matthews.

Cole, Hargrave, Snodgrass & Associates (R). 6218 North Western, Suite 201, Oklahoma City, OK 73118. Tel: (405) 848-1585 Fax: (405) 848-3915. or 512 North Washington Street, Alexandria, VA 22314. Tel: (703) 518-8927 E-mail: chs@flash.net. Principal: Tom Cole.

Competitive Edge Research & Comm. (R). 3550 Camino del Rio North, Suite 304, San Diego, CA 92108. Tel: (619) 584-4000 or (800) 576-CERC Fax: (619) 584-4031 E-mail: 75270.3617@compuserve.com. Principal: John R. Nienstedt.

Conservative Solutions (R). 2839 West Rochelle, Irving, TX 75062. Tel: (214) 255-7913. Principal: Brian Humek.

Cooper & Secrest Assoc. (D). 228 South Washington Street, Suite 330, Alexandria, VA 22314. Tel: (703) 683-7990 Fax: (703) 739-0079 E-mail: asecrest@aol.com. President: Alan M. Secrest.

Corey, Canapary, & Galanis. 447 Sutter Street, San Francisco, CA 94108. Tel: (415) 397-1200 Fax: (415) 433-3809. President: Ed Canapary.

CPC Corporation (R). 9824 South Park Circle, Fairfax Station, VA 22039. Tel: (703) 451-1987 Fax: (703) 455-1986 E-mail: cpccmeb @mail.erols.com. President: Michael E. Belefski.

Craig Group, The. 37 West Broad Street, Suite 480, Columbus, OH 43215-4132. Tel: (614) 241-2222 Fax: (614) 241-2215. Principal: Phillip A. Craig.

Darden Research Corporation. 1534 North Decatur Road, Atlanta, GA 30307. Tel: (404) 377-9294. President: Claibourne Darden.

Richard Day Research (D). PO Box 5090, Evanston, IL 60201. Tel: (708) 328-2329 Fax: (708) 328-8995. President: Richard Day.

DCM Group, The (R). 1320 Old Chain Bridge Road, Suite 220, McLean, VA 22101. Tel: (703) 883-1355 Fax: (703) 883-1850 E-mail: ed@dcm.com. President: Ed DeBolt.

Decision Research (D). 3911 5th Avenue, Suite 300, San Diego, CA 92103. Tel: (619) 682-5343 Fax: (619) 682-5335. or 1828 L Street NW, Suite 402, Washington, DC 20036. Tel: (202) 775-1780. President: Robert Meadow.

Demographic Data Consultants. 530 3rd Avenue South, Suite 7, Nashville, TN 37210-2033. Tel: (615) 726-0777 Fax: (615) 726-0777. Owner: Nancy Hendrix.

Donald Devine Company (R). 919 Prince Street, Alexandria, VA 22314. Tel: (703) 683-6833 or (301) 261-9347 Fax: (703) 684-7642. President: Donald J. Devine.

Dittman Strategic Campaigns (R). 8115 Jewel Lake, DRC Building, Anchorage, AK

99502. Tel: (907) 243-3345 Fax: (907) 243-7172. President: David Lynn Dittman.

Dresner, Wickers & Associates, Inc. (R). 52 Griffin Avenue, Bedford Hills, NY 10507. Tel: (914) 241-9244 Fax: (914) 241-9360 E-mail: dsjw@ aol.com. Principal: Richard Dresner.

Dynamic Marketing and Research Assoc.(D). 114 North Washington Street, Suite 4, Easton, MD 21601. Tel: (410) 819-6606 Fax: (410) 763-8594. President: David A. Dowd.

Eagle Consulting Group, Inc, The (R). 107 North 45th Street, Suite 114, Harrisburg, PA 17111. Tel: (717) 564-3202 Fax: (717) 564-3227. President: Christopher Nicholas.

Emory, Young & Assoc. (D). 400 West 15th Street, Suite 408, Austin, TX 78701. Tel: (512) 474-1431 Fax: (512) 474-7542 E-mail: crosby @eden.com. CEO: W.R. (Peck) Young.

Bryan Eppstein & Company, Inc. (R). 4055 International Plaza, Suite 520, Fort Worth, TX 76109-4800. Tel: (817) 737-3656 Fax: (817) 737-4245. Principal: Bryan Eppstein.

Evans/McDonough Company (EMC) (D). 764 Gillman Street, Berkeley, CA 94710. Tel: (510) 559-1776 Fax: (510) 559-1770. Principal: Alex Evans.

Evets Management Services, Inc. 844 Texas Avenue, Shreveport, LA 71101. Tel: (318) 424-1695. President: Elliott B. Stonecipher.

Fabrizio, McLaughlin & Associates (R). 915 King Street, Alexandria, VA 22314. Tel: (703) 684-4510 Fax: (703) 739-0664 E-mail: info@fabmac.com. Website: http://www.fabmac.com. Principal: John McLaughlin.

Fairbank, Maslin, Maullin & Assoc. (D). 2425 Colorado Avenue, Suite 180, Santa Monica, CA 90404. Tel: (310) 828-1183 Fax: (310) 453-6562 E-mail: fmma@crl.com. Principal: John Fairbank.

Falcon & Hill Research (D). Ellicott Square Building, Suite 522, Buffalo, NY 14203. Tel: (716) 854-1013 or (800) 333-1469 Fax: (716) 854-8869. President: Phillip J. Cook.

Fingerhut, Powers, Smith & Associates (D). 1925 K Street NW, Suite 250, Washington, DC 20006. Tel: (202) 331-3700 Fax: (202) 331-3709. Principal: Frank Powers.

Arthur J. Finkelstein & Associates (R). 16 North Astor, Irvington, NY 10533. Tel: (914) 591-8142 Fax: (914) 591-4013. President: Artrhur Finkelstein.

Frederick/Schneider, Inc (D). 1818 N Street NW, Washington, DC 20036. Tel: (202) 785-3535 Fax: (202) 785-5349. Principal: Keith Frederick.

Garin Hart Yang Research Group (D). 1724 Connecticut Avenue NW, Washington, DC 20009. Tel: (202) 234-5570 Fax: (202) 232-8134 E-mail: hartdc@ix.netcom.com. Principal: Geoffrey Garin.

Gerl, Scotti & Associates (D). PO Box 424, Lewisburg, WV 24901. Tel: (304) 645-7362 Fax: (304) 645-7362. Owner: Jim Gerl.

Gilmore Group. 2324 Eastlake Avenue, E Suite 300, Seattle, WA 98102. Tel: (206) 726-5555. President: Robert Gilmore.

Glick Assoc. (D). 222 Park Avenue South, New York, NY 10003. Tel: (212) 353-9200 or (212) 301-7359 Fax: (212) 477-8235. Principal: Joseph Glick.

GLS Research (D). 233 Wilshire Boulevard, Suite 290, Santa Monica, CA 90401. Tel: (310) 587-3474 Fax: (310) 587-0098 E-mail: 75717.3160@compuserve.com. Executive Vice President: Paul R. Goodwin.

Goldhaber Research Assoc. 1 NFA Park, Amherst, NY 14228. Tel: (716) 689-3311 Fax: (716) 689-3342. Owner: Gerald M. Goldhaber.

Dan Greenblat, Consultant (R). 4182 Pallon Court, San Diego, CA 92124-2703. Tel: (619) 530-2368. Principal: Dan Greenblat.

Greenberg Research, Inc (D). 515 2nd Street NE, Washington, DC 20002. Tel: (202) 547-5200 Fax: (202) 544-7020. President: Stanley B. Greenberg.

Haines Election Services. 8050 Freedom Avenue NW, North Canton, OH 44720. Tel: (800) 260-5540 Fax: (216) 494-0226. Principal: Tom Riehl.

Hamilton & Staff (D). 5335 Wisconsin Avenue NW, Suite 700, Washington, DC 20015. Tel: (202) 686-5900 Fax: (202) 686-7080 E-mail: billham@dgsys.com. President: William R. Hamilton.

Louis Harris & Associates. 111 5th Avenue, 8th Floor, New York, NY 10003. Tel: (212) 539-9600 Fax: (212) 539-9669 E-mail: dkrane @lha.gsbc.com. Principal: David Krane.

Harrison & Goldberg, Inc (D). 2464 Massachusetts Avenue, Cambridge, MA 02141. Tel: (617) 864-1721 Fax: (617) 864-2919. Principal: Tubby Harrison.

Herness & Associates (R). 3555 Highland Fairway Boulevard, Lakeland, FL 33809. Tel: (813) 853-1613. or 2111 Wisconsin Avenue NW, Washington, DC 20007. President: Shaun P. Herness.

Hickman Brown Research, Inc (D). 1350 Connecticut Avenue NW, Suite 206, Washington, DC 20036. Tel: (202) 659-4000 or (213) 443-9983 Fax: (202) 659-1832. President: Harrison Hickman.

Hill Research Consultants (R). 25025 Interstate 45 North 380, The Woodlands, TX 77380. Tel: (713) 363-3840 Fax: (713) 298-1988. Director: David B. Hill.

Independent Opinion Research Comm., Inc (D). PO Box 501, Wrightsville Beach, NC 28480. Tel: (910) 799-9703 Fax: (910) 799-3891. President: Susan K. Bulluck.

Bill Johnson Survey Research, Inc (D). 850 Bronx River Road, Yonkers, NY 10478. Tel: (914) 776-0701. President: William G. Johnson.

Barry Kaplovitz Assoc. 60 Charlesgate West, Boston, MA 02215. Tel: (617) 437-0847. President: Barry Kaplovitz.

Thomas Kielhorn & Assoc. (D). 4400 Hemingway Drive, Suite 231, Oklahoma City, OK 73118. Tel: (405) 840-4236. President: Thomas Kielhorn.

Kitchens Group, The. 1636 Hillcrest Street, Orlando, FL 32803. Tel: (407) 898-3889 Fax: (407) 898-4370. Associate: James T. Kitchens.

Steve Kline Campaigns (D). 1095 Market Street, Suite 612, San Francisco, CA 94103. Tel: (415) 255-8673 Fax: (415) 255-2376. Principal: Steve Kline.

Knox Group. RR 2, Box 1010, Waterbury, VT 05676. Tel: (802) 244-5906 Fax: (802) 244-5906. Principal: Toby Knox.

William Kostka & Associates. 1407 Larimer Square, Denver, CO 80202. Tel: (303) 623-8421 Fax: (303) 573-5426. Chairman: William Kostka.

KRC Research and Consulting (D). 640 5th Avenue, 8th Floor, New York, NY 10019. Tel: (212) 445-8300 Fax: (212) 445-8304. or 1501 M Street NW, Suite 600, Washington, DC 20005. Tel: (202) 739-0200 or (202) 659-8287. Principal: Jim Vanecko (NY), Mark Mallock Brown (DC).

Lake Research, Inc (D). 1730 Rhode Island Avenue NE, Suite 400, Washington, DC 20036. Tel: (202) 776-9066 Fax: (202) 776-9074 E-mail: lakepolls@aol.com. Principal: Celinda Lake.

Lauer, Lalley, Victoria, Inc (D). 7008 Westmoreland Avenue, Suite B, Takoma, MD 20912. Tel: (301) 891-3988. Fax: (301) 891-3887. President: James W. Lauer.

Lawrence Research (R). 1450 North Tustin Avenue, Suite 150, Santa Ana, CA 92705. Tel: (714) 558-3725 Fax: (714) 558-0403. President: Gary C. Lawrence.

Leitner/Braun Research. 262 Wall Street, Princeton, NJ 08540. Tel: (609) 497-0820 Fax: (609) 497-9322. Principal: John H. Leitner.

Lester Telemarketing (D). 19 Business Park Drive, Branford, CT 06405. Tel: (203) 488-5265 Fax: (203) 488-5265. Principal: Joan Marcus.

Allan J. Lichtman (D). 9219 Villa Drive, Bethesda. MD 20817. Tel: (301) 530-8262. Principal: Allan J. Lichtman.

Luntz Research Companies (R). 1000 Wilson Boulevard, Suite 950, Arlington, VA 22209. Tel: (703) 358-0080 Fax: (703) 358-0089. Principal: Frank I. Luntz.

M C Squared Consulting. 120 Dennis Drive, Suite 3, Lexington, KY 40503. Tel: (606) 278-9299 or (800) 370-6071 Fax: (606) 276-3824 E-mail: mc2@mis.net. President: Sam C. McIntosh.

M.O.R. Pace, Inc (R). 31700 Middlebelt, Suite 220, Farmington Hills, MI 48334. Tel: (810) 737-5300 Fax: (810) 737-5326. Principal: Paul Johnson.

Maris, West & Baker, Inc. PO Box 12426, Jackson, MS 39236. Tel: (601) 362-6306 Fax: (601) 981-1902. President: Kenneth E. Sandridge.

Marketing Campaign Strategies, Inc (D). 815 Brazos, Suite 200, Austin, TX 78701. Tel: (512) 476-7797. Principal: Richard Jenson.

Marketing Research Institute (R). 630 East Government Street, Pensacola, FL 32501. Tel: (904) 433-9191 Fax: (904) 433-9778. Principal: Verne R. Kennedy

Marketing Resource Group (R). 225 South Washington Square, Lansing, MI 48933. Tel: (517) 372-4400 Fax: (517) 372-4045 E-mail: mrg@voyager.net. President: David Waymire.

Martin Corporation. 6834 Cantrell, Suite 364, Little Rock, AR 72207. Tel: (501) 329-9426 Fax: (501) 329-9427. Principal: David F. Martin.

Mason Dixon Campaign Polling & Strategy, Inc. 339 Busch's Frontage Road, Suite 204, Annapolis, MD 21401. Tel: (410) 974-4823 Fax: (410) 626-7214. President: Patrick E. Gonzales.

Media Strategies & Research (D). 318 Massachusetts Avenue NE, Washington, DC 20002. Tel: (202) 544-4700 Fax: (202) 544-9222 E-mail: jon@ mediastrategies.com. Principal: Patricia G. Hutchens.

Mellman Group, Inc, The (D). 1000 Thomas Jefferson Street NW, Suite 520, Washington, DC 20007. Tel: (202) 625-0370 Fax: (202) 625-0371 E-mail: Mellman@Mellman. dgsys.com. Principal: Mark S. Mellman.

Meta Information Services (R). PO Box 277037, Sacramento, CA 95827-7037. Tel: (916) 368-9474 Fax: (916) 368-0705. President: Kent Hymas.

Mitchell Research & Communications, Inc (R). 211 Evergreen, PO Box 4066, East Lansing, MI 48823. Tel: (517) 351-4111 Fax: (517) 351-1265. Chairman: Steve Mitchell.

Moore Information (R). 10200 SW Eastridge Street, Suite 210, Portland, OR

97225. Tel: (503) 292-7655 Fax: (503) 291-9038 E-mail: lamour110@aol.com. President: Bob Moore.

Dick Morris (R). 20 Beeholm Road, Redding, CT 06896. Tel: (203) 938-2535 Fax: (203) 938-4055. Principal: Dick Morris.

Multi Quest. 708 Rosa Avenue, Metairie, LA 70005. Tel: (504) 835-3507 or (504) 835-3282 E-mail: pollster@ juno.com. President: John L. Grimm.

Mycon (D). 2320 Ridgeview Road, State College, PA 16801. Tel: (814) 238-5298 or (814) 466-7970 Fax: (814) 466-6609. Principal: Robert O'Connor.

Joseph Napolitan Assoc., Inc (D). 121 Chestnut Street, Springfield, MA 01103. Tel: (413) 732-1232 Fax: (413) 788-4759. President: Joseph Napolitan.

Nason, Lundberg & Associates (R). 320 West Whittier Boulevard, Suite 223, LaHabra, CA 90631. Tel: (714) 578-1270 Fax: (714) 578-1273. Principal: Lois Lundberg.

National Demographic Corporation. PO Box 285, Claremont, CA 91711. Tel: (909) 624-1442 or (805) 237-0330 Fax: (805) 237-9251. Principal: Florence Adams.

National Political Services, Inc. 308 East 30th Street, Suite 4, New York, NY 10016. Tel: (212) 689-7683 Fax: (212) 685-6618. Principal: Joseph Mercurio.

Neighborhood Research and Media (R). 3 Theater Plaza, PO Box 578, Sparta, NJ 07871. Tel: (201) 726-8114/8175 Fax: (201) 726-8967 E-mail: shaftan@ptd.net. Principal: Richard K. Shaftan.

New England Interviewing, Inc. 5 Coliseum Avenue, Nashua, NH 03063. Tel: (603) 889-8222 Fax: (603) 883-1119. President: Joan Greene.

The Paul M. Newman Company (R). 853 West Balda Road, Oak Harbor, WA 98277-7620. Tel: (360) 679-4071 Fax: (360) 679-3722. President: Paul M. Newman.

Numbercrunchers, Inc. (R). 42 North Avenue, New Rochelle, NY 10805. Tel: (914) 235-0800. President: Richard J. Behn.

Opinion Analysts, Inc. (D). 906 Rio Grande, Austin, TX 78701. Tel: (512) 472-9772 Fax: (512) 472-7442 E-mail: opinion@eden.com. President: Jeffrey A. Smith, Ph.D.

Opinion Research of California. 917 Pine Avenue, Long Beach, CA 90813. Tel: (213) 432-0474. Principal: Don McGrew.

Pendragon Consultants (D). 2909 162nd Street, Flushing, NY 11358. Tel: (718) 358-8400. Principal: Arthur Nitzburg.

Penn & Schoen Assoc. (D). 245 East 92nd Street, New York, NY 10128. Tel: (212) 534-4000 Fax: (212) 360-7423. or 516 C Street NE, Suite 300, Washington, DC 200002. Tel: (202) 546-2500 Fax: (202) 543-0526. Principal: Mark Penn.

Personal Marketing Research Inc. 322 Brady Street, Davenport, IA 52801. Tel: (319) 322-1960 Fax: (319) 322-1370 E-mail: permarres@aol.com. or 200 Merle Hay Mall, 3800 Merle, Des Moines, IA 50310. Principal: Patricia E. Duffy.

Platler/Edgington Assoc. 21607 Rambia Vista Drive, Malibu, CA 90265. Tel: (213) 456-0093. Principal: James Platler.

Political Affairs, LLC. 343 3rd Street, Suite 203, Baton Rouge, LA 70802. Tel: (504) 346-6767 Fax: (504) 346-8878. Principal: James Burland.

Political Designs (D). 231 Market Place, Suite 235, San Ramon, CA 94583. Tel: (800) 827-1466 Fax: (510) 551-7633. Principal J. Bradford Senden.

Political Savvy. 410 Ridge Place NE, Albuquerque, NM 87106. Tel: (505) 243-4904 Fax: (505) 888-1376. Principal: Tom Moody.

Polling Report, The. PO Box 42580, Washington, DC 20015. Tel: (202) 237-2000 Fax: (202) 237-2001 E-mail: polling_report @compuserve.com. Principal: Tim Silver.

Potomac Inc. (D). 7940 Norfolk Avenue, Bethesda, MD 20814. Tel: (301) 656-7900 Fax: (301) 656-7903. Principal: G. Keith Haller.

Price Research (D). 2694 Bishop Drive, Suite 250, San Ramon, CA 94583. Tel: (510) 277-0390 Fax: (510) 277-0950. Principal: Kent C. Price.

Victor L. Profughi. Rhode Island College, 600 Mount Pleasant, Providence, RI 02908. Tel: (401) 456-8056 Fax: (401) 456-8379. Principal: Victor L. Profughi.

PSI (R). 421 King Street, Suite 224, Alexandria, VA 22307. Tel: (703) 765-0488 Fax: (703) 660-8910 E-mail: craig@ctufty.com. Website: http://www.ctufty.com. Principal: Craig Tufty.

Public Opinion Strategies, LP (R). 1033 North Fairfax, Suite 120, Alexandria, VA 22314. Tel: (703) 836-7655 Fax: (703) 836-8117. Principal: William D. McInturff.

QS&A Research and Strategy. 5367 Anvil Court, Fairfax, VA 22030. Tel: (703) 502-7610 Fax: (703) 502-0467 E-mail: bquarles@aol.com. Principal: Becky Quarles.

Quest Design Group. PO Box 270, Greenville, RI 02929. Tel: (401) 934-2772. Principal: Bruce R. Daigle.

Quest Opinion Research. 23 Randall Street, Providence, RI 02904. Tel: (401) 949-1384 Fax: (401) 456-8379. Principal: Victor Profughi.

Quick Tally Interactive Systems. 8444 Wilshire, Suite 200, Beverly Hills, CA 90211.

Tel: (310) 653-5303 Fax: (310) 653-2725. Principal: Alan Warshaw.

Raosoft, Inc. 6645 NE Windermere Road, Seattle, WA 98115. Tel: (206) 525-4025 Fax: (206) 525-4947 E-mail: raosoft@raosoft.com. Website: http://www.raosaoft.com. Principal: Catherine McDole.

Raritan Assoc., Inc. (R). 707 South 1st Avenue, Highland Park, NJ 08904. Tel: (908) 846-9539 or (908) 828-5896 Fax: (908) 846-0372. Principal: Stephen A. Salmore

Clinton Reilly Campaigns (D). 704 Sansome, San Francisco, CA 94111. Tel: (415) 397-0431 Fax: (415) 397-1904. President: Clinton Reilly.

Research & Polling, Inc. 7500 Jefferson NE, Courtyard 2, Albuquerque, NM 87109. Tel: (505) 821-5454 Fax: (505) 821-5474. Principal: Brian Sanderoff.

Research Network, The. 1111 East Tennessee Street, Suite 101, Tallahassee, FL 32308. Tel: (904) 681-9955 Fax: (904) 681-9949. or 500 Morris Avenue, Springfield, NJ 07081. Tel: (201) 379-9595 Fax: (201) 379-0446. Principal: Marc Gertz.

Research/Strategy/Management (RSM) (R). 9344 Lanham Severn Road, Lanham, MD 20706. Tel: (301) 306-0844 Fax: (301) 306-0711. Principal: Vincent J. Breglio.

Roberts, Gabbert & Assoc. 1408 North Kingshighway S305, St Louis, MO 63113. Tel: (314) 361-1700. Principal: Michael V. Roberts.

R.A. Robicheaux. 8423 Enterprise Avenue NE, Tuscaloosa, AL 35401. Tel: (205) 345-2877. Principal: Robert A. Robicheaux.

Robinson & Muenster Assoc., Inc (D). 1208 Elkhorn, Sioux Falls, SD 57104-0218. Tel: (605) 332-3386 Fax: (605) 332-8722 E-mail: robinson@rma-inc.com. Principal: Jim Robinson.

Roper Center for Public Opinion Research. PO Box 440, Storrs, CT 06268-0440. Tel: (860) 486-4440 Fax: (860) 486-6308 E-mail: wilbur@opinion.isi.uconn.edu. Website: http://www.lib.uconn.edu/ropercenter/. Principal: Everett C. Ladd.

San Diego Poll. 5409 Hewlett Drive, San Diego, CA 92115. Tel: (619) 582-0080. Principal: Oscar J. Kaplan.

Schroth & Assoc. (D). 420 Connecticut Avenue NW, Suite 212, Washington, DC 20008. Tel: (202) 686-9354 Fax: (202) 686-9356. Principal: Rob Schroth.

Beth Schapiro & Associates (D). 127 Peachtree Street, Suite 610, Atlanta, GA 30303. Tel: (404) 584-5215 Fax: (404) 581-0058 E-mail: bsabeth@ aol.com. Principal: Beth S. Schapiro.

Robert Y. Shapiro. 605 West 113th Street, Suite 21, New York, NY 10025. Tel: (212) 866-1085. Principal: Robert Y. Shapiro.

Shipley & Associates, Inc (D). 919 Congress Avenue, Austin, TX 78701. Tel: (512) 474-7514 Fax: (512) 472-2802. President: George C. Shipley.

Skelton & Associates, Inc (D). 1010 21st Street, Sacramento, CA 95814. Tel: (916) 443-8431 Fax: (916) 443-0106. Principal: Alice Skelton.

SMS Research. 1042 Fort Street Mall, Suite 200, Honolulu, HI 96813. Tel: (808) 537-3356 Fax: (808) 537-2666. Principal: James Dannemiller.

Southwest Research Association. PO Box 721, Lubbock, TX 74408. Tel: (806) 745-2507. Principal: Lisa Nowlin.

Arnold Steinberg & Assoc. (R). 335 Stunt Road, Calabasas, CA 91302. Tel: (818) 591-9100 Fax: (818) 591-9101. Principal: Arnold Steinberg.

Strategic Campaign Initiatives, Inc (D). 12608 Safety Turn, Bowie, MD 20715. Tel: (301) 464-5988 Fax: (301) 464-3040. Principal: Brenda L. Beitzell.

Talmey Drake Research & Strategy, Inc (D). 100 Arapahoe, Suite 4, Boulder, CO 80306. Tel: (303) 443-5300 Fax: (303) 447-9386. Principal: Paul Talmey.

Townsend Raimundo Besler & Usher (D). 1717 I Street, Suite B, Sacramento, CA 95814. Tel: (916) 444-5701 Fax: (916) 444-0382 E-mail: trbu@trbu.com. Website: http://www.trbu.com. Principal: David J. Townsend.

Trotter Research Group (D). 308 Hillwood Avenue, Suite 150, Falls Church, VA 22046. Tel: (703) 538-6575 Fax: (703) 538-6733. Principal: John O'Reilly.

Western Advocates Inc. 1284 Court Street NE, Salem, OR 97301. Tel: (503) 620-3356 or (503) 378-0595. Fax: (503) 598-0298 E-mail: westernadv@aol.com. Principal: Burton Weast.

Western Pacific Research, Inc (R). 4100 Truxton Avenue, Suite 210, Bakersfield, CA 93309. Tel: (805) 327-4141 Fax: (805) 327-3672. Consultant: Mark Abernathy.

Western Wats Center (R). 288 West Center, Provo, UT 84601. Tel: (801) 374-5572 or (888) GOP-WINS Fax: (801) 375-0673. Principal: Ed Ledek.

Whitesides Stonecipher & Assoc. 509 Marshall Street, Suite 716, Shreveport, LA 71101. Tel: (318) 424-8198. Principal: Alan Stonecipher.

Wild Goat Campaigns (D). 6198 Marteney Avenue, Kent, OH 44240. Tel: (216) 677-1155 Fax: (216) 677-1155 E-mail: politx@aol.com. Principal: Scott Walker.

Wilkerson & Assoc. (D). 3339 Taylorsville Road, Louisville, KY 40205. Tel: (502) 459-

3133 Fax: (502) 459-8392. or 4208 Six Forks
Road, Raleigh, NC. Tel: (919) 781-0555.
Principal: Tom Wilkerson.

The Wirthlin Group (R). 1363 Beverly
Road, McLean, VA 22101. Tel: (703) 556-0001
Fax: (703) 506-1071. Principal: Richard B.
Wirthlin.

Scott Wolf and Assoc. (D). 70 President
Avenue, Providence, RI 02906. Tel: (401) 831-
6787. Principal: Scott Wolf.

Overview: Media
and the Political Market Place

The term media has expanded during the past few decades to include not merely print media, historically the oldest form comprising newspapers, journals and newsletters, but also electronic media, comprising the cool medium of television and the hot medium of radio and, more recently, technology-driven forms such as the Internet and the World Wide Web.

It is difficult to define political media as something different from other types of media because all media are, in one form or another, political. The United States, like other Western democracies, is undergoing a rapid politicization of national life. Politics or matters allied to politics dominate electronic and print media news. Politics is the grist of journalistic mills, and it helps to generate and sustain national debate on a variety of topics that transcend the immediate concerns of individuals and families. Political media also set the priorities and national agendas, and channel public interest into policies, programs and personalities. With a nose for wrongdoing and scandal, the media also serve as watchdogs of the nation and a terror for errant politicians. After all, muckraking is an American term.

The media, particularly the technology of communications fueling the new media, have transformed American politics beyond recognition. Most importantly, they have undermined the ability of political parties and traditional political groups and organizations to influence the outcome of elections and the selection of candidates and their ability to control the minds of voters. What is being witnessed is a silent transformation from indirect democracy (through elected representatives mediated through political parties) into a direct Athenian type unmediated democracy.

Teledemocracy is the term coined by political commentators for this transformation. Elements of this emerging democratic process are the electronic town hall meetings, electronic chat rooms and bulletin boards, television sound bites, and call-in telephone numbers attached to television broadcasts. The media have taken over the political education of voters and, implicitly, their political direction. Political parties have become functionless and irrelevant with diminished ability to command political loyalties.

The following section lists several levels of media, each of which has its own strengths and weaknesses:

1. Newspapers
2. Journals and Newsletters
3. Television, including C-Span and all-news cable channels, such as CNN
4. Radio
5. Internet and World Wide Web

In addition, political pundits, commentators and talk show hosts constitute a powerful sixth force in politics. Their influence is enormous and some, like Rush Limbaugh, have devoted fans and acolytes whose ideological fervor is unmatched by more traditional groups.

Television is perhaps the most powerful political medium. More than twice as many people get their political education and information from television as from all other media combined. The McLuhanesque immediacy or all-at-onceness of television reporting and commentary accompanied by strong visual images commands attention in a way that newspapers and journals cannot.

Unfortunately, television's strength is also a source of its weakness. It gives no time for leisurely deliberation or meditation of pros and cons, and does not permit analysis and inquiry, except in a superficial sense. No television story or program can present all the facts relevant to a particular policy or program, let alone its historical and social context. Further, it has to compress news into bite-sized pieces

(hence sound bites) and, in doing so important elements of the story may be skewed or ignored altogether. Lastly, television advertising is the single most important reason for the high costs of political campaigning and is thus the indirect cause of the excesses and abuses of campaign financing. Interestingly, the United States is one of the few Western democracies where candidates do not receive free air time.

Although the framers of the Constitution did not plan it this way, a vigorous and healthy media are the best guarantee for a sound and free government. If Tocqueville were alive today, he would single out the media as one of the great strengths of American democracy.

Media Consultants

Media consultants manage a candidate's television, radio, and print advertisments. Their primary job is to manage the images and messages that the campaign is issuing on a daily basis as well as deal with the numerous media outlets.

If a (D) follows the name of the organization, then the organization either primarily or exclusively assists Democratic candidates. If a (R) follows the name, then it assists primarily or exclusively Republican candidates. No (D) or (R) means the group will handle either party's candidates.

Action Media Inc. Pier 35, Suite 206, San Francisco, CA 94133. Tel: (415) 392-6411 Fax: (415) 392-6459. Principal: Richard Rojas.

Advantage Consultants. 3660 Maguire Boulevard, Suite 103, Orlando, FL 32803. Tel: (407) 895-0077 Fax: (407) 896-4555 E-mail: guetzoe@aol.com. Principal: Douglas Guetzloe.

Advertising Group, The. 141 Deslard Street, Suite 511, Monroe, LA 71201-7339. Tel: (318) 387-1729 Fax: (318) 387-8333. Principal: Penny Doughty.

Alfano Production (R). 2300 North Lincoln, Arlington, VA 22207. Tel: (703) 522-8499 Fax: (703) 522-3971. Principal: Kim Alfano.

All World Consultants. PO Box 2071, Tallahassee, FL 32316. Tel: (850) 222-3475. Principal: Lucius Gantt.

Alliance Pacific Inc. 608 Flour Mill, West 621 Mallon, Spokane, WA 99201. Tel: (509) 325-3220 Fax: (509) 326-5663. Principal: Kerry Lynch Johnson.

Ed Allison Inc. (R). 1341 G Street NW, 2nd Floor, Washington, DC 20005. Tel: (202) 783-1800 Fax: (202) 783-2913. Principal: Ed Allison.

Altamira Communications Group. 9457 Las Vegas Boulevard South, Suite G, Las Vegas, NV 89123-3352. Tel: (702) 263-0333. Principal: Donald Williams.

Arst Public Relations (D). 1798 Scenic Avenue, Suite 314, Berkeley, CA 94709-1323. Tel: (206) 455-9055 Fax: (206) 646-2953. Principal: Jane Arst.

ASV Corporation. 2075 Liddell Drive, Atlanta, GA 30324. Tel: (800) 288-3445 Fax: (404) 876-1715. Principal: Shareen Gustafson.

Austin Sheinkopf, Inc. (D). 379 West Broadway, Suite 305, New York, NY 10012. Tel: (212) 941-6630 Fax: (212) 941-6634 E-mail: hsheink993@aol.com. Principal: Henry A. Sheinkopf.

Avakian & Assoc. (D). 5868 Hallridge Circle, Columbus, OH 43232. Tel: (614) 863-1012 Fax: (617) 925-2957 E-mail: hullonian@ aol.com. Principal: Steve Avakian.

Axelrod and Assoc. (D). 730 North Franklin, Chicago, IL 60610. Tel: (312) 664-7500 Fax:

(312) 664-0174 E-mail: axelro@eworld.com. Principal: David Axelrod.

B.H.I. (D). 2600 Douglas Road, Suite 1007, Coral Gables, FL 33134. Tel: (305) 461-3873 Fax: (305) 461-3970. Principal: Jacqueline Basha.

John P. Bakke. 539 Melody Lane, Memphis, TN 38120. Tel: (901) 682-9509 Fax: (901) 685-2796. Principal: John P. Bakke.

Baraff Communications. 41 Tomahawk Street, Yorktown Heights, NY 10598. Tel: (914) 962-4630 Fax: (914) 245-8927 E-mail: fbaraff@pipeline.com. Franklin L. Baraff.

William Berry Campaigns (D). 921 46th Street, Sacramento, CA 95819. Tel: (916) 737-0707 Fax: (916) 737-0132 E-mail: willberry@msn.com. Principal: Bill Berry.

Blackwelder Communications (R). 1700 Elkhart Drive, Greensboro, NC 27408. Tel: (910) 288-6235 Fax: (919) 282-7533. Principal: Jerry Blackwelder.

Brabender Cox (R). 2100 Wharton Street, Pittsburgh, PA 15203. Tel: (412) 488-6400 Fax: (412) 488-6410. Principal: John A. Brabender.

Bradsell Assoc. (R). 790 Route 518, Skillman, NJ 08558. Tel: (609) 924-4105 Fax: (609) 924-8723. Principal: Robert H. Bradsell.

Bragg, Maddox & Taylor (D). 3250 Wilshire Boulevard, Suite 928, Los Angeles, CA 90010. Tel: (213) 389-6123 Fax: (213) 389-5875. Principal: Felicia Bragg.

Braun Ketchum Public Relations. 11755 Wilshire Boulevard, Suite 2300, Los Angeles, CA 90025. Tel: (310) 444-5000 Fax: (310) 312-8953. or 1225 8th Street, Suite 485, Sacramento, CA 95814. Tel: (916) 449-6168. Principal: Larry Fisher.

Brockmeyer Media Group (R). PO Box 220449, Chantilly, VA 20153-0449. Tel: (703) 803-9247 Fax: (703) 803-9325 E-mail: jjbrock @enols.com. Principal: John Brockmeyer.

Bronrott Communications (D). 4415 Rosedale Avenue, Bethesda, MD 20814. Tel: (301) 652-6016 Fax: (301) 656-0441. Principal: Bill Bronrott.

Brown Giorgetti Consultants (D). 3 Gateway Center, 22nd Floor, Pittsburgh, PA 15222. Tel: (412) 553-6343 Fax: (412) 642-2601. Principal: Nello Giorgetti.

Brown Inc. (D). 720 East Zia Road, Santa Fe, NM 87505. Tel: (505) 982-3410 Fax: (505) 983-1926 E-mail: enlc29a@prodigy.com. Principal: Chris Brown.

Bryant & Clark Advertising (R). 126 North McDowell Street, Charlotte, NC 28204-2211. Tel: (704) 334-8742. Principal: W.E. Bryant Jr.

Paul Buiar Assoc., Inc. 225 West 34th Street, Suite 1310, New York, NY 10122. Tel: (212) 425-2100 Fax: (212) 239-0347. Principal: Paul Buiar.

Burges & Burges Strategists (D). 26100 Lake Shore Boulevard, Cleveland, OH 44132. Tel: (216) 261-3737 Fax: (216) 261-2522 E-mail: burges.burges@worldnet.att.net. Principal: Charlene M. Burges.

Bynum Consulting Group, Inc., The (D). 284 Travis Corners Road, Garrison, NY 10524. Tel: (914) 424-4300 Fax: (914) 424-3850. Principal: Peter Bynum.

C&E Communications. 101 West 6th Street, Suite 402, Austin, TX 78701-2933. Tel: (512) 472-4372 Fax: (512) 473-2098 E-mail: kvidnin@aol.com. Principal: Herb Holland.

California Communications Group (D). 1830 5th Avenue, Sacramento, CA 95818-3826. Tel: (916) 556-1150 or (916) 202-1996 Fax: (916) 441-2256 E-mail: grayr@cwo.com. Principal: Ron Grey.

Campaign Group, Inc. (D). 1600 Locust Street, Philadelphia, PA 19103. Tel: (215) 732-8200 Fax: (215) 790-9969 E-mail: tcgwestbw@aol.com. Principal: Neil Oxman.

Capitol Communications (R). 2648 East Workman Avenue, Suite 124, West Covina, CA 91791. Tel: (818) 919-5249.

Capitol Corporation (R). 1 Fawcett Place, Suite 130, Greenwich, CT 06830-6581. Tel: (203) 661-7962. Principal: Frank Trotta.

Capitol Lights Productions (D). 609 East Washington Avenue, Madison, WI 53703. Tel: (608) 256-7788 Fax: (608) 256-0035. Principal: Ed Garvey.

Carmen Group, The (R). 1401 1st NW, Suite 900, Washington, DC 20005. Tel: (202) 785-0500 Fax: (202) 785-5277. Principal: David Carmen.

Michael Carrier Enterprises (D). 2200 North Classen Boulevard, Suite 1220, Oklahoma City, OK 73106. Tel: (402) 524-7700 Fax: (402) 524-7744. Principal: Michael Carrier.

Thomas Carroll Campaigns. 128 Grant Avenue, Suite 216, Sante Fe, NM 87501. Tel: (505) 983-2203 Fax: (505) 982-2548. Principal: Thomas Carroll.

Chandler Media, Inc. (R). 1835 Marlbrook Drive NE, Atlanta, GA 30307. Tel: (404) 373-7424 Fax: (404) 373-0321. Principal: Ralph Chandler.

Channell & Assoc. (D). 516 DeLeon Drive, El Paso, TX 79912. Tel: (915) 833-0079 Fax: (915) 585-2723. Principal: Tim Channell.

Chesapeake Media (R). 31830 Bittorf Lane, Cordova, MD 21625. Tel: (410) 364-5009 Fax: (410) 364-5971. or 1169 Washington Street, Bath, ME 04530. Tel: (207) 443-9193 E-mail: aray@skipjack.bluecrab.org. Principal: Alex Ray.

Christopherson & Co. 6143 South Willow Drive, Suite 430, Greenwood Village, CO 80111. Tel: (303) 779-4920 Fax: (303) 779-0165. Principal: Dan Christopherson.

Cire Advertising, Inc. (R). 2401 T Circle, Norman, OK 73069. Tel: (405) 236-0836 Fax: (405) 447-4848. Principal: Mike Hammer.

Clarke Communications Group, The. RR 1, PO Box 5Y, East Calais, VT 05650. Tel: (802) 456-1732 Fax: (802) 456-1732 E-mail: ccgroupinc@aol.com. Principal: Rod Clarke.

Cleary & Assoc. (R). 908 Dillon Drive, Omaha, NE 68132. Tel: (402) 397-9200 Fax: (402) 397-9384. Principal: Jim Cleary.

Communication Works (D). 50 Jericho Turnpike, Suite 103, Jericho, NY 11753. Tel: (516) 997-5152 Fax: (516) 997-5154. Principal: Stephen Corrao.

Communications Company, The (D). 511 2nd Street NE, Washington, DC 20002. Tel: (202) 547-4467 Fax: (202) 543-6911. Principal: Jay Rouse.

Conservative Solutions (R). 2305 Southlake Court, Irving, TX 75038-5652. Tel: (214) 255-7913. Principal: Brian Humek.

Cookfair Media, Inc. (R). 536 Buckingham Avenue, Syracuse, NY 13201. Tel: (315) 478-3359 Fax: (315) 478-5236 E-mail: cookfair@aol.com. Principal: John R. Cookfair, III.

Leon Corcos Invasion Entertainment (D). 2727 B Street, Sacramento, CA 95816. Tel: (916) 447-5205. Principal: Leon Corcos.

Coronado Communications (R). 109 Spanish Village, Dallas, TX 75248. Tel: (214) 386-7127. Principal: Dick Leggitt.

Cottington Marti Inc. (R). 2626 East 82nd Street, Suite 121, Minneapolis MN 55425. Tel:

(612) 853-2266 Fax: (612) 853-2262. Principal: Scott Cottington.

Jim Cox & Assoc. (D). 2206 Superior Viaduct, Cleveland, OH 44113. Tel: (216) 241-8060 Fax: (216) 241-5114. Principal: James Cox.

Cox & Assoc. (D). 3625 Manchaca, Suite 302, Austin TX, 78704. Tel: (512) 444-2654 Fax: (512) 444-3533. Principal: Patrick Cox.

Craig Group, The. 37 West Broad Street, Suite 480, Columbus, OH 43215-4132. Tel: (614) 241-2222 Fax: (614) 241-2215. Principal: Philip A. Craig.

Allan B. Crow & Assoc. Inc. (R). 12162 Mendenhal Drive, Baton Rouge, LA 70814. Tel: (504) 273-4564 Fax: (504) 273-4599 E-mail: crowassoc@aol.com. Principal: Allan B. Crow.

Crow & Assoc. (R). 183 East Glenarm, Suite 103, Pasadena, CA 91105. Tel: (818) 500-1100 Fax: (818) 500-1768. Principal: Kathleen Crow.

Cummings Group, The. 1105 NW 44th, Oklahoma City, OK 73118. Tel: (405) 524-9441 Fax: (405) 524-9448. Principal: Ross W. Cummings.

Mike Davis Public Relations, Inc. (D). 3716 National Drive, Suite 118, Raleigh, NC 27612. Tel: (919) 787-6411 Fax: (919) 787-6508 E-mail: 75443.61@ compuserve.com. Principal: Mike Davis.

Deardourff The Media Company (R). 8300 Georgetown Pike, McLean, VA 22102. Tel: (703) 734-1022. Principal: John Deardourff.

Delta Design Group (D). 409 Washington Avenue, Greenville, MS 38701. Tel: (601) 335-6148 Fax: (601) 378-2836 E-mail: nworkman@ dccinfo.com. Principal: Noel Workman.

Democratic Comm. Group, The. 135 Victoria Road, New Britain, CT 06052. Tel: (860) 827-0537 or (860) 827-8552 Fax: (860) 827-0537 E-mail: dmalin@courant.infi.net. Principal: David S. Malinowski.

DGM Communications. 5821 Sylvan Drive, Columbia, SC 29206. Tel: (803) 787-8973 Fax: (803) 252-2016. Principal: Donald G. McLeese.

Direct Response, Inc. (D). 392 A Merrow Road, Tolland, CT 06084. Tel: (860) 875-8530 Fax: (860) 875-6176. Principal: Daniel J. Costello.

Directions By King & Assoc. (D). PO Box 1331, Healdsburg, CA 95448-1331. Tel: (707) 433-9027 Fax: (707) 433-9027 E-mail: kingcall @aol.com. Principal: Rose King.

Dittman Strategic Campaigns (R). 8115 Jewel Lake, DRC Building, Anchorage, AK 99502. Tel: (907) 243-3345 Fax: (907) 243-7172. Principal: David Lynn Dittman.

Doak-Carrier & Assoc. (D). 1000 Thomas Jefferson Street NW, Suite 306, Washington, DC 20007. Tel: (202) 342-7700 Fax: (202) 342-2087 E-mail: doakca@aol.com. Principal: David Doak.

Dolphin Group, Inc. (R). 10866 Wilshire Boulevard, Suite 550, Los Angeles, CA 90024. Tel: (310) 446-4800 Fax: (310) 446-1896. Principal: Lee Stitzenberger.

DPO Inc. (R). 2206 Aldrich Avenue North, Minneapolis, MN 55411. Tel: (612) 529-5090. Principal: Dennis O'Leary.

Dresner, Wickers & Assoc., Inc. (R). 52 Griffin Avenue, Bedford Hills, NY 10507. Tel: (914) 241-9244 Fax: (914) 241-9360 E-mail: dwa1234@aol.com. or 24 Charlton Street, San Carlos, CA 94070. Tel: (415) 595-4709 Fax: (415) 595-4887. Principal: Richard Dresner.

Earworks, Inc. 1479 South Beverly Drive, Suite 302, Los Angeles, CA 90035-9163. Tel: (213) 962-9163 Fax: (213) 962-9163. Principal: Garry South.

Edmonds Associates, Inc. (R). 900 2nd Street NE, Suite 110, Washington, DC 20002. Tel: (202) 371-0110 Fax: (202) 371-9597 E-mail: tomedmonds@aol.com. Principal: Thomas N. Edmonds.

Eidolon Communications (D). 156 5th Avenue, Suite 707, New York, NY 10011. Tel: (212) 633-0404 Fax: (212) 989-7777. Principal: John Graves.

Election Edge, The. PO Box 1691, Corpus Christi, TX 78403. Tel: (512) 883-4236 Fax: (512) 882-7739. Principal: Paul A. Nugent.

F.D.R. Services Inc. (D). 1001 4th Avenue, Suite 2730, Seattle, WA 98154. Tel: (206) 223-0443 Fax: (206) 223-7208 E-mail: hujar@ nwlink.com. Principal: J. Blair Butterworth.

Fairbank, Maslin, Maullin & Assoc. (D). 2425 Colorado Avenue, Suite 180, Santa Monica, CA 90404. Tel: (310) 828-1183 Fax: (310) 453-6562 E-mail: fmma@crl.com. Principal: John Fairbank.

Fingerhut, Powers, Smith & Assoc. (D). 1925 K Street NW, Suite 250, Washington, DC 20006. Tel: (202) 331-3700 Fax: (202) 331-3709. Principal: Frank Powers.

Arthur H. Finkelstein & Assoc. (R). 16 North Astor, Irvington, NY 10533. Tel: (914) 591-8142 Fax: (914) 591-4013. Principal: Ron Finkelstein.

Fitzgerald & Robbins (D). 32 Hampden Street, Springfield, MA 01103. Tel: (413) 737-8757 Fax: (413) 731-1488. Principal: Raul Robbins.

Roy Fletcher (D). 220 Delgado Drive, Baton Rouge, LA 70808. Tel: (504) 769-9301 Fax: (504) 769-1000. Principal: Roy Fletcher.

Fletcher & Rowley Consulting (D). 818 18th Avenue South, Nashville, TN 37203. Tel: (615) 742-9988 Fax: (615) 742-9964 E-mail: 73044.31.01@compuserve.com. Principal: William Fletcher.

Forde and Mollrich (R). 4041 MacArthur Boulevard, Suite 190, Newport Beach, CA 92660. Tel: (714) 476-9064 Fax: (714) 851-9053. Principal: Stu Mollrich.

Milo O. Frank. 1125 Angelo Drive, Beverly Hills, CA 90210. Tel: (310) 550-8970 Fax: (310) 859-1378. Principal: Milo O. Frank.

John Franzen Multimedia (D). 610 C Street NE, Washington, DC 20002. Tel: (202) 543-4430 Fax: (202) 543-8693 E-mail: franzen@ compuserve.com. Principal: John Franzen.

Thomas Frayne & Assoc. (R). 3064 Washington Boulevard, Cleveland Heights, OH 44118. Tel: (216) 932-2388. Principal: Thomas Frayne.

Galanty & Company (D). 1640 5th Street, Santa Monica, CA 90401. Tel: (310) 451-2525 Fax: (310) 451-5020 E-mail: galantyco@ aol.com. Principal: Sidney Galanty.

Garth Group, The. 505 Park Avenue, Suite 8FL, New York, NY 10022-1106. Tel: (212) 838-8800 Fax: (212) 752-1838. Principal: David L. Garth.

Garvey Communications Assoc. (D). PO Box 30036, Springfield, MA 01103. Tel: (413) 736-2245 Fax: (413) 736-2247. Principal: John J. Garvey.

Gatty Communications, Inc. (D). 5460 Harris Farm Lane, Clarksville, MD 21029. Tel: (301) 854-0660 Fax: (301) 843-0662. Principal: Bob Gatty.

Geddings/Mack & Assoc. (D). 602 B King Street, Alexandria, VA 22314. Tel: (703) 836-9811 Fax: (703) 836-9814 E-mail: geddcomm @aol. com. Principal: Kevin Geddings.

Gerl, Scotti & Assoc. (D). PO Box 424, Lewisburg, WV 24901. Tel: (304) 645-7362 Fax: (304) 645-7362. Principal: Jim Gerl.

Lee Gipson. 47 Long Cove Court, Madison, MS 39110. Tel: (601) 853-0563 Fax: (601) 853-2402 E-mail: logohead@aol.com. Principal: Lee Gipson.

Goldman & Assoc. 129 West Virginia Beach Boulevard, Suite 101, Norfolk, VA 23510-2030. Tel: (757) 625-2518 Fax: (757) 625-4336. Principal: Dean S. Goldman.

Goldman Assoc. (D). 4 South Market Street, Boston, MA 02109. Tel: (617) 227-5073 Fax: (617) 227-2379. Principal: Michael Goldman.

Mark Goode Enterprises (R). 1120 Connecticut Avenue NW, Suite 270, Washington, DC 20036. Tel: (202) 466-2616 Fax: (202) 785-3162. Principal: Mark Goode.

Goodman Group, Inc., The (R). 10749 Falls Road, Lutherville, MD 21093. Tel: (410) 296-5330 Fax: (410) 823-7298. or 4604 Richards Court, Tampa, FL 33611. Tel: (813) 805-9505 Fax: (813) 805-9605. Principal: Robert Goodman.

Grant, Inc. (R). PO Box 2688, Lynchburg, VA 24501. Tel: (804) 845-1323. Principal: Al Grant.

Dan Greenblat, Consultant (R). 4182 Pallon Court, San Diego, CA 92124-2703. Tel: (619) 530-2368. Principal: Dan Greenblat.

Greer, Margolis, Mitchell, Burns & Assoc. (D). 1010 Wisconsin Avenue NW, Suite 800, Washington, DC 20007. Tel: (202) 338-8700 Fax: (202) 338-2334. or 11111 Santa Monica Boulevard, Suite 1750, Los Angeles, CA 90025. Tel: (310) 444-0445 Fax: (310) 444-0447. Principal: Frank Greer.

Grossfeld/Severns (D). 350 South Mill Avenue, Tempe, AZ 85281. Tel: (602) 784-4890 Fax: (602) 784-4999 E-mail: grosssev@ goodnet.com. Principal: Bob Grossfeld.

Grunwald Communications (D). 1306 30th Street NW, Washington, DC 20007. Tel: (202) 973-9400 Fax: (202) 973-9408. Principal: Mandy Grunwald.

Hands On Campaign Consulting (D). 2665 Matheson Way, Sacramento, CA 95864. Tel: (916) 484-7895 or (916) 456-2608 Fax: (916) 487-7648. Principal: Chris M. Maupin.

Hicks, Lyons & Partners. PO Drawer 13958, Jackson, MS 39236. Tel: (601) 981-3300 Fax: (601) 981-4735. Principal: Steven Hicks.

Don Hoover & Assoc. (D). 5500 North Western, Suite 210, Oklahoma City, OK 73118. Tel: (405) 848-0632 Fax: (405) 848-0673 E-mail: dhaokl@ aol.com. Principal: Don Hoover.

Hopcraft Communications (D). 3551 N Street, Sacramento, CA 95816. Tel: (916) 457-5546 Fax: (916) 456-6545. Principal: Stephen Hopcraft.

Scott Howell & Company, Inc. (R). 7929 Brookriver Drive, Suite 620, Dallas, TX 75247 Tel: (214) 951-9494 Fax: (214) 688-0555 E-mail: media@scott-howell.com. or 211 North Union Street, Suite 200, Alexandria, VA 22314. Tel: (703) 838-3668. Principal: Scott Howell.

Dan Hunter Creative Services (D). 1101 Walnut, Des Moines, IA 50309. Tel: (515) 288-8908 Fax: (515) 243-4317. Principal: Dan Hunter.

Hurst & Phillips (R). 1440 Foothill Drive, Suite 250, Salt Lake City, UT 84108-2342. Tel: (801) 582-1440 Fax: (801) 582-1441. Principal: Mark Hurst.

Impression Management Consulting. 8615 Forrestal Drive NE, Tuscaloosa, AL 35406-3402. Tel: (205) 345-2861 Fax: (205) 759-1638. Principal: Karen S. Johnson Cartee.

International Communications Group, Inc. (D). 1925 Century Park East, Suite 1850, Los Angeles, CA 90067. Tel: (310) 557-2585 Fax: (310) 557-8623 E-mail: jbrooks@icg.usa.com. Principal: Jean Brooks.

Isenson Assoc. (D). PO Box 564, Olympia, WA 98507. Tel: (360) 426-7115. Principal: Beverly P. Isenson.

J S R Consulting (D). PO Box 101, Port Jervis, NY 12771. Tel: (914) 858-8673 Fax: (914) 856-1361. Principal: Joseph S. Rifkin.

J.G.R. & Assoc. 2600 Douglas Road, Suite 500, Coral Gables, FL 33134. Tel: (305) 446-9234. Principal: Julio G. Rebull.

J.H. Leitner Inc., (D). 149 5th Avenue, 7th Floor, New York, NY 10010. Tel: (212) 388-1300 Fax: (212) 388-9040. Principal: John Leitner.

Jefferson Group, The. 1341 G Street NW, Suite 1100, Washington, DC 20005. Tel: (202) 626-8500 Fax: (202) 626-8578 E-mail: info@jefferson group.com. Principal: Robert E. Carlstrom Jr.

Johnston & Lewis (R). PO Box 81514, San Diego, CA 92138. Tel: (619) 232-3333 Fax: (619) 232-1030. Principal: David Lewis.

Dan Jones & Assoc. 515 South 700 E, Suite 3H, Salt Lake City, UT 84102. Tel: (801) 322-5722 Fax: (801) 322-5725. Principal: Dan Jones.

Just Media. 5050 Kitzmiller Road, New Albany, OH 43054. Tel: (614) 855-7676. Principal: Deborah Beetham.

Grace Kaminkowitz Enterprises. 1143 South Plymouth Court, Suite 501, Chicago, IL 60605. Tel: (312) 987-0038 Fax: (312) 987-1022. Principal: Grace Kaminkowitz.

Barry Kaplovitz Assoc. 60 Charlesgate West, Boston, MA 02215. Tel: (617) 437-0847. Principal: Barry Kaplovitz.

Katz Sheehan Media Inc. 120 Pinewood Trail, Trumbull, CT 06611 3313. Tel: (203) 378-9914. Principal: Susan A. Katz.

Kemper Odell & Assoc. (R). PO Box 507, Sheridan, WY 82801. Tel: (307) 672-9715 Fax: (307) 674-6835. Principal: Cecile Pattison.

Bob Korba Design, Inc. (D). 2214 Euclid Avenue, Austin, TX 78704-5126. Tel: (512) 443-8083. Principal: Bob Korba.

William Kostka & Assoc. 1407 Larimar Square, Denver, CO 80202. Tel: (303) 623-8421 Fax: (303) 573-5426. Principal: William Kostka.

Kranzler Kingsley Communications, Ltd. (D). PO Box 693, Bismarck, ND 58502. Tel: (701) 255-3067 Fax: (701) 255-1022 E-mail: waynek@kkcltd.com. Principal: Wayne Kranzler. Website: http://kkcltd.com

Nicolas Kulibaba Assoc. 9807 Croom Road, Upper Marlboro, MD 20772. Tel: (301) 627-5589. Principal: Nicolas Kulibaba.

LaCorte Communications (R). 3942 Franklin Street, Glendale, CA 91214. Tel: (818) 249-8549 Fax: (818) 249-7577. Principal: Ken LaCorte.

Lacy Communications (R). PO Box 3489, Hamilton, NJ 08619. Tel: (609) 587-7830. Principal: John J. Lacy Jr.

Lake Research, Inc. (D). 1730 Rhode Island Avenue NE, Suite 400, Washington, DC 20036. Tel: (202) 776-9066 Fax: (202) 776-9074 E-mail: lakepolls@aol.com. Principal: Celinda Lake.

Michael Levine Public Relations. 8730 Sunset Boulevard, Los Angeles, CA 90069.

Tel: (310) 659-6400 Fax: (310) 659-1309. Principal: Michael Levine.

Lovgren Advertising, Inc. (R). 120 Regency Parkway, Omaha, NE 68114. Tel: (402) 397-7158 or (800) 366-8488 Fax: (402) 397-0854 E-mail: lovgren@lovgren.com. Principal: Linda H. Lovgren.

MacWilliams Cosgrove Snider Smith Robinson (D). 1150 17th Street NW, Suite 604, Washington, DC 20036. Tel: (202) 887-9201 Fax: (202) 887-9233 E-mail: mcssrds@aol.com. Principal: Matt MacWilliams.

Mandate: Campaign Media (D). PO Box 2124, Woodbridge, VA 22193. Tel: (703) 583-6277 Fax: (703) 583-8504 E-mail: 76046.723@compuserve.com. Principal: Michael R. Shannon.

Marketing and Sales Solutions (R). 85 East Orme, Unit 3 West, St Paul, MN 55118-2303. Tel: (612) 457-8763 Fax: (612) 457-5521. Principal: Mike Barich.

Marketing Resources Group Inc. (R). 225 South Washington Square, Lansing, MI 48933. Tel: (517) 372-4400 Fax: (517) 372-4045 E-mail: mrg.@royager.net. Principal: Thomas H. Shields.

Mason Dixon Camp Polling & Strategy, Inc. 339 Busch's Frontage Road, Suite 204, Annapolis, MD 21201. Tel: (410) 974-4823 Fax: (410) 626-7213. Principal: Patrick E. Gonzales.

Kevin M. McAuliffe Commun. & Editorial Svcs. (D). 451 East 14th Street, Apt 3D, New York, NY 10009. Tel: (212) 677-0921 Fax: (212) 777-5688. Principal: Kevin M. McAuliffe.

McElroy Communications. 2410 K Street, Suite C, Sacramento, CA 95816. Tel: (916) 447-7415 Fax: (916) 447-4944. Principal: Leo McElroy.

McKinnon Media (D). 98 San Jacinto Boulevard, Suite 900, Austin, TX 78701-4039. Tel: (512) 476-9175 Fax: (512) 480-9315. Principal: Mark McKinnon.

Barry McLoughlin Assoc., Inc. 1825 I Street NW, Suite 400, Washington, DC 20006. Tel: (800) 663-3899 Fax: (202) 429-9574. or 116 Village Boulevard, Suite 200, Princeton, NJ 08540. E-mail: communicate@mclomedia.com. Principal: Barry McLoughlin. Website: http://www.mclomedia.com.

Hank McManus Assoc., Inc. (D). 127 East 59th Street, New York, NY 10022. Tel: (212) 755-7730. Principal: Hank McManus.

McNally Temple Assoc., Inc. (R). 1817 Capitol Avenue, Suite A, Sacramento, CA 95814. Tel: (916) 447-8186 Fax: (916) 447-6326. Principal: Raymond M. McNally.

Media & Assoc. (D). 1510 J Street, Suite 125, Sacramento, CA 95814. Tel: (916) 448-1995 Fax: (916) 448-3298 E-mail: vinvotes@midtown.net. Principal: Kevin M. Reikes.

Media Impact. 7510 Old Chester Road, Bethesda, MD 20817. Tel: (301) 229-1740. Principal: James Gray Jr.

Patti Meis, Inc. 3535 NW 58th Street, Suite 1005, Oklahoma City, OK 73112. Tel: (405) 946-3555. Principal: Carol Kilgore.

Mervis & Co. 710 North Plankinton, Suite 300, Milwaukee, WI 53203. Tel: (414) 274-2550. Principal: Michael P. Mervis.

Message & Media (D). 65 Church Street, New Brunswick, NJ 08901. Tel: (908) 246-8291 Fax: (908) 937-6721 E-mail: mandminc@aol.com. Principal: Steve De Micco.

Mica, Dudinsky & Assoc. 305 East Capitol Street SE, Washington, DC 20003. Tel: (202) 543-2143 Fax: (202) 543-3992. or PO Box 756, Winter Park, FL 32790. Tel: (305) 628-3688. Principal: John L. Mica.

Midwest Films, Inc. 804 South Phillips Avenue, Sioux Falls, SD 57104. Tel: (605) 334-4067. Principal: James L. Unzicker.

Bill Miles Assoc., Inc. (D). PO Box 748, Tupelo, MS 38802. Tel: (601) 842-5040. Principal: William T. Miles.

Morris Carick, Inc. (D). 432 Park Avenue South, Suite 1206, New York, NY 10016. Tel: (212) 696-9308 Fax: (212) 696-9147. or 3190 Beachwood Drive, Los Angeles, CA 90034. Tel: (213) 469-1592. Principal: Hank Morris.

Morrison Communications (D). 1800 21st Street, Suite 100, Sacramento, CA 95814. Tel: (916) 736-3005 Fax: (916) 737-1809 E-mail: smorr94@ aol.com. Principal: Steven Morrison.

Moynihan Assoc. 207 East Buffalo Street, Suite 514, Milwaukee, WI 53202. Tel: (414) 272-2700. Principal: Paul J. Moynihan.

Multi Media Services Corporation (R). 915 Kings Boulevard, Alexandria, VA 22314. Tel: (703) 739-2160 Fax: (703) 739-0664. Principal: Anthony Fabrizio.

Murphy Pintak Gautier Hudome Agency Inc., The (R). 7601 Lewinsville Road, Suite 320, McLean, VA 22102. Tel: (703) 556-9600 Fax: (703) 556-4075 E-mail: info@mpgh.com. Principal: Mike Murphy.

Murphy/Powers Media, Inc. (R). 16 North Astor, Irvington, NY 10533. Tel: (914) 591-8142 Fax: (914) 591-4013. Principal: Arthur Finkelstein.

Joseph Napolitan Assoc., Inc. (D). 121 Chestnut Street, Springfield, MA 01103. Tel: (413) 732-1232 Fax: (413) 788-4759. Principal: Joseph Napolitan.

Nason, Lundberg & Assoc. (R). 320 West Whittier Boulevard, Suite 223, LaHabra, CA 90631. Tel: (714) 578-1270 Fax: (714) 578-1273. Principal: Lois Lundberg.

National Media Inc. (R). 211 North Union Street, Suite 200, Alexandria, VA 22314. Tel: (703) 683-4877 Fax: (703) 683-3579 E-mail: robinr@natmedia.com. Principal: Robin D. Roberts.

National Political Services, Inc. 308 East 30th Street, Suite 4, New York, NY 10016. Tel: (212) 689-7683 Fax: (212) 685-6618. Principal: Joseph Mercurio.

Neighborhood Research and Media (R). 3 Theater Plaza, PO Box 578, Sparta, NJ 07871. Tel: (201) 726-8114 Fax: (201) 726-8175 E-mail: shaftan@ptd.net. Principal: Richard K. Shaftan.

Richard E. Neustadt & Assoc. (D). 729 South 3rd Street, Columbus, OH 43206. Tel: (614) 444-2300 Fax: (614) 444-0699. Principal: Richard E. Neustadt.

New West Communications (D). PO Box 3142, Kearney, NE 68848. Tel: (402) 234-6381. Principal: Gary Goldberg.

New West Policy Group L.L.C. 223 East Union Street, Prescott, AZ 86303. Tel: (520) 776-7200 Fax: (520) 776-0146 E-mail: newwest @primenet.com. Principal: Richard T. Mayol.

New York Consultancy (R). 42 North Avenue, New Rochelle, NY 10805. Tel: (914) 632-7000. Principal: Frank Trotta.

Nichols Media Consultants (R). 713 South Cliff Avenue, Sioux Falls, SD 57104. Tel: (605) 339-1841 Fax: (605) 332-3143. Principal: Michael N. Nichols.

Nordlinger Assoc. (D). 1050 17th Street NW, 5th Floor, Washington, DC 20036. Tel: (202) 785-0440 Fax: (202) 785-0477 E-mail: nordlinger@ aol.com. Principal: Gary Nordlinger.

North Woods Advertising (D). 119 North 4th Street, Textile Building, Suite 200, Minneapolis, MN 55401. Tel: (612) 340-9999 Fax:

(612) 340-0857 E-mail: nghillsman@aol.com. Principal: Bill Hillsman.

One Alliance. 465 East High Street, Suite 200, Lexington, KY 40507-1935. Tel: (606) 225-2684 Fax: (606) 225-1335 E-mail: nealliance@uni.com. Principal: Lisa M. Davis.

Pace Marketing & Public Relations. 118 North Gadsden Street, Suite 100, Tallahassee, FL 32301. Tel: (850) 681-8787 Fax: (850) 681-6561. Principal: Andrew A. Pace.

Daniel B. Payne & Co. (D). 20 Park Plaza, Suite 1205, Statler Building, Boston, MA 02116. Tel: (617) 426-5901 Fax: (617) 426-7443 E-mail: polyneco@aol.com. Principal: Daniel B. Payne.

Parsons-Wilson (D). PO Box 66148, St Petersburg, FL 33736-6148. Tel: (813) 363-6100 Fax: (813) 363-6101 E-mail: parwil@ infoursa.com. Principal: Gregory Wilson.

Pendleton Productions, Inc. PO Box 110349, South Station, Anchorage, AK 99511. Tel: (907) 345-3742. Principal: George E. Lukens Jr.

Mary Ann Phillips (D). 89 Osborn Road, Rye, NY 10580. Tel: (914) 967-0692. Principal: Mary Anne Phillips.

Leonard C. Piazza, III/Political Consultant (D). PO Box 72, Luzerne, PA 18709-0072. Tel: (717) 831-6966 E-mail: lcpiazza@aol.com. Principal: Leonard C. Piazza.

Political Advertising & Consulting (R). 115 Shepardson Lane, Alameda, CA 94502. Tel: (510) 814-6195 Fax: (510) 814-6966 E-mail: mbarnespac@aol.com. Principal: Mark Barnes.

Political Affairs, LLC. 343 3rd Street, Suite 203, Baton Rouge, LA 70802. Tel: (504) 346-6767 Fax: (504) 346-8878. Principal: James Burland.

Political Communications (R). 2235 Webster Street, San Francisco, CA 94115. Tel: (415) 567-6301 Fax: (415) 929-0937 E-mail: Harlowell@aol.com. Principal: Harvey H. Hukari.

Politicom, Inc. (D). 84 Spruce Street, Yonkers, NY 10701. Tel: (914) 969-8178. Principal: Jim Surdoval.

Politics Inc. (D). 1920 L Street NW, Suite 700, Washington, DC 20036. Tel: (202) 331-7654 Fax: (202) 659-5559 E-mail: politicsin@ aol.com. Principal: Donald R. Sweitzer.

Potomac Inc. (D). 7940 Norfolk Avenue, Bethesda, MD 20814. Tel: (301) 656-7900 Fax: (301) 656-7903. Principal: G. Keith Haller.

Powell & Weber, Inc. (R). 3287 Keeshen Drive, Los Angeles, CA 90066. Tel: (310) 572-6000 Fax: (310) 572-6002. Principal: Steve Powell.

Public Response Group, Inc. (D). 134 North LaSalle, Chicago, IL 60602. Tel: (312) 630-1118 Fax: (312) 630-1194. Principal: Lloyd Betourney.

Quest Design Group. PO Box 270, Greenville, RI 02929. Tel: (401) 934-2772. Principal: Bruce R. Daigle.

R & M Marketing. 6820 93rd Avenue SE, Mercer Island, WA 98040. Tel: (206) 236-0626. Principal: Ron Mourning.

Reid Strategies. 655 Riverside Drive, Suite 209N, Memphis, TN 38103. Tel: (901) 522-9934 Fax: (901) 529-9413. Principal: Steven Reid.

Clinton Reilly Campaigns (D). 704 Sansome, San Francisco, CA 94111. Tel: (415) 397-0431 Fax: (415) 397-1904. Principal: Clinton Reilly.

Research/Strategy/Management (RSM) (R). 9344 Lanham Severn Road, Lanham, MD

20706. Tel: (301) 306-0844 Fax: (301) 306-0711. Principal: Vincent J. Breglio.

H & G Reich. 127 Mount Hope Boulevard, Hastings on Hudson, NY 10706. Tel: (914) 478-4042 Fax: (914) 478-4081. Principal: Gerri Reich.

Revell Communications (R). 1121 L Street, Suite 806, Sacramento, CA 95814. Tel: (916) 443-3816 Fax: (916) 443-5065. or 2000 L Street NW, Suite 200, Washington, DC 20036. Tel: (202) 785-8240. Principal: Dennis Revell.

Rindy Media (R). 501 North IH 35, Austin, TX 78702. Tel: (512) 472-5715 Fax: (512) 472-8145. Principal: Dean Rindy.

Ringe Media Inc. 14 Sweetwater Road, Burnsville, NC 28714. Tel: (800) 352-4698 Fax: (704) 675-9271. Principal: Don Ringe.

River Bank, Inc. (R). 14463 Black Ankle Road, Mount Airy, MD 21771. Tel: (301) 829-0033 Fax: (301) 829-0021 E-mail: iansweinschel@worldnet.att.net. Principal: Ian Weinschel.

Robbett & Rosenthal (D). PO Box 71, Green Farm, CT 06436. Tel: (203) 222-7406. or 517 East 81st Street, Suite 5W, New York, NY 10028. Tel: (212) 535-7113 E-mail: robbett &ross@aol.com. Principal: Bart Robbett.

Roberts, Gabbert & Assoc. 1408 North Kingshighway S305, St Louis, MO 63113. Tel: (314) 361-1700. Principal: Michael V. Roberts.

Robinson Communications (D). 10080 North Wolfe Road, SW3 140, Cupertino, CA 95014. Tel: (408) 252-9530 Fax: (408) 252-9531. Principal: Richard Robinson. Website: http://politicalindex.com.robinson.

Rothstein & Co. (D). 2101 Connecticut Avenue, Suite 32, Washington, DC 20008. Tel: (202) 232-9096 Fax: (202) 328-9064 E-mail: rothstein@isismedia.com. Principal: Joe Rothstein.

Michael Rowan (D). 406 East 73rd Street, New York, NY 10021. Tel: (212) 988-3158. Principal: Michael Rowan.

Russo Marsh & Assoc., Inc. (R). 770 L Street, Suite 950, Sacramento, CA 95814. Tel: (916) 441-3734 Fax: (916) 441-6057 E-mail: rmrinc@ns.com. Principal: Sal Russo.

Sandler Innocenzi (R). 705 Prince Street, Alexandria, VA 22314. Tel: (703) 684-0633 Fax: (703) 684-1343 E-mail: b4gop@aol.com. Principal: Jim Innocenzi.

Sautter Communications (D). 3623 Everett Street NW, Washington, DC 20008. Tel: (202) 244-3111 Fax: (202) 244-4220 E-mail: sauttercom@aol.com. Principal: Chris Sautter.

Savage Concepts. 4315 Oakhill Drive, Jackson, MS 39209. Tel: (601) 982-5107. Principal: Judy Kay Jefferson.

Seder/Laguens (D). 1817 Adams Mill Road NW, 2nd Floor, Washington, DC 20009. Tel: (202) 232-0300 Fax: (202) 232-8682 E-mail: dlaguens@ aol.com. Principal: Deno Seder.

Severin/Aviles Assoc., Inc. (R). 630 3rd Avenue, 3rd Floor, New York, NY 10017-6705. Tel: (212) 755-2280 Fax: (212) 755-2295. Principal: James T. Severin III.

Shea & Assoc. (D). 1205 Statler Building, 20 Park Plaza, Boston, MA 02116. Tel: (617) 695-9350 Fax: (617) 426-7443. Principal: Michael P. Shea.

Bernard Sheredy Media. 57 Hill Avenue, Johnson City, NY 13790. Tel: (607) 723-1333 Fax: (607) 723-1360. Principal: Bernard J. Sheredy.

Paul Shone & Assoc. Inc. (D). 141 Putnam Avenue, Cambridge, MA 02139. Tel: (617) 492-3736 Fax: (617) 834-1004. Principal: Paul Shone.

Shortt Comm. Group, Ltd. PO Box 14120, Savannah, GA 31416. Tel: (912) 232-9390 Fax: (912) 232-8213 E-mail: mshortt@ ix.netcom.com. Principal: Michael L. Shortt.

Sipple Strategic Communications (R). 2600 Virginia Avenue NW, Suite 512, Washington, DC 20037. Tel: (202) 338-8833. Principal: Don Sipple.

Smith & Harroff, Inc. (R). 11 Canal Center Plaza, Suite 104, Alexandria, VA 22314. Tel: (703) 683-8512 Fax: (703) 683-4622 E-mail: eblakely@mindspring.com. Principal: J. Brian Smith.

Sound of Birmingham. 3625 5th Avenue South, Birmingham, AL 35222. Tel: (205) 595-8497. Principal: Don Mosley.

Special Forces Communications (R). 2100 Susquehanna Road, Abington, PA 19001. Tel: (215) 572-0717. Principal: Mark R. Weaver.

Speech Dynamics. 111 West 57th Street, New York, NY 10019. Tel: (212) 759-3996. Principal: Dorthy Sarnoff.

Squier/Knapp Ochs Communications (D). 511 2nd Street NE, Washington, DC 20002. Tel: (202) 547-4970. Principal: Robert Squier.

Standing Ovations: Exec. Speaking Training. 511 Hilltop Terrace, Alexandria, VA 22301. Tel: (703) 548-1265 Fax: (703) 549-1265. Principal: Carol M. Simpson.

Stardot Consulting Ltd. 2888 Bluff Street, Suite 116, Boulder, CO 80301-1227. Tel: (800) 598-4005 Fax: (303) 415-9811 E-mail: info@ stardot.com. Principal: Luke Seemann. Website: http://www.stardot.com.

Arnold Steinberg & Assoc. (R). 335 Stunt Road, Calabasas, CA 91302. Tel: (818) 591-9100 Fax: (818) 591-9101. Principal: Arnold Steinberg.

Stevens, Reed, Curcio & Company (R). 201 North Union Street, Suite 400, Alexandria, VA 22314. Tel: (703) 683-8326 Fax: (703) 683-8826 E-mail: gscompany@aol.com. Principal: Greg Stevens.

Strategy & Campaign Management Group, The (D). 1 Sutter Street, Suite 800, San Francisco, CA 94104. Tel: (415) 421-4515 Fax: (415) 421-5466 E-mail: campstrat1@aol.com. Principal: John D. Whitehurst.

Strother/Duffy/Strother (D). 1400 I Street NW, Suite 450, Washington, DC 20005. Tel: (202) 626-5650 Fax:: (202) 639-8974 E-mail: rdsfilms@aol.com. Principal: Raymond Strother.

Struble Oppel Donovan Communications (D). 700 7th Street SE, Washington, DC 20003. Tel: (202) 544-2300 Fax: (202) 547-2804. or 2743 NE 20th Avenue, Portland, OR 97212. Tel: (503) 284-2834 Fax: (503) 284-3380. Principal: Karl Struble.

Stevens Schriefer Group, The (R). 10142 South Union, Alexandria, VA 22314. Tel: (703) 548-9777 Fax: (703) 548-8944. Principal: Stuart Stevens.

George Strong & Assoc. 2242 Bartlett, Houston, TX 77098. Tel: (713) 526-3606 Fax: (713) 528-3688 E-mail: gstrong@political.com. Principal: George Strong.

Sutherland MultiMedia (D). 7750 Broadway, San Antonio, TX 78209. Tel: (210) 820-3278 Fax: (210) 820-3375. Principal: Tucker Sutherland.

Ken Swope & Assoc. (D). 22 Edgewood Road, Marblehead, MA 01945. Tel: (617) 631-4292 Fax: (617) 631-3960. Principal: Ken Swope.

Tammany Hall. 916 Seagirl Boulevard, Far Rockaway, NY 11691-5632. Tel: (718) 327-0310 Fax: (718) 327-2857. Principal: Bill Mark.

Target Enterprises (R). 16501 Ventura Boulevard, Suite 515, Encino, CA 90068. Tel: (818) 905-0005 or (213) 462-1234 Fax: (818) 905-1444. Principal: David Bienstock.

Taurus Productions. 107 South 7th Street, Colorado Springs, CO 80905. Tel: (719) 633-3842 Fax: (719) 633-3896. Principal: Ginger Kathrens.

Television Communicators Media Training. PO Box 5437, Friendship Station NW, Washington, DC 20016-5437. Tel: (202) 966-6616. Principal: Robert D. Wechter.

Thompson Communications, Inc. (R). PO Box 5, 200 West Jefferson Street, Marshfield, MO 65706. Tel: (417) 859-5428 Fax: (417) 468-7577. Principal: John P. Thompson.

Timbes & Yeager, Inc. 263 North Conception Street, PO Box 2305, Mobile, AL 36603. Tel: (205) 432-7577 Fax: (205) 432-7570. Principal: W.N. Yeager.

Tobe TV (D). 12 Marion Terrace, Brookline, MA 02146. Tel: (617) 232-5547 Fax: (617) 277-5725 E-mail: tobetv@bu.edu. Principal: Tobe Berkovitz.

Totalcom, Inc. PO Box 20101, 922 20th Avenue, Tuscaloosa, AL 35402. Tel: (205) 345-7363 Fax: (205) 345-7373. or 100 Washington Street, Suite 303, Huntsville, AL 35801. Tel: (205) 534-6383. Principal: Jimmy Warren.

Townsend Group, Inc., The (R). Box 517, Deer Hill Road, Cornwall on Hudson, NY 12520. Tel: (914) 534-3513 Fax: (914) 534-4149. Principal: Jay Townsend.

Townsend Hermocillo Raimundo & Usher (D). 1717 I Street, Suite B, Sacramento, CA 95814. Tel: (916) 444-5701 Fax: (916) 444-0382 E-mail: trbu@dpbu.com. Principal: David J. Townsend. Website: http://www.trbu.com.

Trainor Assoc. (R). 39 Pike Street, Providence, RI 02903. Tel: (401) 454-1700 Fax: (401) 454-0033. Principal: Michael F. Trainor.

Trippi McMahon & Squier (D). 1029 North Royal Street, Suite 350, Alexandria, VA 22314. Tel: (703) 519-8600 Fax: (703) 519-8604 E-mail: info@tmsnewmedia.com. Principal: Joe Trippi.

Trudy L. Mason, Consulting (D). 205 East 78 Street, New York, NY 10021. Tel: (212) 744-8841 Fax: (212) 737-4650. Principal: Trudy L. Mason.

Varied Directions, Inc. 69 Elm Street, Camden, ME 04843. Tel: (207) 236-8506. Principal: David Hoffman.

Video Base International (D). PO Box 687, Prince Street Station, New York, NY 10012-5801. Tel: (212) 941-7445 Fax: (212) 941-8455 E-mail: salhunter@ aol.com. Principal: Sally Hunter.

Jack Walsh & Assoc., Inc. (D). 22 Richmond Street, West Roxbury, MA 02132. Tel: (617) 325-1050 Fax: (617) 325-0387. Principal: Jack Walsh.

David Weeks & Company (R). 114 West 7th Street, Suite 700, Austin, TX 78701. Tel: (512) 477-6540 Fax: (512) 477-6572 E-mail: dmwks@ aol.com. Principal: David Weeks.

Gus Weill Inc. PO Box 82009, Baton Rouge, LA 70884. Tel: (504) 769-7020 Fax: (504) 769-7796. Principal: Gus Weill.

Weiner & Weiner Inc. 7809 Jefferson Highway, Suite F 2, Baton Rouge, LA 70806. Tel: (504) 928-6931 Fax: (504) 928-6937. Principal: Gary K. Weiner.

West Rogers Marketing/Communications (R). 6075 Poplar Avenue, Suite 122, Memphis, TN 38119. Tel: (901) 682-3839 Fax: (901) 682-0605. Principal: Becky West.

Whistlestop Communications, Inc. (R).
1810 Broad Ripple Avenue, Suite 13/PO Box
802, Indianapolis, IN 46206-0802. Tel: (317)
259-0781 Fax: (317) 259-0754 E-mail: whistle@
whistlestopgop.com. Principal: Keith L.
Shallenberger.

Joe Slade White and Company, Inc. (D).
130 West 88th Street, New York, NY 10024.
Tel: (212) 580-1052 Fax: (212) 877-2167. or
901 North Pitt Street, Suite 170, Alexandria,
VA 22314. Tel: (703) 548-0012 Fax: (703) 548-
8151. Principal: Joe Slade.

Wilkes Company, The. PO Box 6933,
Lubbock, TX 79493-6933. Tel: (806) 765-5298
Fax: (806) 744-4902 E-mail: 74167.177@
compuserve.com. Principal: Morris Wilkes.

Wilson Grand Communications (R). 407
North Washington Street, Alexandria, VA
22314. Tel: (800) 678-9276 or (703) 739-0330
Fax: (703) 739-0332 E-mail: winelects@
aol.com. Principal: Paul O. Wilson.

Winn Consultancy. 1934 Mosswood Way,
Bowling Green, KY 42101. Tel: (502) 782-
9583. Principal: Larry J. Winn.

Winner/Wagner & Associates Campaigns.
1000 Potomac Street NW, Suite 401, Washington, DC 20007. Tel: (202) 333-2533 Fax: (202)
342-0763. Principal: Paul Mandabach.

Winning Image (R). 1629 K Street NW,
Suite 1100, Washington, DC 20006. Tel: (202)
785-6717. Principal: Chris Kielich.

Woodward & McDowell. 111 Anza Boulevard, Suite 406, Burlingame, CA 94010. Tel:
(650) 340-0470 Fax: (650) 340-1740. or 11444
West Olympic Boulevard, Suite 1018, Los
Angeles, CA 90064. Tel: (310) 445-8885 Fax:
(310) 445-8870. Principal: Richard S.
Woodward.

Yankee Communications (R). 240 Bonita
Drive, Bakersfield, CA 93305. Tel: (805) 334-
1776 Fax: (805) 326-1997. Principal: Jimmy
Yee.

Doug Zabel & Assoc. (D). 1501 Barton
Springs Road, Suite 121, Austin, TX 78704.
Tel: (512) 495-9499. Principal: Doug Zabel.

Zimmerman & Markman (D). 1250 6th
Street, Santa Monica, CA 90401. Tel: (310)
451-2522 Fax: (310) 451-7494. Principal: Bill
Zimmerman.

Political Journals and Newsletters

The following list contains leading political journals, magazines and newsletters. In addition to this extensive listing, the reader should consult individual political parties, political associations, political science research institutes, and think tanks for minor journals and newsletters that are not listed here.

Access Reports
1975. Biweekly. $325. Access Reports, Inc, 1624 Dogwood Lane, Lynchburg, VA 24503-1924. Tel: (804) 384-5334 Fax: (804) 384-8272. Editor: Harry Hammitt. ISSN: 0364-7625. Content: Coverage of the Freedom of Information Act and privacy issues relating to disclosure of government information.

AD Action News and Notes
1989. Weekly. $20.00. Americans for Democratic Action, 1625 K Street NW, Suite 210, Washington, DC 20006-1604. Tel: (202) 785-5980 Fax: (202) 785-5969. Editor: Amy Isaacs. Content: Coverage of ADA activities and programs.

ADA Today
1947. Quarterly. $20.00. Americans for Democratic Action, 1625 K Street NW, Suite 210, Washington, DC 20006-1604. Tel: (202) 785-5980 Fax: (202) 785-5969. Editor: Valerie Dulk. ISSN: 0896-3134. Content: News reports on ADA activities, including legislative lobbying efforts.

Against the Current
1979. Bimonthly. $20.00. Center for Change, 7012 Michigan Avenue, Detroit, MI 48210-2872. Tel: (313) 841-0160 Fax: (313) 841-8884. Editor: David Finkel. ISSN: 0739-4853. Content: Discussions of movements and motivations for political and social change.

Almanac of American Politics
1972. Biennial. $50. National Journal, 1501 M Street NW, Suite 300, Washington, DC 20005-1709. Tel: (202) 739-8400 Fax: (202) 739-8474. Editor: Eleanor Evans. ISSN: 0362-076X. Content: Biographies of governors and members of Congress.

Almanac of Federal PACs
1986. Biennial. $240. Amward Publications, 2030 Clarendon Boulevard, Suite 401, Arlington, VA 22201-2911. Tel: (703) 525-7227 Fax: (703) 525-3536. Editor: Edward Zuckerman. ISSN: 0362-076X. Content: Financial data and background information on federal PACS.

America Votes
1956. Biennial. $149.50. Congressional Quarterly, 1414 22nd Street NW, Washington, DC 20037-1096. Tel: (202) 887-8500 Fax: (202) 728-1863. Editor: Richard Scammon. ISSN: 0065-678X. Content: Details of votes cast by state and congressional district.

American Enterprise
1990. Bimonthly. $28. American Enterprise Institute for Public Policy Research, 1150 17th Street NW, Washington, DC 20036-4603. Tel: (202) 862-5887 Fax (202) 862-7177. Editor: Karlyn Keene. ISSN: 1043-3572. Content: Research reports on public policy issues.

American Journal of Political Science
1950. Quarterly. $30. University of Wisconsin Press, Journals Division, 114 North Murray Street, Madison, WI 53715-1137. Tel: (608) 262-4952 Fax: (608) 265-5277. Editor: Kenneth S. Meier. ISSN: 0092-5853. Content: Scholarly articles focusing on American politics and methodology.

American Lobbyists Directory
1989. $175. Gale Research Inc, 835 Penobscot Building, 645 Griswold Street, Detroit, MI 48226-4094. Tel: (313) 961-2242 Fax: (313) 961-6241. Editor: Robert Wilson. ISSN: 1045-3679. Content: Activities of registered lobbyists at federal and state levels.

American Political Report
1971. Biweekly. $195. American Political Research Corp, 4715 Cordell Avenue, Bethesda, MD 20814-3016. Tel: (301) 654-4990 Fax: (301) 656-0822. Editor: Kevin Phillips. ISSN: 8755-562X. Content: Analyses of American political trends and movements.

American Political Science Review
1903. Quarterly. $154. American Political Science Association, 1527 New Hampshire Avenue NW, Washington DC 20036-1206. Tel: (202) 483-2512 Fax: (202) 483-2657. Editor: G. Bingham Powell. ISSN: 0003-0554. Content: Scholarly studies covering all fields of political science.

American Politics Quarterly
1973. Quarterly. $54. Sage Publications, Inc, 2455 Teller Road, Thousand Oaks, CA 91320-2218. Tel: (805) 499-9774 Fax: (805) 499-0871. Editor: James C. Garand. ISSN: 0044-7803. Content: Basic research into all aspects of the American political system.

American Prospect
1990. Bimonthly. $25. American Prospect, Inc, 6 University Road, Cambridge, MA 02138-5731. Tel: (617) 547-2950 Fax: (617) 547-3896. Editor: Scott Stossel. ISSN: 1049-7258. Content: Liberal perspectives on politics and public policy issues.

American Sentinel
1971. 22 times a year. $87. Sentinel Communications, Inc, 15113 Steele Creek Road, Charlotte, NC 28273-6855. Tel: (704) 587-0898 Fax: (704) 587-0195. ISSN: 1079-6509. Content: Reports on left wing activities.

American Spectator
1967. Monthly. $35. American Spectator, 2020 14th Street N, Suite 750, Arlington, VA 22201-2515. Tel: (703) 243-2733 Fax: (703) 243-6814. Editor: R. Emmett Tyrrell, Jr. ISSN: 0148-8414. Content: Investigative studies from a conservative viewpoint.

America's Future
1959. Bimonthly. $15. America's Future, 7800 Bonhomme Avenue, St Louis, MO 63105-1906. Tel: (314) 725-6003 Fax: (314) 721-3373. Editor: F.R. Duplantier. ISSN: 0003-1593. Content: Views of public affairs issues from a conservative perspective.

Annals of the American Academy of Political and Social Science
1891. Bimonthly. $51. Sage Publications, Inc, 2455 Teller Road, Thousand Oaks, CA 91320-2218. Tel: (805) 499-0721 Fax: (805) 499-0871. Editor: Richard D. Lambert. ISSN: 0002-7162. Content: Interdisciplinary discussions of public policy issues.

APSA Departmental Services Program, Survey of Departments
1971. Annual. $23.50. American Political Science Association, 1527 New Hampshire Avenue NW, Washington, DC 20036. Tel: (202) 483-2512 Fax: (202) 483-2657. Editor: Sheilah Mann. ISSN: 0094-7954. Content: Survey results e.g. salary, enrollment of political science departments.

APSA Directory of Department Chairpersons
1927. Annual. $28.50. American Political Science Association, 1527 New Hampshire Avenue NW, Washington, DC 20036. Tel: (202) 483-2512 Fax: (202) 483-2657. Editor: Patricia Spellman. ISSN: 0196-5255. Content: Directory

information on political science chairpersons at four year institutions.

Ballot Access News
1985. 13 times a year. $9. Coalition for Free & Open Elections, PO Box 470296, San Francisco, CA 94147-0296. Tel: (415) 922-9779 Fax: (415) 441-4268. Editor: Richard Winger. ISSN: 1043-6898. Content: Legal developments affecting third parties.

BIPAC Politics
1964. Quarterly. $30. Business Industry Political Action Committee, 888 16th Street NW, Washington, DC 20006-4604. Tel: (202) 833-1880 Fax: (202) 833-2338. Editor: Carol Farouchar. ISSN: 0032-3276. Content: Coverage of political trends and developments impacting the business community.

Boston Review
1975. Bimonthly. $15. Boston Review, c/o Kim Cooper, 33 Harrison Avenue, Boston, MA 02111. Tel: (617) 253-3642 Fax: (617) 252-1549. Editor: Joshua Cohen. ISSN: 0734-2306. Content: Radical democratic views of political issues.

Brookings Review Magazine
1982. Quarterly. $17.95. Brookings Institution Press, 1775 Massachusetts Avenue NW, Washington, DC 20036-2188. Tel: (202) 797-6258 Fax: (202) 797-6004. Editor: Brenda Szittya. ISSN: 0745-1253. Content: Public policy studies aimed at lawmakers.

California Journal
1970. Monthly. $35. Information for Public Affairs, Inc, 2101 K Street, Sacramento, CA 95816-4920. Tel: (916) 444-2840. Editor: A. G. Block. ISSN: 0008-1205. Content: Nonpartisan coverage of the politics and personalities of California.

California Political Week
1979. Weekly. $90. California Political Week, PO Box 1468, Beverly Hills, CA 90213-1468. Tel: (310) 659-0205 Fax: (310) 657-4340. Editor: Dick Rosengarten. ISSN: 0195-6175.

Content: Analyses of public policy trends in California and other western states.

Campaigns & Elections
1980. 10 times a year. $40. C & E Publishing Corp, 1511 K Street NW, Suite 1020, Washington, DC 20005-1401. Tel: (202) 638-7788 Fax: (202) 638-4668. Editor: Ron Faucheux. ISSN: 0197-0771. Content: Management strategies and techniques for political professionals.

Cato Journal
1981. 3 times a year. $24. Cato Institute, 1000 Massachusetts Avenue NW, Washington, DC 20077-0172. Tel: (202) 842-0200 Fax: (202) 842-3490. Editor: James A. Dom and Monika Vanberg. ISSN: 0273-3072. Content: Interdisciplinary studies aimed at policy analysts.

City Journal
1990. Quarterly. $20. Manhattan Institute, 52 Vanderbilt Avenue, New York, NY 10017-3808. Tel: (212) 599-7000 Fax: (212) 599-3494. Editor: Myron Magnet. ISSN: 1060-8540. Content: Articles focusing on urban public policy issues.

Common Cause Magazine
1970. Quarterly. $12. Common Cause, 2030 M Street NW, Washington, DC 20036-3380. Tel: (202) 736-5714 Fax: (202) 659-3716. Editor: Vicki Kemper. ISSN: 0271-9592. Content: Investigative reports of government misconduct.

Comparative Political Studies
1968. Bimonthly. $59. Sage Publications, 2455 Teller Road, Thousand Oaks, CA 91320-2218. Tel: (805) 499-0721 Fax: (805) 499-0871. Editor: James A. Caporaso. ISSN: 0010-4140. Content: Articles by scholars engaged in cross-national studies.

Comparative Politics
1968. Quarterly. $30. CUNY Graduate School, 33 West 42nd Street, New York, NY 10036-8003. Tel: (212) 642-2355 Fax: (212) 642-1980. Editor: I. L. Markovitz. ISSN: 0010-4159.

Content: Comparative studies conducted by leading political science specialists.

Congress & the Presidency
1972. 2 times a year. $15. American University, School of Public Affairs, Washington, DC 20016. Tel: (202) 885-6250 Fax: (202) 885-1037. Editor: Susan Hammond & Martha Kumar. ISSN: 0734-3469. Content: Research reports on the Presidency.

Congressional Digest
1921. 10 times a year. $53.50. Congressional Digest Corp, 3231 P Street NW, Washington, DC 20007. Tel: (202) 333-7332 Fax: (202) 625-6670. Editor: Page B. Robinson. ISSN: 0010-5899. Content: Pro and con articles on major issues before the Congress.

Congressional Quarterly Almanac
1948. Annual. $315. Congressional Quarterly, Inc, 1414 22nd Street NW, Washington, DC 20037. Tel: (202) 432-2250 ext. 621 Fax: (202) 785-4415. ISSN: 0095-6007. Content: Summaries of congressional actions.

Congressional Quarterly Service
1945. Weekly. $1,095. Congressional Quarterly, Inc, 1414 22nd Street NW, Washington, DC 20037-1096. Tel: (202) 887-8500 Fax: (202) 728-1863. Editor: Neil Brown. ISSN: 0010-5910. Content: Coverage of congressional events and votes.

Congressional Quarterly Weekly Report
1956. Weekly. Comes with Congressional Quarterly Service. Congressional Quarterly, Inc, 1414 22nd Street NW, Washington, DC 20037. Tel: (202) 432-2250 ext. 621 Fax: (202) 785-4415. ISSN: 0010-5910. Content: Voting records of members of Congress.

Conservative Chronicle
1985. Weekly. $45. Hampton Publishing Company, 9 2nd Street NW, PO Box 29, Hampton, IA 50441-0029. Tel: (515) 456-2585 Fax: (515) 456-2587. Editor: Joseph P. Roth. ISSN: 0888-7403. Content: Articles by syndicated conservative columnists.

Conservative Review
1990. Bimonthly. $29. Council for Social & Economic Studies, 1133 13th Street NW, Suite C2, Washington, DC 20005-4207. Tel: (202) 371-2700 Fax: (202) 371-1523. Editor: Frederic N. Smith. ISSN: 1047-5990. Content: Coverage of the current political scene from a conservative perspective.

CQ Researcher
1923. 48 times a year. $314. Congressional Quarterly, Inc, 1414 22nd Street NW, Washington, DC 20037-1096. Tel: (202) 887-8500 Fax: (202) 728-1863. Editor: Sandra Stencil. ISSN: 1056-2036. Content: Broad coverage of current political issues.

Current
1960. 10 times a year. $32. Helen Dwight Reid Educational Foundation, 1319 18th Street NW, Washington, DC 20036-1802. Tel: (202) 296-6267 Fax: (202) 296-5149. Editor: Joyce Horn. ISSN: 0011-3131. Content: Reprints of articles on public policy issues.

Democratic Left
1972. Bimonthly. $8. Democratic Socialists of America, 180 Varick Street, 21st Floor, New York, NY 10014-4606. Tel: (212) 727-8610 Fax: (212) 227-4205. Editor: Michael Lighty. ISSN: 0164-3207. Content: Articles addressing topics of interest to the democratic left.

Directory of Political Newsletters
1990. Irregular. $45. Government Research Service, 214 SW 6th Avenue, Suite 301, Topeka, KS 66603-3719. Tel: (913) 232-7720 Fax: (913) 232-1615. Editor: Lynn Hellebust. ISSN: 1071-796X. Content: Listings of newsletters focusing on public policies and politics.

Dissent
1954. Quarterly. $22. Foundation for the Study of Independent Social Ideas, 521 5th Avenue, New York, NY 10175-0003. Tel: (212) 595-3084 Fax: (212) 595-3084. Editor: Irving Howe. ISSN: 0012-3846. Content: Left-wing magazine offering independent views of politics in America.

Evans/Novak Political Report
1967. Biweekly. $247. Eagle Publishing, Inc, 422 1st Street SE, Suite 300, Washington, DC 20003-1803. Tel: (202) 546-5005 Fax: (301) 424-4297. ISSN: 0014-3650. Content: Latest news on topical political issues.

Focus
1972. Monthly. $15. Joint Center for Political Studies, 1090 Vermont Avenue NW, Suite 1100, Washington, DC 20005-4905. Tel: (202) 789-3500. Editor: Jane Lewin. ISSN: 0740-0195. Content: Political studies aimed at blacks and other minorities.

Freedom Socialist
1967. Quarterly. Free to qualified individuals. Freeway Hall Publications, 5018 Rainier Avenue South, Seattle, WA 98118-1927. Tel: (206) 722-2453 Fax: (206) 723-7691. Editor: Andrea Bauer. ISSN: 0272-4367. Content: Articles advocating active feminism.

Gallup Poll Monthly
1965. Monthly. $95. Gallup Organization, Inc, PO Box 628, 47 Hulfish Street, Princeton, NJ 08542-0628. Tel: (609) 924-9600 Fax: (609) 683-9256. Editor: Leslie C. McAneny. ISSN: 1051-2616. Content: Overviews of polls conducted by the Gallup Organization.

George
1995. Monthly. $24. George Magazine, 1632 Broadway, 41st Floor, New York, NY 10019-6818. Tel: (212) 767-6100 Fax: (212) 767-5622. Editor: John F. Kennedy Jr. ISSN: 1084-662X. Content: Profiles of personalities who shape public issues.

Governing
1987. Monthly. $39.95. Congressional Quarterly, Inc, 2300 N Street NW, Suite 760, Washington, DC 20037-1122. Tel: (202) 862-8802 Fax: (202) 862-0032. Editor: Peter Harkness. ISSN: 0894-3842. Content: Analyses of trends in formulation of public policies.

Grass Roots Campaigning
1979. Monthly. $36. Campaign Consultants, PO Box 7281, Little Rock, AR 72217-7281. Tel: (501) 225-3996 Fax: (501) 225-5167. Editor: Jerry L. Russell. Content: Techniques and tactics of running political campaigns.

Green Party Newsletter
1973. Quarterly. $25. Green Party USA, 981 Old Indian Trail, Suite 103, Aurora, IL 60506. Tel: (630) 896-4819. Editor: Lowell Mathes. Content: Official national newsletter of the Green Party USA.

Guide to the American Left
1969. Annual. $25. Editorial Research Service, PO Box 2047, Olathe, KS 66051-2047. Tel: (913) 829-0609 Fax: (913) 829-0609. Editor: Laird Wilcox. ISSN: 0894-4547. Content: Listings of organizations, institutions and publications associated with liberal causes.

Guide to the American Right
1969. Annual. $25. Editorial Research Service, PO Box 2047, Olathe, KS 66051-2047. Tel: (913) 829-0609 Fax: (913) 829-0609. Editor: Laird Wilcox. ISSN: 0894-4547. Content: Listings of organizations, institutions and publications associated with conservative causes.

Harvard Political Review
1969. Quarterly. $15. Harvard Political Review, 79 John F. Kennedy Street, Cambridge, MA 02138-5801. Tel: (617) 495-2454 Fax: (617) 496-3692. Editor: John Turner. ISSN: 0090-1032. Content: Nonpartisan studies of political thought.

Headway
1988. Monthly. $30. Richberg Communications, Inc, 13555 Bammel North Houston Road, Suite 227, Houston, TX 77066-2957. Tel: (281) 444-4265 Fax: (281) 583-9534. Editor: Gwen Daye Richardson. ISSN: 1087-2353. Content: Conservative political opinions aimed at minority groups.

Heterodoxy
1992. Monthly. $25. Center for the Study of Popular Culture, PO Box 67398, Los Angeles,

CA 90067-0398. Tel: (310) 843-3499 Fax: (310) 843-3692. Editor: David Throwitz. ISSN: 1069-7268. Content: Caustic articles on the subject of political correctiveness.

Hill, The
1994. Weekly. $100. The Hill, 733 15th Street NW, Suite 1140, Washington, DC 20005. Tel: (202) 628-8500 Fax: (202) 628-8503. Editor: Martin Tolchin. Content: Newspaper coverage of Capitol Hill.

Hillary Clinton Quarterly
1992. Quarterly. $15. Maracom, PO Box 2642, Concord, NH 03302-2642. Tel: (603) 225-8940. Editor: Frank Marafiote. ISSN: 1067-0777. Content: News and commentary on the first lady.

Hotline
1987. Daily. $4,397. National Journal, 3129 Mount Vernon, Alexandria, VA 22305. Tel: (202) 739-8531. Editor: Robert Balkin. Content: Daily briefings on key events in American politics.

Human Events
1944. Weekly. $49.95. Phillips Publishing, Inc, 7811 Montrose Road, Potomac, MD 20854. Tel: (301) 340-2100 Fax: (301) 424-5059. Editor: Thomas S. Winter. ISSN: 0018-7194. Content: Conservative viewpoints of domestic political issues.

Illinois Issues
1975. Monthly. $35.95. University of Illinois at Springfield, Brookens 440, Springfield, IL 62794. Tel: (217) 786-6084 or (217) 786-7435 Fax: (217) 786-7257. Editor: Caroline Gheradini. ISSN: 0738-9663. Content: Coverage of the issues and personalities in Illinois politics.

In Depth
1991. 3 times a year. $12. Washington Institute, 1015 18th Street NW, Suite 300, Washington, DC 20036-5204. Tel: (202) 293-7440 Fax: (202) 293-9393. Editor: Richard L. Rubenstein. ISSN:

1055-9809. Content: Nonpartisan examinations of public policy issues.

Inside Alabama Politics
1985. 39 times a year. $83. Inside Alabama Politics, PO Box 66200, Mobile, AL 36660-1200. Tel: (334) 473-4269 Fax: (334) 479-8822. Editor: Bessie Ford. ISSN: 0884-030X. Content: Analyses of Alabama political trends.

Intellectual Activist
1979. Bimonthly. $24. TIA Publications, Inc, PO Box 262, Lincroft, NJ 07738-0262. Tel: (908) 842-6610 Fax: (908) 842-6381. Editor: Robert Trainski. ISSN: 0730-2355. Content: Articles advocating the rights of individuals in society.

Interpretation
1970. Tri-quarterly. $29. Interpretation, Inc, 6530 Kissena Boulevard, Queens College, Flushing, NY 11367-1575. Tel: (718) 997-5547. Editor: Hilail Gildin. ISSN: 0020-9635. Content: Studies of political philosophy.

Jack Anderson Confidential
1984. Semimonthly. $98. Target Publishing, Inc, PO Box 887, Springville, UT 84663-0887. Tel: (415) 463-2200 Fax: (415) 463-0173. Editor: Tom Walton. ISSN: 1064-4458. Content: Inside information on Washington politics.

John Birch Society Bulletin
1958. Monthly. $20. John Birch Society, 770 North Westhill Boulevard, Appleton, WI 54914-6521. Tel: (414) 749-3780 Fax: (414) 749-3785. Editor: John McManus. ISSN: 0449-0754. Content: Activities, tactics and strategies of the John Birch Society.

Journal of Democracy
1990. Quarterly. $29. Johns Hopkins University Press, 2715 North Charles Street, Baltimore, MD 21218-4363. Tel: (410) 516-6964 Fax: (410) 516-6968. Editor: Marc F. Plattner. ISSN: 1045-5736. Content: Studies on the trends in democratic governments.

Journal of Political Science
1973. Annual. $14.95. College of Charleston, 66 George Street, Department of Political Science, Charleston, SC 29424-0100. Tel: (803) 953-5724 Fax: (803) 953-8140. Editor: Martin Slann. ISSN: 0098-4612. Content: Theme-based studies of political issues.

Journal of Politics
1938. Quarterly. $30. University of Texas Press, PO Box 7819, Austin, Texas 78713-7819. Tel: (512) 471-4531 Fax: (512) 320-0668. Editor: Edward Portis. ISSN: 0022-3816. Content: Broad coverage of a wide range of political issues.

Kiplinger Washington Newsletter
1923. Weekly. $73. Kiplinger Washington Editors, 1729 H Street NW, Washington, DC 20006. Tel: (301) 887-6400 Fax: (301) 559-9272. Editor: Austin Kiplinger. ISSN: 0023-1770. Content: Studies assessing the impact of Washington politics on the business sector.

Leader in Action
1981. 3 times a year. $20. American Association of University Women, 1111 16th Street NW, Washington, DC 20037. Tel: (202) 785-7740. Editor: Jodi Lipson. ISSN: 8755-2620. Content: Strategies for starting and managing grassroots movements.

Liberty
1987. Bimonthly. $19.50. Liberty Publishing, PO Box 1181, Port Townsend, WA 98368-0981. Tel: (360) 385-5097 Fax: (360) 385-3704. Editor: R. W. Bradford. ISSN: 0894-1408. Content: Traditional libertarian views on culture and politics.

Limbaugh Letter
1993. Monthly. $29.95. EFM Media Management, 366 Madison Avenue, 7th Floor, New York, NY 10017-3122. Tel: (212) 661-7500 Fax: (212) 563-9166. Editor: Rush Limbaugh. ISSN: 1065-0377. Content: Articles reflecting viewpoints of the conservative commentator.

Long Term View
1992. Quarterly. $10. Massachusetts School of Law, 500 Federal Street, Woodland Park, Andover, MA 01810-1017. Tel: (508) 681-0800 Fax: (508) 681-6330. Editor: Douglas Velvel. Content: Extensive discussions on a single public policy issue.

Madison Review
1995. Quarterly. $20. James Madison Institute for Public Policy, PO Box 13894, Tallahassee, FL 32317-3894. Tel: (904) 386-3131 Fax: (904) 381-1807. Editor: Thomas Dye. ISSN: 1083-3684. Content: Studies of the principles of limited government at the state and local levels.

Michigan Journal of Political Science
1980. Semiannual. $12. University of Michigan Political Science Department, 5620 Haven Hall, Ann Arbor, MI 48109-1045. Tel: (313) 764-6386. Editor: Emily Metzgar. ISSN: 0733-4486. Content: Discussions of political issues from viewpoint of students.

Militant
1928. Weekly. $45. 408 Printing & Publishing Corp, 410 West Street, New York, NY 10014-2570. Tel: (212) 929-8994 Fax: (212) 727-0150. Editor: Greg McCartan. ISSN: 0026-3885. Content: Articles addressing the needs of working people.

Mother Jones
1976. Bimonthly. $18. Foundation for National Progress, 731 Market Street, Suite 600, San Francisco, CA 94103-2002. Tel: (415) 665-6637 Fax: (415) 665-6696. Editor: Jeffrey Klein. ISSN: 0362-8841. Content: Investigative articles exposing abuses of power in government.

Nation
1865. Weekly. $48. Nation, Inc, 72 5th Avenue, New York, NY 10011-8004. Tel: (212) 242-8400 Fax: (212) 463-9712. Editor: Katrina Vanden Heuvel. ISSN: 0027-8378. Content: Traditional liberal analyses of public policy issues.

National Journal
1969. Weekly. $624. National Journal, Inc, 1501 M Street NW, Suite 300, Washington, DC 20005-1709. Tel: (202) 833-8069 Fax: (202) 739-8540. Editor: Richard Frank. ISSN: 0360-4217. Content: In depth coverage of issues of national importance.

National Political Science Review
1989. Annual. $22. Transaction Publishers, Rutgers State University, New Brunswick, NJ 08903. Tel: (908) 445-2280 Fax: (908) 445-3138. Editor: George Persons. ISSN: 0896-629X. Content: Examinations of theoretical aspects of politics as applied to disadvantaged groups.

National Review
1955. Biweekly. $57. National Review, Inc, 150 East 35th Street, New York, NY 10016-4178. Tel: (212) 679-7330 Fax: (212) 889-7514. Editor: John O'Sullivan. ISSN: 0028-0038. Content: Traditional conservative perspectives on political matters.

National Voter
1951. Quarterly. $15. League of Women Voters of the US, 1730 M Street NW, Suite 1000, Washington, DC 20036-4587. Tel: (202) 429-1965 Fax: (202) 429-0854. ISSN: 0028-0372. Content: Comprehensive coverage of selected national and local issues.

New American
1985. Biweekly. $39. American Opinion Publishing, Inc, 770 North Westhill Boulevard, Appleton, WI 54914-5785. Tel: (920) 749-3789 Fax: (920) 749-3785. Editor: Gary Benoit. ISSN: 0885-6540. Content: News and political commentary from a right wing perspective.

New Political Science
1978. Quarterly. $30. Columbia University, Department of Political Science, 420 West 118th Street, Room 733, New York, NY 10027-7213. Tel: (212) 280-3644. Editor: Florindo Volpacchio. ISSN: 0739-3148. Content: Progressive perspectives on current political developments.

New Republic
1914. Weekly. $70. New Republic, Inc, 1220 19th Street NW, Suite 600, Washington, DC 20036-2474. Tel: (202) 331-7494 Fax: (202) 331-0275. Editor: Rick Hertzberg. ISSN: 0028-6583. Content: Moderately liberal perspectives on contemporary political topics.

News & Letters
1955. 10 times a year. $3. News & Letters, 59 East Van Buren Street, Chicago, IL 60605-1212. Tel: (312) 663-0839. Editor: Olga Domanski. ISSN: 0028-8969. Content: Analyses of political events from a Marxist Humanist perspective.

Oklahoma Observer
1969. Semimonthly. $25. Troy Enterprises Company, PO Box 53371, Oklahoma City, OK 73152-3371. Tel: (405) 525-5582. Editor: Frosty Troy. ISSN: 0030-1795. Content: Commentary on government and politics in Oklahoma.

Peacework
1972. Monthly. $10. American Friends Service Committee/Massachusetts, 2161 Massachusetts Avenue, Cambridge, MA 02140-1336. Tel: (617) 661-6130. Editor: Pat Farren. ISSN: 0748-0725. Content: Grassroots peace and social justice newsletter.

People
1891. Semimonthly. $5. Socialist Labor Party, 711 West Evelyn Avenue, Suite 209, Sunnyvale, CA 94086-6140. Tel: (408) 245-2047 Fax: (408) 245-2049. Editor: Robert Bills. ISSN: 0199-350X. Content: News features on public policy issues affecting working people.

Perot Periodical
1993. Quarterly. $15. Perot Periodical, PO Box 435, Bronx, NY 10471-0435. Tel: (718) 548-4360 Fax: (718) 548-4360. Editor: Micah Sifry. ISSN: 10471-0435. Content: Independent reports on Ross Perot and his movement.

Perspectives on Political Science
1973. Quarterly. $45. Heldref Publications, 1319 18th Street NW, Washington, DC 20036-

1802. Tel: (202) 296-6267 Fax: (202) 296-5149. Editor: Lisa Culp Neikirk. ISSN: 1045-7097. Content: Reviews of books focusing on political thought.

Policy Review

1977. Quarterly. $27. Heritage Foundation, 214 Massachusetts Avenue NE, Washington, DC 20002-4999. Tel: (202) 546-4400 Fax: (202) 608-6136. Editor: Adam Meyerson. ISSN: 0146-5945. Content: Articles on private sector and local government alternatives to the federal bureaucracy.

Policy Studies Journal

1972. Quarterly. $24. University of Illinois at Urbana-Champaign, 361 Lincoln Hall, Urbana, IL 61801. Tel: (217) 359-8541 Fax: (217) 244-5712. Editor: Don Hadwiger. ISSN: 0190-292X. Content: Studies of applied alternative public policies.

Policy Studies Review

1981. Quarterly. $22. Policy Studies Organization, 702 South Wright Street, Urbana, IL 61801-3631. Tel: (217) 359-8541 Fax: (217) 244-5712. Editor: Allen Rosenbaum. ISSN: 0278-4416. Content: Articles examining causes and effects of alternative public policies.

Political Behavior

1979. Quarterly. $46. Plenum Publishing Corp, 233 Spring Street, New York, NY 10013-1520. Tel: (212) 620-8000 Fax: (212) 463-0742. Editor: Diana C. Mutz. ISSN: 0190-9320. Content: Interdisciplinary studies with an emphasis on empirical and theoretical work.

Political Finance & Lobby Reporter

1980. 24 times a year. $327. Amward Publications, Inc, 2030 Clarendon Boulevard, Suite 401, Arlington, VA 22201. Tel: (703) 525-7227 Fax: (703) 525-3536. Editor: Edward Zuckerman. ISSN: 0270-353X. Content: Developments in campaign finance practices.

Political Psychology

1979. Quarterly. $73.50. Blackwell Publishers, 238 Main Street, Cambridge, MA 02142-1016.

Tel: (617) 547-7110 Fax: (617) 547-0789. Editor: Stanley Renshon. ISSN: 0162-895X. Content: Examinations of the links between psychology and political science.

Political Pulse

1985. Semimonthly. $265. Political Pulse, 926 J Street, Suite 1214, Sacramento, CA 95814-2708. Tel: (916) 446-2048 Fax: (916) 446-5302. Editor: Bud Lembke. ISSN: 8756-9248. Content: Newsletter covering California politics and government.

Political Research Quarterly

1948. Quarterly. $20. Western Political Science Association, 252 Orson Spencer Hall, University of Utah, Salt Lake City, UT 84112-1103. Tel: (801) 581-7031 Fax: (801) 581-6957. Editor: Walt Stone. ISSN: 1065-9129. Content: Scholarly studies on all aspects of political science.

Political Resource Directory

1987. Annual. $95. Political Resources, Inc, PO Box 3177, Burlington, VT 05401-0031. Tel: (802) 660-2869 Fax: (802) 864-9502. Editor: Carol Hese. ISSN: 0898-4271. Content: Detailed directory of information on political organizations.

Political Science Quarterly

1886. Quarterly. $39. Academy of Political Science, 475 Riverside Drive, Suite 1274, New York, NY 10115-1298. Tel: (212) 870-3526 Fax: (212) 870-2202. Editor: Cerentha Harris. ISSN: 0032-3195. Content: Academic articles and essays on a variety of public policy issues.

Political Science Reviewer

1971. Annual. $10. Intercollegiate Studies Institute, 3901 Centerville Road, PO Box 4431, Wilmington, DE 19807-1938. Tel: (302) 652-4600 Fax: (302) 652-1760. Editor: George W. Carey (TME). ISSN: 0091-3715. Content: Essays reviewing major academic works in politics and law.

Political Woman Hotline

1992. Biweekly. $45. Political Woman, 276

Chatterton Parkway, White Plains, NY 10606-2012. Tel: (914) 285-9761 Fax: (914) 285-9763. Editor: Antonia Stolper. ISSN: 1069-6652. Content: Articles tracing trends in the women's political movement.

Politics & Society
1970. Quarterly. $54. Sage Publications, Inc, 2455 Teller Road, Thousand Oaks, CA 91320-2218. Tel: (805) 499-9774 Fax: (805) 499-0871. ISSN: 0032-3292. Content: Articles presenting alternative views of political systems.

Politics in America
1982. Annual. $60. Congressional Quarterly, Inc, 1414 22nd Street NW, Washington, DC 20037-1096. Tel: (202) 887-8500 Fax: (202) 728-1863. Editor: Philip D. Duncan. ISSN: 1064-6809. Content: Profiles of members of Congress.

Polity
1968. Quarterly. $20. Northeastern Political Science Association, University of Massachusetts, 426 Thompson Hall, Amherst, MA 01003-7520. Tel: (413) 545-1354 Fax: (413) 545-4902. Editor: M.J. Peterson. ISSN: 0032-3497. Content: Coverage of all aspects of American political thought.

Popular Government
1931. Quarterly. $20. Institute of Government, CB 3300, Knapp Building, University of North Carolina, Chapel Hill, NC 27599-0001. Tel: (919) 966-4119 Fax: (919) 962-2707. Editor: Anne M. Dellinger. ISSN: 0032-4515. Content: Articles covering North Carolina state and local government.

Presidential Studies Quarterly
1965. Quarterly. Free to qualified individuals. Center for the Study of the Presidency, 208 East 75th Street, New York, NY 10021-2925. Tel: (212) 249-1200. Editor: R. Gordon Hoxie. ISSN: 0360-4918. Content: Historical views of the Presidency.

Progressive
1909. Monthly. $30. The Progressive, Inc, 409

East Main Street, Madison, WI 53703-2899. Tel: (608) 257-4626 Fax: (608) 257-3373. Editor: Matthew Rothschild. ISSN: 0033-0736. Content: Interviews with prominent activists and investigative reports from a left-wing perspective.

Progressive Review
1966. 10 times a year. $18. Progressive Review, 1739 Connecticut Avenue NW, Washington, DC 20009-1126. Tel: (202) 232-5544 Fax: (202) 234-6222. Editor: Sam Smith. ISSN: 0889-2202. Content: Articles emphasizing progressive alternatives to current political system.

PS: Political Science & Politics
1968. Quarterly. Free with membership. American Political Science Association, 1527 New Hampshire Avenue NW, Washington, DC 20036-1206. Tel: (202) 483-2512 Fax: (202) 483-2657. Editor: Robert Hauck. ISSN: 1049-0965. Content: Scholarly analyses of contemporary political issues.

Publius
1971. Quarterly. $25. Lafayette College, Meyner Center, Easton, PA 18042-1785. Tel: (610) 250-5598 Fax: (610) 559-4048. Editor: John Kincaid. ISSN: 0048 -. Content: Studies and analyses of federalism and intergovernmental relations.

Radical America
1967. Quarterly. $22. Alternative Education Project, Inc, 1 Summer Street, Somerville, MA 02143-1704. Tel: (617) 628-6586 Fax: (617) 628-6585. Editor: Margaret Cerullo. ISSN: 0033-7617. Content: Left-wing observations of political and cultural issues.

Reason
1968. Monthly. $19.95. Reason Foundation, 3415 South Sepulveda Boulevard, Suite 400, Los Angeles, CA 90034-6060. Tel: (310) 391-2245 Fax: (310) 391-4395. Editor: Virginia Postrel. ISSN: 0048-6906. Content: Libertarian views of national political issues.

Resist
1967. 10 times a year. $15. Resist, 1 Summer Street, Somerville, MA 02143-1704. Tel: (617) 623-5110. Editor: Tatiana Schreiber. ISSN: 0897-2613. Content: Articles on topics and issues relating to peace and justice.

Review of Politics
1939. Quarterly. $25. University of Notre Dame, Box B, Notre Dame, IN 46556. Tel: (219) 631-6623 Fax: (219) 631-8609. Editor: Walter Nicgorski. ISSN: 0034-6705. Content: Critical analyses of political ideas, institutions and techniques.

Right Guide
1993. Annual. $78.45. Economics America, 612 Church Street, Ann Arbor, MI 48104-3002. Tel: (313) 995-0865. Editor: Dirk A. Wilcox. ISSN: 1064-7414. Content: Directory of conservative and libertarian organizations.

Roll Call
1955. 2 times a week. $225. Economist Group, 25 St James Street, London SW1A 1HG England. Tel: (44) (171) 830-7000 Fax: (44) (171) 839-2968. Editor: Stacy Mason. ISSN: 0035-788X. Content: Latest news on congressional activities.

Rothenberg Political Report
1978. Weekly. $197. Stuart Rothenberg, Publisher, 13305 Morning Field Way, Potomac, MD 20854-6379. Tel: (202) 546-2822. Editor: Stuart Rothenberg. ISSN: 1051-4287. Content: Reports on House and Senate campaigns and elections.

Socialist
1993. Bimonthly. Free with membership. Socialist Party USA, 516 West 25th Street, Suite 404, New York, NY 10001-5525. Tel: (212) 691-0776 Fax: (212) 691-0776. ISSN: 0884-6154. Content: Articles promoting socialism in America.

Southeastern Political Review
1973. Quarterly. $18. Georgia Political Science Association, Georgia Southern University, Suite 8101, Statesboro, GA 30460-8101. Tel: (912) 681-5698 Fax: (912) 681-5348. Editor: Roger Pajari. ISSN: 0730-2177. Contents: Articles of general interest on all subfields of political science.

Southern Partisan
1979. Quarterly. $14. Southern Partisan, PO Box 11708, Columbia, SC 29211-1708. Tel: (803) 254-3660 Fax: (803) 256-9220. Editor: Richard Quinn Sr. ISSN: 0739-1714. Content: Articles reflecting agrarian and conservative intellectual tradition of the Old South.

Southern Political Report
1978. 24 times a year. $157. Southern Political Report, PO Box 15507, Washington, DC 20003-0507. Tel: (202) 547-8098. Editor: Hastings Wyman Jr. ISSN: 0739-3938. Content: Articles covering the politics and politicians of the 12 southern states.

Spotlight
1960. Weekly. $40. Cordite Fidelity, Inc, 300 Independence Avenue SE, Washington, DC 20003-1010. Tel: (202) 544-1794. Editor: Vincent Ryan. ISSN: 0191-6270. Content: Populist views of public policy issues.

State Government News
1958. 10 times a year. $39. Council of State Governments, PO Box 11910, Iron Works Pike, Lexington, KY 40578-1910. Tel: (606) 244-8000 Fax: (606) 244-8001. Editor: Elaine Stuart. Content: News reports from all branches of state government for all 50 states.

State Legislatures
1975. Monthly. $49. National Conference of State Legislatures, 1560 Broadway, Suite 700, Denver, CO 80202. Tel: (303) 830-2200 Fax: (303) 863-8003. Editor: Karen Hansen. ISSN: 0147-6041. Content: Commentary and analysis of state issues and politics.

Studies in American Political Development
1986. 2 times a year. $32. Cambridge University Press/New York, 40 West 20th Street, New York, NY 10011-4211. Tel: (212) 924-

3900 Fax: (212) 691-3239. Editor: Stephen Skowronek. Content: Studies of political change and institutional development in America.

Washington Monthly

1969. 10 times a year. $30. Washington Monthly Company, 1611 Connecticut Avenue NW, Washington, DC 20009-1048. Tel: (202) 462-0128 Fax: (202) 332-8413. Editor: John Meacham. ISSN: 0043-0633. Content: Investigative reports reflecting traditional liberal values.

Weekly Standard

1995. Weekly. $80. Weekly Standard, PO Box 500, Radnor, PA 19088-0500. Tel: (610) 293-8500 Fax: (610) 293-6212. Editor: Bill Kristol. ISSN: 1083-3013. Content: Coverage of political issues from a conservative viewpoint.

Who's Who in American Politics

1968. Biennial. $240. Reed Elsevier Directories, 121 Chanlon Road, New Providence, NJ 07974-1541. Tel: (908) 464-6800 Fax: (908) 464-3553. ISSN: 0000-0205. Content: Biographies of American political leaders.

Women & Politics

1980. Quarterly. $36. Haworth Press, Inc, 10 Alice Street, Binghamton, NY 13904-1580. Tel: (607) 722-5857 Fax: (607) 722-6362. Editor: Janet M. Clark. ISSN: 0195-7732. Content: Comparative studies of the women's political movement focusing on interdisciplinary topics.

Women's Political Times

1976. Quarterly. $20. National Womens Political Caucus, 1211 Connecticut Avenue NW, Suite 425, Washington, DC 20036-2701. Tel: (202) 898-1100. Editor: Pat Reilly. ISSN: 0195-1688. Content: Information on issues affecting women legislators and policy makers.

Z Magazine

1987. 11 times a year. $26. Institute for Social & Cultural Communications, 116 St Botolph Street, Suite 1, Boston, MA 02115-4818. Tel: (617) 787-4531 Fax: (617) 787-4531. Editor: Lydia Sargent. ISSN: 1056-5507. Content: Critical essays on major political issues from an independent political perspective.

Books

This selected list of books covers 1996 and 1997. The entries are listed alphabetically by author within the following categories:

Congress
Constitution
Elections
Foreign Relations
General Government and Politics
Media and Politics
Political Parties
Political Thought
President
Supreme Court
U.S. Military

Congress

Burnham, James. *Congress and The American Tradition.* Washington, DC: Regnery Publishing, 1996. (ISBN 0895267179).

Dodd, Lawrence C. and Bruce I. Oppenheimer, eds. *Congress Reconsidered.* Washington, DC: CQ Press, 1997. (ISBN 1568022034).

Feinberg, Barbara S. *Term Limits for Congress?* New York: Twenty-First Century Books, 1996. (ISBN 0805040994).

Foerstel, Karen. *Climbing the Hill: Gender Conflict in Congress.* Westport, CT: Greenwich, 1996. (ISBN 0275949141).

Foley, Michael. *Congress and The Presidency: Institutional Politics in a Separated System.* New York: St Martin's, 1996. (ISBN 0719038847).

Gill, LaVerne McCain. *African American Women in Congress.* New Brunswick, NJ: Rutgers University Press, 1997. (ISBN 0813523524).

Hibbing, John R. *Congress As Public Enemy: Public Attitudes Toward American Political Institutions.* New York: Cambridge University Press, 1996. (ISBN 0521482992).

Kaptur, Marcy. *Women of Congress: A 20th Century Odyssey.* Washington, DC: Congressional Quarterly Press, 1996. (ISBN 0871879891).

Kessler, Ronald. *Inside Congress: The Shocking Scandals, Corruption and Abuse of Power Behind the Scenes on Capitol Hill.* New York: Pocket Books, 1997. (ISBN 0671003852).

Loomis, Burdett A. *The Contemporary Congress.* New York: St Martin's, 1996. (ISBN 0312123051).

Maraniss, David. *Tell Newt to Shut Up.* New York: Simon & Schuster, 1996. (ISBN 0684832933).

Miller, William L. *Arguing About Slavery: The Great Battle in the United States Congress.* New York: Knopf, 1996. (ISBN 0394569229).

Thurber, James A. *Rivals for Power.* Washington, DC: CQ Press, 1996. (ISBN 1568021526).

Wright, Jim. *Balance of Power.* New York: Turner Publishing, 1996. (ISBN 1570362785).

Constitution

Bond, James Edward. *No Easy Walk to Freedom.* Westport, CT: Praeger, 1997. (ISBN 0275957039).

Cohen, Joshua, ed. *Constitution, Democracy and State Power.* Brookfield, VT: Ashgate, 1996. (ISBN 1852783427).

Cortner, Richard C. *The Kingfish and the Constitution.* Westport, CT: Greenwood, 1996. (ISBN 0313298424).

De Grazia, Sebastian. *A Country with No Name.* New York: Pantheon Book, 1997. (ISBN 0679419772).

Evans, James R. *Back to the Future: Reclaiming America's Constitutional Heritage.* Ottawa, IL: Jameson Books, 1997. (ISBN 0915463784).

Grasso, Kenneth L. and Cecilia R. Castillo. *Liberty Under Law.* Lantham, MD: University Press of America, 1997. (ISBN 0761806911).

Griffin, Stephen M. *American Constitutionalism.* Princeton, NJ: Princeton University Press, 1996. (ISBN 0691002401).

Halpern, Thomas and Brian Levin. *The Limits of Dissent.* Amherst, MA: Aletheia Press, 1996. (ISBN 1880831171).

Lazare, Daniel. *The Frozen Republic: How the Constitution is Paralyzing Democracy.*

New York: Harcourt Brace, 1996. (ISBN 0151000859).

Lyons, Oren. *Exiled in the Land of the Free: Democracy, Indian Nations and the U.S. Con-stitution.* New York: Clear Light Publishers, 1997. (ISBN 0940666502).

McDowell, Gary L. and Sharon Noble, eds. *Reason and Republicanism.* Lanham, MD: Rowan & Littlefield, 1997. (ISBN 0847685209).

Mueller, Dennis C. *Constitutional Democracy.* New York: Oxford University Press, 1996. (ISBN 019509588X).

Smoke, Stephen. *Bill of Rights and Responsibilities.* New York: General Publishing, 1996. (ISBN 1881649865).

U.S. Capitol Historical Society. *The Bill of Rights.* Charlottesville: University Press of Virginia, 1997. (ISBN 081391759X).

Vladovich, Simon. *U.S. Citizenship Handbook.* 2nd ed. New York: Vladovich International Publishing, 1997. (ISBN 0962375330).

Weir, William. *A Well Regulated Militia.* North Haven, CT: Archon Books, 1997. (ISBN 0208024239).

Elections

Ansolabehere, Stephen. *Going Negative: How Political Advertisements Shrink and Polarize the Electorate.* New York: Free Press, 1996. (ISBN 0029007321).

Ceaser, James W. *Losing to Win: The 1996 Elections and American Politics.* Lanham, MD: Rowman & Littlefield Publishers, 1997. (ISBN 0847684067).

Christian, Spencer. *Electing Our Government.* New York: St Martin's Press, 1996. (ISBN 0312143249).

De la Garza, Rodolfo O. *Ethnic Ironies: Latino Politics in the 1992 Elections.* Boulder, CO: Westview, 1996. (ISBN 0813330122).

Drew, Elizabeth. *Whatever It Takes: The Real Struggle for Political Power in America.* New York: Viking Penguin, 1997. (ISBN 0670875368).

Glaser, James M. *Race, Campaign Politics and the Realignment in the South.* New Haven, CT: Yale University Press, 1996. (ISBN 0300063989).

Greir, R. R. Bob. *The Blood, Sweat and Tears of Political Victory and Defeat.* Lanham, MD: University Press of America, 1996. (ISBN 0761803610).

Hohenberg, John. *Reelecting Bill Clinton: Why America Chose a "New" Democrat.* Syracuse, NY: Syracuse University Press, 1997. (ISBN 0815604912).

Holbrook, Thomas. *Do Campaigns Matter?* Thousand Oaks, CA: Sage Publications, 1996. (ISBN 0803973454).

Klinker, Philip A., ed. *Midterm: The Elections of 1994 in Context.* Boulder, CO: Westview, 1996. (ISBN 0813328187).

Menendez, Albert J. *The Perot Voters and the Future of American Politics.* New York: Prometheus, 1996. (ISBN 1573920444).

Morris, Dick. *Behind the Oval Office: Winning the Presidency in the Nineties.* New York: Macmillan Library Reference, 1997. (ISBN 0786211024).

Pomper, Gerald M. *The Election of 1996.* Chatham, NJ: Chatham House, 1997. (ISBN 1566430569).

Foreign Relations

Abu-Lebdeh, Hatem Shareef. *Conflict and Peace in the Middle East: National Perceptions and United States-Jordan Relations.* Lanham, MD: University Press of America, 1997. (ISBN 0761808116).

Arbatov, Alexei G. *Taming Armageddon?: Revising the U.S.-Russian Nuclear Relationship.* Cambridge, MA: MIT Press, 1997. (ISBN 022011492).

Cornish, Paul. *Partnership in Crisis: The U.S., Europe and the Fall and Rise of NATO.* London: Royal Institute of International Affairs, 1997. (ISBN 185567467X).

Foot, Rosemary. *The Practice of Power: U.S. Relations With China Since 1949.* New York: Oxford University Press, 1997. (ISBN 0198292929).

Hudson, Valerie M. *Culture and Foreign Policy.* Boulder, CO: Lynne Rienner, 1997. (ISBN 1555876404).

Joyner, Christopher and Ethel Theis. *Eagle over the Ice.* Hanover, NH: University Press of New England, 1997. (ISBN 0874517788).

Klingberg, Frank L. *Positive Expectations of America's World Role.* Lantham, MD: University Press of America, 1996. (ISBN 0761802622).

Knott, Stephen F. *Secret and Sanctioned: Covert Operations and the American Presidency.* New York: Oxford University Press, 1996. (ISBN 0195100980).

McDougall, Walter A. *Promised Land, Crusader State.* Boston: Houghton Mifflin, 1997. (ISBN 0395830850).

Newsom, David D. *The Public Dimension of Foreign Policy.* Bloomington: Indiana University Press, 1996. (ISBN 0253329604).

Pells, Richard H. *Not Like Us: How Europeans Loved, Hated and Transformed American Culture Since World War II.* New York: Basic Books, 1997. (ISBN 0465001645).

Przystup, James J. and Kim R. Holmes. *Between Diplomacy and Deterrence: Strategies for U.S. Relations with China.* Washington, DC: Heritage Foundation, 1997. (ISBN 089195242X).

Robinson, William I. *Promoting Polyarchy: Globalization, U.S. Intervention and Hegemony.* New York: Cambridge University Press, 1996. (ISBN 0521566916).

Schmertz, Eric J. *President Reagan and the World.* Westport, CT: Greenwood Publishing Group, 1997. (ISBN 0313301158).

Small, Melvin. *Democracy and Diplomacy.* Baltimore: Johns Hopkins University Press, 1996. (ISBN 0801851777).

Sterns, Monteagle. *Talking to Strangers: Improving American Diplomacy at Home and Abroad.* Princeton, NJ: Princeton University Press, 1996. (ISBN 0691011303).

Thomas, A. M. *The American Predicament: Apartheid and United States Foreign Policy.* Brookfield, VT: Ashgate, 1997. (ISBN 1855219417).

General Government and Politics

Abshire, David M. *Putting America's House in Order: The Nation As a Family.* Westport, CT: Greenwood, 1996. (ISBN 0275954315).

Cardenas, Jose A. *Texas School Finance Reform: An IDRA Perspective.* San Antonio, TX: Intercultural Development Research, 1997. (ISBN 1878550632).

Chalfont, William Y. *Cheyennes at Dark Water Creek: The Last Fight of the Red River War.* Norman: University of Oklahoma Press, 1997. (ISBN 0806128755).

Chomsky, Noam. *Class Warfare; Interviews with David Barsamian.* Monroe, ME: Common Courage Press, 1996. (ISBN 1567510930).

Davis, Phillip J., ed. *Political Issues in America Today: The 1990s Revisited.* New York: St Martin's Press, 1996. (ISBN 0719042259).

Dees, Morris. *Gathering Storm: The Story of America's Militia Network.* New York: HarperCollins, 1996. (ISBN 006017403X).

Dershowitz, Alan. *The Vanishing American Jews: In Search of Jewish Indentity for the Next Century.* Boston: Little Brown & Company, 1997. (ISBN 0316181331).

Dionne, E. J., Jr. *They Only Look Dead: Why Progressives Will Dominate the Next Political Era.* New York: Simon & Schuster, 1996. (ISBN 0684807688).

Dolbeare, Kenneth M. *U.S.A. 2012: After the Middle-Class Revolution.* Chatham, NJ: Chatham House, 1996. (ISBN 1566430364).

Drew, Elizabeth. *Showdown.* New York: Simon & Schuster Trade, 1997. (ISBN 0684815184).

Evans, M. Stanton. *The Theme Is Freedom: Religion, Politics and the American Tradition.* Washington, DC: Regnery Publishing, 1996. (ISBN 0895264978).

Frum, David. *What's Right: The New Conservative Majority and the Remaking of America.* New York: Basic Books, 1996. (ISBN 0465041973).

Graetz, Michael J. *The Decline (and Fall?) of the Income Tax.* New York: W. W. Norton, 1997. (ISBN 0393040615).

Green, John C. *Religion and the Culture Wars: Dispatches from the Front.* Lanham, MD: Rowman & Littlefield, 1996. (ISBN 0847682676).

Larson, Robert W. *Red Cloud: Warrior-Statesman of the Dakota Sioux.* Norman: University of Oklahoma Press, 1997. (ISBN 0806129301).

MacInnes, Gordon. *Wrong for All the Right Reasons: How White Liberals Have Been Undone by Race.* New York: New York University Press, 1996. (ISBN 0814755437).

McGrew, John. *Uncommon Remedies for America's Ills: Futuring for the New Millennium.* New York: New Vista Press, 1997. (ISBN 0936544082).

National Research Council Staff. *Proliferation Concerns: Assessing U.S. Efforts to Help Contain Nuclear and Other Dangerous Materials and Technologies in the Former Soviet Union.* Washington, DC: National Academy Press, 1997. (ISBN 0309057418).

Nobles, Gregory H. *American Frontiers.* New York: Hill & Wang, 1997. (ISBN 0809024713).

Novak, Michael. *Unmeltable Ethnics: Politics and Culture in American Life.* New Brunswick, NJ: Transaction, 1996. (ISBN 1560007737).

Pearsall, Marilyn. *The Other Within Us: Feminist Perspectives on Women and Aging.* New York: HarperCollins, 1997. (ISBN 0813381630).

Pertusati, Linda. *In Defense of Mohawk Land: Ethnopolitical Conflict in Native North America.* Albany: State University of New York Press, 1996. (ISBN 0791432122).

Reed, Ralph. *Active Faith: How Christians Are Changing the Face of American Politics.* New York: Free Press, 1996. (ISBN 0684827581).

Simpson, Brooks D. *Let Us Have Peace: Ulysses S. Grant and the Politics of War and Reconstruction, 1861-1868.* Chapel Hill: University of North Carolina Press, 1997. (ISBN 0807846295).

Skocpol, Theda. *Boomerang: Clinton's Health Security Effort and the Turn Against Government in U.S. Politics.* New York: W. W. Norton & Company, 1996. (ISBN 0393039706).

Steel, Brent. *Public Lands Management in the West: Citizens, Interest Groups and Values.* Westport, CT: Greenwood Publishing Group, 1997. (ISBN 0275956954).

Steineger, Jack E. *Houdini and the Federal Budget Hoax: A Special Report to Reveal the Magic of Using Your Social Security Pension to Hide the Federal Deficit and Much More.* American Patriot Publishing, 1997. (ISBN 0965747131).

Svingen, Orlan. *The Northern Cheyenne Indian Reservation, 1877-1900.* Boulder: University Press of Colorado, 1997. (ISBN 0870814869).

Thiemann, Ronald F. *Religion in Public Life: A Dilemma for Democracy.* Washington, DC: Georgetown University Press, 1996. (ISBN 0878406107).

Vila, Bryan and Cynthia Morris, eds. *Capital Punishment in the United States.* Westport, CT: Greenwood, 1997. (ISBN 0313299420).

Wade, Edwin L. *Constitution 2000: A Federalist Proposal for the Next Century.* New York: Let's Talk Sense Publishing, 1996. (ISBN 0964737256).

Walton, Hanes. *African-American Power and Politics: The Political Context Variable.* New York: Columbia University Press, 1997. (ISBN 0231104197).

Winograd, Morley. *Taking Control: Politics in the Information Age.* New York: Henry Holt, 1996. (ISBN 0805044892).

Media & Politics

Cappella, Joseph M. *Spiral of Criticism: The Press and the Public Good.* New York: Oxford University Press, 1997. (ISBN 0195090632).

Croteau, David. *Media/Society: Industries, Images and Audiences.* Thousand Oaks, CA: Pine Forge Press, 1997. (ISBN 0803990650).

Davis, Richard. *The Press and American Politics: The New Mediator.* Upper Saddle River, NJ: Prentice Hall, 1996. (ISBN 0131859439).

Dearing, James W. and Everett M. Rogers. *Agenda-Setting.* Thousand Oaks, CA: Sage, 1996. (ISBN 0761905626).

Dunham, Corydon B. *Fighting for the First Amendment.* Westport, CT: Praeger, 1997. (ISBN 0275960277).

Flink, Stanley E. *Sentinel Under Siege.* Boulder, CO: Westview, 1997. (ISBN 081333344X).

Graeber, Doris A. *Mass Media and American Politics.* Washington, DC: CQ Press, 1997. (ISBN 0871877686).

Graham, Tim. *Pattern of Deception: The Media's Role in the Clinton Presidency.* Alexandria, VA: Media Research Center, 1996. (ISBN 0962734837).

Grant, Bob. *Let's Be Heard: The King of Conservative Talk Radio Speaks Out to America!* New York: Pocket Books, 1997. (ISBN 0671537210).

Hindman, Elizabeth. *Rights Vs. Responsibilities.* Westport, CT: Greenwood, 1997. (ISBN 0313299226).

Iyengar, Shanto and Richard Reeves, eds. *Do the Media Govern?* Thousand Oaks, CA: Sage Publications, 1997. (ISBN 0803956061).

Katz, Jon. *Media Rants: Post-Politics in the Digital Nation.* San Francisco: Hardwired, 1997. (ISBN 1888869127).

Nussbaum, Martha C. *Poetic Justice: The Literary Imagination and Public Life.* Boston: Beacon Press, 1997. (ISBN 0807041092).

Streitmatter, Rodger. *Mightier Than the Sword.* Boulder, CO: Westview, 1997. (ISBN 0813332109).

Winters, Paul A., ed. *The Media and Politics.* New York: Greenhaven Press, 1996. (ISBN 1565103831).

Woodward, Gary C. *Perspectives on American Political Media.* Boston: Allyn and Bacon, 1997. (ISBN 0205262503).

Political Parties

Barbour, Haley. *Agenda for America: A Republican Direction for the Future.* Washington, DC: Regnery Publishing, 1996. (ISBN 0895267217).

Bibby, John. *Politics, Parties and Elections in America.* New York: Nelson-Hall, 1996. (ISBN 0830414347).

Blondel, Jean, ed. *Party and Government.* New York: St Martin's, 1996. (ISBN 031215917X).

Caddell, Patrick H. *The Fire This Time: The Failure of Two-Party Politics.* New York: Grove/Atlantic, 1996. (ISBN 0871136392).

Carville, James. *We're Right, They're Wrong: A Progressive Program.* New York: Random House, 1996. (ISBN 0679769781).

Crewe, Ivor. *SDP: The Birth, Life and Death of the Social Democratic Party.* New York: Oxford University Press, 1997. (ISBN 0198293135).

Galderisi, Peter F., Robert Q. Herzberg and Peter McNamara. *Divided Government.* Lanham, MD: Rowan & Littlefield Publishing, 1996. (ISBN 0847682951).

George, John. *American Extremists.* Amherst, NY: Prometheus Books, 1996. (ISBN 1573920584).

Gimpel, James G. *National Elections and the Anatomy of American State Party Systems.* Pittsburgh: University of Pittsburgh Press, 1996. (ISBN 0822939401).

Rosenstone, Steven J. *Third Parties in America.* Princeton, NJ: Princeton University Press, 1996. (ISBN 0691026130).

Ryden, David K. *Representatives in Crisis.* Albany: State University of New York Press, 1996. (ISBN 0791430598).

Savage, Sean. *Truman and the Democratic Party.* Lawrence: University Press of Kentucky, 1997. (ISBN 0813109418).

Smith, Oran P. *Rise of Baptist Republicanism.* New York: New York University Press, 1997. (ISBN 0814780733).

Witcover, Jules. *The Year the Dream Died: Revisiting 1968 in America.* New York:

Warner Books, 1997. (ISBN 0446518492).

Wand, Xi. *The Trial of Democracy: Black Suffrage and Northern Republicans, 1860-1910.* Athens: University of Georgia Press, 1997. (ISBN 082031837X).

Political Thought

Bowman, Scott R. *The Modern Corporation and American Political Thought.* University Park: Penn State University Press, 1996. (ISBN 0271014725).

Brown, Richard D. *The Strength of a People.* University of North Carolina Press, 1996. (ISBN 0807822612).

Coats, Wendell, J., Jr. *Statesmanship: Six Modern Illustrations of a Modified Ancient Ideal.* Susquehanna, PA: Susquehanna University Press, 1996. (ISBN 0945636849).

Kruman, Marc W. *Between Authority and Liberty.* Chapel Hill: University of North Carolina Press, 1997. (ISBN 0807823023).

Lind, Michael. *Hamilton's Republic.* New York: Free Press, 1997. (ISBN 0684831600).

Richardson, Elliot L. *Reflections of a Radical Moderate.* New York: Pantheon, 1996. (ISBN 0679428208).

Schall, James V. *At the Limits of Political Philosophy: From "Brilliant Errors" to Things of Uncommon Importance.* Washington, DC: Catholic University Press, 1996. (ISBN 0813208327).

Young, James P. *Reconsidering American Liberalism.* Boulder, CO: Westview, 1996. (ISBN 0813306485).

Zuckert, Michael P. *The Natural Rights Republic.* Notre Dame, IN: University of

Notre Dame Press, 1996. (ISBN 0268014809).

President

Cimbala, Stephen J. *Clinton and Post-Cold War Defense.* Westport, CT: Greenwood, 1996. (ISBN 0275950069).

Cwiklik, Robert. *Bill Clinton: President of the 90s.* Millbrook, NY: Millbrook Press, Inc, 1997. (ISBN 0761301461).

Denton, Robert E., Jr., ed. *The Clinton Presidency: Images and Communication Strategies.* CT: Greenwood, 1996. (ISBN 0275951103).

Evans-Pritchard, Ambrose. *The Secret Life of Bill Clinton: His Legacy and Its Roots.* Washington, DC: Regnery Publishing, 1997. (ISBN 0895264080).

Ferrell, Robert H. *Ill-Advised: Presidential Health and Public Trust.* Columbia: University of Missouri Press, 1996. (ISBN 0826210651).

Flowers, Gennifer. *Sleeping with the President: My Intimate Years with Bill Clinton.* New York: Anonymous Press, Inc, 1997. (ISBN 1889801003).

Hubbell, Webb. *Friends in High Places: Our Journey from Little Rock to Washington, DC.* New York: William Morrow & Company, 1997. (ISBN 0688157491).

Hutchinson, Earl O. *Betrayed: A History of Presidential Failure to Protect Black Lives.* Boulder, CO: Westview, 1996. (ISBN 0813324661).

Judson, Karen. *Ronald Reagan.* New York: Enslow Publishers, Inc, 1997. (ISBN 0894908359).

Kurz, Kenneth. *The Reagan Years A to Z.* Lowell, MA: Lowell House, 1997. (ISBN 1565658159).

Landau, Elaine. *Bill Clinton and His Presidency.* Philadelphia, PA: Franklin Watts Inc, 1997. (ISBN 053120295X).

Lerner, Max. *Thomas Jefferson: America's Philosopher-King.* New Brunswick, NJ: Transaction, 1996. (ISBN 156000262X).

McIver, Stuart B. *Rating the Presidents: Every Chief Executive Ranked in Order of Influence.* New York: Carol Publishing, 1996. (ISBN 0806517999).

Melvin, David. *George Bush and the Guardianship Presidency.* New York: St Martin's, 1996. (ISBN 0312129610).

Morris, Roger. *Partners in Power: The Clintons and Their America.* Henry Holt, 1996. (ISBN 0805028048).

Noonan, Peggy. *What I Saw at the Revolution: A Political Life in the Reagan Era.* New York: Fawcett Book Group, 1997. (ISBN 0449001008).

Pemberton, William E. *Exit with Honor: The Life and Presidency of Ronald Reagan.* Armonk, NY: M. E. Sharpe Inc, 1997. (ISBN 076560096X).

Pfiffner, James P. *The Strategic Presidency: Hitting the Ground Running.* Lawrence: University Press of Kansas, 1996. (ISBN 0700607684).

Pfiffner, James P. and Roger H. Davidson. *Understanding the Presidency.* New York: Longman, 1997. (ISBN 0673998991).

Reagan, Michael. *The City on a Hill: Fulfilling Ronald Reagan's Vision for America.* Nashville, TN: Thomas Nelson Inc, 1997. (ISBN 0785272364).

Reeves, Richard. *Running in Place: How Bill Clinton Disappointed America.* New York: Andrews & McMeel, 1996. (ISBN 0836210913).

Renshon, Stanley A. *High Hopes: The Clinton Presidency and the Politics of Ambition.* New York: New York University Press, 1996. (ISBN 0814774636).

Renshon, Stanley A. *The Psychological Assessment of Presidential Candidates.* New York: New York University Press, 1996. (ISBN 0814774695).

Schmertz, Eric J. *Ronald Reagan's America: Vol. I.* Westport, CT: Greenwood Publishing Group, 1997. (ISBN 0313301174).

Sidey, Hugh. *The Presidents of the United States of America.* Washington, DC: White House Historical Association, 1996. (ISBN 0912308575).

Smith, Neal. *Mr. Smith Went to Washington: From Eisenhower to Clinton.* Ames: Iowa State University Press, 1996. (ISBN 0813824796).

Stewart, James B. *Blood Sport: The President and His Adversaries.* New York: Touchstone Press, 1997. (ISBN 0684831392).

Sufrin, Mark. *The Story of George Bush: The Forty-First President of the United States.* New York: Gareth Stevens Inc, 1997. (ISBN 0836814789).

Sundquist, James L., ed. *Back to Gridlock?: Governance in the Clinton Years.* Washington, DC: Brookings, 1996. (ISBN 0815782330).

Thomas, Evan. *Back from the Dead: How Clinton Survived the Republican Revolution.* New York: Grove/Atlantic, 1997. (ISBN 0871136899).

Thomas, Norman C. *The Politics of the Presidency.* Washington, DC: Congressioonal Quarterly, 1996. (ISBN 1568023162).

Warshaw, Shirley A. *Powersharing: White House-Cabinet Relations in the Modern Presidency.* Albany: State University of New York Press, 1996. (ISBN 0791428699).

Whitney, David C. *The American Presidents.* New York: Reader's Digest, 1996. (ISBN 0895778637).

Wilson, Robert A. *Character Above All: Ten Presidents from FDR to George Bush.* New York: Simon & Schuster, 1996. (ISBN 0684814110).

Wymbs, Norman E. *Ronald Reagan's Crusade.* New York: Skyline Publications, Inc, 1997. (ISBN 1889936006).

Supreme Court

Barton, David. *Original Intent: The Courts, the Constitution and Religion.* New York: Wallbuilders, 1996. (ISBN 0925279501).

Berger, Raoul. *Government by Judiciary.* Indianapolis: Liberty Fund Press, 1997. (ISBN 0865971439).

Bigel, Alan J. *Justices William J. Brennan Jr. and Thurgood Marshall on Capital Punishment.* Lanham, MD: University Press of America, 1997. (ISBN 0761806148).

Caplan, Lincoln. *Up Against the Law.* New York: Twentieth Century Fund Press, 1997. (ISBN 0820284099).

Franck, Matthew J. *Against the Imperial Judiciary: The Supreme Court vs. the Sovereignty of the People.* Lawrence: University Press of Kansas, 1996. (ISBN 0700607617).

Harrison, Maureen, ed. *Freedom of Speech Decisions of the United States Supreme Court.* New York: Excellent Books, 1996. (ISBN 1880780097).

Katzman, Robert A. *Courts and Congress.* Washington, DC: Brookings, 1997. (ISBN 0815748655).

Leahy, James E. *Freedom Fighters of the United States Supreme Court: Nine Who Championed Individual Rights.* Jefferson, NC: McFarland & Company, 1996. (ISBN 0786402067).

Maroon, Suzy. *Supreme Court of the United States.* New York: Thomasson-Grant, 1996. (ISBN 0965030806).

Maveety, Nancy. *Justice Sandra Day O'Connor: Strategist on the Supreme Court.* Lantham, MD: Rowman & Littlefield, 1996. (ISBN 0847681955).

McGurn, Barrett. *America's Court.* Golden, CO: Fulcrum, 1997. (ISBN 155591263X).

McKeever, Robert J. *Raw Judicial Power?: The Supreme Court and American Society.* New York: St Martin's, 1996. (ISBN 0719048737).

O'Brien, David M. *Storm Center: The Supreme Court in American Politics.* New York: W. W. Norton, 1996. (ISBN 039396891X).

Ragan, Sandra L., ed. *The Lynching of Language: Gender, Politics and Power in the Hill-Thomas Hearings.* Urbana: University of Illinois Press, 1996. (ISBN 0252021266).

Schultz, David A. and Christopher E. Smith. *The Jurisprudential Vision of Justice Antonin Scalia.* Lantham, MD: Rowan & Littlefield, 1996. (ISBN 0847681319).

Schwartz, Bernard. *Decision: How the Supreme Court Decides Cases.* New York: Oxford University Press, 1996. (ISBN 0195098595).

Sunderland, Lane V. *Popular Government and the Supreme Court.* Lawrence: University Press of Kansas, 1996. (ISBN 0700607439).

Tushnet, Mark V. *Making Civil Rights Law: Thurgood Marshall and the Supreme Court, 1936-1961.* New York: Oxford University Press, 1996. (ISBN 0195104684).

Wilkins, David E. *American Indian Sovereignty and the U.S. Supreme Court.* Austin: University of Texas Press, 1997. (ISBN 0292791097).

U.S. Military

Cave, Dorothy. *Four Trails to Valor.* Las Cruces, NM: Yucca Tree Press, 1997. (ISBN 1881325229).

Clarke, Charles F. *Above a Common Soldier: Frank and Mary Clark in the American West and Civil War from Their Letters, 1847-1872.* Albuquerque: University of New Mexico Press, 1997. (ISBN 0826317995).

Crouchet, Jack. *Vietnam Stories: A Judge's Memoir.* Niwot: University Press of Colorado, 1997. (ISBN 0870814532).

Flynn, Kelly. *Proud to Be.* New York: Random House, 1997. (ISBN 0375501096).

Harrell, Margaret C. *New Opportunities for Millitary Women: Effects Upon Readiness, Cohesion, and Morale.* Santa Monica, CA: Rand, 1997. (ISBN 0833025589).

Herek, Gregory M., Jared B. Jobe and Ralph M. Carney. *Out in Force: Sexual Orienta-*

tion and the Military. Chicago: University of Chicago Press, 1996. (ISBN 0226400476).

Kelly, Arthur L. *Battlefire: Combat Stories from World War II.* Lexington: University Press of Kentucky, 1997. (ISBN 0813120349).

McDaid, Hugh. *Smart Weapons: Top Secret History of Remote Contolled Airborne Weapons.* New York: Barnes & Noble Books, 1997. (ISBN 076070760X).

Poole, H. J. *The Last Hundred Yards: The NCO's Contribution to Warfare.* Emerald Isle, NC: Posterity Press, 1997. (ISBN 0963869523).

Schuster, R. J. *An Act of Betrayal: America's Involvement in the Bay of Pigs.* New York: Tri Star Books, 1997. (ISBN 1889987018).

Westeider, James E. *Fighting on Two Fronts: African Americans and the Vietnam War.* New York: New York University Press, 1997. (ISBN 0814793010).

Reference Books

The following list of leading political reference works is arranged alphabetically in the following categories:

General Guides to the Literature
Abstracts and Indexes
Almanacs
Atlases
Bibliographies
Biographies
Catalogs
Dictionaries
Directories
Encyclopedias
Handbooks and Guides
Profiles
Quotations
Statistics
Trivia

General Guides to the Literature

Holler, Frederick L. *Information Sources of Political Science*. 4th edition. Santa Barbara, CA: ABC-Clio, 1986.

Describes more than 2,400 reference works and bibliographies in the field of political science with indexes by author, subject, title and type of reference.

York, Henry E. *Political Science: A Guide to Reference and Information Sources, Print and Electronic*. New York: Libraries Unlimited, 1990.

Describes 805 major sources on political science.

Abstracts and Indexes

Comprehensive Retrospective Index to Journals in Political Science, 1886-1974. Carrollton, 1978.

Eight-volume reference set indexing over 115,000 articles in political science. Six volumes provide title keyword and author indexes. Most of the journals indexed are in English. Helpful in doing a quick historical search for information.

PAIS. *PAIS International in Print*. Public Affairs Information Service, 1990.

Formerly the PAIS Index. Covers public and social policy materials, including books, periodicals, pamphlets, microfiche, and reports of public and private agencies, published in English, French, German, Italian, Portuguese and Spanish. Updated monthly. Also available in electronic formats: CD-ROM, Online (DIALOG, OCLC and RLG) and magnetic tape.

UNESCO. *International Political Science Abstracts*. New York: UNESCO, 1952-.

Quarterly publication that abstracts more than 5,000 articles in 600 journals worldwide. Broken down into six categories: political science, political thought, government and public administration, government process, international relations and area studies.

United States Political Science Documents. Pittsburgh: University of Pittsburgh Press, 1975-.

Annual two-volume indexing/abstracting service covers 120 scholarly political science journals published in the United States. Generally two to three years out of date. Includes subject, author, geographic and source indexes. Also available online via DIALOG where it is updated quarterly.

Almanacs

Barone, Michael and Grant Ujifusa, eds. *The Almanac of American Politics: The Representatives and the Governors, their Records and Election Results, their States and Districts.* Washington, DC: National Journal, Biennial.

Well-written review of congressional and administrative policies, personalities and institutions. Includes maps, photographs, statistics and overview articles.

Shields-West, Eileen. *The World Almanac of Presidential Campaigns.* New York: World Almanac/St. Martin's Press, 1992.

An interesting array of facts, anecdotes, scandals and mudslinging in the races for the White House. Each campaign discusses credentials, conventions, campaigns, party symbols, songs, slogans and campaign expenditures.

The World Almanac of US Politics. New York: World Almanac/Funk and Wagnalls, Biennial.

Packed with useful data on Congress, the Federal government, the judiciary and important state and city governments.

Atlases

Bureau of the Census. *Congressional District Atlas.* Washington, DC: Government Printing Office, 1960-.

Maps of current congressional districts.

Martis, Kenneth C. and Gregory A. Elmes, eds. *The Historical Atlas of State Power in Congress, 1790-1990.* Washington, DC: Congressional Quarterly, 1993.

Documents through maps the changes in state

political representation and power in the House of Representatives. Part of the United States Congress Bicentennial Atlas Project.

Martis, Kenneth C., ed. *The Historical Atlas of Political Parties in the United States Congress, 1789-1989.* New York: Macmillan, 1989.

Companion volume to the above. Includes national political party maps for each Congress with pie charts showing party percentages.

Martis, Kenneth C., ed. *The Historical Atlas of United States Congressional Districts, 1789-1983.* New York: Free Press, 1982.

Maps the changes in congressional districts in accordance with population growth.

Bibliographies

Cox, Elizabeth M., ed. *Women in Modern American Politics: A Bibliography, 1900-1995.* Washington, DC: Congressional Quarterly, 1997.

Contains 5,985 entries on the role of women in US Politics from 1894 when the first three women were elected to state legislatures to the present day. Citations are drawn from books, journal articles, research reports and dissertations.

The Democratic and Republican Parties in America: A Historical Bibliography. Santa Barbara, CA: ABC-Clio, 1986.

1,600 abstracts organized in five chapters drawn from ABC-PolSci database.

Englefield, Dermot and Gavin Drewry, eds. *Information Sources in Politics and Political Science: A Worldwide Survey.* London: Butterworths, 1984

Contains 24 bibliographic essays covering English language publications with emphasis on the United Kingdom.

Eccleshal, Robert and Michael Kenny, eds. *Western Political Thought: Bibliographical Guide to Research.* Manchester, England: Manchester University Press, 1995.

Provides a good, although not comprehensive, survey of political literature since 1945 on the history of political thought in the Western tradition.

Goehlert, Robert U., Fenton S. Martin and John R. Sayre, eds. *Members of Congress: A Bibliography.* Washington, DC: Congressional Quarterly, 1996.

Lists more than 9,000 journal articles, books, dissertations and essays on members of Congress from 1774 through 1995.

International Bibliography of Political Science. New York: Routledge, 1953-.

The standard bibliography in the field which merged with the *London Bibliography of the Social Sciences* in 1990. Highly selective and generally two to four years out of date. Scans more than 2,000 journals worldwide.

Martin, Fenton S. and Robert U. Goehlert, eds. *How to Research Congress.* Washington, DC: Congressional Quarterly, 1996.

Martin, Fenton S. and Robert U. Goehlert, eds. *How to Research the Presidency.* Washington, DC: Congressional Quarterly, 1996.

The two companion volumes include key information on researching Congress and the Presidency. Each has two parts: The first part contains concise descriptions of secondary reference and finding tools. The second part examines primary sources and finding tools and serves as a guide to specific characteristics of the institution.

Biographies

Benewick, Robert and Philip Green, eds. *The Routledge Dictionary of Twentieth-Century Political Thinkers.* London: Routledge, 1992.

Examines political thought during the 20th century through biographical profiles of the most eminent political thinkers from Adler to Zetkin.

Congress of the United States. *Biographical Directory of the United States Congress, 1774-1989.* Bicentennial Edition. Washington, DC: Government Printing Office, 1989.

Comprehensive record of over 11,000 members of US Congress from 1789 to 1989 and members of the Continental Congress from 1774 to 1789.

Day, Glenn, ed. *Minor Presidential Candidates and Parties of 1992.* Jefferson, NC: McFarland, 1992.

Profiles unconventional or alternative presidential candidates, some of them crackpots.

Duncan, Phil, ed. *Politics in America, 1998: The 105th Congress.* Washington, DC: Congressional Quarterly, 1997.

Includes profiles of all members of US Congress and examines their legislative priorities, personal style and achievements.

Havel, James T., ed. *US Presidential Campaigns and the Elections: A Biographical and Historical Guide.* New York: Macmillan Library Reference, 1996.

A survey of US Presidential Elections from 1789 to 1992. The first volume, *The Candidates,* contains an alphabetically arranged list of individuals who have sought the presidency and the vice presidency. The second volume, *The Elections,* provides a summary of each election and gives data on primary, general and electoral college balloting.

Joint Center for Political Studies. *Black Elected Officials: A National Roster.* Washington, DC: Joint Center for Political and Economic Studies, 1992.

A guide to the names and addresses of more than 7,500 African-American elected officials at all levels.

Utter, Glenn H. and Charles Lockhart, eds. *American Political Scientists: A Dictionary.* Westport, CT: Greenwood Press, 1993.

A collection of short, bio-bibliographical sketches of 171 political science scholars. Each of the signed articles includes a summary of the subject's accomplishments, but no personal history.

Who's Who in AmericanPolitics, 1997-1998. 2 vols. New York: R. R. Bowker/Reed Reference Publishing, Biennial.

Includes biographical data on more than 28,000 persons active in US politics at all levels.

Catalogs

Reilly Jr., Bernard F., ed. *American Political Prints, 1766-1866: A Catalog of Collections in the Library of Congress.* Boston: G. K. Hall, 1991.

Editorial cartoons in the Library of Congress for the century ending with the Civil War.

Dictionaries

Ashford, Nigel and Stephen Davies, eds. *A Dictionary of Conservative and Libertarian Thought.* London: Routledge, Chapman and Hall, 1991.

100 entries on classic conservative and libertarian ideas.

Blake, Fay M. and H. Morton Newman, eds. *Verbis Non Factis: Words Meant to Influence Political Choices in the United States, 1800-1980.* New York: Scarecrow, 1984.

1,000 American political slogans covering 180 years, arranged chronologically with indexes by political party, name of candidate and keyword.

Comfort, Nicholas, ed. *Brewer's Politics: A Phrase and Fable Dictionary.* New York: Cassell/Sterling, 1993.

A dictionary of over 5,000 political terms with pithy, entertaining and humorous definitions. International in scope.

Dickason, Paul and Paul Clancy, eds. *The Congress Dictionary: The Ways and Meanings of Capitol Hill.* New York: John Wiley, 1993.

A to Z guide to the language of politics on the Hill.

Elliot, Jeffrey M. and Sheikh R. Ali, eds. *The Presidential-Congressional Political Dictionary.* Santa Baraba, CA: ABC-Clio, 1984.

Contains 12 chapters, each covering a cluster of words and concepts with an interpretative commentary.

Evans, Graham and Jeffrey Newnham, eds. *The Dictionary of World Politics: A Reference Guide to Concepts, Ideas and Institutions.* New York: Simon & Schuster, 1991.

Defines 600 ideas, concepts and institutions essential to an understanding of world politics.

Filler, Louis, ed. *Dictionary of American Conservatism.* Philadelphia: Philosophical Library, 1987.

Lively but controversial publication that serves as a companion to Filler's *A Dictionary of American Social Change.*

Hill, Kathleen Thompson and Gerald N. Hill, eds. *Real Life Dictionary of American Politics: What They are Saying and What it Really Means.* New York: General Publishing Group, 1994.

1,300 words important in American politics with lively commentary.

Kravitz, Walter, ed. *Congressional Quarterly's American Congressional Dictionary.* Washington, DC: Congressional Quarterly, 1993.

Arranged alphabetically from Absence of Quorum to Zone Whip, the dictionary defines more than 900 terms with numerous cross-references.

O'Laughlin, John. *Dictionary of Geopolitics*. Westport, CT: Greenwood Press, 1994.

A glossary of political concepts, theories and policies. Each entry provides detailed analysis of the origin and influence of the term discussed.

Plano, Jack C. and Milton Greenberg, eds. *The American Political Dictionary*. New York: Holt, 1989.

A popular reference work since 1962 providing an overview of the US political system. Contains 1,200 A to Z entries that explain key terms, concepts, agencies, court cases and laws.

Renstron, Peter G. and Chester B. Rogers, eds. *The Electoral Politics Dictionary*. Santa Barbara, CA: ABC-Clio, 1989.

Covers 440 terms relating to political culture, public opinion, political participation, elections, political campaigns, political parties, interest groups and mass media.

Riff, R. A., ed. *Dictionary of Modern Political Ideologies*. New York: St. Martin's Press, 1987.

Describes 43 political ideologies, ranging from Bonapartism to Islamic Fundamentalism, that have influenced political thinking since the Enlightenment.

Robertson, David, ed. *A Dictionary of Modern Politics*. New York: Taylor & Francis, 1985.

Defines 400 entries with informative commentary. The emphasis is on political ideas and important people and institutions associated with them.

Safire, William, ed. *Safire's New Political Dictionary: The Definitive Guide to the New Language of Politics*. New York: Random House, 1993.

A comprehensive guide to the words of US politics by a noted political commentator and wordsmith.

Shafritz, Jay M., ed. *The HarperCollins Dictionary of American Government and Politics*. New York: HarperCollins, 1992.

A lexicon of politics covering biography, political science jargon, legal and legislative terms, federal agencies and public institutions. Supersedes *Dorsey Dictionary of American Government and Politics*, 1988, also by Jay Shafritz.

Shafritz, Jay M., Phil Williams and Ronald S. Calinger, eds. *The Dictionary of 20th Century World Politics*. New York: Henry Holt, 1993.

Covers more than 4,000 entries on people, theories and ideas that have influenced politics in the 20th century.

Young, Michael L., ed. *The American Dictionary of Campaigns and Elections*. New York: Hamilton Press, 1987.

Defines 725 major terms and concepts associated with campaigns and elections under seven headings: Campaign Processes, Media and Politics, Polling and Public Opinion, Electoral Strategies and Tactics, Parties and PACs, Voting and Political Behavior, and Money and Politics.

Directories

Guide to Political Videos. New York: Pacifica Communications, 1993.

Includes reviews of 400 political videos.

Hess, Carol, ed. *The Political Resource Directory: A Compilation of Political Professional Organizations*. Washington, DC: Political Resources, 1993.

A directory of political professional organizations providing services and products to politicians. Includes 7,400 listings of which 3,000 are organizations and 4,400 are individuals.

Wilcox, Derek Arend, Joshua Shackman and Penelope Nass, eds. *The Right Guide: A Guide to Conservative and Right-of-Center Organizations.* Ann Arbor, MI: Economics America, 1993.

Profiles more than 500 conservative organizations and institutions.

Wilcox, Laird, ed. *A Guide to the American Right: Directory and Bibliography.* New York: Editorial Research Service, 1986.

-----. *A Guide to the American Left: Directory and Bibliography.* New York: Editorial Research Service, 1986.

Lists of organizations and their addresses.

Encyclopedias

Bacon, Donald C., Roger H. Davidson and Morton Keller, eds. *The Encyclopedia of the United States Congress.* 4 vols. New York: Simon & Schuster, 1995.

Comprises 1,056 alphabetically arranged articles, including 247 biographies, by 550 political scholars. Also includes 900 illustrations, charts and graphs.

Bogdanor, Vernon, ed. *The Blackwell Encyclopedia of Political Institutions.* London: Basil Blackwell, 1987.

A succinct guide to the central concepts that drive politics in advanced industrialized countries. Covers 600 topics.

Buhle, Mary Jo, Paul Buhle and Dan Georgakas, eds. *Encyclopedia of the American Left.* New York: Garland, 1990.

Contains approximately 600 articles dealing with major movements, organizations, concepts, events and personalities of the radical American left from the Civil War to the end of the 1980s.

Clucas, Richard A., ed. *Encyclopedia of American Political Reform.* Santa Barbara, CA: ABC-Clio, 1996.

Covers movements and ideas relating to the reform of US politics and government from the 1960s to the present. Phrases and key terms are defined and major reformers and their ideas are profiled.

Congressional Quarterly. *Congress A to Z: A Ready Reference Encyclopedia.* Washington, DC: Congressional Quarterly, 1993.

A desk reference on US Congress that includes information on committees and lawmaking as well as short biographies.

Delury, George E., ed. *World Encyclopedia of Political Systems and Parties.* 2 vols. New York: Facts On File, 1987.

Describes in some detail electoral systems and political parties in over 150 countries as they existed in the mid-1980s.

Dennis, J. Derbyshire and Ian Derbyshire, eds. *Political Systems of the World.* New York: St Martin's Press, 1996.

Second edition of a work that appeared in the United Kingdom in 1990. Provides extensive information on political parties, voting, elections, and political history of 145 countries.

Greene, Jack P., ed. *Encyclopedia of American Political History: Studies of the Principal Movements and Ideas.* 3 vols. New York: Scribner's, 1984.

An impressive compilation of 90 long survey articles covering such broad topics as civil rights, machine politics, suffrage, separation of church and state, populism, federalism and the New Deal.

Hawksworth, Mary and Maurice Hogan, eds. *Encyclopedia of Government and Politics.* 2 vols. New York: Routledge, 1992.

Covers contemporary trends in political theory, ideology and policies in 84 essay-length articles arranged under 10 major headings.

Klingman, William K. *Encyclopedia of the McCarthy Era.* New York: Facts on File, 1996.

Includes a chronology of events from 1919 to 1960, a short bibliography and 18 appendices giving the text of critical documents.

Krieger, Joel, ed. *The Oxford Companion to the Politics of the World.* New York: Oxford University Press, 1993.

Outstanding survey of the global political landscape by 500 specialists from 40 countries. Includes 650 well-written articles, with particular emphasis on political concepts.

Kruschke, Earl R. *Encyclopedia of Third Parties in the United States.* Santa Barbara, CA: ABC-Clio, 1991.

Profiles 81 political parties that have existed at one time or another in the United States outside the Republican Party and the Democratic Party

Kurian, George Thomas and Jeffrey D. Schultz, eds. *The Encyclopedia of the Republican Party.* 2 vols. Armonk, NY: M. E. Sharpe, 1996.

-----. *The Encyclopedia of the Democratic Party.* 2 vols. Armonk, NY: M. E. Sharpe, 1996.

Authoritative works giving a wide range of information on the history of the two principal political parties in the United States. Covers elections, standard bearers, party platforms and conventions.

Levy, Peter B. *Encyclopedia of the Reagan-Bush Years.* Westport, CT: Greenwood Press, 1996.

A factual review of the years 1981-1989. Includes tables, charts, photographs and a timeline.

Levy, Leonard W. and Louis Fisher, eds. *Encyclopedia of the American Presidency.* 4 vols. New York: Simon and Schuster, 1993.

Contains over 1,000 articles dealing with the presidents, the presidency, and the major issues and events that have shaped the office over the years.

Lipset, Seymour Martin, ed. *Encyclopedia of Democracy.* 4 vols. Washington, DC: Congressional Quarterly Books, 1995.

Traces the evolution of democracy and democratic ideology from ancient Greece to modern day. Includes over 400 articles on the many forms of representative government.

Maisel, L. Sandy and Charles Bassett, eds. *Political Parties and Elections in the United States. An Encyclopedia.* 2 vols. New York: Garland, 1991.

Contains 1,200 articles by 250 scholars on political parties and elections from Colonial times to the present. Includes biographies as well as entries on political movements, concepts and legislative issues.

Makinson, Larry and Joshua P. Goldstein, eds. *Open Secrets: The Encyclopedia of Congressional Money and Politics.* Washington, DC: Congressional Quarterly, 1992.

Identifies and catalogs the sources of congressional campaign contributions in the historic 1994 elections. Includes campaign finance profiles of all 535 members of Congress and more than 2,000 charts and graphs.

Milled, David, ed. *The Blackwell Encyclopedia of Political Thought.* New York: Blackwell, 1997.

350 articles on important concepts, ideologies, doctrines, theories and movements central to Western, especially British, political tradition.

Schlesinger Jr., Arthur M., Fred L. Israel and David J. Frent, eds. *Running for President: The Candidates and their Images.* 2 vols. New York: Simon & Schuster, 1994.

A detailed historical reference work on each election in US history. Volume I covers 1789 to 1896 and Volume II covers the 20th century.

Silbey, Joel H., ed. *Encyclopedia of the American Legislative System: Studies of the Principal Structures, Processes and Policies of Congress and State*

Legislatures since the Colonial Era. 3 vols. New York: Scribner's, 1994.

Contains essay-length articles on Congress and the legislative process.

Snyder, Louis, ed. *Encyclopedia of Nationalism.* New York: Paragon House, 1990.

Contains 250 essays on nationalism in politics and history from the 19th century to the present.

Handbooks and Guides

Appleton, Andrew M. and Daniel S. Ward, eds. *State Party Profiles: A 50-state Guide to Development, Organization and Resources.* Washington, DC: Congressional Quarterly, 1997.

Survey of the development and performance of parties at the state level. Illustrates the diversity of state political systems and the nature of political change.

Austin, Erik W. and Jerome W. Clubb, eds. *Political Facts of the United States since 1789.* New York: Columbia University Press, 1986.

Provides historical facts and figures about national leadership, state parties, parties and elections, foreign affairs, wealth, revenue, taxation and public expenditures and demographics.

Jenkins, Russell, John J. Virtes and Frederick W. Campano, eds. *The National Review Politically Incorrect Reference Guide: Your Handbook for the Right Information Sources.* New York: National Review Books, 1993.

Handbook covering hundreds of topics both of general interest and of particular interest to conservatives.

Nelson, Michael. *The Presidency and the Political System.* Washington, DC: Congressional Quarterly, 1997.

Reflects the most recent scholarship on the presidency, especially in the context of changing political dynamics.

Thomas, Norman C. and Joseph A. Pika, eds. *The Politics of the Presidency.* Washington, DC: Congressional Quarterly, 1997.

An in-depth study of the Bill Clinton presidency that explores his political style.

Wyman, Hastings, ed. *The Guide to Southern Politics.* Lanham, MD: University Press of America, 1989.

Covers politics and elections in the American South.

Profiles

Foundation for Public Affairs. *Public Interest Profiles, 1996-97.* Washington, DC: Congressional Quarterly, 1996.

Provides information on 233 public interest organizations divided into 12 chapters. A number of political organizations are included.

Quotations

Baker, Daniel B., ed. *Political Quotations: A Collection of Notable Sayings on Politics from Antiquity to 1989.* Detroit: Gale, 1990.

More than 4,000 quotations, more than one-third dating after World War II.

Eigen, Lewis and Jonathan P. Siegel, eds. *The Macmillan Dictionary of Political Quotations.* New York: Macmillan, 1993.

A compendium of 11,000 quotations organized in 99 chapters ranging from abortion to welfare.

Henning, Charles, ed. *The Wit and Wisdom of Politics.* New York: Fulcrum, 1989.

Eclectic and serendipitous collection of quotations on themes somewhat loosely associated with politics.

Jay, Anthony, ed. *The Oxford Book of Political Quotations.* New York: Oxford University Press, 1996.

4,000 political quotations arranged alphabetically by name of author with a keyword-in-context index.

Platt, Suzey, ed. *Respectfully Quoted: A Dictionary of Quotations from the Library of Congress.* Washington, DC: Congressional Quarterly, 1992.

Quotations garnered by the Congressional Research Service in response to requests from members of Congress. A delightful and authoritative quotations collection.

Statistics

Brace, Kimball W. and the Staff of the Election Data Service, eds. *The Election Data Book: A Statistical Portrait of Voting in America.* Washington, DC: Bernan Press, 1993.

An essential source of statistics for presidential, congressional, senatorial and gubernatorial races. The core information is divided into individual state chapters organized around a series of 10 tables. Three additional sections are a summary chapter for the United States, election data for the 70 counties with the largest populations, and color maps.

Cook, Rhodes, ed. *America Votes: A Handbook of Contemporary Election Statistics.* Washington, DC: Congressional Quarterly, 1998.

Includes detailed results from the 1995 and 1996 elections for president, governor, US Senate and US House of Representatives compiled state-by-state and county-by-county.

McGillivray, Alice V. and Richard M. Scammon, eds. *America at the Polls, 1960-1996: Kennedy to Clinton. A Handbook of Presidential Elections Statistics.* Washington, DC: Congressional Quarterly, 1998.

-----. *America at the Polls, 1920-1956: Harding to Eisehower. A Handbook of Presidential Election Statistics.* Washington, DC: Congressional Quarterly, 1994.

Includes comprehensive election results from 1920 to 1996 organized by state and presented with county-by-county data.

Scott, Thomas G., ed. *The Pursuit of the White House: A Handbook of Presidential Election Statistics and History.* Westport, CT: Greenwood Press, 1987.

Covers 50 presidential elections between 1789 and 1984. Divided into two major sections: the first deals with elections and the second with candidates, parties and states. The first six chapters are divided by historical periods with detailed data on primaries, conventions and general elections. The last three chapters profile the 213 candidates who sought the presidency during this period.

Stanley, Harold W. and Richard G. Niemi, eds. *Vital Statistics on American Politics, 1997-1998.* Washington, DC: Congressional Quarterly, 1998.

Features over 200 tables covering the spectrum of US politics.

Trivia

Villard, ed. *The Book of Political Lists.* New York: *George Magazine*, 1998.

An entertaining, playful and informative compilation of political facts and figures.

Publishers

Few publishers engage in the publication of exclusively political works. Therefore, the following list of publishers includes ones that have a history of publishing political works in a diverse area including public policy, women's studies, political biography, etc.

ABC-Clio
130 Cremona Drive
Santa Barbara, CA 933117
(805) 968-1911 or (800) 422-2546
(805) 685-9685 (Fax)
Website: http://www.abc-clio.com

Mailing Address:
P O Box 1911
Santa Barbara, CA 93116-1911

Editorial Office:
501 Cherry Street, Suite 350
Denver, CO 80222
(303) 333-3003
(303) 333-4037 (Fax)
Founded: 1955

Ablex Publishing Corp
355 Chestnut Street
Norwood, NJ 07648
(201) 767-8450
(201) 767-8450 (Fax)
Founded: 1976

Academy of Political Science
475 Riverside Drive, Suite 1274
New York, NY 10115

(212) 875-2500
(212) 870-2202 (Fax)
Founded: 1880

Addison-Wesley Longman
1 Jacob Way
Reading, MA 01867-3999
(617) 944-3700
(617) 944-9338 (Fax)
Website: http://www.awl.com

Branch Offices:
10 Bank Street, 9th Floor
White Plains, NY 10606-1951
(914) 997-2600
(914) 997-2192 (Fax)

2725 Sand Hill Road
Menlo Park, CA 94025-7092
(415) 854-0300
(415) 614-2909 (Fax)
Founded: 1942

The AEI Press
1150 17th Street NW
Washington, DC 20036
(202) 862-5800 or (800) 223-2336
(202) 862-7177 (Fax)
Website: http://aei.org/press.htm
Founded: 1943

Aldine de Gruyter
200 Saw Mill River Road
Hawthorne, NY 10532
(914) 747-0110

(914) 747-1326 (Fax)
Founded: 1961

Almanac Publishing
PO Box 3785
Washington, DC 20037
(202) 296-2297
(202) 223-3504 (Fax)
Website: http://www.maximov.com/almanac
Founded: 1986

The Apex Press
777 United Nations Plaza, Suite 3C
New York, NY 10017
(914) 271-6500 or (800) 316-2739

Editorial Office:
52 Grand Street
Croton on Hudson, NY 10520
Founded: 1985

Ashgate Publishing
Old Post Road
Brookfield, VT 05036
(802) 276-3162 or (800) 535-9544
(802) 276-3837 (Fax)
Website: http://www.ashgate.com
Founded: 1979

Bantam Books
Division of Bantam Doubleday Dell
1540 Broadway
New York, NY 10036
(212) 354-6500 or (800) 223-6834
(212) 302-7985 (Fax)
Website: http://www.bantam.com
Founded: 1945

Barnes & Noble Books
120 5th Avenue, 4th Floor
New York, NY 10011
(212) 633-3300
(212) 727-4838 (Fax)

Website: http://www.barnesandnoble.com
Founded: 1873

Basic Books
Subsidiary of Perseus Books Group
10 East 53rd Street, 23rd Floor
New York, NY 10022-5299
(212) 207-7600
(212) 207-7703 (Fax)
Website: http://www.hcacademic.com/basic.htm
Founded: 1951

Beacon Press
25 Beacon Street
Boston, MA 02108
(614) 742-2110
(614) 723-3097 (Fax)
Website: http://www.uua.org/beacon
Founded: 1854

Blackwell Publishers
238 Main Street
Cambridge, MA 02142
(614) 547-7110
(614) 547-0789 (Fax)
Website: http://www.blackwellpublishers.co.uk
Founded: 1984

The Brookings Institution
1775 Massachusetts Avenue NW
Washington, DC 20036-2188
(202) 797-6000 or (800) 275-1447
(202) 797-6195 (Fax)
Website: http://www.brook.edu
Founded: 1916

Burgess International Group
7110 Ohms Lane
Edina, MN 55439-2143
(612) 831-1344
(612) 831-3167 (Fax)
Founded: 1925

California Institute of Public Affairs
PO Box 189040
Sacramento, CA 95818
(916) 442-2472
(916) 442-2478 (Fax)
Website: http://www.igc.org/cipa
Founded: 1969

California State University Press
The Press at California State University
Fresno, CA 93740-0099
(209) 278-3056
(209) 278- 6758 (Fax)
Founded: 1982

Cambridge University Press
40 West 20th Street
New York, NY 10011-4512
(212) 924-3900 or (800) 221-4512
(212) 692-3239 (Fax)
Website: http://www.cup.cam.ac.uk
Founded: 1584

Cassell Publishing
127 West 24th Street, 4th Floor
New York, NY 10011
(212) 924-0020
(212) 924-1221 (Fax)
Founded: 1851

The Catholic University of America Press
240 Leahy Hall
620 Michigan Avenue NE
Washington, DC 20064
(202) 319-5052
(202) 319-4985 (Fax)
Website: gopher://vmsgopher.cua.edu/
    11gopher_root_cupr
Founded: 1939

Cato Institute
1000 Massachusetts Avenue NW
Washington, DC 20001-5403
(202) 842-0200

(202) 842-3490 (Fax)
Website: http://www.cato.org
Founded: 1977

Center for Strategic and International Studies
1800 K Street NW, Suite 400
Washington, DC 20006
(202) 775- 3119
(202) 775-3199 (Fax)
Website: http://www.csis.org
Founded: 1962

Chadwyck-Healey
1101 King Street, Suite 380
Alexandria, VA 22314
(703) 683-4890 or (800) 752-0515
(703) 683-7589 (Fax)
Website: http://www.chadwyck.com
Founded: 1974

Chatham House Publishers
PO Box 1
Chatham, NJ 07928
(201) 635-2059
(201) 635- 9366 (Fax)
Website: http://www.gti.net/chatham
Founded: 1979

Chicago Review Press
814 North Franklin
Chicago, IL 60610
(312) 337-0747/ 0748 or (800) 888-4741
(312) 337-5985 (Fax)
Founded: 1973

Columbia University Press
562 West 113th Street
New York, NY 10025
(212) 666-1000 or (800) 944-8648
(212) 316-9422 (Fax)
Website: http://www.cc.columbia.edu/cu/cup
Founded: 1893

Congressional Information Service
4520 East-West Highway
Bethesda, MD 20814-3389
(301) 654-1550 or (800) 638-8380
(301) 654-4033 or (301) 657-3203 (Fax)
Website: http://www.cispubs.com
Founded: 1969

Congressional Quarterly Books
1414 22nd Street NW
Washington, DC 20037
(202) 887-8500 or (800) 638-1710
(202) 887-6706 (Fax)
Website: http://www.cq.com
Founded: 1945

Contemporary Books
2 Prudential Plaza, Suite 1200
Chicago, IL 60601
(312) 540-4500 or (800) 540-9440
(800) 998-3103 (Fax)
Founded: 1947

The Continuum Publishing Group
370 Lexington Avenue, Suite 1700
New York, NY 10017-6503
(212) 953-5858 or (800) 937-5557
(212) 953-5944 (Fax)
Website: http://www.continuum-books.com
Founded: 1979

Cornell University Press
512 East State Street
Ithaca, NY 14850
(607) 277-2338
(607) 277-2374 (Fax)
Website: http://cornellpress.cornell.edu
Founded: 1869

Council of State Governments
PO Box 11910
3572 Iron Works Pike
Lexington, KY 40578-1910
(606) 244-8000 or (800) 800-1910

(606) 244-8001
Website: http://www.csg.org
Founded: 1935

CQ Staff Directories
815 Slaters Lane
Alexandria, VA 22314
(703) 739-0900 or (800) 252-1722
(703) 739-0234 (Fax)
Founded: 1959

Walter de Gruyter
200 Saw Mill River Road
Hawthorne, NY 10532
(914) 747-0110
(914) 747-1326 (Fax)
Website: http://www.degruyter.de
Founded: 1971

Doubleday
Division of Bantam Doubleday Dell
1540 Broadway
New York, NY 10036
(212) 354-6500 or (800) 223-6834
(212) 302-7985 (Fax)
Website: http://www.bantam.com
Founded: 1897

Duke University Press
PO Box 90660
Durham, NC 27708-0660
(919) 687-3600
(919) 688-4574 (Fax)
Website: http://www.duke.edu/web/dupress
Founded: 1921

The Dushkin Publishing Group
Sluice Dock
Guilford, CT 06437
(203) 453-4351
(203) 453-6000 (Fax)
Website: http://www.dushkin.com
Founded: 1971

M. Evans & Co
216 East 49th Street
New York, NY 10017
(212) 688-2810
(212) 486-4544 (Fax)
Founded: 1963

Facts On File
11 Penn Plaza
New York, NY 10001
(212) 967-8800
(212) 967-8107 (Fax)
Website: http://www.factsonfile.com
Founded: 1940

Fitzroy Dearborn
70 East Walton Street
Chicago, IL 60611
(312) 587-0131 or (800) 850-8102
(312) 587-1049 (Fax)
Website: http://www.fitzroydearborn.com
Founded: 1994

Fordham University Press
University Box L
Bronx, NY 10458-5172
(718) 817-4780 or (800) 247-6553
(718) 817-4785 (Fax)
Founded: 1907

Free Press
See Simon & Schuster

Garland Publishing
717 5th Avenue, 25th Floor
New York, NY 10022
(212) 751-7447
(212) 308-9399 (Fax)
Website: http://www.garland.com
Founded: 1969

Georgetown University Press
3619 O Street NW

Washington, DC 20007
(202) 687-6251/5889 or (800) 246-9606
(202) 687-6340 (Fax)
Founded: 1966

Greenwood Publishing Group
Includes Greenwood Press, Praeger Publishers,
    Quorum Books, Auburn House, Bergin &
    Garvey
PO Box 5007
88 Post Road West
Westport, CT 06881
(203) 226-3571 or (800) 225-5800
(203) 222-1502 (Fax)
Website: http://www.greenwood.com
Founded: 1967

Harcourt Brace
Includes Academic Press, Holt Rinehart &
    Winston, Johnson Reprint
6277 Sea Harbor Drive
Orlando, FL 32887
(407) 345-2000 or (800) 225-5425
(407) 352-3445 (Fax)
Website: http://www.harcourtbrace.com

New York Office:
15 East 26th Street
New York, NY 10010
(212) 592-1000
(212) 592-1010 (Fax)

Fort Worth Office:
City Center Tower II
301 Commerce Street, Suite 3700
Fort Worth, TX 76102
(817) 334-7500
(817) 334-0947 (Fax)
Founded: 1919

HarperCollins
Includes Westview Press, HarperSanFrancisco
10 East 53rd Street
New York, NY 10022
(212) 207-7000 or (800) 242-7737
(212) 207-7617 (Fax)

Website: http://www.harpercollins.com
Founded: 1817

Harvard University Press
79 Garden Street
Cambridge, MA 02138-1499
(617) 495-2600 or (800) 448-2242
(617) 495-5898 or (617) 496-4677
Website: http://www.hup.harvard.edu
Founded: 1913

Heritage Foundation
214 Massachusetts Avenue NE
Washington, DC 20002-4999
(202) 546-4400
(202) 546-8328 (Fax)
Website: http://www.heritage.org
Founded: 1973

Holmes & Meier
160 Broadway, East Building
New York, NY 10038
(212) 374-0100 or (800) 698-7781
(212) 374-1313 (Fax)
Founded: 1969

Henry Holt & Co
115 West 18th Street
New York, NY 10011
(212) 288-9200 or (800) 488-5233
(212) 633-0748 (Fax)
Website: http://www.henryholt.com
Founded: 1988

Hoover Institution Press
Stanford University
Stanford, CA 94305-6010
(415) 723-3373
(415) 723-1687 (Fax)
Website: http://www-hoover.stanford.edu/
   presswebsite/hooverpress2.html
Founded: 1962

Houghton Mifflin Co
222 Berkeley Street
Boston, MA 02116
(617) 351-5000 or (800) 225-3362
(617) 351-1125 (Fax)
Website: http://www.hmco.com
Founded: 1832

Hudson Institute
PO Box 26-919
Indianapolis, IN 46226
(317) 545-1000
(317) 545-9639 (Fax)
Website: http://www.hudson.org
Founded: 1961

Humanities Press International
165 1st Avenue
Atlantic Highlands, NJ 07716-1289
(908) 872-1441
(908) 872-0717 (Fax)
Website: http://www.humanitiespress.com
Founded: 1952

Huntington House
104 Row 2 Suite A-1 and A-2
Lafayette, LA 70508
(318) 237-7049 or (800) 709-4009
(318) 237-7060 (Fax)
Founded: 1982

ICS Press
Division of Institute for Contemporary Studies
720 Market Street, 4th Floor
San Francisco, CA 94102
(415) 981-5553 or (800) 326-0263
(415) 986-4878 (Fax)
Founded: 1974

**Interuniversity Consortium for Political and
Social Research**
University of Michigan Institute for Social
   Research
PO Box 1248

Ann Arbor, MI 48106
(313) 763-5010
(313) 764-8041 (Fax)
Website: http://www.icpsr.umich.edu
Founded: 1962

JAI Press
PO Box 1678
55 Old Road Post Road, No 2
Greenwich, CT 06936
(203) 661-7602
(203) 661-0792 (Fax)
Website: http://www.jai.press
Founded: 1975

The Johns Hopkins University Press
2715 North Charles Street
Baltimore, MD 21218-4319
(410) 516-6900
(410) 516-6968 (Fax)
Website: http://www.jhu.edu/~jhupress
Founded: 1878

Augustus M. Kelley
PO Box 1048
Fairfield, NJ 07004-1048
(201) 685-7202

New York Branch:
1140 Broadway, Room 901
New York, NY 10001-7504
(212) 685-7202
Founded: 1947

Lake View Press
PO Box 578279
Chicago, IL 60657-8279
(312) 935-2694
Founded: 1982

Peter Lang Publishing
275 7th Avenue
New York, NY 10001-6708
(212) 647-7700

(212) 647-7707 (Fax)
Website: http://www.peterlang.com
Founded: 1982

Liberty Fund
8335 Allison Pointe Trail, Suite 300
Indianapolis, IN 46250-1687
(317) 842-0880 or (800) 955-8335
(317) 579-6060 (Fax)
ISBN prefix: 0-913966; 0-86597
Founded: 1975

Libraries Unlimited
PO Box 6633
Englewood, CO 80155-6633
(303) 770-1220 or (800) 237-6124
(303) 220-8843 (Fax)
Website: http://www.lu.com
Founded: 1964

Little, Brown & Co
3 Center Plaza
Boston, MA 02108-2084
(617) 227-0730 or (800) 343-9204
(617) 227-4633 (Fax)
Website: http://www.littlebrown.com

Branch Office:
1271 Avenue of the Americas
New York, NY 10020
(212) 522-8700
(212) 522-2067 (Fax)
Founded: 1837

Louisiana State University Press
PO Box 25053
Baton Rouge, LA 70894-5053
(504) 388-6294
(504) 388-6461 (Fax)
Website: http://www.lsu.edu/guests/lsupress/
   index.html
Founded: 1935

McFarland & Co
PO Box 611
Jefferson, NC 28640
(910) 246-4460 or (800) 235-2187
(910) 246-5018 (Fax)
Website: http://www.mcfarlandpub.com
Founded: 1979

McGraw-Hill Book Company
1221 Avenue of the Americas
New York NY, 10020-1095
(212) 512-2000
Website: http://www.bookstore.mcgraw-hill.com

Professional Book Group:
11 West 19th Street
New York, NY 10011
(212) 337-6000
Founded: 1873

Macmillan Publishing
See Simon & Schuster

Madison Books
Subsidiary of University Press of America
4720 Boston Way
Lanham, MD 20706
(301) 459-3366 or (800) 462-6420
(301) 459-2118 (Fax)
Founded: 1985

Madison House
2016 Winnebago Street
Madison, WI 53704
(608) 244-6210 or (800) 604-1776
(608) 244-7050 (Fax)
Founded: 1988

Monthly Review Press
122 West 27th Street
New York, NY 10001
(212) 691-2555 or (800) 670-9499
(212) 727-3676 (Fax)

Website: http://igc.apc.org/monthlyreview
Founded: 1949

William Morrow & Co
1350 Avenue of the Americas
New York, NY 10019
(212) 261-6500 or (800) 843-9389
(212) 261-6595 (Fax)
Website: http://www.williammorrow.com
Founded: 1926

Nelson-Hall Publishers
111 North Canal Street
Chicago, IL 60606
(312) 930-9446
(312) 930-5903 (Fax)
Founded: 1909

The New Press
450 West 41st Street
New York, NY 10036
(212) 629-8802
(212) 268-6349 (Fax)
Website: http://www.wwnorton.com/newpress/
    welcome.htm
Founded: 1992

New York University Press
70 Washington Square South
New York, NY 10012
(212) 998-2575
(212) 995-3833 (Fax)
Website: http://www.nyupress.nyu.edu
Founded: 1916

Northern Illinois University Press
De Kalb, IL 60115
(815) 753-1826
(815) 753-1845 (Fax)
Website: gopher://cron.cso.niu.edu/11/univ_press
Founded: 1965

W. W. Norton & Co
500 5th Avenue

New York, NY 10110
(212) 354-5500 or (800) 233-4830
(212) 869-0856 (Fax)
Website: http://www.wwnorton.com
Founded: 1923

The Oryx Press
4041 North Central Avenue, Suite 700
Phoenix, AZ 85012-3397
(602) 265-2651 or (800) 279-6799
(602) 265-6250 (Fax)
Website: http://www.oryxpress.com
Founded: 1975

Oxford University Press
198 Madison Avenue
New York, NY 10016
(212) 726-6000
(212) 726-6445 (Fax)
Website: http://www.oup-usa.org
Founded: 1896

Pantheon Books
Division of Random House
201 East 50th Street
New York, NY 10022
(212) 751-2600 or (800) 638-6460
(212) 572-6030 (Fax)
Founded: 1942

F. E. Peacock Publishers
115 West Orchard Street
Itasca, IL 60143-1780
(708) 775-9000
(708) 775-9003 (Fax)
Founded: 1967

Penguin-Putnam
Includes Dutton, Viking, Penguin USA, Putnam
375 Hudson Street
New York, NY 10014
(212) 366-2000
(212) 366-2666 (Fax)

Website: http://www.penguinputnam.com
Founded: 1852 (Dutton)

Pennsylvania State University Press
820 North University Drive
University Park, PA 16802
(814) 865-1327 or (800) 326-9180
(814) 863-1408 (Fax)
Founded: 1956

Perseus Books
10 East 53rd Street
New York, NY 10022
(212) 207-7600
(212) 207-7703 (Fax)
Founded: 1997

Pioneer Institute for Public Policy Research
85 Devonshire Street, 8th Floor
Boston, MA 02109
(617) 723-2277
(617) 723-1880 (Fax)
Founded: 1987

Political Research Associates
120 Beacon Street, Suite 202
Somerville, MA 02143
(617) 661-9313
(617) 661-0059 (Fax)
Founded: 1981

Political Risk Services
6320 Fly Road East
Syracuse, NY 13057
(315) 431-0511
(315) 431-0200 (Fax)
Website: http://www.prsgroup.com
Founded: 1979

Princeton University Press
Princeton, NJ 08540
(609) 258-4900 or (800) 777-4726
(609) 258-6305 (Fax)

Website: http://pup.princeton.edu
Founded: 1905

Public Citizen
1600 20th Street NW
Washington, DC 20009
(202) 588-2000
(202) 588-7798 (Fax)
Founded: 1971

Rand Corp
1700 Main Street
Santa Monica, CA 90406
(310) 393-0411
(310) 451-6996 (Fax)
Website: http://www.rand.org
Founded: 1948

Random House
Divisions include: A.A. Knopf, Crown Publishing,
    Times Books, Ballantine Books and Pantheon
201 East 50th Street
New York, NY 10022
(212) 751-2600 or (800) 726-0600
(212) 572-8700 (Fax)
Website: http://www.randomhouse.com
Founded: Random House, 1925; Crown, 1933;
    Knopf, 1915; Ballantine, 1925; Pantheon, 1942

Regnery Publishing
422 1st Street SE, Suite 300
Washington, DC 20003
(202) 546-5005 or (800) 462-6420
(202) 546-8759 (Fax)
Founded: 1947

Lynne Rienner Publishers
1800 30th Street, Suite 314
Boulder, CO 80301
(303) 444-6684
(303) 444-0824 (Fax)
Website: http://www.rienner.com
Founded: 1984

Routledge
29 West 35th Street
New York, NY 10001-2299
(212) 244-3326
(212) 563-2269 (Fax)
Website: http://www.routledge.com
Founded: 1836

Rowman & Littlefield
Subsidiary of University Press of America
4720 Boston Way
Lanham, MD 20706
(301) 459-3366 or (800) 462-6420
(301) 459-2118 (Fax)
Website: http://www.romanlittlefield.com
Founded: 1969

Russell Sage Foundation
112 East 64th Street
New York, NY 10021-7383
(212) 750-6000 or (800) 666-2211
(212) 371-4761 (Fax)
Website: http://epn.org/sage.html
Founded: 1907

Rutgers University Press
Building 4161, Livingston Campus
New Brunswick, NJ 08903-5062
(908) 445-7762
(908) 445-7039 (Fax)
Founded: 1936

Sage Publications
2455 Teller Road
Thousand Oaks, CA 91320
(805) 499-0721
(805) 499-0871 (Fax)
Website: http://www.sagepub.com
Founded: 1964

St Martin's Press
175 5th Avenue
New York, NY 10010
(212) 674-5151 or (800) 221-7745

(212) 420-9314 (Fax)
Website: http://www.stmartins.com
Founded: 1952

M. E. Sharpe
80 Business Park Drive
Armonk, NY 10504
(914) 273-1800 or (800) 541-6563
(914) 273-2106 (Fax)
Website: http://www.mesharpe.com
Founded: 1958

Simon & Schuster
A Viacom Company
Divisions include: Prentice Hall, Macmillan and
    Scribner's
120 Avenue of the Americas
New York, NY 10020
(212) 698-7000 or (800) 223-2348
(212) 698-7007 (Fax)
Website: http://www.simonandschuster.com
Founded: Simon & Schuster, 1924; Prentice Hall,
    1913; Scribner's, 1846; Macmillan,1869

SIRS
PO Box 2348
Boca Raton, FL 33427-2348
(561) 994-0079 or (800) 232-7477
(561) 994-4704 (Fax)
Website: http://www.sirs.com
Founded: 1973

Stanford University Press
Stanford, CA 94305-2235
(415) 723-9434
(415) 725-3457 (Fax)
Website: http://www.sup.org
Founded: 1925

Syracuse University Press
1600 Jamesville Avenue
Syracuse, NY 13244-5160
(315) 443-5541 or (800) 365-8929
(315) 443-5545 (Fax)

Website: http://www.syr.edu/www-syr/aboutsu/
    supress/contents.htm
Founded: 1943

Temple University Press
1601 North Broad Street, USB 306
Philadelphia, PA 19122
(215) 204-8787 or (800) 447-1656
(215) 204-4719 (Fax)
Website: http://www.temple.edu/tempress/
    index.html
Founded: 1969

Times Books
Division of Random House
201 East 50th Street
New York, NY 10022
(212) 572-1623 or (800) 733-3000
(212) 572-4949 (Fax)
Founded: 1959

Transaction Publishers
Rutgers University
Building 4051
New Brunswick, NJ 08903
(908) 445-2280
(908) 445-3138 (Fax)
Website: http://www.transactionpub.com
Founded: 1962

Twentieth Century Fund Press
41 East 70th Street
New York, NY 10021
(212) 535-4441
(212) 535-7534 (Fax)
Founded: 1984

University of Alabama Press
PO Box 870380
Tuscaloosa, AL 35487
(205) 348-5180
(205) 348-9201 (Fax)
Website: http://www.uapress.ua.edu
Founded: 1945

University of California Press
2120 Berkeley Way
Berkeley, CA 94720
(510) 642-4247 or (800) 822-6657
(510) 643-7127 (Fax)
Website: http://www-ucpress.berkeley.edu
Founded: 1893

University of Chicago Press
5801 Ellis Avenue
Chicago, IL 60637
(773) 702-7700/7603 or (800) 621-2736
(773) 702-9756 (Fax)
Website: http://www.press.uchicago.edu
Founded: 1891

University of Delaware Press
Associated University Presses
440 Forsgate Drive
Cranbury, NJ 08512
(609) 655-4770
(609) 655-8366 (Fax)
Founded: 1922

University of Georgia Press
330 Research Drive
Athens, GA 30602-4901
(706) 369-6130
(706) 369-6131 (Fax)
Website: http://www.ugapress.uga.edu
Founded: 1938

University of Hawaii Press
2840 Kolowalu Street
Honolulu, HI 96822
(808) 956-8255 or (800) 956-2840
(800) 650-7811 (Fax)
Website: http://www2.hawaii.edu/uhpress/search
Founded: 1947

University of Illinois Press
1325 South Oak
Champaign, IL 61820
(217) 333-0950

(217) 244-8082 (Fax)
Website: http://www.press.uillinois.edu
Founded: 1918

University of Massachusetts Press
PO Box 429
Amherst, MA 01004-0429
(413) 545-2217
(413) 545-1226 (Fax)
Website: http://www.umass.edu/umpress
Founded: 1964

University of Michigan Press
PO Box 1104
839 Greene Street
Ann Arbor, MI 48106
(313) 764-4392
(313) 936-0456 (Fax)
Website: http://www.press.umich.edu
Founded: 1930

University of Nebraska Press
312 North 14th Street
Lincoln, NE 68588-0484
(402) 472-3581
(402) 472-0308 (Fax)
Website: http://nebraskapress.unl.edu
Founded: 1941

University of North Carolina Press
PO Box 2288
Chapel Hill, NC 27515-2288
(919) 966-3561
(919) 966-3829
Website: http://sunsite.unc.edu/uncpress/
    home.html
Founded: 1922

University of Notre Dame Press
Notre Dame, IN 46556
(219) 631-6346
(219) 631-8148 (Fax)
Website: http://www.nd.edu/~ndpress
Founded: 1949

University of Oklahoma Press
1005 Asp Avenue
Norman, OK 73019-0445
(405) 325-5111
(405) 325-4000 (Fax)
Website: http://www.ou.edu/oupress
Founded: 1928

University of Pennsylvania Press
Blockley Hall
423 Guardian Drive
Philadelphia, PA 19104-6097
(215) 898-6261
(215) 898-0404 (Fax)
Founded: 1869

University of South Carolina Press
937 Assembly Street
Carolina Plaza, 8th Floor
Columbia, SC 29208
(803) 777-5243
(803) 777-0160 (Fax)
Founded: 1944

University of Texas Press
PO Box 7819
Austin, TX 78713-7819
(512) 471-7233
(512) 320-0668 (Fax)
Website: http://www.utexas.edu/depts/utpress
Founded: 1950

University of Utah Press
101 University Service Building
Salt Lake City, UT 84112
(801) 581-6771
(801) 581-3365 (Fax)
Website: http://www.media.utah.edu/upress
Founded: 1949

University of Wisconsin Press
114 North Murray Street
Madison, WI 53715-1199
(608) 262-4928

(608) 262-7560 (Fax)
Website: http://www.wisc.edu/wisconsinpress
Founded: 1937

University Press of America
Includes Scarecrow Press, Madison Books,
    National Book Network, and Rowman &
    Littlefield
4720 Boston Way
Lanham, MD 20706
(301) 459-3366
(301) 459-2118
Website: http://www.univpress.com
Founded: 1950

University Press of Kansas
2501 West 15th Street
Lawrence, KS 66049-3904
(913) 864-4154
(913) 864-4586 (Fax)
Founded: 1946

The University Press of Kentucky
663 South Limestone Street
Lexington, KY 40508-4008
(606) 257-2951
(606) 257-2984 (Fax)
Website: http://www.uky.edu/universitypress
Founded: 1943

University Press of Mississippi
3825 Ridgewood Road
Jackson, MS 39211-6492
(601) 982-6205 or (800) 737-7788
(601) 982-6217 (Fax)
Website: http://www.upress.state.ms.us
Founded: 1970

University Press of New England
23 South Main Street
Hanover, NH 03755-2048
(603) 643-7100
(603) 643-1540 (Fax)

Website: http://www.dartmouth.edu/acad-inst/
    upne
Founded: 1970

The University Press of Virginia
PO Box 3608
University Station
Charlottesville, VA 22903
(804) 924-3468/3469
(804) 982-2655 (Fax)
Website: http://www.upress.virginia.edu
Founded: 1963

Vanderbilt University Press
PO Box 1813, Station B
Nashville, TN 37235
(615) 322-3585
(615) 343-8823 (Fax)
Website: http://www.vanderbilt.edu/publications/
    vupress/welcome/about_press.html
Founded: 1940

Westview Press
Division of Perseus Books
5500 Central Avenue
Boulder, CO 80301-2877
(303) 444-3541
(303) 449-3356 (Fax)
Website: http://hcacademic.com/westview.htm
Founded: 1975

World Almanac Books
1 International Boulevard, Suite 444
Mahwah, NJ 07495
(201) 529-6860
(201) 529-6901 (Fax)
Website: http://www.facts.com/k3ref.htm
Founded: 1986

Yale University Press
302 Temple Street
New Haven, CT 06511
(203) 432-0960
(203) 432-0948 (Fax)
Website: http://www.yale.edu.yup
Founded: 1908

Print, Radio, and Television Commentators

This section contains the names and contact information for leading commentators (or pundits) from print (newspaper and news magazines), radio, and television. Each individual is listed in only his or her primary medium.

There are two exceptions to this general rule. The first is when a commentator from one medium is the primary host for another, then he or she may be listed in two places. For example, Patrick Buchanan is a syndicated newspaper columnist and is listed in that section, but he is also the primary host of the television show *Crossfire* and is listed there too.

The second exception is when the person is not a commentator in their primary medium, but is one in their secondary one. For example, Mara Liason's primary medium is radio where she is a reporter for NPR, therefore she is not listed in the radio section. However, Ms. Liason is a featured panelist on *Fox Sunday News* and so she is listed there.

Print Commentators

Jonathan Alter
Newsweek
251 West 57th Street
New York, NY 10019-6999
(212) 445-4000

Fred Barnes
The New Republic
1220 19th Street NW, Suite 600
Washington, DC 20036
(202) 331-7494

James Barnes
National Journal
1501 M Street NW
Washington, DC 20005
(202) 739-8544

Dan Balz
The Washington Post
1150 15th Stret NW
Washington, DC 20071
(202) 334-6000

Michael Barone
U.S. News & World Report
2400 N Street NW
Washington, DC 20037
(202) 955-2000

Laurence I. Barrett
Time
1271 Avenue of the Americas
New York, NY 10020-1392
(212) 522-1212

Arnold Beichman
The Washington Times
3600 New York Avenue NE
Washington, DC 20002
(202) 636-3000

Tom Bethell
American Spectator
PO Box 549
Arlington, VA 22216
(540) 243-3733

Gloria Borger
U.S. News & World Report
2400 N Street NW
Washington, DC 20037
(202) 955-2000

David Broder
The Washington Post
1150 15th Street NW
Washington, DC 20071
(202) 334-6000

Patrick Buchanan
Tribune Media Service
435 North Michigan Avenue, Suite 1400
Chicago, IL 60611

William F. Buckley Jr.
National Review
150 East 35th Street
New York, NY 10016
(212) 679-7330

Stephen Chapman
Tribune Media Service
435 North Michigan Avenue, Suite 1400
Chicago, IL 60611

Eleanor Clift
Newsweek
251 West 57th Street
New York, NY 10019-6999
(212) 445-4000

Alexander Cockburn
The Nation
72 5th Avenue
New York, NY 10011
(212) 242-8400

Richard Cohen
The Washington Post
1150 15th Street NW

Washington, DC 20071
(202) 334-6000

Ann Devroy
The Washington Post
1150 15th Street NW
Washington, DC 20071
(202) 334-6000

Helen Dewar
The Washington Post
1150 15th Street NW
Washington, DC 20071
(202) 334-6000

E. J. Dionne Jr.
The Washington Post
1150 15th Street NW
Washington, DC 20071
(202) 334-6000

Maureen Dowd
The New York Times
229 West 43rd Street
New York, NY 10036
(212) 556-1234

Elizabeth Drew
The New York Times
229 West 43rd Street
New York, NY 10036
(212) 556-1234

William J. Eaton
Los Angeles Times
Times Mirror Square
Los Angeles, CA 90053
(213) 237-5000

Thomas B. Edsall
The Washington Post
1150 15th Street NW
Washington, DC 20071
(202) 334-6000

Rowland Evans
Chicago Sun-Times
401 North Wabash Avenue

Chicago, IL 60611
(312) 321-3000

Suzanne Fields
Los Angeles Times
Times Mirror Square
Los Angeles, CA 90053
(213) 237-5000

Howard Fineman
Newsweek
251 West 57th Street
New York, NY 10019-6999
(212) 445-4000

Sara Fritz
Los Angeles Times
Times Mirror Square
Los Angeles, CA 90053
(213) 237-5000

David Gergen
U.S. News & World Report
2400 N Street NW
Washington, DC 20037
(202) 955-2000

Jack Germond
National Journal
1501 M Street NW
Washington, DC 20005
(202) 739-8544

Paul Gigot
The Wall Street Journal
200 Liberty Street
New York, NY 10281
(212) 416-2000

Meg Greenfield
The Washington Post
1150 15th Street NW
Washington, DC 20071
(202) 334-6000

Ralph Z. Hallow
The Washington Times
3600 New York Avenue NE

Washington, DC 20002
(202) 636-3000

Nat Hentoff
The Village Voice
36 Cooper Square
New York, NY 10003
(212) 475-3300

Hendrik Hertzberg
The New Republic
1220 19th Street NW, Suite 600
Washington, DC 20036
(202) 331-7494

Christopher Hitchins
The Nation
72 5th Avenue
New York, NY 10011
(212) 242-8400

David Hoffman
The Washington Post
1150 15th Street NW
Washington, DC 20071
(202) 334-6000

Michael Isikoff
The Washington Post
1150 15th Street NW
Washington, DC 20071
(202) 334-6000

Douglas Jehl
Los Angeles Times
Times Mirror Square
Los Angeles, CA 90053
(213) 237-5000

Tom Kenworthy
The Washington Post
1150 15th Street NW
Washington, DC 20071
(202) 334-6000

James J. Kilpatrick
Universal Press Syndicate
4250 Main Street, Suite 700

Kansas City, MO 64111
(816) 932-6600

Michael Kinsley
The New Republic
1220 19th Street NW, Suite 600
Washington, DC 20036
(202) 331-7494

Joe Klein
The New Yorker
20 West 43rd Street
New York, NY 10036
(212) 840-3800

Morton Kondracke
Roll Call
1257-B National Press Building
Washington, DC 20045
(202) 737-1888

Bill Kristol
Public Interest
1112 16th Street NW, Suite 530
Washington, DC 20036
(202) 785-8555

David Lauter
Los Angeles Times
Times Mirror Square
Los Angeles, CA 90053
(213) 237-5000

Nicholas Lemann
The Atlantic
77 North Washington Street
Boston, MA 02114
(617) 854-7700

John Leo
U.S. News & World Report
2400 N Street NW
Washington, DC 20037
(202) 955-2000

Max Lerner
Los Angeles Times
Times Mirror Square

Los Angeles, CA 90053
(213) 237-5000

Anthony Lewis
The New York Times
229 West 43rd Street
New York, NY 10036
(212) 556-1234

Ed Magnuson
Time
1271 Avenue of the Americas
New York, NY 10020-1392
(212) 522-1212

Mary McGrory
The Washington Post
1150 15th Street NW
Washington, DC 20071
(202) 334-6000

William McGurn
National Review
150 East 35th Street
New York, NY 10016
(212) 679-7330

Michael McQueen
The Wall Street Journal
200 Liberty Street
New York, NY 10281
(212) 416-2000

Frank J. Murray
The Washington Times
3600 New York Avenue NE
Washington, DC 20002
(202) 636-3000

Jack Nelson
Los Angeles Times
Times Mirror Square
Los Angeles, CA 90053
(213) 237-5000

Timothy Noah
The New Republic
1220 19th Street NW, Suite 600

Washington, DC 20036
(202) 331-7494

Michael Novak
Forbes
60 5th Avenue
New York, NY 10011
(212) 620-0220

Robert Novak
Chicago Sun-Times
401 North Wabash Avenue
Chicago, IL 60611
(312) 321-3000

Jeremiah O' Leary
The Washington Times
3600 New York Avenue NE
Washington, DC 20002
(202) 636-3000

Michael Oreskes
The New York Times
229 West 43rd Street
New York, NY 10036
(212) 556-1234

Raymond Price
The New York Times
229 West 43rd Street
New York, NY 10036
(212) 556-1234

Wesley Pruden
The Washington Times
3600 New York Avenue NE
Washington, DC 20002
(202) 636-3000

Susan Rasky
The New York Times
229 West 43rd Street
New York, NY 10036
(212) 556-1234

William Raspberry
The Washington Post
1150 15th Street NW

Washington, DC 20071
(202) 334-6000

Paul Craig Roberts
The Washington Times
3600 New York Avenue NE
Washington, DC 20002
(202) 636-3000

Steven U. Roberts
U.S. News & World Report
2400 N Street NW
Washington, DC 20037
(202) 955-2000

David Rogers
The Wall Street Journal
200 Liberty Street
New York, NY 10281
(212) 416-2000

William A. Rusher
Newspaper Enterprise Association
200 Madison Avenue
New York, NY 10016
(212) 293-8500

William Safire
The New York Times
229 West 43rd Street
New York, NY 10036
(212) 556-1234

Robert J. Samuelson
Newsweek
251 West 57th Street
New York, NY 10019-6999
(212) 445-4000

William Schneider
National Journal
1501 M Street NW
Washington, DC 20005
(202) 739-8544

Gerald Seib
The Wall Street Journal
200 Liberty Street

New York, NY 10281
(212) 416-2000

Mark Shields
The Washington Post
1150 15th Street NW
Washington, DC 20071
(202) 334-6000

David Shribman
The Wall Street Journal
200 Liberty Street
New York, NY 10281
(212) 416-2000

Hugh Sidey
Time
1271 Avenue of the Americas
New York, NY 10020-1392
(212) 522-1212

Glenn Simpson
Insight
3600 New York Avenue NE
Washington, DC 20002
(202) 636-3000

Joseph Sobran
National Review
150 East 35th Street
New York, NY 10016
(212) 679-7330

Burt Solomon
National Journal
1501 M Street NW
Washington, DC 20005
(202) 739-8544

Thomas Sowell
Scripps-Howard News Service
1090 Vermont Avenue NW, Room 1000
Washington, DC 20005
(202) 408-1484

Jennifer Spevacek
The Washington Times
3600 New York Avenue NE

Washington, DC 20002
(202) 636-3000

Cal Thomas
Los Angeles Times
Times Mirror Square
Los Angeles, CA 90053
(213) 237-5000

Robin Toner
The New York Times
229 West 43rd Street
New York, NY 10036
(212) 556-1234

Emmett R. Tyrrell Jr.
American Spectator
PO Box 549
Arlington, VA 22216
(540) 243-3733

Steven Waldman
Newsweek
251 West 57th Street
New York, NY 10019-6999
(212) 445-4000

Ben Wattenberg
Newspaper Enterprise Association
200 Madison Avenue
New York, NY 10016
(212) 293-8500

Bernard Weinraub
The New York Times
229 West 43rd Street
New York, NY 10036
(212) 556-1234

Ben Whalen
Insight
3600 New York Avenue NE
Washington, DC 20002
(202) 636-3000

Tom Wicker
The New York Times
229 West 43rd Street

New York, NY 10036
(212) 556-1234

George Will
Newsweek
251 West 57th Street
New York, NY 10019-6999
(212) 445-4000

Jules Witcover
National Journal
1501 M Street NW
Washington, DC 20005
(202) 739-8544

Lawrence Zuckerman
Time
1271 Avenue of the Americas
New York, NY 10020-1392
(212) 522-1212

Radio Commentators

Fred Barnes
What's the Story?
1030 15th Street, Suite 700
Washington, DC 20005
(202) 408-0944
(202) 408-1087 (Fax)

Art Bell
The Art Bell Show
PO Box 4755
Pahrump, NV 89041-4755
(702) 727-8499 (Fax)

Jim Bohannan
The Jim Bohannan Show
1755 South Jefferson Davis Highway
Suite 1200
Arlington, VA 22202
(703) 413-8300

Derry Brownfield
The Derry Brownfield Show

1030 15th Street, Suite 700
Washington, DC 20005
(202) 408-0944
(202) 408-1087 (Fax)

Pat Choate
Washington, The Week Ahead
3 River Street
White Springs, FL 32086
(904) 397-4300
(904) 397-4149 (Fax)

Jack Christy
USA Radio Daily
2290 Springlake, Suite 107
Dallas, TX 75234
(214) 484-3900

Michael Cromartie
Faith & Freedom
1030 15th Street, Suite 700
Washington, DC 20005
(202) 408-0944
(202) 408-1087 (Fax)

Blanquita Cullom
BQ, View
1030 15th Street, Suite 700
Washington, DC 20005
(202) 408-0944
(202) 408-1087 (Fax)

Mario Cuomo
The Mario Cuomo Show
1370 Avenue of the Americas, 22nd Floor
New York, NY 10019
(212) 833-5400
(212) 833-4944 (Fax)

Mark Davis
The Mark Davis Show
2221 East Lamar Boulevard, Suite 406
Arlington, TX 76006
(817) 695-1820

Alan Dershowitz
The Alan Dershowitz Show
1370 Avenue of the Americas, 22nd Floor
New York, NY 10019

(212) 833-5400
(212) 833-4944 (Fax)

Frank Donatelli
Talking Politics
1030 15th Street, Suite 700
Washington, DC 20005
(202) 408-0944
(202) 408-1087 (Fax)

Tom Gresham
Gun Talk
354 Turnpike Street
Canton, MA 02021
(781) 828-4546
(781) 828-3822 (Fax)

Bob Grant
The Bob Grant Show
1440 Broadway
New York, NY 10018
(212) 642-4500
(212) 642-4486 (Fax)

Bo Gritz
The Bo Gritz Show
354 Turnpike Street
Canton, MA 02021
(781) 828-4546
(781) 828-3822 (Fax)

Gil Gross
The Gil Gross Show
51 West 52nd Street
New York, NY 10019
(212) 975-6085
(212) 975-3515 (Fax)

Ira Flatow
The Talk of the Nation
635 Massachusetts Avenue NW
Washington, DC 20001
(202) 414-2000

Stefan Halper
This Week from Washington
1030 15th Street, Suite 700
Washington, DC 20005

(202) 408-0944
(202) 408-1087 (Fax)

Kevin Hamblin
Kevin Hamblin Talk Show
PO Box 100037
Denver, CO 80250-0037
(800) IM-ANGRY
(303) 758-4099
(303) 758-9423 (Fax)

Chuck Harder
For the People
PO Box 150
Tampa, FL 33601-0150

Paul Harvey
Paul Harvey News and Comment
333 North Michigan Avenue
Chiago, IL 60601
(312) 899-4085

Jim Hightower
Hightower & Associates
1800 West 6th Street
Austin, TX 78703
(800) TALK-YES
(512) 477-5588
(512) 478-8536 (Fax)

Don Imus
Imus in the Morning
34-12 36th Street
Astoria, NY 11106
(800) 370-4687
(714) 706-7690

Earl Jackson
Across America
1030 15th Street, Suite 700
Washington, DC 20005
(202) 408-0944
(202) 408-1087 (Fax)

Brian Lehrer
On the Media
1 Centre Street
New York, NY 10007

(212) 669-7800
(212) 669-3312 (Fax)

Michael Lewan
Talking Points
1030 15th Street, Suite 700
Washington, DC 20005
(202) 408-0944
(202) 408-1087 (Fax)

G. Gordon Liddy
The G. Gordon Liddy Show
PO Box 3649
Washington, DC 20007
(800) GGLIDDY
(800) 937-GFAX (Fax)

Rush Limbaugh
The Rush Limbaugh Show
2 Penn Plaza, 17th Floor
New York, NY 10121
(800) 282-2882
(212) 563-9166

Marlin Maddoux
The Marlin Maddoux Commentary
2290 Springlake, Suite 107
Dallas, TX 75234
(214) 484-3900

Steve Major
The Steve Major Show
1030 15th Street, Suite 700
Washington, DC 20005
(202) 408-0944
(202) 408-1087 (Fax)

Mary Matalin
The Mary Matalin Show
1755 Jefferson Davis Highway
Arlington, VA 22202
(800) 600-MARY
(703) 413-8535 (Fax)

Alan Nathan
Battling the Left & Right
1030 15th Street, Suite 700
Washington, DC 20005

(202) 408-0944
(202) 408-1087 (Fax)

Kojo Nnamdi
Public Interest
4400 Massachusetts Avenue NW
Washington, DC 20016
(202) 885-1200

Gary Nolan
Nolan at Night
1030 15th Street, Suite 700
Washington, DC 20005
(202) 408-0944
(202) 408-1087 (Fax)

Oliver North
The Oliver North Show
1030 15th Street, Suite 700
Washington, DC 20005
(202) 408-0944
(800) 510-TALK
(202) 408-1087 (Fax)

Michael Novak
Faith & Freedom
1030 15th Street, Suite 700
Washington, DC 20005
(202) 408-0944
(202) 408-1087 (Fax)

Charles Osgood
Osgood File
51 West 52nd Street
New York, NY 10019
(212) 975-6095
(212) 975-3515 (Fax)

Phil Paleologos
America, Good Morning
354 Turnpike Street
Canton, MA 02021
(781) 828-4546
(781) 828-3822 (Fax)

Michael Reagan
The Michael Reagan Show
PO Box 6061-405
Sherman Oaks, CA 91413

(800) 468-MIKE
(818) 461-5493 (Fax)

Diane Rehm
The Diane Rehm Show
4400 Massachusetts Avenue NW
Washington, DC 20016
(202) 885-1200

Jim Roberts
Profile
1030 15th Street, Suite 700
Washington, DC 20005
(202) 408-0944
(202) 408-1087 (Fax)

Mike Siegel
The Mike Siegel Show
354 Turnpike Street
Canton, MA 02021
(781) 828-4546
(781) 828-3822 (Fax)

Tom Snyder
The Late Late Radio Show
51 West 52nd Street
New York, NY 10019
(212) 975-6085
(212) 975-3515 (Fax)

Doug Stephen
The Doug Stephen Show
1030 15th Street, Suite 700
Washington, DC 20005
(202) 408-0944
(202) 408-1087 (Fax)

Ray Suarez
The Talk of the Nation
635 Massachusetts Avenue NW
Washington, DC 20001
(202) 414-2000

Dave Teeuwen
Dateline Washington
1030 15th Street, Suite 700
Washington, DC 20005
(202) 408-0944
(202) 408-1087 (Fax)

Armstrong Williams
The Right Side
545 East John Carpenter Freeway, Suite 450
Irving, TX 75062
(214) 831-1920
(214) 831-8626 (Fax)

Television Commentators

Fred Barnes
The Beltway Boys
400 North Capitol Street NW, Suite 500
Washington, DC 20001
(202) 824-6300

Wolf Blitzer
Late Edition with Wolf Blitzer
820 1st Street NE
Washington, DC 20002

Ken Bode
Washington Week in Reveiw
3700 South Four Mile Run Drive
Arlington, VA 22206
(703) 998-2600
(703) 998-3401 (Fax)

Ed Bradley
60 Minutes
51 West 52nd Street
New York, NY 10019
(212) 975-4321
(212) 945-8714 (Fax)

Patrick Buchanan
Crossfire
820 1st Street NE
Washington, DC 20002
(202) 898-7655
(202) 898-7611 (Fax)

Alan Colmes
Hannity & Colmes
400 North Capitol Street NW, Suite 500

Washington, DC 20001
(202) 824-6300

Sam Donaldson
This Week
1717 DeSales Street NW
Washington, DC 20036
(202) 222-7100

Hugh Downs
20/20
77 West 66th Street
New York, NY 10023-6298
(212) 456-7777
(212) 456-6850 (Fax)

Rowland Evans
Evans, Novak, Shields & Hunt
820 1st Street NE
Washington, DC 20002
(202) 898-7622
(202) 515-2919 (Fax)

Steve Fox
60 Minutes
51 West 52nd Street
New York, NY 10019
(212) 975-4321
(212) 945-8714 (Fax)

Paul Gigot
NewsHour with Jim Lehrer
3620 South 27th Street
Arlington VA 22206
(703) 998-2844

Bryant Gumbel
Public Eye
51 West 52nd Street
New York, NY 10019
(212) 975-4321
(212) 945-8714 (Fax)

Sean Hannity
Hannity & Colmes
400 North Capitol Street NW, Suite 500
Washington, DC 20001
(202) 824-6300

Brit Hume
Special Report with Brit Hume
400 North Capitol Street NW, Suite 500
Washington, DC 20001
(202) 824-6300

Al Hunt
The Capitol Gang
820 1st Street NE
Washington, DC 20002
(202) 898-7628
(202) 898-7611 (Fax)

Jesse Jackson
Both Sides with Jesse Jackson
820 1st Street NE
Washington, DC 20002
(202) 515-2804
(202) 515-2919 (Fax)

Bernard Kalb
Reliable Sources
820 1st Street NE
Washington, DC 20002

Larry King
Larry King Live
820 1st Street NE
Washington, DC 20002
(202) 898-7690

Morton Kondracke
The Beltway Boys
400 North Capitol Street NW, Suite 500
Washington, DC 20001
(202) 824-6300

Ted Koppel
Nightline
1717 DeSales Street NW
Washington, DC 20036
(202) 222-7000

Bill Kristol
This Week
1717 DeSales Street NW
Washington, DC 20036
(202) 222-7100

Mara Liasson
Fox News Sunday
400 North Capitol Street NW, Suite 500
Washington, DC 20001
(202) 824-6300

Bill Maher
Politically Incorrect
7800 Beverly Boulevard
Los Angeles, CA 90036

John McLaughlin
The McLaughlin Group
1211 Connecticut Avenue NW, Suite 810
Washington, DC 20036
(202) 457-0870

Chris Matthews
Hardball with Chris Matthews
1825 K Street NW, Suite 1003
Washington, DC 20006
(202) 776-7426
(202) 467-0601 (Fax)

Robert Novak
Crossfire
820 1st Street NE
Washington, DC 20002
(202) 898-7655
(202) 898-7611 (Fax)

Bill O'Reilly
The O'Reilly Factor
400 North Capitol Street NW, Suite 500
Washington, DC 20001
(202) 824-6300

Jane Pauley
Dateline NBC
30 Rockefeller Plaza
New York, NY 10112
(212) 664-4444
(212) 664-2648 (Fax)

Stone Phillips
Dateline NBC
30 Rockefeller Plaza
New York, NY 10112

(212) 664-4444
(212) 664-2648 (Fax)

Bill Press
Crossfire
820 1st Street NE
Washington, DC 20002
(202) 898-7655
(202) 898-7611 (Fax)

Dan Rather
48 Hours
51 West 52nd Street
New York, NY 10019
(212) 975-4321
(212) 945-8714 (Fax)

Geraldo Rivera
Rivera Live
1825 K Street NW, Suite 1003
Washington, DC 20006
(202) 776-7426
(202) 467-0601 (Fax)

Cokie Roberts
This Week
1717 DeSales Street NW
Washington, DC 20036
(202) 222-7100

Pat Robertson
700 Club
977 Centerville Turnpike
Virginia Beach, VA 23463
(757) 226-7000

Tim Russert
Meet the Press
4001 Nebraska Avenue NW
Washington, DC 20016
(202) 885-4548
(202) 362-2009 (Fax)

Morley Safer
60 Minutes
51 West 52nd Street
New York, NY 10019
(212) 975-4321
(212) 945-8714 (Fax)

Diane Sawyer
20/20
77 West 66th Street
New York, NY 10023-6298
(212) 456-7777
(212) 456-6850 (Fax)

Bob Schieffer
Face the Nation
2020 M Street NW
Washington, DC 20036
(202) 457-4481

Jon Scott
Fox In Depth
400 North Capitol Street NW, Suite 500
Washington, DC 20001
(202) 824-6300

Mark Shields
Evans, Novak, Shields & Hunt
820 1st Street NE
Washington, DC 20002
(202) 898-7622
(202) 515-2919 (Fax)

Travis Smiley
BET Tonight
1900 W Place NE
Washington, DC 20018
(202) 608-2000
(202) 608-2599 (Fax)

Tony Snow
Fox News Sunday
400 North Capitol Street NW, Suite 500
Washington, DC 20001
(202) 824-6300

Leslie Stahl
60 Minutes
51 West 52nd Street
New York, NY 10019
(212) 975-4321
(212) 945-8714 (Fax)

George Stephanopolous
This Week
1717 DeSales Street NW

Washington, DC 20036
(202) 222-7100

Mike Wallace
60 Minutes
51 West 52nd Street
New York, NY 10019
(212) 975-4321
(212) 945-8714 (Fax)

Barbara Walters
20/20
77 West 66th Street
New York, NY 10023-6298
(212) 456-7777
(212) 456-6850 (Fax)

Ben Wattenberg
Think Tank with Ben Wattenberg
1150 17th Street NW, Suite 1050
Washington, DC 20036
(202) 775-4945

George Will
This Week
1717 DeSales Street NW
Washington, DC 20036
(202) 222-7100

Juan Williams
Fox News Sunday
400 North Capitol Street NW, Suite 500
Washington, DC 20001
(202) 824-6300

Internet Resources

The Internet is an ever-expanding and ever-changing new media that offers increased access to political information around the world. The selected list below is divided into three sub-groups: Government Websites, Non-Government Websites, and Newsgroups. In addition to the listings that appear in this chapter, the reader is reminded that many more website addresses are contained within the entries in other chapters such as third parties, political science research institutes, etc.

GOVERNMENT WEBSITES

CENSUS BUREAU
Website: http://www.census.gov

CENTRAL INTELLIGENCE AGENCY
Website: http://www.odci.gov/cia/

DEPARTMENT OF AGRICULTURE
Website: http://www.usda.gov

DEPARTMENT OF COMMERCE
Website: http://www.doc.gov

DEPARTMENT OF DEFENSE
Website: http://www.defenselink.mil

DEPARTMENT OF EDUCATION
Website: http://www.ed.gov

DEPARTMENT OF ENERGY
Website: http://www.doe.gov

DEPARTMENT OF HEALTH AND HUMAN SERVICES
Website: http://www.dhhs.gov

DEPARTMENT OF HOUSING AND URBAN DEVELOPMENT
Website: http://www.hud.gov

DEPARTMENT OF INTERIOR
Website: http://www.doi.gov/index.html

DEPARTMENT OF JUSTICE
Website: http://www.usdoj.gov

DEPARTMENT OF LABOR
Website: http://www.dol.gov

DEPARTMENT OF STATE
Website: http://www.state.gov

DEPARTMENT OF TRANSPORTATION
Website: http://www.dot.gov

DEPARTMENT OF TREASURY
Website: http://www.ustreas.gov

DEPARTMENT OF VETERANS' AFFAIRS
Website: http://www.va.gov

THE FEDERAL BUREAU OF INVESTIGATION
Website: http://www.fbi.gov

FEDWORLD INFORMATION SERVICES
Website: http://www.fedworld.gov

THE HOUSE OF REPRESENTATIVES
Website: http://www.house.gov

INTERNAL REVENUE SERVICE
Website: http://www.irs.gov

JOINT CHIEFS OF STAFF
Website: http://www.dtic.mil/jcs

THE LIBRARY OF CONGRESS
Website: http:// www.loc.gov

THE PRESIDENT OF THE UNITED STATES
Website: http://www.whitehouse.gov

THE SENATE OF THE UNITED STATES
Website: http://www.senate.gov

THE SUPREME COURT OF THE UNITED STATES
Website: http://www.uscourts.gov

UNITED STATES AIR FORCE
Website: http://www.af.mil

UNITED STATES ARMY
Website: http://www.army.mil

UNITED STATES COAST GUARD
Website: http://www.uscg.mil

UNITED STATES MARINE CORPS
Website: http://www.usmc.mil

UNITED STATES NAVY
Website: http://www.navy.mil

NON-GOVERNMENT WEBSITES

ALBION MONITOR
Website: http://www.monitor.net/monitor/
Content: Full-text studies on political issues from an independent point of view.

ALLPOLITICS
Website: http://allpolitics.com/1998/index.html
Content: Comprehensive coverage of political events from CNN and Time Warner.

AMERICAN JOURNAL OF POLITICAL SCIENCE
Website: http://www.sbs.ohio-state.edu/polisci/ajps/content.htm
Content: Abstracts of scholarly articles on political philosophy from the official journal of the Midwest Political Science Association.

AMERICAN NEWSPEAK
Website: http://www.scn.org/news/newspeak/
Content: Satirical articles on the state of American politics.

AMERICAN POLITICAL SCIENCE REVIEW
Website: http://www.ssc.msu.edu/~apsr/
Content: Abstracts from the quarterly journal of the

American Political Science Association, offering comprehensive coverage of all aspects of the political scene.

AMERICAN PROSPECT
Website: http://epn.org:80/prospect.html
Content: Full-text articles providing a liberal perspective on contemporary issues.

AMERICAN SPECTATOR
Website: http://www.spectator.org/
Content: Investigative studies with a conservative perspective.

APSA NET
Website: http://www.apsanet.org/
Content: Resources and activities of the American Political Science Association.

ATLANTIC UNBOUND
Website: http://www.theatlantic.com/atlantic/election/connection/
Content: Feature articles from the *Atlantic Monthly* relating to public policy.

BAD SUBJECTS
Website: http://english-www.hss.cmu.edu/bs/
Content: Articles projecting progressive political convictions.

BOSTON REVIEW
Website: http://www-polisci.mit.edu/BostonReview/
Content: Full-text studies reflecting egalitarian convictions.

C-SPAN
Website: http://www.c-span.org/
Content: Comprehensive coverage of congressional activities by the C-SPAN television network.

CAPITOL HILL BLUE
Website: http://www.capitohillblue.com/index.htm
Content: Articles containing cynical views of the current political scene.

CAPITOL STEPS
Website: http://www.capsteps.com/
Content: Humorous looks at political issues by current and former congressional staffers.

CENTER FOR RESPONSIVE POLITICS
Website: http://www.crp.org/index.html-ssi
Content: Articles on the role money plays in lobbying and elections.

CIVIC PRACTICES NETWORK
Website: http://fount.journalism.wisc.edu/cpn/cpn.html
Content: Practical methods for public problem-solving at the local level.

COMMON CAUSE MAGAZINE
Website: http://www.commoncause.org/
Content: Investigative stories by the activist group on political misconduct.

CONCORD COALITION
Website: http://www.concordcoalition.org/
Content: Activities of coalition dedicated to eliminating federal budget deficits.

CONGRESS ACTION
Website: http://www.aimnet.com:80/~jbv/congress_action.html
Content: Conservative newsletter offering full-text articles alerting interested people to actions pending in Congress.

CONGRESSIONAL QUARTERLY'S AMERICAN VOTER
Website: http://www.cq.com/
Content: Complete coverage of all activities of the United States Congress.

CONSERVATIVE NET
Website: http://www.ConservativeNet.com/
Content: Search engine to conservative sites on the Web.

CONSERVATIVE REVIEW
Website: http://www.erols.com/conrev/
Content: Latest insights from influential conservative policymakers.

DEEP POLITICS
Website: http://www.copi.com/~deepbook.html
Content: News and pro-activist commentary covering current political events.

DEMOCRACY NETWORK
Website: http://www.democracynet.org/about.html
Content: Forum for public officials, citizens and candidates to debate issues of local, state and national importance.

DISSENT
Website: http://www.igc.apc.org/dissent/
Content: Full-text articles reflecting sharp left-wing view of current issues.

DRUDGE REPORT
Website: http://www.drudgereport.com/
Content: Political headlines, rumors and links to columnists by name.

E.POLITICS
Website: http://www.epolitics.com/
Content: Current reports on the legislative and regulatory actions of the federal government.

ELECTNET
Website: http://www.electnet.org/
Content: Non-profit (non-partisan) source of information for state and local politics.

FREE-MARKET.NET
Website: http://www.free-market.com/directory/
Content: Resources covering the spectrum of libertarian and free-market ideas.

FREEDOM DAILY
Website: http:fff.org/freedom/daily/
Content: Selected full-text articles offering a libertarian perspective on the role of government.

GEORGE
Website: http://www.georgemag.com/index2.html
Content: Politics with a focus on personalities.

GREEN PARTIES OF NORTH AMERICA
Website: http://www.greens.org/
Content: Official site of the Green Parties.

HARVARD POLITICAL REVIEW
Website: http://harvard.edu/~hpr/main.html
Content: Full-text articles presenting in-depth studies of public policy issues.

THE HILL
Website: http://www.hillnews.com/
Content: Non-partisan news reports analyzing the actions of Congress.

IDEA HOUSE
Website: http://www.public-policy.org/~ncpa/
Content: Background information on issues before Congress compiled by the National Center for Policy Analysis.

INTELLECTUAL CAPITAL
Website: http://www.intellectualcapital.com/
Content: Articles providing wide range of perspectives on contemporary political matters.

JOURNAL OF POLITICS
Website: http://www.utexas.edu/utpress/journals/jjop.html
Content: Tables of contents from previous and forthcoming issues of the official journal of the Southern Political Science Association.

LIBERTARIAN ENTERPRISE
Website: http://www.webleyweb.com/tle/index.html
Content: Full-text articles on political matters from the Libertarian point of view.

MICHIGAN JOURNAL OF POLITICAL SCIENCE
Website: http://www.umich.edu/~mjps/index.html
Content: Full-text articles on a wide range of political topics submitted by students from around the country.

MID-ATLANTIC INFOSHOP
Website: http://burn.ucsd.edu/~mai/
Content: Guide to sites of interest to anarchists, anti-authoritarians, and other social change activists.

MR. JEFFERSON'S CHALLENGE HOME PAGE
Website: http://users.aol.com/mrjeffchlg/index.htm
Content: Full-text articles focusing on the nation's changing social and political climate.

MODERN MAN
Website: http://www.geocities.com/CapitolHill/3839/whatsnew.htm
Content: Full-text articles reflecting the middle of the American political spectrum.

MOJOWIRE
Website: http://www.mojones.com/
Content: Investigative articles from the electronic version of *Mother Jones* magazine.

MONEY & POLITICS
Website: http://www.pflr.com/
Content: Information on campaign financing and PACs.

NATION
Website: http://www.thenation.com/
Content: Selected full-text articles with a liberal orientation.

NATIONAL COMMITTEE FOR AN EFFECTIVE CONGRESS
Website: http://www.ncec.org/

Content: Current reports on candidates advocating progressive politics.

NATIONAL GAY AND LESBIAN TASK FORCE
Website: http://www.ngltf.org/
Content: Official site of the National Gay and Lesbian Task Force.

NATIONAL JOURNAL'S CLOAKROOM
Website: http://cloakroom.com/
Content: Commentary, news and resource materials on politics and policy.

NATIONAL POLITICAL INDEX
Website: http://www.politicalindex.com/index.htm
Content: An index of substantive political information for voters, activitists, consultants, lobbyists, politicians, political scientists, and reporters. It includes listings of national political parties, political activitist groups and political science departments.

NATIONAL REVIEW
Website: http://www.nationalreview.com/
Content: Conservative views on political issues and cultural trends.

NEW AMERICAN
Website: http://www.jbs.org/tna.htm
Content: Selected articles from the official magazine of the John Birch Society.

NEW POLITICAL SCIENCE
Website: http://gramercy.ios.com/~urbsoc/NPS/Home.html
Content: Tables of contents from recent issues, offering articles aimed at academics and activists interested in the study and practice of political change.

NEW REPUBLIC
Website: http://magazines.enews.com/magazines/tnr/
Content: Selected full-text articles from the liberal journal.

POLICY.COM
Website: http://www.policy.com/
Content: A public policy information resource offering comprehensive news analysis.

POLICY REVIEW
Website: http://www.heritage.org/heritage/p_review/

Content: Complete articles specializing in the study of private-sector and local-government alternatives to the federal system.

POLITICAL METHODOLOGY SOCIETY/WORKING PAPERS/JOURNAL
Website: http://wizard.ucr.edu/polmeth/polmeth.html
Content: Abstracts of working papers and conference programs from an arm of the American Political Science Association.

POLITICAL RESEARCH QUARTERLY
Website: http://www.u.arizona.edu/~prq/
Content: Tables of contents and abstracts of original research covering all areas of political science.

POLITICAL RESOURCES ON THE NET
Website: http://www.agora.stm.it/politic/
Content: Links to political parties, organizations, governments and the media.

POLITICAL SCIENCE MANUSCRIPTS
Website: http://www.TCNJ.EDU/~psm/
Content: Links to scholarly political science abstracts and manuscripts.

POLITICAL SCIENCE QUARTERLY
Website: http://epn.org/psq.html
Content: Full-text featured articles on government, politics and public policy.

POLITICS 1
Website: http://www.politics1.com/
Content: Comprehensive links to presidential, gubernatorial, U.S. Senate & congressional candidates and political parties.

POLS GUIDE
Website: http://www.trincoll.edu/~pols/guide/home.html
Content: Guide for students and professionals to resource materials pertaining to politics, government and law.

PRESIDENTIAL STUDIES QUARTERLY
Website: http://www.cspresidency.org/presquar.htm
Content: Complete texts of scholarly articles on the U.S. Presidency.

PRICE POLITICAL REVIEW
Website: http://www.geocities.com/CapitolHill/2533/pprissue.html

Content: Results and analysis of presidential and senate elections.

PROGRESSIVE
Website: http://www.progressive.org
Content: Featured full-text articles from the current issue of the left-wing magazine.

PROJECT VOTE SMART
Website: http://www.vote-smart.org/
Content: Information on the performance of over 13,000 political leaders.

PS: POLITICAL SCIENCE & POLITICS
Website: http://www.apsanet.org/PS/ps.html
Content: Tables of contents for current issues of the trade journal produced by the American Political Science Association.

REASON
Website: http://www.reasonmag.com/
Content: Full-text articles from a libertarian perspective.

REVIEW OF POLITICS
Website: http://www.nd.edu/~rop/
Content: Abstracts of articles with an emphasis on the philosophical and historical approach to politics.

ROLL CALL
Website: http://www.rollcall.com/
Content: Full-text articles from the publication covering the U.S. Congress.

SLATE
Website: http://www.slate.com/
Content: Full-text articles on a variety of political topics.

TURN LEFT
Website: http://www.cjnetworks.com/~cubsfan/liberal.html.
Content: Home of liberal thought on the Web.

VOTELINK
Website: http://www.votelink.com/
Content: Online discussions and voting regarding current public policy issues.

WASHINGTON WEEKLY
Website: http://www.federal.com/
Content: Complete articles focusing on citizen initiatives and third party alternatives.

WEEKLY STANDARD
Website: http://www.weeklystandard.com/
Content: Selected full-text articles from a conservative point of view.

WOMEN & POLITICS
Website: http://www.westga.edu/~wandp/w+p.html
Content: Abstracts of articles analyzing the role of women in politics.

Z MAGAZINE
Website: http://www.lbbs.org/zmagst.htm
Content: Amalgam of articles reflecting independent views of the political scene.

NEWSGROUPS

news:alt.abortion
news:alt.abortion.inequity
news:alt.activism
news:alt.activism.children
news:alt.activism.d
news:alt.activism.death-penalty
news:alt.alien.visitors
news:alt.aliens.imprisoned
news:alt.anarchism
news:alt.bork
news:alt.building.gov-issues
news:alt.building.law
news:alt.cable-tv.re-regulate
news:alt.censorship
news:alt.child-support
news:alt.culture.us.1960s
news:alt.culture.us.1970s
news:alt.culture.us.1980s
news:alt.current-events.bosnia
news:alt.current-events.clinton.whitewater
news:alt.current-events. haiti
news:alt.current-events.usa
news:alt.dads-rights
news:alt.destroy.the.earth
news:alt.drugs
news:alt.education.disabled
news:alt.education.home-school.christian
news:alt.education.ib.econ
news:alt.education.industry.comp
news:alt.education.university.vision2020
news:alt.fan.bob-dole

news:alt.fan.dan.quayle
news:alt.fan.g-gordon-liddy
news:alt.fan.newt-gingrich
news:alt.fan.noam-chomsky
news:alt.fan.ronald-reagan
news:alt.fan.rush-limbaugh.tv-show
news:alt.flame.right-wing-conservatives
news:alt.freedom.of.information.act
news:alt.games.tradewars
news:alt.government.abuse
news:alt.journalism.newspapers
news:alt.journalism.objective
news:alt.journalism.print
news:alt.law-enforcement.traffic
news:alt.mens-rights
news:alt.org.earth-first
news:alt.org.food-not-bombs
news:alt.org.sierra-club
news:alt.pissed.federal.employees
news:alt.planning.urban
news:alt.politics.bush
news:alt.politics.clinton
news:alt.politics.correct
news:alt.politics.datahighway
news:alt.politics.democrats
news:alt.politics.democrats.clinton
news:alt.politics.democrats.d
news:alt.politics.democrats.governors
news:alt.politics.democrats.house
news:alt.politics.democrats.senate
news:alt.politics.drinking-age
news:alt.politics.economics
news:alt.politics.elections
news:alt.politics.equality
news:alt.politics.greens
news:alt.politics.homosexuality
news:alt.politics.immigration
news:alt.politics.libertarian
news:alt.politics.libertarian.gay
news:alt.politics.media
news:alt.politics.org.batf
news:alt.politics.org.btaf
news:alt.politics.org.ccr
news:alt.politics.org.cia
news:alt.politics.org.covert
news:alt.politics.org.fbi
news:alt.politics.org.misc
news:alt.politics.org.nsa
news:alt.politics.org.un

news:alt.politics.perot
news:alt.politics.radical-left
news:alt.politics.reform
news:alt.politics.scorched-earth
news:alt.politics.sex
news:alt.politics.socialism.mao
news:alt.politics.socialism.trotsky
news:alt.politics.usa.congress
news:alt.politics.usa.constitution
news:alt.politics.usa.misc
news:alt.politics.usa.newt-gingrich
news:alt.politics.usa.republican
news:alt.prisons
news:alt.radio.talk
news:alt.revisionism
news:alt.revolution.american.second
news:alt.rush-limbaugh
news:alt.save.the.earth
news:alt.sex.senator-exon
news:alt.soc.ethics
news:alt.society.anarchy
news:alt.society.civil-disob
news:alt.society.civil-liberty
news:alt.society.conservatism
news:alt.society.labor-unions
news:alt.society.mental-health
news:alt.society.paradigms
news:alt.society.resistance
news:alt.society.revolution
news:alt.society.sovereign
news:alt.speech.debate
news:alt.survival
news:alt.tv.public-access
news:alt.war
news:alt.war.civil.usa
news:courts.usa.config
news:courts.usa.federal.supreme
news:courts.usa.state.ohio.appls-8th
news:courts.usa.state.ohio.config
news:courts.usa.state.ohio.supreme
news:dc.politics
news:fedreg.agriculture
news:fedreg.commerce
news:fedreg.defense
news:fedreg.education
news:fedreg.energy
news:fedreg.environ
news:fedreg.finance
news:fedreg.general

news:fedreg.govern
news:fedreg.health
news:fedreg.humanserv
news:fedreg.interior
news:fedreg.labor
news:fedreg.legal
news:fedreg.lists
news:fedreg.misc
news:fedreg.science
news.fedreg.tocs
news.fedreg.transport
news:info.firearms.politics
news:misc.activism.militia
news:misc.activism.progressive
news:misc.education
news:misc.education.adult
news:misc.education.home-school.misc
news:misc.headlines
news:misc.immigration.misc
news:misc.immigration.usa
news:misc.survivalism
news:mn.politics
news:nvc.politics
news:or.politics
news:seattle.politics
news:shamash.jewishweek
news:shamash.newsflash
news:shamash.zionline
news:soc.culture.usa
news:soc.history.war.world-war-ii
news:soc.org.nonprofit
news:soc.politics
news:soc.politics.arms-d
news:soc.rights.alien
news:soc.rights.human
news:talk.politics.animals
news:talk.politics.china
news:talk.politics.crypto
news:talk.politics.guns
news:talk.politics.libertarian
news:talk.politics.medicine
news:talk.politics.mideast
news:talk.politics.misc
news:talk.politics.soviet
news:talk.politics.theory
news:talk.politics.tibet
news:tnn.forum.global-brain
news:tw.bbs.soc.politics

Political Prizes and Awards

The following list of political prizes and awards are those that are given by non-governmental organizations and governmental agencies. Please note that many political associations give awards for leading advocates of their cause or for rising young members. Those awards have not been listed here because of the overlap with the chapter on political associations. Additionally, military honors are not included in the listings, but several veterans' awards are. The criteria for the award is included for each entry.

Achievement of the Year Award
Association of Government Accountants
2200 Mount Vernon Avenue
Alexandria, VA 22301-1314
(703) 684-6931
(703) 548-9367 (Fax)

Awarded annually in order to recognize individuals displaying leadership and achievement in government service financial management.

American Community Leadership
National Association of Towns and Townships
444 North Capitol Street NW, Suite 294
Washington, DC 20001
(202) 624-3550
(202) 624-3554 (Fax)
E-mail: natat@sso.org

Given to local and small community officials that display a high level of commitment, creativity, and leadership within their field of service.

AMVETS Silver Helmet Awards
AMVETS National Headquarters
4647 Forbes Boulevard
Lanham, MD 20706-9961
(301) 459-9600
(301) 459-5578 (Fax)

Was created to acknowledge individuals who distinguished themselves by making Congressional contributions in the areas of Americanism, national defense, civil service, and peace.

Annual Awards for Distinction in Financial Management
United States Department of the Treasury
Financial Management Service
Washington, DC 26228
(202) 622-2000

f.1985; this annual award is provided to non-Treasury government officials who have excelled in the areas of credit fund management.

Philip Arrow Award
United States Department of Labor
Secretary's Honor Awards Committee
200 Constitution Avenue NW, Room N5470
Washington, DC 20210
(202) 219-6741
(202) 219-8127 (Fax)

f. 1972; an annual honor bestowed upon people illustrating consistently outstanding service over a period of 15 years or more to the Department of Labor.

Assistant Secretary's Award for Excellence in Information Systems Management
United States Department of State
Peripe, Room 2803
2201 C Street NW
Washington, DC 20520
(202) 647-3412
(202) 647-1010 (Fax)

Annual award presented to Foreign and Civil services employees in information systems management positions that have excelled in their service to the government.

Award of Heroism
United States Department of State
Peripe, Room 2803
2201 C Street NW
Washington, DC 20520
(202) 647-3412
(202) 647-1010 (Fax)

Presented to state, AID, and USIA employees and Marine Guardsmen assigned to US Embassies who have illustrated a high level of heroism during emergency situations.

Award of Merit/Distinguished Service Award
National Council of Senior Citizens
8403 Colesville Road, Suite 1200
Silver Spring, MD 20910-3314
(301) 578-8837
(301) 578-8911 (Fax)
Website: www.ncscinc.org

f. 1963; to recognize the dedication of Senators and Representatives in helping America's elderly.

Award of Valor
United States Department of State
Peripe, Room 2803
2201 C Street NW
Washington, DC 20520

(202) 647-3412
(202) 647-1010 (Fax)

Presented to state, AID and USIA employees and Marine Guardsmen assigned to US embassies who have demonstrated a high degree of bravery, perseverance, and valor under emergency situations.

James A. Baker III/Howard Wilkins Award for Excellence in the Direction and Management of Overseas Missions
United States Department of State
Peripe, Room 2803
2201 C Street NW
Washington, DC 20520
(202) 647-3412
(202) 647-1010 (Fax)

Awarded to Deputy Chiefs of Missions achieving excellence in service to ambassadors and in operating as charge d'affaires.

Barbed Wire Award
American Ex-Prisoners of War
3201 East Pioneers Parkway, Suite 40
Arlington, TX 76010-5396
(817) 649-2979
(817) 649-0109 (Fax)
E-mail: pow@flash.net

f. 1988; this annual award is presented to the Congress member who provided the most help and legislative support for POWs.

Capital Award
Society for Human Resource Management
606 North Washington Street
Alexandria, VA 22314
(703) 548-3440
(703) 836-0367 (Fax)

Awarded annually to people who provided a high degree of leadership, determination, and management skills to the development of state or chapter legislative affairs programs.

Wilbur J. Carr Award
United States Department of State
Peripe, Room 2803
2201 C Street NW
Washington, DC 20520
(202) 647-3412
(202) 647-1010 (Fax)

Given to retiring State Department officers
who served with determination and distinction
during their careers.

Census Award of Excellence
United States Department of Commerce
Bureau of the Census
Federal Building 3, Room 3280
Washington, DC 20233
(301) 457-3701
(301) 457-3742 (Fax)

f. 1986; an annual recognition of government
employees whose efforts have greatly advanced the goals of the Census Bureau.

Winston Churchill Memorial Award
National Center for Public Policy Research
300 I Street NE, Suite 3
Washington, DC 20002
(202) 543-1286
(202) 543-4779 (Fax)
E-mail: ncppr@aol.com
Website: www.nationalcenter.inter.net

f. 1982; this award is provided to an individual
who has made the greatest and most selfless
contributions to freedom and human rights
policy.

Civil Government Award
American Society of Civil Engineers
1015 15th NW, Suite 600
Washington, DC 20005
(202) 789-2200
(800) 548-2723
(202) 289-6797 (Fax)
E-mail: itaylor@asce.org

f.1963; this annual award is bestowed upon an
individual who has excelled in both engineering
and elected or appointed civil government
positions.

Justice Tom C. Clark Award
Federal Bar Association
District of Columbia Chapter
1815 H Street NW, Suite 408
Washington, DC 20006
(202) 638-0252
(202) 775-0295 (Fax)

f. 1959; this annual award is presented to
career lawyers who have performed outstanding service to the US government.

COGEL Award
Council on Governmental Ethics Laws
10951 West Pico Boulevard, Suite 120
Los Angeles, CA 90064
(310) 470-6590
(310) 475-3752 (Fax)
E-mail: sterngs@aol.com
Website: www.cogel.org

f. 1983; an award created in order to recognize
individuals providing distinguished service in the
promotion of government and candidate ethical
conduct.

Congressional Award
Small Business Council of America
480 Hampton Lane, 7th Floor
Bethesda, MD 20814
(301) 951-9325
(301) 654-7354

f. 1981; to recognize the efforts of a Congressman or Senator in regards to small business
federal tax matters.

Congressman of the Year
National Multiple Sclerosis Society
733 3rd Avenue

New York, NY 10017-3288
(212) 986-3240
(212) 986-7981 (Fax)
E-mail: nat@nmss.org
Website: www.nmss.org

f. 1984; an annual award created in order to recognize Congress members who displayed outstanding support for research, rehabilitation services, and legislation beneficial to people with multiple sclerosis.

Congressperson of the Year
Association of Free Community Papers
401 North Michigan Avenue
Chicago, IL 60611-4267
(312) 644-6610
(312) 245-1083 (Fax)

Awarded to congresspersons and legislative officials who have met distinction in governmental promotion and financial management.

William L. Dawson Award for Legislative Development
Congressional Black Caucus Foundation
Special Events Director
1004 Pennsylvania Avenue SE
Washington, DC 20003
(202) 675-6735
(202) 547-3806 (Fax)

f. 1973; this award is presented to the individual who makes the greatest contributions in the area of minority legislation development.

Decoration for Exceptional Public Service
United States Department of Defense
Defense Special Weapons Agency
c/o MP
6801 Telegraph Road
Alexandria, VA 22310-3398
(703) 325-7591
(703) 325-6295 (Fax)
E-mail: moore@hq.dswa.mil

f. 1971; to recognize the achievements of those in service to public responsibility, especially as it pertains to citizenship and patriotism.

Department of Defense Distinguished Service Award
United States Department of Defense
Armed Forces Decorations and Awards, Civilian
The Pentagon, Room 5E589
Washington, DC 20350
(703) 695-4111
(703) 695-6049 (Fax)

Presented to civilian employees who have exhibited exceptional levels of dedication and efficiency in service to the US government and the Department of Defense.

Dirksen Center Award for Meritorious Service
Everett McKinley Dirksen Congressional Leadership Research Center
Dirksen Congressional Center
301 South 4th Street, Suite A
Pekin, IL 61554-4219
(309) 347-7113
(309) 347-6432 (Fax)
E-mail: evdirksen@pekin.net

Created to recognize the outstanding achievements of individuals seeking the preservation of the United States Congress.

Arthur S. Flemming Award
Downtown Jaycees of Washington, DC
1612 K Street NW, Suite 202
Washington, DC 20006
(202) 728-1135
(202) 833-1835 (Fax)

f. 1948; to recognize government employees 40 years old or younger that have performed outstanding service.

Equal Employment Opportunity Award
United States Department of State
Peripe, Room 2803
2201 C Street NW
Washington, DC 20520
(202) 647-3412
(202) 647-1010 (Fax)

Annual award presented to Department of State employees who have made great strides in the areas of affirmative action and equal opportunity.

Excellence in Government Leadership Award
Association of Free Community Papers
401 North Michigan Avenue
Chicago, IL 60611-4267
(312) 644-6610
(312) 245-1083 (Fax)

Presented to government officials that have displayed high levels of leadership, ethical standards, and management skills.

Gaius Petronius Award
National Hamiltonian Party
24669 West 10 Mile Road, Suite 3
Southfield, MI 48034
(810) 352-7196

f. 1968; an annual award presented to individuals in recognition for their "general retention of sanity" while serving the government.

Global Statesman Award
Campaign for United Nations Reform
418 7th Street SE
Washington, DC 20003
(202) 546-3956
(202) 546-3749 (Fax)

f. 1978; in order to recognize House and Senate members with perfect world order voting records.

Golden Bulldog Award
Watchdogs of the Treasury, Inc.
1010 Wisconsin Avenue NW, Suite 900
Washington, DC 20007
(202) 337-9400
(202) 337-4508 (Fax)

f. 1964; to recognize US Congress members who strive for strong economy and defense.

Golden Carrot Award
Public Voice for Food and Health Policy
1101 14th Street NW, Suite 710
Washington, DC 20005
(202) 371-1840
(202) 371-1910 (Fax)
E-mail: pvoice@ix.netcom.com
Website: www.public.voice.org/pvoice.html

f. 1983; to recognize Congress members displaying leadership in progressive food safety, nutrition, and agriculture policy leadership.

Goldsmith Prize for Investigative Reporting
Goldsmith Awards Program
Joan Shorenstein Center on the Press, Politics, and Public Policy
John F. Kennedy School of Government
Harvard University
Cambridge, MA 02138
(617) 495-1329
(617) 495-8696 (Fax)
Website: ksgwww.harvard.edu/~presspol/home.htm

f. 1991; presented annually every March, this award honors journalists whose work has promoted ethical and efficient government, just political practice, and public policy.

Government Achievement Award
National Hemophilia Foundation
Soho Building
Greene Street, Suite 303
New York, NY 10012-3813

(212) 219-8180
(212) 966-9247 (Fax)

f. 1988; for the purpose of recognizing individuals involved in hemophilia legislation or government related administration.

Government Affairs Award

National Association of the Remodeling
    Industry
4900 Seminary Road, Suite 320
Alexandria, VA 22311
(703) 575-1100
(703) 575-1121 (Fax)

Given to government officials who have had significant involvement with legislation to the professional remodeling industry.

Government Affairs and Public Service Award

National Rehabilitation Association
633 South Washington Street
Alexandria, VA 22314
(703) 836-0850
(703) 836-0848 (Fax)
Website: www.nationalrehab.com

f. 1981; this award is presented to government officials who strive through legislative and other means to improve services for disabled Americans.

Government Civil Engineer of the Year Award

American Society of Civil Engineers
1015 15th NW, Suite 600
Washington, DC 20005
(202) 789-2200
(800) 548-2723
(202) 289-6797 (Fax)
E-mail: itaylor@asce.org

Recognizes the public service achievements of government civil engineers.

Government Executive Leadership Award

Government Executive
1501 M Street NW, Suite 300
Washington, DC 20005

f. 1991; to recognize the career achievements of federal employees; focuses on service in regards to leadership, public policy goals, intra-government communication and public image.

Government Relations ACA/Carl D. Perkins Award

American Counseling Association
5999 Stevenson Avenue
Alexandria, VA 22304-3300
(703) 823-9800
(703) 823-0252 (Fax)

Established to recognize public officials involved in supporting counseling policy legislation.

John H. Heinz Award

National Organization for Victim Assistance
1757 Park Road
Washington, DC 20010
(202) 232-6682
(202) 462-2255 (Fax)

Recognizes federal government employees and public government officials in their efforts towards victim services and rights.

Hubert H. Humphrey Award

American Pharmaceutical Association
2215 Constitutional Avenue NW
Washington, DC 20037
(202) 628-4410
(202) 783-2351 (Fax)

f. 1978; with the purpose of recognizing group members who make outstanding contributions in government and legislative service.

Roger W. Jones Award for Executive Leadership
American University
School of Public Affairs
Ward Circle Building, Room 104
4400 Massachusetts Avenue NW
Washington, DC 20016
(202) 885-2940
(202) 885-2353 (Fax)

f. 1978; to recognize annually two individuals who have great achievements while serving the federal government.

Labor, Management, Government Social Responsibility Awards
Martin Luther King Jr. Center for Nonviolent Social Change
449 Auburn Avenue NE
Atlanta, GA 30312
(404) 524-1956
(404) 526-8940
(404) 522-6932 (Fax)

f.1989; a merger of three previous awards, it currently recognizes companies, labor groups, and government officials that made outstanding strides in the areas of freedom, nonviolence, and economic justice.

Leadership in Human Services Awards
American Public Welfare Association
Melissa Montgomery
810 1st Street NE, Suite 500
Washington, DC 20002-4267
(202) 682-0100
(202) 289-6555 (Fax)

Annual award presented to government policy makers on the national and state level who illustrate outstanding efforts in assisting poor Americans.

Legislator of the Year
Vietnam Veterans of America
1224 M Street NW
Washington, DC 20005-5783
(202) 628-2700
(202) 628-5881 (Fax)

f. 1984; this annual award is presented to one legislative official who provided tremendous advocacy for positive veteran legislation.

National Congressional Award
National Recreation and Park Association
2775 South Quincy Street, Suite 300
Arlington, VA 22206
(703) 820-4940
(703) 671-6772 (Fax)
E-mail: info@nrpa.org

Presented to a member of the US Senate or House in recognition of that individual's outstanding efforts and leadership regarding park, recreation, and conservation efforts.

NWRA Distinguished Service Award
National Water Resources Association
3800 North Fairfax Drive, Suite 4
Arlington, VA 22203-1703
(703) 524-1544
(703) 524-1548 (Fax)
E-mail: nwra@dgs.dgsys.com

f. 1987; to honor federal and state officials who made significant contributions to the development and conservation of American water resources.

Outstanding Advocate Award
National Easter Seal Society
230 West Monroe Street, Suite 1800
Chicago, IL 60606
(312) 726-6200
(312) 726-1494 (Fax)
E-mail: sara@ness.org
Website: seals.com

f. 1993; this award honors legislators seeking to significantly better the lives of disabled Americans.

Outstanding CPA in Government Award

American Bar Association
750 North Lake Shore Drive
Chicago, IL 60611
(312) 988-6137
(312) 988-6281 (Fax)

f. 1989; to annually recognize an individual for outstanding government service.

Mary D. Pinkard Leader in Federal Equity Award

Federally Employed Women
Legal & Education Fund
PO Box 4830
Washington, DC 20008
(202) 462-5235

Recognizes the achievements of federal employees in the advancement of equality, especially in regards to government.

Johanna Cooke Plaut Community Leadership Award

National Easter Seal Society
230 West Monroe Street, Suite 1800
Chicago, IL 60606
(312) 726-6200
(312) 726-1494 (Fax)
E-mail: sara@ness.org
Website: seals.com

Presented to disabled government officials and community service personnel who illustrate exceptional leadership abilities.

President's Award for Distinguished Federal Service

United States Office of Personnel Management
Performance Management & Incentive
Awards Division
1900 E Street NW, Room 7412
Washington, DC 20415
(202) 606-2720
(202) 606-2395 (Fax)
Website: www.opm.gov

f. 1957; this award acts as one of the highest achievements bestowed upon career federal employees by recognizing their outstanding service and ability.

President's Award for Exceptional Service

United States Office of Personnel Management
Performance Management & Incentive
Awards Division
1900 E Street NW, Room 7412
Washington, DC 20415
(202) 606-2720
(202) 606-2395 (Fax)
Website: www.opm.gov

f. 1984; to recognize individuals who have displayed acts of heroism and selflessness, performed extraordinary achievements, and/or provided outstanding service to the United States.

Program Excellence Awards

International City Management Association
777 North Capitol Street NE, Suite 500
Washington, DC 20002-4201
(202) 962-3566
(202) 962-3500 (Fax)
E-mail: mbowman@icma.org

f. 1986; to recognize local government administrators in their efforts to create successful programs, especially in regards to the disadvantaged, public safety, citizenship, and education.

Public Policy Award

American Society for Training and
  Development
1640 King Street
Alexandria, VA 22313-2043
(703) 683-8100
(703) 683-8103 (Fax)
Website: www.astd.org

Recognizes outstanding public service by legislative or executive officials in the area of human resource development.

Ernest Thompson Seton Awards

International Association of Fish and Wildlife
  Agencies
444 North Capitol Street NW, Suite 544
Washington, DC 20001
(202) 624-7890
(202) 624-7890 (Fax)
E-mail: iafish@aol.com

f. 1977; this award recognizes government
agencies that promote wildlife management
policies and public awareness on wildlife
issues.

Solar Congressman of the Year, Solar Salute

Solar Energy Industries Association
122 C Street NW, 4th Floor
Washington, DC 20001
(202) 383-2600
(202) 386-2670 (Fax)

f. 1973; to recognize a Congress member who
has actively supported and provided leadership
for solar energy promotion.

State Public Official Award for Significant Legislative Achievement

American Association of Retired Persons
601 E Street NW, Suite A1 300
Washington, DC 20049
(202) 434-3200
(202) 434-6460 (Fax)

Given to a public official who, through legislative or administrative means, has made significant contributions to assisting the elderly.

Taxpayer's Best Friend/Taxpayer's Friend/ Big Spender

National Taxpayer's Union
108 North Alfred Street
Alexandria, VA 22314
(703) 683-5700
(703) 683-5722 (Fax)
Website: www.ntu.org

f. 1979; to recognize those in Congress trying
to limit federal spending; offers "Best Friend"
status to the two top spending reduction advocates, "Friend" status to the top tenth, and "Big
Spender" for the bottom tenth Congressional
spenders.

Touchdown Club Mr. Sam Award

Touchdown Club
Capital Hilton Hotel
1001 16th Street
Washington, DC 20036
(202) 624-9766
(202) 624-9769 (Fax)

f.1961; the award recognizes government
official who contributes to sports through
leadership and example.

Veterans Employment Awards

United States Department of Labor
Secretary's Honor Awards Committee
200 Constitution Avenue NW, Room N5470
Washington, DC 20210
(202) 219-6741
(202) 219-8127 (Fax)

An annual award presented to government
employees who made outstanding achievements
in the area of veterans' employment.

Edgar Wayburn Award

Sierra Club
Executive Office Manager
85 2nd Street, 2nd Floor
San Francisco, CA 94105-3441
(415) 776-2211
(415) 776-0350 (Fax)

f. 1970; an annual award created to recognize
an executive or legislative government official
who has illustrated outstanding service in areas
concerning the environment and conservation.

White House Fellows
President's Commission on White House
    Fellowships
712 Jackson Place, NW
Washington, DC 20503
(202) 395-4522
(202) 395-6179 (Fax)
E-mail: almanac@ace.esusda.gov
Website: www.whitehouse.gov/white_house/
    wh_fellows/html/fellows1.html

f. 1964; to recognize highly motivated individuals desiring to become personally involved in government affairs, as well as assist them in reaching these goals.

Political Statistics

There is no shortage of political statistics that could have been selected for inclusion in this section of the book. Political scientists, pollsters, and politicians spend much of their time creating and studying the numbers of politics. However, many of the numbers that are studied today are gone and forgotten tomorrow. A new public opinion poll supplants the one taken only a few days ago. The tables of information, which were selected, were done so in order to pass on information about the historical and current state of politics in America. Therefore, public opinion polls, which are by their nature fleeting, have been excluded in favor of more permanent information.

Table 1: State Provisions for Initiative, Referendum, and Recall

Table 2: Governor's Terms, Limits, and Powers

Table 3: Gains/Losses by President's Party in Midterm Elections, 1862-1994

Table 4: Term Limits in State Legislatures

Table 5: Partisan Division of Governors and State Legislatures

Table 6: Financial Activity of Democratic Party, 1983-1994

Table 7: Financial Activity of Republican Party, 1983-1994

Table 1: State Provisions for Initiative, Referendum, and Recall

State	Initiative*	Referendum**	Recall
AL	no	n/a	n/a
AK	Direct	Leg., Petition	All but judges
AZ	Direct	Leg., Petition	All elected
AR	Direct	Leg., Petition	n/a
CA	Direct	Leg., Petition	All elected
CO	Direct	Leg.	All elected
CT	n/a	Leg.	n/a
DE	n/a	Leg.	n/a
FL	n/a	Leg.	n/a
GA	n/a	Leg.	All elected
HI	n/a	Leg., Petition	n/a
ID	n/a	Leg., Petition	All but judges
IL	Direct	Leg.	n/a
IN	n/a	Leg.	n/a
IA	n/a	Leg.	n/a
KS	n/a	Leg.	All but judges
KY	n/a	Leg., Petition	n/a
LA	n/a	Leg.	All but certain judges
ME	Indirect	Leg., Petition	n/a
MD	n/a	Leg., Petition	n/a
MA	Indirect	Leg., Petition	n/a
MI	Direct, Indirect	Leg., Petition	All but certain judges
MN	n/a	Leg.	n/a
MS	Indirect	Leg.	n/a
MO	Direct	Leg., Petition	n/a

Table 1, continued: State Provisions for Initiative, Referendum, and Recall

State	Initiative*	Referendum**	Recall
MT	Direct	Leg., Petition	All officials
NE	Direct	Leg., Petition	n/a
NV	Direct, Indirect	Leg., Petition	All public officers
NH	n/a	Leg.	n/a
NJ	n/a	Leg.	n/a
NM	n/a	Leg., Petition	n/a
NY	n/a	Leg.	n/a
NC	n/a	Leg.	n/a
ND	Direct	Leg., Petition	All elected
OH	Direct, Indirect	Leg., Petition	n/a
OK	Direct	Leg., Petition	n/a
OR	Direct	Leg., Petition	All elected
PA	n/a	Leg.	n/a
RI	n/a	Leg.	Some elected
SC	n/a	Leg.	n/a
SD	Direct	Leg., Petition	n/a
TN	n/a	Leg.	n/a
TX	n/a	Leg.	n/a
UT	Direct, Indirect	Leg., Petition	n/a
VT	n/a	Leg.	n/a
VA	n/a	Leg.	n/a
WA	Direct, Indirect	Leg., Petition	All but certain judges
WV	n/a	Leg.	n/a
WI	n/a	Leg.	n/a
WY	Indirect	Leg., Petition	All elected

*A direct initiative is directly placed on the ballot.   An indirect one is first submitted to the legislature for approval and if rejected to the people.

**Legislative referendums are measures placed on the ballot by the legislature.   Referendum by petition allows measures to be placed on the ballot by collecting a certain number of signatures.

Table 2: Governor's Terms, Limits, and Powers

State	Length of Term in 1900	Length of Term in 1998	Year of Change	Maximum Number of Consecutive Terms	Line Item Veto
AL	2	3	1902	2	No
AK	n/a	4	n/a	2	Yes
AZ	n/a	4	1970	2	Yes
AR	2	4	1984	2	Yes
CA	4	4	n/a	2	Yes
CO	2	4	1958	2	Yes
CT	2	4	1950	No Limit	Yes
DE	4	4	n/a	2	Yes
FL	4	4	n/a	2	No
GA	2	4	1942	2	Yes
HI	n/a	4	n/a	2	Yes
ID	2	4	1946	No Limit	Yes
IL	4	4	n/a	No Limit	Yes
IN	4	4	n/a	No Limit	No
IA	2	4	1974	No Limit	Yes
KS	2	4	1974	2	Yes
KY	4	4	n/a	2	Yes
LA	4	4	n/a	2	Yes
ME	2	4	1958	2	No
MD	4	4	n/a	2	Yes
MA	1	4	1920/1966	2	Yes
MI	2	4	1966	2	Yes
MN	2	4	1962	No Limit	Yes
MS	4	4	n/a	2	Yes
MO	4	4	n/a	2	Yes
MT	4	4	n/a	n/a	Yes
NE	2	4	1966	2	Yes

Table 2, continued: Governor's Terms, Limits, and Powers

State	Length of Term in 1900	Length of Term in 1998	Year of Change	Maximum Number of Consecutive Terms	Line Item Veto
NV	4	4	n/a	2	No
NH	2	4		No Limit	No
NJ	3	4	1949	2	Yes
NM	n/a	4	1916/1970	2	Yes
NY	2	4	1938	No Limit	Yes
NC	4	4	n/a	2	No
ND	2	4	1964	No Limit	Yes
OH	2	4	1958	2	Yes
OK	n/a	4	n/a	2	Yes
OR	4	4	n/a	2	Yes
PA	4	4	n/a	2	Yes
RI	1	4	1912/1995	No Limit	No
SC	2	4	1926	2	Yes
SD	2	4	1974	2	Yes
TN	1	4	1954	2	Yes
TX	2	4	1974	No Limit	Yes
UT	4	4	n/a	3	Yes
VT	2	4		No Limit	No
VA	2	4		1	Yes
WA	4	4	n/a	No Limit	Yes
WV	4	4	n/a	2	Yes
WI	2	4	1970	No Limit	Yes
WY	4	4	n/a	No Limit	Yes

Table 3: Gains/Losses by President's Party in Midterm Elections, 1862-1994

Year	President's Party	Gain/Loss in House	Gain/Loss in Senate
1862	Republican	-3	8
1866	Republican	-2	0
1870	Republican	-31	-4
1874	Republican	-96	-8
1878	Republican	-9	-6
1882	Republican	-33	3
1886	Democrat	-12	3
1890	Republican	-85	0
1894	Republican	-116	-5
1898	Republican	-21	7
1902	Republican	9	3
1906	Republican	-28	4
1910	Republican	-57	-10
1914	Democrat	-59	5
1918	Democrat	-19	-6
1922	Republican	-75	-8
1926	Republican	-10	-6
1930	Republican	-49	-8
1934	Democrat	9	20
1938	Democrat	-71	-6
1942	Democrat	-55	-9
1946	Democrat	-55	-23
1950	Democrat	-29	-6
1954	Republican	-18	-2
1958	Republican	-48	-13
1962	Democrat	-4	3
1966	Democrat	-47	-4
1970	Republican	-12	2
1974	Republican	-48	-5
1978	Democrat	-15	-3
1982	Republican	-26	1
1986	Republican	-5	-8
1990	Republican	-8	-1
1994	Democrat	-53	-8
1998	Democrat	5	0

Table 4: Term Limits in State Legislatures

State	Lower House	Upper House	Year Passed	Percentage Supported	Year It Takes Effect	Break in Service
AZ	8	8	1992	74	2000	2 years
AR	6	8	1992	60	1998	Lifetime
CA	6	8	1990	52	1996	Lifetime
CO	8	8	1990	71	1998	4 years
FL	8	8	1992	77	2000	2 years
ID	8/15*	8/15*	1994	59	2000	Contingent
ME	8	8	1993	63	1996	2 years
MA	8	8	1994	51	2002	2 years
MI	6	8	1992	59	1998	Lifetime
MS	8	8	1995		2003	2 years
MO	8	8	1992	74	2000	Lifetime
MT	8/16*	8/16*	1992	67	2000	Contingent
NE	8	n/a**	1994	68	2002	4 years
NV	12	12		70	1998	Lifetime
OH	8	8	1992	68	2000	4 years
OK	12***	12***	1990	67	2002	Lifetime
OR	6	8	1992	69	1998	Lifetime
SD	8	8	1992	63	2000	2 years
UT	12	12	1994		2006	2 years
WA	6/12*	8/14*	1992	52	1998	Contingent
WY	6/12*	12/14*	1992	77	1998	Contingent

*The first number represents the maximum number of years in that particular house and the second number represents the maximum number of total years of service in both houses.

**Nebraska has a unicameral legislature.

***Oklahoma has a maximum of 12 years of service in any combination of service in the two houses.

Table 5:   Partisan Division of Governors and State Legislatures

State	Governor (Party)	Upper House Membership		Lower House Membership	
		Dem.	Rep.	Dem.	Rep.
AL	Don Siegelman (D)	23	12	69	36
AK	Tony Knowles (D)	8	15	16	24
AZ	Jane Dee Hull (R)	14	16	20	40
AR	Mike Huckabee (R)	29	6	77	23
CA	Gray Davis (D)	25	15	48	32
CO	Bill Owens (R)	15	20	25	40
CT	John G. Rowland (R)	20	16	96	55
DE	Thomas R. Carper (D)	13	8	15	26
FL	Jeb Bush (R)	15	25	47	73
GA	Roy Barnes (D)	33	23	102	78
HI	Benjamin Cayetano (D)	23	2	39	12
ID	Dick Kempthorne (R)	4	31	12	58
IL	George Ryan (R)	27	32	62	56
IN	Frank O'Bannon (D)	19	31	53	47
IA	Tom Vilsack (D)	20	30	44	56
KS	Bill Graves (R)	13	27	48	77
KY	Paul Patton (D)	20	18	66	34
LA	Mike Foster (R)	25	14	78	27
ME	Angus King (I)	20	14	79	71
MD	Parris Glendening (D)	33	13	107	34
MA	Paul Cellucci (R)	33	7	131	28
MI	John Engler (R)	15	23	52	58
MN	Jesse Ventura (I)	42	24	63	71
MS	Kirk Fordice (R)	34	18	83	36
MO	Mel Carnahan (D)	17	16	86	76
MT	Marc Racicot (R)	18	32	41	59
NE*	Mike Johanns (R)	n/a	n/a	n/a	n/a

Table 5, continued: Partisan Division of Governors and State Legislatures

State	Governor (Party)	Upper House Membership		Lower House Membership	
		Dem.	Rep.	Dem.	Rep.
NV	Kenny Guinn (R)	9	12	28	14
NH	Jeanne Sheheen (D)	13	11	153	246
NJ	Christine Todd Whitman (R)	16	24	32	48
NM	Gary Johnson (R)	25	17	40	30
NY	George Pataki (R)	26	35	98	52
NC	James B. Hunt Jr. (D)	35	15	65	55
ND	Edward Schafer (R)	18	31	36	64
OH	Robert Taft (R)	12	21	40	59
OK	Frank Keating (R)	33	15	61	40
OR	John Kitzhaber (D)	12	17	25	34
PA	Tom Ridge (R)	20	30	100	103
RI	Lincoln Almond (R)	42	8	86	13
SC	Jim Hodges (D)	26	20	56	68
SD	William Janklow (R)	13	22	18	51
TN	Don Sundquist (R)	18	15	59	40
TX	George Bush (R)	15	16	79	71
UT	Michael Leavitt (R)	11	18	21	54
VT	Howard Dean (D)	17	13	77	67
VA	Jim Gilmore (R)	19	21	50	49
WA	Gary Locke (D)	27	22	49	49
WV	Cecil Underwood (R)	29	5	75	25
WI	Tommy Thompson (R)	17	16	44	55
WY	Jim Geringer (R)	10	20	17	43
TOTAL	17-D, 31-R, 2-I	1021	912	2868	2557

*Nebraska has a unicameral nonpartisan legislature.

Table 6: **Financial Activity of Democratic Party, 1983-1994** (millions in current dollars)

Period	Raised	Spent	Contributors	Coordinated Expenditures*
1983-1984	84.4	83.7	2.6	9.0
1985-1986	57.0	57.8	1.7	9.0
1987-1988	116.1	109.9	1.8	17.9
1989-1990	76.9	81.6	1.5	8.7
1991-1992	162.2	156.8	2.0	28.0
1993-1994	131.3	129.7	2.2	21.1

*Party money spent on behalf of federal candidates in a coordinated manner with the candidates.

Table 7: **Financial Activity of Republican Party, 1983-1994** (millions in current dollars)

Period	Raised	Spent	Contributors	Coordinated Expenditures*
1983-1984	289.0	291.9	4.9	20.1
1985-1986	255.2	255.8	3.4	14.3
1987-1988	257.5	251.4	3.4	22.7
1989-1990	206.4	213.5	2.9	10.7
1991-1992	254.8	246.4	3.0	33.8
1993-1994	245.6	234.7	2.8	20.4

*Party money spent on behalf of federal candidates in a coordinated manner with the candidates.

The 1998 State of the Union Address of President William J. Clinton

January 27, 1998

Mr. Speaker, Mr. Vice President, members of the 105th Congress, distinguished guests, my fellow Americans:

Since the last time we met in this chamber, America has lost two patriots and fine public servants. Though they sat on opposite sides of the aisle, Representatives Walter Capps and Sonny Bono shared a deep love for this House and an unshakable commitment to improving the lives of all our people. In the past few weeks they've both been eulogized. Tonight, I think we should begin by sending a message to their families and their friends that we celebrate their lives and give thanks for their service to our nation.

For 209 years it has been the President's duty to report to you on the state of the Union. Because of the hard work and high purpose of the American people, these are good times for America. We have more than 14 million new jobs; the lowest unemployment in 24 years; the lowest core inflation in 30 years; incomes are rising; and we have the highest homeownership in history. Crime has dropped for a record five years in a row. And the welfare rolls are at their lowest levels in 27 years. Our leadership in the world is unrivaled. Ladies and gentlemen, the state of our Union is strong.

With barely 700 days left in the 20th century, this is not a time to rest. It is a time to build, to build the America within reach: an America where everybody has a chance to get ahead with hard work; where every citizen can live in a safe community; where families are strong, schools are good and all young people can go to college; an America where scientists find cures for diseases from diabetes to Alzheimer's to AIDS; an America where every child can stretch a hand across a keyboard and reach every book ever written, every painting ever painted, every symphony ever composed; where government provides opportunity and citizens honor the responsibility to give something back to their communities; an America which leads the world to new heights of peace and prosperity.

This is the America we have begun to build; this is the America we can leave to our children-- if we join together to finish the work at hand. Let us strengthen our nation for the 21st century.

Rarely have Americans lived through so much change, in so many ways, in so short a time. Quietly, but with gathering force, the ground has shifted beneath our feet as we have moved into an Information Age, a global economy, a truly new world.

For five years now we have met the challenge of these changes as Americans have at every turning point--by renewing the very idea of America: widening the circle of opportunity, deepening the meaning of our freedom, forging a more perfect union.

We shaped a new kind of government for the Information Age. I thank the Vice President for his leadership and the Congress for its support in building a government that is leaner, more flexible, a catalyst for new ideas--and most of all, a government that gives the American people the tools they need to make the most of their own lives.

We have moved past the sterile debate between those who say government is the enemy and those who say government is the answer. My fellow Americans, we have found a third way. We have the smallest government in 35 years, but a more progressive one. We have a smaller government, but a stronger nation. We are moving steadily toward an even stronger America in the 21st century: an economy that offers opportunity, a society rooted in responsibility and a nation that lives as a community.

First, Americans in this chamber and across our nation have pursued a new strategy for prosperity: fiscal discipline to cut interest rates and spur growth; investments in education and skills, in science and technology and transportation, to prepare our people for the new economy; new markets for American products and American workers.

When I took office, the deficit for 1998 was projected to be $357 billion, and heading higher. This year, our deficit is projected to be $10 billion, and heading lower. For three decades, six Presidents have come before you to warn of the damage deficits pose to our nation. Tonight, I come before you to announce that the federal deficit--once so incomprehensibly large that it had 11 zeroes--will be, simply, zero. I will submit to Congress for 1999 the first balanced budget in 30 years. And if we hold fast to fiscal discipline, we may balance the budget this year--four years ahead of schedule.

You can all be proud of that, because turning a sea of red ink into black is no miracle. It is the product of hard work by the American people, and of two visionary actions in Congress--the courageous vote in 1993 that led to a cut in the deficit of 90 percent--and the truly historic bipartisan balanced budget agreement passed by this Congress. Here's the really good news: If we maintain our resolve, we will produce balanced budgets as far as the eye can see.

We must not go back to unwise spending or untargeted tax cuts that risk reopening the deficit. Last year, together we enacted targeted tax cuts

so that the typical middle class family will now have the lowest tax rates in 20 years. My plan to balance the budget next year includes both new investments and new tax cuts targeted to the needs of working families: for education, for child care, for the environment.

But whether the issue is tax cuts or spending, I ask all of you to meet this test: Approve only those priorities that can actually be accomplished without adding a dime to the deficit.

Now, if we balance the budget for next year, it is projected that we'll then have a sizeable surplus in the years that immediately follow. What should we do with this projected surplus? I have a simple four-word answer: Save Social Security first. Thank you.

Tonight, I propose that we reserve 100 percent of the surplus--that's every penny of any surplus--until we have taken all the necessary measures to strengthen the Social Security system for the 21st century. Let us say to all Americans watching tonight--whether you're 70 or 50, or whether you just started paying into the system--Social Security will be there when you need it. Let us make this commitment: Social Security first. Let's do that together.

I also want to say that all the American people who are watching us tonight should be invited to join in this discussion, in facing these issues squarely, and forming a true consensus on how we should proceed. We'll start by conducting nonpartisan forums in every region of the country--and I hope that lawmakers of both parties will participate. We'll hold a White House Conference on Social Security in December. And one year from now I will convene the leaders of Congress to craft historic, bipartisan legislation to achieve a landmark for our generation--a Social Security system that is strong in the 21st century. Thank you.

In an economy that honors opportunity, all Americans must be able to reap the rewards of prosperity. Because these times are good, we can afford to take one simple, sensible step to help millions of workers struggling to provide for their families: We should raise the minimum wage.

The Information Age is, first and foremost, an education age, in which education must start at birth and continue throughout a lifetime. Last year, from this podium, I said that education has to be our highest priority. I laid out a 10-point plan to move us forward and urged all of us to let politics stop at the schoolhouse door. Since then, this Congress, across party lines, and the American people have responded, in the most important year for education in a generation--expanding public school choice, opening the way to 3,000 new charter schools, working to connect every classroom in the country to the Information Superhighway, committing to expand Head Start to a million children, launching America Reads, sending literally thousands of college students into our elementary schools to make sure all our 8-year-olds can read.

Last year I proposed, and you passed, 220,000 new Pell Grant scholarships for deserving students. Student loans, already less expensive and easier to repay, now you get to deduct the interest. Families all over America now can put their savings into new tax-free education IRAs. And this year, for the first two years of college, families will get a $1,500 tax credit--a HOPE Scholarship that will cover the cost of most community college tuition. And for junior and senior year, graduate school, and job training, there is a lifetime learning credit. You did that and you should be very proud of it.

And because of these actions, I have something to say to every family listening to us tonight: Your children can go on to college. If you know a child from a poor family, tell her not to give up--she can go on to college. If you know a young couple struggling with bills, worried they won't be able to send their children to college, tell them not to give up--their children can go on to college. If you know somebody who's caught in a dead-end job and afraid he can't afford the classes necessary to get better jobs for the rest of his life, tell him not to give up--he can go on to college. Because of the things that have been done, we can make college as universal in the 21st century as high school is today. And, my friends, that will change the face and future of America.

We have opened wide the doors of the world's best system of higher education. Now we must make our public elementary and secondary schools the world's best as well by raising standards, raising expectations, and raising accountability.

Thanks to the actions of this Congress last year, we will soon have, for the very first time, a voluntary national test based on national standards in 4th grade reading and 8th grade math. Parents have a right to know whether their children are mastering the basics. And every parent already knows the key: good teachers and small classes.

Tonight, I propose the first ever national effort to reduce class size in the early grades. Thank you.

My balanced budget will help to hire 100,000 new teachers who have passed a state competency test. Now, with these teachers--listen--with these teachers, we will actually be able to reduce class size in the 1st, 2nd, and 3rd grades to an average of 18 students a class, all across America.

If I've got the math right, more teachers teaching smaller classes requires more classrooms. So I also propose a school construction tax cut to help communities modernize or build 5,000 schools.

We must also demand greater accountability. When we promote a child from grade to grade who hasn't mastered the work, we don't do that child any favors. It is time to end social promotion in America's schools.

Last year, in Chicago, they made that decision--not to hold our children back, but to lift them up. Chicago stopped social promotion, and started mandatory summer school, to help students who are behind to catch up. I propose, I propose to help other communities follow Chicago's lead. Let's say to them: Stop promoting children who don't learn, and we will give you the tools to make sure they do.

I also ask this Congress to support our efforts to enlist colleges and universities to reach out to disadvantaged children, starting in the 6th grade, so that they can get the guidance and hope they need so they can know that they, too, will be able to go on to college.

As we enter the 21st century, the global economy requires us to seek opportunity not just at home, but in all the markets of the world. We must shape this global economy, not shrink from it. In the last five years, we have led the way in opening new markets, with 240 trade agreements that remove foreign barriers to products bearing the proud stamp "Made in the USA." Today, record high exports account for fully one-third of our economic growth. I want to keep them going, because that's the way to keep America growing and to advance a safer, more stable world.

All of you know, whatever your views are, that I think this a great opportunity for America. I know there is opposition to more comprehensive trade agreements. I have listened carefully and I believe that the opposition is rooted in two fears: first, that our trading partners will have lower environmental and labor standards which will give them an unfair advantage in our market and do their own people no favors, even if there's more business; and, second, that if we have more trade, more of our workers will lose their jobs and have to start over. I think we should seek to advance worker and environmental standards around the world. I have made it abundantly clear that it should be a part of our trade agenda. But we cannot influence other countries' decisions if we send them a message that we're backing away from trade with them.

This year, I will send legislation to Congress, and ask other nations to join us, to fight the most intolerable labor practice of all--abusive child labor. We should also offer help and hope to those Americans temporarily left behind by the global marketplace or by the march of technology, which may have nothing to do with trade. That's why we have more than doubled funding for training dislocated workers since 1993--and if my new budget is adopted, we will triple funding. That's why we must do more, and more quickly, to help workers who lose their jobs for whatever reason.

You know, we help communities in a special way when their military base closes. We ought to help them in the same way if their factory closes. Again, I ask the Congress to continue its bipartisan work to consolidate the tangle of training programs we have today into one single G.I. Bill for Workers, a simple skills grant so people can, on their own, move quickly to new jobs, to higher incomes and brighter futures.

We all know in every way in life change is not always easy, but we have to decide whether we're going to try to hold it back and hide from it

or reap its benefits. And remember the big picture here: While we've been entering into hundreds of new trade agreements, we've been creating millions of new jobs.

So this year we will forge new partnerships with Latin America, Asia, and Europe. And we should pass the new African Trade Act--it has bipartisan support. I will also renew my request for the fast track negotiating authority necessary to open more new markets, create more new jobs, which every President has had for two decades.

You know, whether we like it or not, in ways that are mostly positive, the world's economies are more and more interconnected and interdependent. Today, an economic crisis anywhere can affect economies everywhere. Recent months have brought serious financial problems to Thailand, Indonesia, South Korea, and beyond.

Now, why should Americans be concerned about this? First, these countries are our customers. If they sink into recession, they won't be able to buy the goods we'd like to sell them. Second, they're also our competitors. So if their currencies lose their value and go down, then the price of their goods will drop, flooding our market and others with much cheaper goods, which makes it a lot tougher for our people to compete. And, finally, they are our strategic partners. Their stability bolsters our security.

The American economy remains sound and strong, and I want to keep it that way. But because the turmoil in Asia will have an impact on all the world's economies, including ours, making that negative impact as small as possible is the right thing to do for America--and the right thing to do for a safer world.

Our policy is clear: No nation can recover if it does not reform itself. But when nations are willing to undertake serious economic reform, we should help them do it. So I call on Congress to renew America's commitment to the International Monetary Fund. And I think we should say to all the people we're trying to represent here that preparing for a far-off storm that may reach our shores is far wiser than ignoring the thunder until the clouds are just overhead.

A strong nation rests on the rock of responsibility. A society rooted in responsibility must first promote the value of work, not welfare. We can be proud that after decades of finger-pointing and failure, together we ended the old welfare system. And we're now we replacing welfare checks with paychecks.

Last year, after a record four-year decline in welfare rolls, I challenged our nation to move 2 million more Americans off welfare by the year 2000. I'm pleased to report we have also met that goal, two full years ahead of schedule.

This is a grand achievement, the sum of many acts of individual courage, persistence and hope. For 13 years, Elaine Kinslow of Indianapolis, Indiana, was on and off welfare. Today, she's a dispatcher with a van company. She's saved enough money to move her family into a good neighborhood, and she's helping other welfare recipients go to work. Elaine Kinslow and all those like her are the real heroes of the welfare revolution. There are millions like her all across America. And I'm happy she could join the First Lady tonight. Elaine, we're very proud of you. Please stand up.

We still have a lot more to do, all of us, to make welfare reform a success--providing child care, helping families move closer to available jobs, challenging more companies to join our welfare-to-work partnership, increasing child support collections from deadbeat parents who have a duty to support their own children. I also want to thank Congress for restoring some of the benefits to immigrants who are here legally and working hard--and I hope you will finish that job this year.

We have to make it possible for all hard-working families to meet their most important responsibilities. Two years ago, we helped guarantee that Americans can keep their health insurance when they change jobs. Last year, we extended health care to up to 5 million children. This year, I challenge Congress to take the next historic steps.

One hundred sixty million of our fellow citizens are in managed care plans. These plans save money and they can improve care. But medical decisions ought to be made by medical doctors, not insurance company accountants. I urge this Congress to reach across the aisle and write into law a Consumer Bill of Rights that says this: You have the right to know all your medical options, not just the cheapest. You have the right to choose the doctor you want for the care you need. You have the right to emergency room care, wherever and whenever you need it. You have the right to keep your medical records confidential. Traditional care or managed care, every American deserves quality care.

Millions of Americans between the ages of 55 and 65 have lost their health insurance. Some are retired; some are laid off; some lose their coverage when their spouses retire. After a lifetime of work, they are left with nowhere to turn. So I ask the Congress: Let these hard-working Americans buy into the Medicare system. It won't add a dime to the deficit--but the peace of mind it will provide will be priceless.

Next, we must help parents protect their children from the gravest health threat that they face: an epidemic of teen smoking, spread by multimillion-dollar marketing campaigns. I challenge Congress: Let's pass bipartisan, comprehensive legislation that improve public health, protect our tobacco farmers, and change the way tobacco companies do business forever. Let's do what it takes to bring teen smoking down. Let's raise the price of cigarettes by up to $1.50 a pack over the next 10 years, with penalties on the tobacco industry if it keeps marketing to our children.

Tomorrow, like every day, 3,000 children will start smoking, and 1,000 will die early as a result. Let this Congress be remembered as the Congress that saved their lives.

In the new economy, most parents work harder than ever. They face a constant struggle to balance their obligations to be good workers--and their even more important obligations to be good parents. The Family and Medical Leave Act was the very first bill I was privileged to sign into law as President in 1993. Since then, about 15 million people have taken advantage of it, and I've met a lot of them all across this country. I ask you to extend that law to cover 10 million more workers, and to give parents time off when they have to go see their children's teachers or take them to the doctor.

Child care is the next frontier we must face to enable people to succeed at home and at work.

Last year, I co-hosted the very first White House Conference on Child Care with one of our foremost experts, America's First Lady. From all corners of America, we heard the same message, without regard to region or income or political affiliation: We've got to raise the quality of child care. We've got to make it safer. We've got to make it more affordable.

So here's my plan: Help families to pay for child care for a million more children. Scholarships and background checks for child care workers, and a new emphasis on early learning. Tax credits for businesses that provide child care for their employees. And a larger child care tax credit for working families. Now, if you pass my plan, what this means is that a family of four with an income of $35,000 and high child care costs will no longer pay a single penny of federal income tax.

I think this is such a big issue with me because of my own personal experience. I have often wondered how my mother, when she was a young widow, would have been able to go away to school and get an education and come back and support me if my grandparents hadn't been able to take care of me. She and I were really very lucky. How many other families have never had that same opportunity? The truth is, we don't know the answer to that question. But we do know what the answer should be: Not a single American family should ever have to choose between the job they need and the child they love.

A society rooted in responsibility must provide safe streets, safe schools, and safe neighborhoods. We pursued a strategy of more police, tougher punishment, smarter prevention, with crime-fighting partnerships with local law enforcement and citizen groups, where the rubber hits the road. I can report to you tonight that it's working. Violent crime is down, robbery is down, assault is down, burglary is down--for five years in a row, all across America. We need to finish the job of putting 100,000 more police on our streets.

Again, I ask Congress to pass a juvenile crime bill that provides more prosecutors and probation officers, to crack down on gangs and guns and drugs, and bar violent juveniles from buying guns for life. And I ask you to dramati-

cally expand our support for after-school programs. I think every American should know that most juvenile crime is committed between the hours of 3:00 in the afternoon and 8:00 at night. We can keep so many of our children out of trouble in the first place if we give them someplace to go other than the streets, and we ought to do it.

Drug use is on the decline. I thank General McCaffrey for his leadership. And I thank this Congress for passing the largest antidrug budget in history. I ask you to join me in a groundbreaking effort to hire 1,000 new border patrol agents and to deploy the most sophisticated available new technologies to help close the door on drugs at our borders.

Police, prosecutors, and prevention programs, as good as they are, they can't work if our court system doesn't work. Today there are large number of vacancies in the federal courts. Here is what the Chief Justice of the United States wrote: Judicial vacancies cannot remain at such high levels indefinitely without eroding the quality of justice. I simply ask the United States Senate to heed this plea, and vote on the highly qualified judicial nominees before you, up or down.

We must exercise responsibility not just at home, but around the world. On the eve of a new century, we have the power and the duty to build a new era of peace and security. But, make no mistake about it, today's possibilities are not tomorrow's guarantees. America must stand against the poisoned appeals of extreme nationalism. We must combat an unholy axis of new threats from terrorists, international criminals and drug traffickers. These 21st century predators feed on technology and the free flow of information and ideas and people. And they will be all the more lethal if weapons of mass destruction fall into their hands.

To meet these challenges, we are helping to write international rules of the road for the 21st century, protecting those who join the family of nations and isolating those who do not. Within days, I will ask the Senate for its advice and consent to make Hungary, Poland, and the Czech Republic the newest members of NATO. For 50 years, NATO contained communism and kept America and Europe secure. Now these three formerly communist countries have said yes to democracy. I ask the Senate to say yes to them-- our new allies.

By taking in new members and working closely with new partners, including Russia and Ukraine, NATO can help to assure that Europe is a stronghold for peace in the 21st century.

Next, I will ask Congress to continue its support for our troops and their mission in Bosnia. This Christmas, Hillary and I traveled to Sarajevo with Senator and Mrs. Dole and a bipartisan congressional delegation. We saw children playing in the streets, where two years ago they were hiding from snipers and shells. The shops are filled with food; the cafes were alive with conversation. The progress there is unmistakable--but it is not yet irreversible.

To take firm root, Bosnia's fragile peace still needs the support of American and allied troops when the current NATO mission ends in June. I think Senator Dole actually said it best. He said, "This is like being ahead in the 4th quarter of a football game. Now is not the time to walk off the field and forfeit the victory."

I wish all of you could have seen our troops in Tuzla. They're very proud of what they're doing in Bosnia. And we're all very proud of them. One of those brave soldiers is sitting with the First Lady tonight--Army Sergeant Michael Tolbert. His father was a decorated Vietnam vet. After college in Colorado, he joined the Army. Last year, he led an infantry unit that stopped a mob of extremists from taking over a radio station that is a voice of democracy and tolerance in Bosnia. Thank you very much, Sergeant, for what you represent.

In Bosnia and around the world, our men and women in uniform always do their mission well. Our mission must be to keep them well-trained and ready, to improve their quality of life, and to provide the 21st century weapons they need to defeat any enemy.

I ask Congress to join me in pursuing an ambitious agenda to reduce the serious threat of weapons of mass destruction. This year, four decades after it was first proposed by President Eisenhower, a comprehensive nuclear test ban is within reach. By ending nuclear testing we can help to prevent the development of new and more dangerous weapons and make it more difficult for non-nuclear states to build them.

I'm pleased to announce four former Chairmen of the Joint Chiefs of Staff--Generals John Shalikashvili, Colin Powell, and David Jones, and Admiral William Crowe--have endorsed this treaty. And I ask the Senate to approve it this year.

Together, we also must also confront the new hazards of chemical and biological weapons, and the outlaw states, terrorists and organized criminals seeking to acquire them. Saddam Hussein has spent the better part of this decade, and much of his nation's wealth, not on providing for the Iraqi people, but on developing nuclear, chemical, and biological weapons--and the missiles to deliver them. The United Nations weapons inspectors have done a truly remarkable job, finding and destroying more of Iraq's arsenal than was destroyed during the entire Gulf War. Now Saddam Hussein wants to stop them from completing their mission.

I know I speak for everyone in this chamber, Republicans and Democrats, when I say to Saddam Hussein: You cannot defy the will of the world. And when I say to him: You have used weapons of mass destruction before; we are determined to deny you the capacity to use them again.

Last year, the Senate ratified the Chemical Weapons Convention to protect our soldiers and citizens from poison gas. Now we must act to prevent the use of disease as a weapon of war and terror. The Biological Weapons Convention has been in effect for 23 years now. The rules are good, but the enforcement is weak. We must strengthen it with a new international inspection system to detect and deter cheating.

In the months ahead, I will pursue our security strategy with old allies in Asia and Europe, and new partners from Africa to India and Pakistan, from South America to China. And from Belfast, to Korea to the Middle East, America will continue to stand with those who stand for peace.

Finally, it's long past time to make good on our debt to the United Nations. More and more, we are working with other nations to achieve common goals. If we want America to lead, we've got to set a good example. As we see so clearly in Bosnia, allies who share our goals can also share our burdens. In this new era, our freedom and independence are actually enriched, not weakened, by our increasing interdependence with other nations. But we have to do our part.

Our founders set America on a permanent course toward "a more perfect union." To all of you I say it is a journey we can only make together--living as one community. First, we have to continue to reform our government--the instrument of our national community. Everyone knows elections have become too expensive, fueling a fundraising arms race. This year, by March 6th, at long last the Senate will actually vote on bipartisan campaign finance reform proposed by Senators McCain and Feingold. Let's be clear: A vote against McCain and Feingold is a vote for soft money and for the status quo. I ask you to strengthen our democracy and pass campaign finance reform this year.

At least equally important, we have to address the real reason for the explosion in campaign costs--the high cost of media advertising. To the folks watching at home, those were the groans of pain in the audience. I will formally request that the Federal Communications Commission act to provide free or reduced-cost television time for candidates who observe spending limits voluntarily. The airwaves are a public trust, and broadcasters also have to help us in this effort to strengthen our democracy.

Under the leadership of Vice President Gore, we've reduced the federal payroll by 300,000 workers, cut 16,000 pages of regulation, eliminated hundreds of programs and improved the operations of virtually every government agency. But we can do more. Like every taxpayer, I'm outraged by the reports of abuses by the IRS. We need some changes there--new citizen advocacy panels, a stronger taxpayer advocate, phone lines open 24 hours a day, relief for innocent taxpayers. Last year, by an overwhelming bipartisan margin, the House of Representatives passed sweeping IRS reforms. This bill must not now languish in the Senate. Tonight I ask the Senate: follow the House, pass the bipartisan package as your first order of business.

I hope to goodness before I finish I can think of something to say, "follow the Senate" on, so I'll be out of trouble.

A nation that lives as a community must value all its communities. For the past five years, we have worked to bring the spark of private enterprise to inner city and poor rural areas --with community development banks, more commercial loans in the poor neighborhoods, cleanup of polluted sites for development. Under the continued leadership of the Vice President, we propose to triple the number of empowerment zones, to give business incentives to invest in those areas.

We should also should give poor families more help to move into homes of their own, and we should use tax cuts to spur the construction of more low-income housing.

Last year, this Congress took strong action to help the District of Columbia. Let us renew our resolve to make our capital city a great city for all who live and visit here. Our cities are the vibrant hubs of great metropolitan areas. They are still the gateways for new immigrants, from every continent, who come here to work for their own American Dreams. Let's keep our cities going strong into the 21st century. They're a very important part of our future.

Our communities are only as healthy as the air our children breathe, the water they drink, the Earth they will inherit. Last year, we put in place the toughest-ever controls on smog and soot. We moved to protect Yellowstone, the Everglades, Lake Tahoe. We expanded every community's right to know about the toxins that threaten their children. Just yesterday, our food safety plan took effect, using new science to protect consumers from dangers like E. coli and salmonella.

Tonight, I ask you to join me in launching a new Clean Water Initiative, a far-reaching effort to clean our rivers, our lakes, our coastal waters for our children.

Our overriding environmental challenge tonight is the worldwide problem of climate change, global warming, the gathering crisis that requires worldwide action. The vast majority of scientists have concluded unequivocally that if we don't reduce the emission of greenhouse gases, at some point in the next century we'll disrupt our climate and put our children and grandchildren at risk. This past December, America led the world to reach a historic agreement committing our nation to reduce greenhouse gas emissions through market forces, new technologies, energy efficiency. We have it in our power to act right here, right now. I propose $6 billion in tax cuts and research and development to encourage innovation, renewable energy, fuel-efficient cars, energy-efficient homes.

Every time we have acted to heal our environment, pessimists have told us it would hurt the economy. Well, today our economy is the strongest in a generation, and our environment is the cleanest in a generation. We have always found a way to clean the environment and grow the economy at the same time. And when it comes to global warming, we'll do it again.

Finally, community means living by the defining American value--the ideal heard round the world that we are all created equal. Throughout our history, we haven't always honored that ideal and we've never fully lived up to it. Often it's easier to believe that our differences matter more than what we have in common. It may be easier, but it's wrong.

What we have to do in our day and generation to make sure that America becomes truly one nation--what do we have to do? We're becoming more and more and more diverse. Do you believe we can become one nation? The answer cannot be to dwell on our differences, but to build on our shared values. We all cherish family and faith, freedom and responsibility. We all want our children to grow up in a world where their talents are matched by their opportunities.

I've launched this national initiative on race to help us recognize our common interests and to bridge the opportunity gaps that are keeping us from becoming one America. Let us begin by recognizing what we still must overcome. Discrimination against any American is un-American. We must vigorously enforce the laws that make it illegal. I ask your help to end the backlog at the Equal Employment Opportunity Commission. Sixty thousand of our fellow citizens are waiting in line for justice, and we should act now to end their wait.

We also should recognize that the greatest progress we can make toward building one America lies in the progress we make for all Americans, without regard to race. When we open the doors of college to all Americans, when we rid all our streets of crime, when there are jobs available to people from all our neighborhoods, when we make sure all parents have the child care they need, we're helping to build one nation.

We, in this chamber and in this government, must do all we can to address the continuing American challenge to build one America. But we'll only move forward if all our fellow citizens--including every one of you at home watching tonight--is also committed to this cause.

We must work together, learn together, live together, serve together. On the forge of common enterprise Americans of all backgrounds can hammer out a common identity. We see it today in the United States military, in the Peace Corps, in AmeriCorps. Wherever people of all races and backgrounds come together in a shared endeavor and get a fair chance, we do just fine. With shared values and meaningful opportunities and honest communication and citizen service, we can unite a diverse people in freedom and mutual respect. We are many; we must be one.

In that spirit, let us lift our eyes to the new millennium. How will we mark that passage? It just happens once every thousand years. This year, Hillary and I launched the White House Millennium Program to promote America's creativity and innovation, and to preserve our heritage and culture into the 21st century. Our culture lives in every community, and every community has places of historic value that tell our stories as Americans. We should protect them. I am proposing a public-private partnership to advance our arts and humanities, and to celebrate the millennium by saving American's treasures, great and small.

And while we honor the past, let us imagine the future. Think about this--the entire store of human knowledge now doubles every five years. In the 1980s, scientists identified the gene causing cystic fibrosis--it took nine years. Last year, scientists located the gene that causes Parkinson's Disease--in only nine days. Within a decade, "gene chips" will offer a road map for prevention of illnesses throughout a lifetime. Soon we'll be able to carry all the phone calls on

Mother's Day on a single strand of fiber the width of a human hair. A child born in 1998 may well live to see the 22nd century.

Tonight, as part of our gift to the millennium, I propose a 21st Century Research Fund for path-breaking scientific inquiry--the largest funding increase in history for the National Institutes of Health, the National Science Foundation, the National Cancer Institute.

We have already discovered genes for breast cancer and diabetes. I ask you to support this initiative so ours will be the generation that finally wins the war against cancer, and begins a revolution in our fight against all deadly diseases.

As important as all this scientific progress is, we must continue to see that science serves humanity, not the other way around. We must prevent the misuse of genetic tests to discriminate against any American.   And we must ratify the ethical consensus of the scientific and religious communities, and ban the cloning of human beings.

We should enable all the world's people to explore the far reaches of cyberspace. Think of this--the first time I made a State of the Union speech to you, only a handful of physicists used the World Wide Web. Literally, just a handful of people. Now, in schools, in libraries, homes and businesses, millions and millions of Americans surf the Net every day. We must give parents the tools they need to help protect their children from inappropriate material on the Internet. But we also must make sure that we protect the exploding global commercial potential of the Internet. We can do the kinds of things that we need to do and still protect our kids.

For one thing, I ask Congress to step up support for building the next generation Internet. It's getting kind of clogged, you know. And the next generation Internet will operate at speeds up to a thousand times faster than today.

Even as we explore this inner space in a new millennium we're going to open new frontiers in outer space. Throughout all history, humankind has had only one place to call home--our planet Earth. Beginning this year, 1998, men and women from 16 countries will build a foothold in the heavens--the international space station. With its vast expanses, scientists and engineers will

actually set sail on an unchartered sea of limitless mystery and unlimited potential.

And this October, a true American hero, a veteran pilot of 149 combat missions and one, five-hour space flight that changed the world, will return to the heavens. Godspeed, John Glenn. John, you will carry with you America's hopes. And on your uniform, once again, you will carry America's flag, marking the unbroken connection between the deeds of America's past and the daring of America's future.

Nearly 200 years ago, a tattered flag, its broad stripes and bright stars still gleaming through the smoke of a fierce battle, moved Francis Scott Key to scribble a few words on the back of an envelope--the words that became our national anthem. Today, that Star Spangled Banner, along with the Declaration of Independence, the Constitution and the Bill of Rights, are on display just a short walk from here. They are America's treasures and we must also save them for the ages.

I ask all Americans to support our project to restore all our treasures so that the generations of the 21st century can see for themselves the images and the words that are the old and continuing glory of America; an America that has continued to rise through every age, against every challenge, of people of great works and greater possibilities, who have always, always found the wisdom and strength to come together as one nation--to widen the circle of opportunity, to deepen the meaning of our freedom, to form that "more perfect union." Let that be our gift to the 21st century.

God bless you, and God bless the United States.

Republican Response to President Clinton's State of the Union Address

Delivered by Senate Majority Leader Trent Lott of Mississippi
January 27, 1998

Family, Faith and Freedom

Tonight I'd like to share with you our plans, here in the Congress, for a safer, stronger, and more prosperous America.

Those plans are shaped by our commitment to family, to faith, and to freedom. And they highlight some real differences, between the Republican Party and the President, concerning what government should do--and how much of your money government should take.

Big Government or families? More taxes or more freedom?

We believe the choice is clear: The first priority of your representatives in Washington must be to fight for the interests of the American family.

That's why one of the first things we'll tackle is REAL reform of the IRS. I'll have more to say about that later, but the bottom line is this:

We... are... going to stop the abuses the IRS is inflicting on American taxpayers.

You've got our word on it!

Also... we'll be building on the progress of the last few years, when our Republican Congress, working with the nation's governors, took some historic first steps.

We took the first step in transforming welfare into workfare.

We started reducing taxes, especially for families with children. And with considerable difficulty, we finally worked out a long-term agreement with the President for a balanced budget.

We protected Medicare. And in that same way, we're going to protect Medicare, this year, against any changes that would imperil its financial stability.

We strengthened education opportunities for disabled youngsters, launched a long-overdue reform of the nation's troubled foster care system, made adoption easier, and encouraged alternatives to abortion.

We proved that people of good will and strong faith can work together to deal with the problems that face our nation and our neighborhoods.

But we have only just BEGUN the difficult job of stopping Big Government, making it more responsive, and--perhaps hardest of all--rebuilding the trust you used to have in your elected officials.

That's especially important when it comes to education, to taxes, and to the twin plagues of drugs and crime.

Those are the three areas where the American people are most dissatisfied... and where our freedom is most threatened.

Parents--and good teachers, as well--are dissatisfied with schools where kids don't learn, and in many cases, where they aren't even safe. When one-quarter--one out of four--of our high school students can barely read, isn't it obvious the current system isn't working?

I know we are all fed up with the criminal justice system that has tragically failed to halt the poisonous epidemic of drugs that is undermining family life in our country. Violent crime is turning the Land of the Free into the Land of the Fearful.

Today's workers and today's savers are angry and disillusioned with a tax code that benefits only tax lawyers and Big Government...

Let's take a look at the typical family budget.

The typical family pays more than 38 percent of its income in taxes.

That's nearly forty cents of every dollar. That's not just bad policy. It's immoral. Our tax system should not penalize marriage, hard work, or savings, not to mention your efforts to keep up with the cost of living. We believe these high taxes mean less freedom overall.

And yet, President Clinton now wants the government to spend billions of dollars more. But I don't have to tell you, if the government spends more, you'll wind up getting taxed more.

You know that. He knows that.

Instead, Republicans want you--the people who work hard for the money --to keep more of what you earn. The President seems to think that Big Government can solve all your children's problems if you will just give government more of your money--and more control over your lives. Nonsense!

We think the best things for safe, healthy children are healthy, stable families--not more government programs that require parents to work longer, take home less, and spend less time with the kids. That's why we fought for a $500 per child tax credit last year.

Once again, the choice is clear: Big Government? Or families? More taxes? Or more freedom?

The American people elected us in the Congress to listen to you and then to lead. So while we listen respectfully to the President's ideas, we can not wait on them.

One example is the drug crisis. With all due respect, for the past five years, we've had all kinds of wrong signals.

It took the President four years to admit the need to reduce the tax burden on the American people, as we finally did in the Balanced Budget Act last year. That was a welcome reversal of the pile-on-the-taxes approach of his first four years in office.

But you know that Americans are still over-taxed... over-regulated... and over-governed.

This chart shows how the income of the federal government, over the last 30 years, has gone up almost 1,000 percent. But during the same period, family incomes rose only half as much. Government has gotten fat, while families are working overtime just to stay where they were.

We believe hard-working Americans deserve a break. So our focus in 1998 will be to increase family income by CUTTING taxes and making government more accountable for the way it spends your money.

But tax relief is only the first step.

As I said earlier... the only way to limit government and expand individual freedom is to eliminate the IRS as we know it today.

It... is... morally wrong for a free people to live in fear of any government agency.

It... is... morally wrong for citizens in a democracy to be presumed guilty until proven innocent.

But IRS reform alone isn't enough.

The real problem lies with the tax code itself.

It is too long...

It is too complicated...

It is simply unfair.

It punishes achievement... It discourages work... savings... and innovation.

As Republicans, we pledge to replace the tax code with a new system that is fair, consistent, easy to understand, and less frightening to the American taxpayer--a tax code that will end the fear and encourage savings and investment.

Finally, because the Republican balanced budget plan is now working, we should commit, here and now, not to spend any budget surplus on unnecessary government programs.

If there is a surplus, we should use part of it to

pay down the national debt, and return the rest to you, the taxpayer. After all, it is your money.

Like those tax proposals, the Republican education plan proposes the same fundamental change from what we have now. As a father, and a prospective grandfather, I realize that nothing is more important than the education of our young people.

Washington today has more than 750 education programs, in 39 different bureaucracies.

That just doesn't make sense.

And it doesn't make sense for Washington to tax the people in your community and, then, give the money back with strings attached. We want to cut those strings and to remove the out-of-date rules and restrictions that hold back our schools from the future.

For example, if your community needs to build new schools or rehabilitate old ones, YOU should be able to do that.

If you want to offer merit pay for great teachers, YOU should be able to do that too.

We've heard a lot from the President about testing.

But he thinks Washington should administer the tests. Wrong again.

We think that you-- the parents, the teachers and local officials-- should do the job.

Republicans in Congress strongly support that kind of state testing, just as we support an even more important kind: Periodic testing for teachers. You won't hear much about that from the President. On this subject, the President disagrees with us. And, we disagree with him.

But good teachers--like my Mother, who taught public elementary school for 19 years-- don't object to testing. They want it. They say, teacher testing will be a key step in implementing the kind of merit pay program that attracts star teachers.

They also say, even the best teachers can't get good results when their school is a dangerous, violent place. We hope the President, this year, will finally see the wisdom in our proposal to give freedom of choice to low-income families whose children are stuck in dead-end, drug-ridden schools.

Because we care so deeply about those families, we want them to have the same option exercised by both President Clinton and Vice President Gore, who chose the schools their children attended.

Parental choice and involvement are absolutely essential, but choice in education does not mean abandoning our public schools.

It simply means moving decision-making away from Washington, and back to you at your family's kitchen table.

That's the first and most important step to launching an era of education renewal that will equip our schools and our students to lead America and the world into the new century.

But don't forget, today's young people confront a danger even worse than poor education. Teen drug abuse has become epidemic, and there are no safe havens from this insidious modern plague. Overall, teenage drug use has nearly doubled since 1992 and, perhaps most frightening of all, nearly half of all 17-year-olds say they could buy marijuana in just an hour's time.

Like the president, I want to stop youth smoking, but the narcotics problem is a far greater threat to teenagers.

First, to solve the drug crisis, we have to start with the family, the school, and with our churches and synagogues.

Studies show that teens in families that eat together, play together, and pray together are the ones least likely to try drugs.

When the battle against drug abuse is first waged at home, the war is half won.

Second, schools must be drug-free. We must demand absolute accountability and zero tolerance for any drug abuse on school grounds.

Third, there is the critical role of the federal government. We've simply got to be more aggressive in guarding our national borders. Along with that, we must be more vigilant in arresting and prosecuting anyone--yes, anyone-- who sells this poison.

And fourth, it's time to get tough on society's predators.

We must end parole for violent criminals, crack down on juvenile criminals, increase prison capacity, make the death penalty a real threat, and impose mandatory penalties for crimes committed with a gun.

If we are honestly committed to protecting the

innocent, we must do more to punish the guilty.

By combining national leadership with community activism, we can--and we will--save America, one child and one neighborhood at a time.

We don't pretend to have all the answers here in Washington, but I guarantee you we will ask the right questions.

For example, there's the issue of child-care. We say, give families more flexibility in the way they work and care for their children.

But how do we do it?

* First and foremost, cut the tax burdens on the American family. Don't force both parents to work, and work longer hours, when they could have more time at home with their kids.

* Give stay-at-home parents the same tax breaks and benefits available to parents who use day care. After all, all moms work--whether at home or in an outside job.

* Let employees negotiate flex-time and comp-time arrangements. Help small businesses provide on-site day care. And make it easier--and more profitable--for older Americans to provide child care for growing families.

We're taking this common-sense approach because, as parents and grandparents ourselves, we've learned it takes parents, and parental choice, to raise a child in today's world.

Of course, there are dangers in today's world that demand strong national leadership. Just last week, Pope John Paul's visit to Cuba reminded us that, despite the collapse of communism, tonight the future remains very uncertain over much of the globe.

Let me make one thing clear to Saddam Hussein--or anyone else who needs to be told: Despite any current controversy, this Congress will vigorously support the President in full defense of America's interests throughout the world.

By the same token, we will ask the President to work with us in considering ways to stop the threats of terrorism, international narcotics, and the spread of weapons of mass destruction.

As hard as it is to believe, right now, our country has no national defense against missiles carrying nuclear, chemical, or biological warheads.

Those who hate America most--in Iraq, Iran, and elsewhere--they know that.

President Clinton, I urge you to reconsider your opposition to defending America from missile attack. Join us in taking the steps that will actually deploy a missile defense system for the United States.

There are at least a dozen other important subjects the Congress will deal with in the months ahead. For example, ending the dreadful practice of partial-birth abortions. I urge our Democratic colleagues in the Senate to help us override the President's veto of that legislation.

In addition, we're committed to more positive reforms in health care, protection of worker's rights and paychecks, reform of bankruptcy laws, and legislation to combat teen smoking.

All the while, we're going to concentrate on what we call oversight. Which means finding out why you aren't getting your money's worth from government. And why so much of your hard-earned money goes for programs filled with fraud and abuse.

Last year, for example, the Administration admitted it paid out $23 billion dollars in ineligible Medicare claims--that's in one year alone--and spent another $5 billion dollars in improper payments in just one welfare program.

That's--just--intolerable!

We... intend... to... make... government accountable,

From the classrooms to the courts.

From the clerks to the President's Cabinet.

From the post office to the Presidency.

This isn't a matter of Republicans versus Democrats. It's a question of whether we will learn from past mistakes, in order to restore the great institutions... and the cherished values--family, faith, and freedom--that for so long have held us together as a nation.

The President is right to point out our heroes tonight... but there are some others who should not be forgotten. Twenty-five years ago... next month... a small band of Americans returned home after long captivity in Southeast Asia.

Some broken in body... but never broken in spirit... those returning Prisoners of War reminded us, through our cheers and our tears, just how PRECIOUS... we hold our freedom.

Now the world has changed greatly--and greatly for the better--in those twenty-five years.

But we must remember WHY it changed-- WHY we can now look to the century ahead with high hopes--and just WHY we are the envy of the world.

The reason is that Americans, we the people, have been willing to sacrifice everything to protect our families, to practice our faith, and to defend our freedom.

What those heroes fought to preserve, we must now work to recover and strengthen:

By renewing American education...

Restoring the security of the American family...

And rebuilding the kind of government that works with you... and for you....

The kind of government you can trust.

Thank you for listening.

Good night . . . and God bless you all.

Name/Organization Index

Geographic Index

Political Market Place USA

Third Parties 28, 32, 34, 37, 43,
45

North Dakota
Democratic Party 11
Federal Election Committee and
State Election Bodies 141
League of Women Voters 147
Media Consultants 188
Political Science Research
Institutes 113
Political Statistics 274, 276, 280
Republican Party 22
Third Parties 37, 43

Ohio
Democratic Party 11
Federal Election Committee and
State Election Bodies 141
League of Women Voters 148
Media Consultants 182-3, 185-6,
188, 190
Political Action Committees 85,
94-5, 98
Political Associations 50, 56, 69,
71
Political Consultants & Campaign
Managers 151, 157, 162, 165-
6, 168
Political Science Research
Institutes 101-2, 104, 106,
109-10
Political Statistics 274, 276, 278,
280
Public Opinion and Campaign
Pollsters 172, 174, 178
Republican Party 23
Third Parties 28, 30, 32, 34, 37,
41, 43, 45, 47

Oklahoma
Democratic Party 11
Federal Election Committee and
State Election Bodies 141
League of Women Voters 148
Media Consultants 184-5, 187,
189
Political Associations 58
Political Consultants & Campaign
Managers 154, 167
Political Science Research
Institutes 106, 113
Political Statistics 274, 276, 278,
280
Public Opinion and Campaign
Pollsters 172, 174
Publishers 239
Republican Party 23
Third Parties 37, 43

Oregon
Democratic Party 11
Federal Election Committee and
State Election Bodies 142
League of Women Voters 148
Media Consultants 193
Political Action Committees 96
Political Associations 64
Political Consultants & Campaign
Managers 150, 160-2, 167
Political Science Research
Institutes 106
Political Statistics 274, 276, 278,
280
Public Opinion and Campaign
Pollsters 175, 178
Republican Party 23
Think Tanks 128
Third Parties 34, 37, 39, 43

Pennsylvania
Democratic Party 12
Federal Election Committee and
State Election Bodies 142
League of Women Voters 148
Media Consultants 183-4, 191,
193
Political Action Committees 96,
99
Political Associations 53-4, 58,
60, 62-4, 75, 79
Political Consultants & Campaign
Managers 150, 152, 156, 158,
166
Political Science Research
Institutes 106-8, 114
Political Statistics 274, 276, 280
Public Opinion and Campaign
Pollsters 171, 173, 176
Publishers 236, 238, 240
Republican Party 23
Third Parties 28, 30, 32, 34, 37-
8, 40-1, 43, 45, 47

Puerto Rico
Democratic Party 12
Federal Election Committee and
State Election Bodies 142
Republican Party 23

Rhode Island
Democratic Party 12
Federal Election Committee and
State Election Bodies 142
League of Women Voters 148
Media Consultants 191, 194
Political Consultants & Campaign
Managers 163-4, 168
Political Science Research
Institutes 101, 107

Political Statistics 274, 276, 280
Public Opinion and Campaign
Pollsters 177, 179
Republican Party 23
Third Parties 28, 32, 34, 37, 43,
47

South Carolina
Democratic Party 12
Federal Election Committee and
State Election Bodies 142
League of Women Voters 148
Media Consultants 185
Political Associations 67
Political Consultants & Campaign
Managers 151, 153, 156, 162
Political Science Research
Institutes 102, 109, 114
Political Statistics 274, 276, 280
Public Opinion and Campaign
Pollsters 171
Publishers 240
Republican Party 23
Third Parties 37, 43

South Dakota
Democratic Party 12-3
Federal Election Committee and
State Election Bodies 142
League of Women Voters 148
Media Consultants 190
Political Consultants & Campaign
Managers 152
Political Science Research
Institutes 114
Political Statistics 274, 276, 278,
280
Public Opinion and Campaign
Pollsters 177
Republican Party 23
Third Parties 37, 44

Tennessee
Democratic Party 13
Federal Election Committee and
State Election Bodies 142
League of Women Voters 148
Media Consultants 183, 186,
191, 194
Political Action Committees 86,
89, 90
Political Associations 76
Political Consultants & Campaign
Managers 151, 164
Political Science Research
Institutes 114-5
Political Statistics 274, 276, 280
Public Opinion and Campaign
Pollsters 171-2
Publishers 241

342

Key Subject Index